The Greatest Briton

Why, man, he doth bestride the narrow world
Like a Colossus; and we petty men
Walk under his huge legs.
(*Julius Caesar*)

The Greatest Briton

ESSAYS ON
WINSTON CHURCHILL'S LIFE
AND POLITICAL PHILOSOPHY

Jeremy Havardi

SHEPHEARD-WALWYN (PUBLISHERS) LTD

First published in 2009 by
Shepheard-Walwyn (Publishers) Ltd
107 Parkway House, Sheen Lane,
London SW14 8LS

British Library Cataloguing in Publication Data
A catalogue record of this book
is available from the British Library

ISBN: 978-0-85683-265-9

Typeset by Alacrity,
Sandford, Somerset
Printed and bound through
s|s|media limited, Wallington, Surrey

Contents

To Sir Martin Gilbert
– a man to whom all Churchill scholars are indebted

Introduction

Churchill and the war on terror

THE EVENTS of September 11th 2001 have left an indelible imprint on the modern psyche. On that deadly autumn morning, nineteen Islamist terrorists carried out the single most devastating attack on American soil, claiming the lives of nearly three thousand people. In a well co-ordinated and planned operation, they assaulted the heart of the American political and economic system by attacking the Pentagon and the World Trade Centre. These attacks, a classic example of asymmetric warfare, were rightly described as 'an act of war' and not just an act of terror.[1] For many Americans, they induced a heightened sense of national vulnerability that was reminiscent of Britain's experience in the Blitz.

In the aftermath of the atrocity one wartime leader loomed large in the American imagination: Winston Churchill. Speaking to survivors of the attack on the Pentagon, Donald Rumsfeld said: 'At the height of peril to his own nation, Winston Churchill spoke of their finest hour. Yesterday, America and the cause of human freedom came under attack.'[2] The phrase 'cause of human freedom' would have struck a chord with Churchill. Churchill often portrayed Britain's struggle against Nazi Germany in simple moral terms. In his famous broadcast announcing the imminent 'Battle of Britain', he declared that nothing less than 'the survival of Christian civilisation' was at stake. He told Parliament that if Britain lost, 'the whole world, including the United States' would 'sink into the abyss of a new dark age'.[3]

President Bush appeared certain of the significance of 9/11. What was at stake in the war on terror was nothing less than the survival of the same freedoms that were threatened in 1940. 'Every civilised nation has a part in this struggle,' he declared, 'because every civilised nation has a stake in its outcome.' The war on terror was a pledge 'for the freedom and security of [the] country and the

I

civilised world'. For Al Qaeda 'attacked not just our people but all freedom-loving people everywhere in the world'. On the eve of the invasion of Afghanistan, President Bush told the American people: 'We will not waver, we will not tire, we will not falter, and we will not fail.' He was echoing Churchill's resonant declaration in 1941: 'We shall not fail or falter; we shall not weaken or tire.'

Both men were using Manichean phraseology in which the battles to come reflected simple moral opposites: good versus evil, freedom versus slavery, liberty versus tyranny. For many in Britain's modern secular culture, this terminology often appears alien and discomfiting, a throwback to the moral certainties of Victorian times. But as the embodiment of British resolve and indomitability, it is likely that Churchill would have approved of Bush's 9/11 phraseology, if not all of the President's subsequent policies. Though not a religious man, Churchill was profoundly aware of the potency of language and its role in political leadership.

Parallels were also drawn between the behaviour of New York mayor Rudy Giuliani and that shown by Churchill at the height of the Blitz. Giuliani will be remembered on 9/11 for his consoling words and his unwavering belief that New Yorkers would emerge stronger from their shattering experience. Like Churchill, Giuliani learnt the vital importance of *appearing* certain of victory. Without downplaying the havoc the terrorists had wrought, Giuliani talked and walked with an air of authority and inner belief. As the late Lord Jenkins put it: 'What Giuliani succeeded in doing is what Churchill succeeded in doing in that dreadful summer of 1940. He managed to create the illusion that we were bound to win.'4 In 1940, Churchill did the same. He sent out a memo ordering his staff not to appear sullen, dejected or defeatist but to radiate confidence in Britain's cause and its ability to survive. It was a confidence trick – but it worked.

Giuliani admitted in an interview that Churchill had long been his hero although he 'never used to tell people that'. Churchill had 'helped him a lot, before, during and after' the September 11th attacks. He admired the way that he 'had revived the spirit of the British people when it was down ... and [I] used Churchill to teach me how to reinvigorate the spirit of a dying nation.'5 *Time* magazine named Giuliani Man of the Year for 2001 and his popularity enabled him to pose as the Republicans' 'security' candidate in the race for the 2008 presidency.

It was therefore no accident that many Americans turned to Churchill after 9/11. It helped that he was a half American on his mother's side and that he had often romanticised the links between the English speaking peoples. Americans remembered that as a war leader he was indomitable, courageous, vigorous, optimistic and possessed of a deep moral conviction about the causes he espoused. They admired his pristine moral clarity in arguing that accommodation with Nazism was impossible and that appeasing Hitler was a short sighted betrayal of British values. For Churchill viewed Hitler, not as a simple-minded nationalist, but as one of a terrifying new brigade of ideological revolutionaries.

Today Europe, and the wider world, faces an unnerving challenge from the forces of radical Islam. Like Nazism, radical Islam (or Islamism) seeks no long term accommodation with its foe and demands no redress for merely localised grievances. Instead its jihadist supporters want to create a global Islamic state ruled by Sharia law, one in which the central freedoms of secular, Western societies are eradicated. This goal 'requires terror and unrelenting terror until its ends are achieved'.[6]

The advocates of radical Islam reject the separation of church and state, the notion that beliefs can ever be confined to the private realm. In their pure Islamic state, all behaviour must be in rigid conformity to the perceived tenets of the faith. Any values which conflict with their interpretation of Islamic law, such as freedom of speech, religious pluralism, democracy and sexual liberalism must be abolished. Radical Islam is therefore an inherently totalitarian ideology with religious foundations.

Like Nazism, Islamism is inherently anti-Semitic at its core. In the writings of leading Islamist ideologues, such as Muhammad Wahhab, Sayyid Qutb and Ruhollah Khomeini, the Jew is portrayed as a demonic enemy of Muslims and a malignant influence in the world. Jews are seen as having a treacherous and deceitful character, making them ripe for political suppression or eventual slaughter. Depictions of the Jew in the Arab world today frequently borrow the most virulent images from Nazi newspapers.[7] Like the Nazis, Islamists thrive on a victim centred theory of history to explain and justify their murderous obsessions. Just as the Nazis lamented the Treaty of Versailles for emasculating German power, the Islamists point to the abolition of the Caliphate in 1924 as the starting point for their jihadist crusade.[8] The call to arms against a perceived enemy, whether Jews

or infidels, has a seductive power for Muslim radicals, just as it did
for Germans in the 1930s.

Churchill would certainly have grasped the Islamic dimension to
today's terror threat. As a young man in Sudan, he noted certain characteristics of Islamic rule that repelled him and was unsparing in his
choice of words: 'How dreadful are the curses which Mohammed-
anism lays on its votaries. Besides the fanatical frenzy, which is as
dangerous in a man as hydrophobia in a dog, there is this fearful
fatalistic apathy. Improvident habits, slovenly systems of agriculture,
sluggish methods of commerce, and insecurity of property exist
wherever the followers of the Prophet rule or live.'

He also condemned the Islamic law that stipulated that 'every
woman must belong to some man as his absolute property', arguing
that this hindered 'the final extinction of slavery'. Despite his
favourable comments about the bravery of individual Muslim
soldiers, he believed that Islam paralysed 'the social development of
those who [followed] it'. In summary, there was 'no stronger retrograde force in the world'. In today's politically correct age, it is safe
to assume that no Western leader would offer such a damning critique, at least not in public.

Churchill also realised that as a 'militant and proselytising' faith,
it was a potent rallying cry for its devotees.9 In *The History of the
Malakand Field Force* he wrote that whereas Christianity 'must always
exercise a modifying influence on men's passions', Islam, 'increases,
instead of lessening, the fury of intolerance'. He went on: 'It was
originally propagated by the sword, and ever since, its votaries have
been subject, above the people of all other creeds, to this form of
madness.'10 His description of the Pashtun fakir, Mullah Mastun
('the Mad Mullah') as 'a wild enthusiast, convinced alike of his divine
mission' who 'preached a crusade against the infidel' could easily be
applied to jihadist leaders today.11

Together with Egypt and Pakistan, the epicentre of twentieth-
century radical Islam was Saudi Arabia. As Colonial Secretary,
Churchill met the founder of the Saudi state, Ibn Saud, and in his
dealings with him became familiar with the doctrine of Wahhabism.
He wrote that this form of Islam bore comparison to 'the most
militant form of Calvinism' and that Wahhabis held, as 'an article of
faith', the need to kill those who disagreed with their ideas.

The Wahhabis were 'austere, intolerant, well-armed, and bloodthirsty' and believed they had to 'kill all those who [did] not share

their opinions' as well as 'make slaves of their wives and children'. He listed those who were affected: 'Women have been put to death in Wahabi villages for simply appearing in the streets. It is a penal offence to wear a silk garment. Men have been killed for smoking a cigarette.'[12] This was a perceptive comment on how much radical Islam was motivated by a rejection of Western values, practices and freedoms.[13]

Churchill then would have had much to say about the West's current 'long war' against extremism. But today's neo-conservatives have become somewhat misty-eyed when comparing George Bush and Winston Churchill. Despite his love of grand oratory and occasional Manichean terminology, Churchill rarely spoke of democracy and freedom in messianic tones. While he mentioned God on occasions, he was not an essentially religious man and his reverence for liberty and the Constitution was couched most often in pragmatic and secular terms.

Moreover, Churchill had a thoroughgoing knowledge of international affairs and wrote numerous articles on nearly every major conflict of his times. Before taking up his seat in the House of Commons, he had already acquired intimate knowledge of wars in Cuba, South Africa, Afghanistan and Sudan. This gave him an air of authority when he spoke up on colonial issues in Parliament. By contrast, Bush, like Neville Chamberlain, took office with little knowledge or experience of foreign issues.[14]

Churchill, more than Bush, sought to bridge the political divide on many occasions, refusing to be the plaything of any one political party. He was a coalitionist during the grave struggles of the Second World War, bringing together politicians from across the political divide so as to forge a more effective and representative government. After 9/11, Bush won cross-party support for his war on terror. But this support evaporated towards the end of his first term amid recriminations over domestic and foreign policy.

Above all, Churchill was an intellectual as well as a man of action. He was a biographer, novelist, historian and journalist, a master of words and an oratorical genius who famously became his own speechwriter. Though no intellectual slouch, Bush became famous for his lack of verbal dexterity and inarticulate manner. And, despite the similarities between Nazism and radical Islam, the challenge posed to Western civilisation between 1939 and 1945 was on a monumentally different scale to that posed by militant Islam today.

At their height, the Axis powers might have overrun Europe and the Far East, while seizing control of the Middle East's oil supplies, posing the ultimate threat to the Allies. That is not comparable to the current jihadist terror assault, which will need to be defeated, or contained, by a combination of military, economic and ideological pressures. Globalised terror cannot be defeated on the battlefield alone.

In some respects, radical Islam more closely resembles Soviet Communism. Both share a utopian belief in the redemption of humanity, with communism raising man from the 'despond' of capitalism and radical Islam reclaiming humanity from the perceived shackles of secular life. The advocates of both doctrines espouse the use of violence to achieve political change, regarding the killing of fellow travellers as a necessary stage to redemption. Just as Stalin inflicted terror on members of the communist party, so too jihadists have murdered moderate Muslims for rejecting puritanical Islam.[15] And both communists and Islamists have sought to make inroads within Western societies by the subtle use of propaganda and subversion.

As a life-long opponent of communism, Churchill would have understood this form of cultural intimidation. He wrote that the Bolshevik aim of global revolution could be pursued in peacetime or war. As he put it, a Bolshevist peace was only 'another form of war'.[16] If the Bolsheviks could not work by military means they would 'employ every device of propaganda in their neighbours' territories' to ensure those countries were 'poisoned internally'.[17]

Despite not being a conventional neo-con, Churchill was a bitter opponent of tyranny in any form. As such, he would have certainly approved of the principled stand taken by the Western alliance against Al Qaeda. But would he have approved of the 2003 war in Iraq? Certainly politicians on both sides of the Atlantic invoked Churchill's vigorous stand against appeasement to justify regime change against Saddam Hussein. On the eve of war in March 2003, President Bush declared: 'In this century, when evil men plot chemical, biological and nuclear terror, a policy of appeasement could bring destruction of a kind never before seen on this earth.'[18]

At the same time, Tony Blair offered the flipside of Neville Chamberlain's Munich speech by condemning 'appeasement in our time'. Chamberlain was, according to Blair, a 'good man who made the wrong decision'. He spelt out the crucial lessons of appeasement:

'The lesson we learnt then was that if, confronted by a threat, we back away because we assume that our ... peaceful intentions are matched by those threatening us, the threat only grows, and at a later time has to be confronted again, but in a far more deadly and dangerous form.'[19] On the other side of the Atlantic, Richard Perle warned of Saddam Hussein: 'The danger that springs from his capabilities will only grow as he expands his arsenal. A pre-emptive strike against Hitler at the time of Munich would have meant an immediate war, as opposed to the one that came later. Later was much worse.'[20]

What all these politicians overlooked was that Churchill had already experienced a dispiriting military entanglement in Iraq. After the First World War Britain was awarded the mandate for Mesopotamia (Iraq) and maintained an imperial presence there for a number of years. But in 1920 a coalition of Iraqi insurgents declared a jihad against the British and parts of Iraq rebelled against colonial rule. The uprising was swiftly put down, albeit at considerable cost to British troops.

As Colonial Secretary, Churchill took over responsibility for reaching a political settlement in Iraq but often expressed grave doubts about the mandate. At one point he declared: 'We have not got a single friend in the press upon the subject, and there is no point of which they make more effective use to injure the government. Week after week and month after month for a long time to come we shall have a continuance of this miserable, wasteful, sporadic warfare...'[21] These sound like the sentiments of many a politician and General after the 2003 invasion.

We should sometimes be wary of those who wrap themselves in a Churchillian mantle in order to promote controversial policies. But in general, Churchill remains profoundly relevant to political debate in the twenty first century. During a public career spanning sixty years, he confronted many of the issues that concern us today: the Northern Ireland peace process, the Arab-Israeli conflict, the future of Iraq, the response to terrorism, European unity, the special relationship with America, welfare reform and taxation to name but a few. This volume will show how he grappled with these, and other, problems and how some of his thinking remains apposite for a modern generation. Above all, it is the aim of this book to dispel the many myths that surround the Churchill legend and, in so doing, offer a more rounded portrait of this multifaceted genius.

NOTES

1 This was how President Bush described the attacks in a live address to the nation on September 11th 2001.
2 A. Roberts, *Secrets of Leadership*, p.xvii.
3 Speeches VI, pp.6231-8.
4 J. Ramsden, *Man of the Century*, p.586.
5 A. Thompson, 'I looked out of the window and saw this nuclear cloud', in *Daily Telegraph*, February 12th 2002.
6 M. Desai, *Rethinking Islamism*, p.12.
7 See the short documentary *Obsession* by Wayne Kopping and Raphael Shore (2006).
8 In 1923, Turkey's leader, Kemal Ataturk, formally dissolved the Ottoman Sultanate, creating a secular republic with himself as President. A year later he dissolved the Muslim Caliphate, the political leadership of the global Muslim community since the time of Muhammad, as part of his modernisation.
9 W. Churchill, *The River War II*, pp.248-50.
10 W. Churchill, *The Story of the Malakand Field Force*, p.40.
11 *Ibid.*, p.39.
12 Speeches III, p.3102.
13 By comparison, contemporary *bien pensant* opinion blames Western foreign policy for this Islamist aggression.
14 L. Olson, 'Why Winston Wouldn't Stand For W', *Washington Post*, July 1st 2007.
15 Islamists are attempting to dominate the cultural sphere, setting up schools to propagate Saudi Wahhabism, forcing through Sharia law in civil matters and using 'human rights' to ring fence Islam from criticism.
16 *Evening News*, July 28th 1920.
17 Companion IV (ii), p.1099.
18 J. Weisberg, *The Bush Tragedy*, p.233.
19 Tony Blair, Speech, March 1st 2003.
20 *Daily Telegraph*, August 9th 2002.
21 Companion IV (ii), p.1199.

CHAPTER ONE
The Promise of Youth

WINSTON SPENCER-CHURCHILL was born at Blenheim Palace on November 30th 1874, the first son of Randolph Churchill and Jennie Jerome. He was the grandson of an aristocrat, the 7th Duke of Marlborough, and was proud to trace his descent from the illustrious John Churchill, the 1st Duke of Marlborough, who died in 1722.

He was educated at St George's school in Ascot before attending Harrow at the age of 13. He received mixed reports during his five years there but excelled at history, English and fencing. He rarely received parental visits but developed a close relationship with his beloved nanny, Mrs Everest. In 1893 he enrolled at Sandhurst Military Academy and within two years, he had been commissioned into the 4th Hussars. While on leave in 1895, he travelled to Cuba, where he wrote dispatches for the *Daily Graphic*. He witnessed the Cuban insurrection against the Spanish authorities and developed a love of Havana cigars which would last for the rest of his life.

He went to India and, in 1897, fought in the North-West Frontier against Pashtun tribesmen. From his experiences there he wrote his first book, *The Story of the Malakand Field Force*. A year later, he saw action at Omdurman in Sudan under Lord Kitchener, which led to his second book, *The River War*. In his account, he condemned Kitchener's tactics as inhumane, in particular his decision to disinter the corpse of the Mahdi. In 1899 he stood, unsuccessfully, as a Tory candidate in a by-election at Oldham.

He then travelled as a correspondent to South Africa at the start of the Second Boer War, where he was commissioned to write for the *Morning Post*. He was subsequently captured and imprisoned by the Boer authorities but managed to escape captivity, becoming an overnight sensation when he turned up safe in Portuguese controlled Lorenço Marques. He returned to South Africa, where he took part in the relief of Ladysmith and saw action in Pretoria. He wrote two further books about his experiences, *From London to Ladysmith* and *Ian Hamilton's March*.

In 1900 he was elected as Conservative MP for Oldham and went on a speaking tour of the United States and Canada.

Was Churchill a neglected child?

CHURCHILL OFTEN DESCRIBED himself as a child of the Victorian age and nowhere is this more evident than in his relationship with his parents. Winston's mother, the American Jennie Jerome was, in the words of her grandson, 'a woman of exceptional beauty in an age of famous beauties'.[1] Her father, Leonard Jerome, was a self-made American millionaire stockbroker who had won and lost fortunes on the US stock exchange and whose political career involved a stint as US ambassador in Trieste. Jennie's great grandmother was said to be an Iroquois Indian, though this claim has recently been questioned.[2]

Jennie was 19 when she met Randolph Churchill at a regatta at Cowes on the Isle of Wight. The younger son of the 7th Duke of Marlborough, Randolph had been an MP since 1873, and a rapid ascent up the 'greasy pole' led to his appointment as Chancellor of the Exchequer under Lord Salisbury. A year later a reckless mis-judgement led to his swift downfall and within a few years, he entered political oblivion. Together Jennie and Randolph, with all their influential connections, became thoroughly immersed in the London social circuit, something that would have an impact on the young Winston.

In *My Early Life* Winston describes both his parents in glowing terms. His mother was a 'fairy princess' and 'radiant being' who shone 'like the evening star'.[3] His father, Lord Randolph Churchill, was a career politician and Winston later wrote that he took his politics 'almost unquestioningly from him'. Churchill described him as 'the greatest and most powerful influence' in his early life and 'conceived an intense admiration and affection for him'.[4]

But Winston's idolisation of his parents was tempered by their frequent absences during his early years. Some of Winston's letters from his various schools 'abound in pathetic requests for letters and for visits' but both parents were too busy to visit him.[5] Lady Randolph was caught up in the world of fashionable society while Randolph was absorbed in high politics. Of course in many ways Winston was spoiled, as one would expect for someone of his class and background. He was brought up in the luxury of Blenheim Palace and enjoyed frequent holidays abroad and on the Isle of Wight. He also had an indulgent nanny, Mrs Everest, to cater for his every need. In this sense, he was not a victim of parental neglect.

But his parents rarely visited him at school and Winston took offence. His letters home contained a variety of requests for attention, money and visits, often using a blatant form of emotional manipulation to get his way. In 1886 Winston asked his mother to attend his school play. Jennie replied that she could not do so because she was hosting a dinner party in London but Winston was persistent: 'Now you know I was always your darling and you can't find it in your heart to give me a denial. I want you to put off the dinner party...'[6] To the young boy's chagrin, Jennie ended up hosting the dinner party.

In another letter, the 12-year-old Churchill expressed his desire to watch the 1887 Jubilee. He urged his mother to pull strings for him, assuring her that 'you love me too much to disappoint me'.[7] On this occasion he was more successful. Typical of his requests was one he made in a letter to his father in 1889: 'I do hope both you and Mamma will come as last speech day nobody came to see me and it was vy dull. You have never been to see me...'[8]

In another letter, Winston had demanded to be at home for Christmas rather than be sent abroad. In a typically demanding manner, he declared that he had no intention of going abroad and added: 'If you in spite of my entreaties force me to go I will do as little as I can and the holidays will be one continual battle.' Winston's overbearing tone elicited a sharp response from his mother: 'When one wants something in this world, it is not by delivering ultimatums that one is likely to get it.'[9]

In truth, Churchill's parents paid young Winston little attention while he was at school but as Celia Sandys has pointed out: 'Neglectful though this may seem in the twentieth century, Victorian parents, once they had dispatched their sons to school, did not feel obliged to spend their time going to see them.'[10] It was normal for the boys of upper-middle-class families to be sent to public schools for a term at a time, during which they would not be expected to see their parents.

If Winston enjoyed only brief glimpses of his mother's affections, those with his father were rarer still. He regretted not having a closer relationship with his father and not living long enough to know him intimately. When Randolph died in 1895, Winston wrote that his 'dreams of comradeship with him, of entering Parliament at his side and in his support' came to an end. Winston later claimed that he had had but two or three *deep* conversations with Randolph and, after the latter's death, all that remained was to 'pursue his aims and vindicate his memory'.[11]

Evidence of the remoteness of father and son comes in a letter written by Winston on finding out that he was to go to Harrow and not Winchester. 'Did you', Winston enquires, 'go to Harrow or Eton?'[12] Randolph Churchill remarks in the official biography how strange it was that a boy of 13 would not know of his father's choice of schooling, while Winston himself found out indirectly of his father's choice for him.

On the rare occasions that his father corresponded with him, it was often to rebuke him for some personal failing. Randolph once returned one of his son's letters with the following note: 'This is a letter which I shall not keep but return to you that you may from time to time review its pedantic and overgrown schoolboy style.'[13] He even suggested in another letter that Winston substitute 'Father' for 'Papa' in his letters.[14]

The most famous example of fatherly displeasure followed Churchill's entrance into the Sandhurst military academy. In June 1893 Churchill had taken the entrance exam for the third time and, though his marks were too low for an infantry cadetship, he gained one for the cavalry. Winston was relieved but his father offered a stern and destructive rebuke. In his letter, Randolph reprimanded his son for his 'slovenly happy-go-lucky harum scarum style of work', while no longer attaching 'the slightest weight' to anything he said about his own acquirements and exploits. He then warned his son that if he did not abandon 'his idle useless unprofitable life' he would become 'a mere social wastrel' and 'degenerate into a shabby unhappy & futile existence.'[15]

Winston was clearly affected by the sternness of this rebuke and merely promised his father that he would try to improve. Randolph did little to deserve his son's hero worship. But Winston still felt that his father owned 'the key to everything or almost everything worth having' even if the admiration was all one way. When Winston showed his father signs of comradeship, he was 'frozen into stone'.[16]

Jennie made up for her former aloofness by assisting Winston during the early part of his public career. While he was serving in India she sent him dozens of volumes from the world's famous authors, as well as 27 volumes of the *Annual Register*. She later served as his literary agent, helping to find him a suitable newspaper to publish his articles on the Malakand war, as well as a publisher for his early books. While Churchill's relations with his mother improved in his twenties, he had no opportunity to repair relations with his father. Randolph died after a lingering illness in 1895, with Winston declaring that he would seek 'to lift again the flag I found lying on a stricken field'.[17]

Without doubt though, the spirit of Randolph Churchill hovered over Winston in the early stages of his political career. In 1901 Churchill delivered his maiden speech in the House of Commons on the Boer War. At the end, he thanked the House for their attention: 'I cannot sit down without saying how very grateful I am for the kindness and patience with which the House has heard me, and which have been extended to me, I well know, not on my own account, but because of a certain splendid memory which many Hon Members still preserve.'[18]

During the first half of the next decade, Churchill would write a biography of his father while starting out on his own political journey. In a sense, this was no mere coincidence. Churchill sought to vindicate his father's life and career while showing himself, with respect to his core political beliefs, to be his father's son. After all, they both endorsed similar causes: Tory democracy, army retrenchment, Ulster and cross party coalition. But Randolph needed political rehabilitation for he was best remembered for his reckless resignation and later decline. Winston's filial piety ensured he would get it.

In the preface he wrote: 'I have thought it my duty, so far as possible, to assemble once and for all the whole body of historical evidence required for the understanding of Lord Randolph Churchill's career. Scarcely anything of material consequence has been omitted, and such omissions as have been necessary are made for others' sakes and not his own...'[19] Of course this was disingenuous for material was suppressed which would have done posthumous damage to Randolph's reputation. Winston appears to have believed that his father died from the effects of tertiary syphilis but no such revelation could have been made in respectable society. It was a final act of loving kindness from son to father.

Was Churchill a school dunce?

'I AM ALL FOR the public schools but I do not want to go there again.' This comment in his autobiography *My Early Life* neatly encapsulated Churchill's unhappiness at school and his dislike of the traditional curriculum. For the slightly unorthodox and precocious 'young man in a hurry', public school life was too rigid and constraining to be of real satisfaction. He enjoyed some subjects but hated others and his resulting boredom led to reports of slovenliness and a lack of diligence. Throughout his early years, Churchill's defiant attitude was a constant source of frustration to his teachers. Their frequent disappointment has helped foster the belief that Churchill was an intellectually feeble school dunce and that his rise to power was a miracle for an uneducated boy. In the film *Young Winston*, based on Churchill's autobiography, we see how the intrepid 13-year-old fared in the Classics entrance exam to Harrow:

> I wrote my name at the top of the page. I wrote down the number of the question 'I'. But thereafter I could not think of anything connected with it that was either relevant or true. Incidentally there arrived from nowhere in particular a blot and several smudges. I gazed for two whole hours at this sad spectacle; and then merciful ushers collected my piece of foolscap with all the others and carried it up to the Headmaster's table.

Churchill tells us: 'It was from these slender indications of scholarship that Mr. Welldon drew the conclusion that I was worthy to pass into Harrow...'[20] The account is interesting for what it leaves out, for he was also examined in algebra and 'a very easy arithmetic paper'.[21] However, he was placed in the lowest division of the fourth (or bottom) form, which was a rather 'unpretentious situation'.[22]

But was Churchill's rather uncharacteristic modesty no more than a clever ploy to enhance his political career? His son certainly believed so: 'Just as his greatest friend, F.E. Smith, was wont to exaggerate the poverty of his youth,' Randolph Churchill wrote, 'Winston was inclined to exaggerate his own early ignorance.' He went on: 'Both no doubt subconsciously felt in later years that their brilliant successes would be enhanced, set against a somber background of poverty and stupidity.'[23]

The myth of the intellectually deficient schoolboy is easily exploded when one reads the less self effacing passages of *My Early Life*. His frequent poor subject reports and exam lapses had less to do with poor ability and more to do with a lack of interest in the school curriculum. And where Churchill's interest could not be engaged, he would simply refuse to try. Churchill revealed the following in his autobiography: 'I would have liked to have been examined in history, poetry and writing essays,' subjects in which he would have excelled. But the examiners 'were partial to Latin and mathematics'. Churchill continued: 'I would have willingly displayed my knowledge' but the examiners 'sought to expose my ignorance'.[24]

Churchill's partiality to favourite subjects, and contemptuous dislike of others, explains why he did not receive glowing reports from his frustrated teachers. As he admitted in *My Early Life*, 'Where my reason, imagination or interest were not engaged, I would not or I could not learn...' And, as one of his tutors put it at the time, Winston's problem was not a lack of ability but a 'fitful' energy.[25]

In particular, Churchill hated the emphasis on classics in the public school curriculum. As one of his contemporaries remembered, 'to shy at Latin was a serious obstacle to success', for he was as a result a 'late starter'.[26] Another of his contemporaries at Harrow remembered that he 'really hated much of the school curriculum' and that it seemed 'a shocking waste to spend so much time on dead languages and so little on his native tongue'.[27] His hatred of classics has an amusing ring to it. At the age of seven he thought that the practice of declining Latin words was 'rigmarole' and, on hearing that Gladstone read Homer for fun, he thought that this 'served him right'.[28] He claimed that in twelve years of education, he never wrote a Latin verse or learnt Greek, except the alphabet, a stubborn attitude that would accompany him throughout his school career.

This stubborn attitude was also reflected in his school behaviour, which was often marked by a defiance of authority. At his first school, St George's in Ascot, there is evidence of young Winston's mischievous behaviour. In his first report the headmaster noted that, while Winston was 'very truthful', he was also 'a regular pickle' who had 'not fallen into school ways yet'.[29] According to one of Churchill's contemporaries at St George's, young Winston had a 'quarrelsome attitude' which 'got on everyone's nerves'.[30]

The following year, despite his improvement, he could still be 'troublesome' while his headmaster stated that he could not 'be trusted to behave himself anywhere'.[31] At Harrow Churchill was the recipient of corporal punishment which was sometimes administered by the Head of House. On one occasion Churchill was 'whipped' by his Head of House, Nugent Hicks; after receiving his first lashing, he said to Hicks, 'I shall be a greater man than you.' Hicks replied: 'You can take two more for that.'

One of his contemporaries at Harrow summed up his memory of Churchill's school behaviour: 'He consistently broke almost every rule made by masters or boys, was quite incorrigible, and had an unlimited vocabulary of "back chat", which he produced with dauntless courage on every occasion of remonstrance.'[32]

When Churchill applied himself to subjects of interest, such as the humanities, his reports were encouraging. In his last report at St George's in Ascot for summer 1883, his history and geography were 'very good' and 'very fair' respectively.[33] Both history and geography were 'very good' (report of June 1884) and, in the same report, spelling was improved although his writing was 'full of corrections & untidy.'[34] Even in subjects which he claimed to hate, there is evidence that Churchill was no dunce. In revising for his Harrow entrance exam, Winston found that he was 'forward' rather than backward in his study of Euclid, and in preparatory exams at that time he came first in many subjects, including algebra, English and Bible history.[35] He claimed to enjoy chemistry and, in one of his earliest letters to his mother, he wrote: 'It seems so funny that two gases should make water.'[36]

Winston also demonstrated his remarkable memory by successfully reciting twelve hundred lines of Macaulay's *Lays of Ancient Rome*, winning a school prize in the process. One of Winston's Harrovian contemporaries said that, while people teaching him literature could remember a line or two of a Shakespeare play, 'Winston could quote whole scenes straight off; nor was he slow to take advantage of his remarkable gift of memory' for, if a master misquoted a passage, 'Winston would instantly correct him'.[37] While at Harrow, he had also finished fouth out of twenty-five for the Shakespeare prize (for the lower class), beating a number of older boys.

Churchill's powers of expression were on display in other ways. While at Harrow, he sent notes on current events to the school magazine *The Harrovian* which were, in the words of one contemporary, 'extraordinarily witty and well expressed'.[38] It is not for nothing that Dr Welldon is said to have talked of Winston's 'love and veneration for the English language'.[39] His love of the language owed something to Mr Robert Somervell, the lower school English master at Harrow. As a result of being in the bottom form at Harrow, Churchill learned English under Somervell, whose duty consisted in 'teaching the stupidest boys the most disregarded thing – namely, to write mere English'. As a result of Somervell's training, Churchill claimed to have mastered the 'essential structure of the ordinary British sentence', which was 'a noble thing'.[40]

There is early evidence, too, of his outstanding oratorical ability. As Canon Tomlin recalls: 'The one vivid memory that I have of him, corroborated independently by two of my Harrow friends, is of this small red haired, snub nosed, jolly faced youngster darting up during a house debate, against all the rules, before he had been a year in the house, to refute one of his seniors and carrying all before him with a magnificent speech.'[41] Churchill did not particularly distinguish himself at Harrow but he was certainly described as 'a marked boy' whose 'great ability was recognised by at any rate some masters'.[42]

Churchill, then, was not so much stupid as stubborn. He had a special gift for the English language and history and he impressed his peers with his oratorical technique. Sebastian Haffner is therefore a little wide of the mark in suggesting that Churchill left school 'uneducated' and that a Harrow education 'was wasted on him'.[43] But, as Randolph Churchill remarked in the official biography, 'No one could make him do or learn anything against his will.'[44] Ultimately that spirit of stubbornness and rebellion, and unyielding love of the English language, would remain with Churchill for the rest of his life.

Was Churchill an unrepentant jingoist in the 'River War'?

I have tried to gild war... But there was nothing dulce et decorum about the Dervish dead; nothing of the dignity of unconquerable manhood... Yet these were as brave men as ever walked the earth.[45]

AFTER COMPLETING his military training at Sandhurst, Churchill became embroiled in a series of imperial wars in India, Sudan and South Africa. This suited the young subaltern for he was eager for decoration and military glory. In 1898 there was a new focus for

imperial activity in the Sudan where Sir Herbert Kitchener, the
Egyptian Sirdar (commander), was leading an expedition. Kitchener's
aims were twofold. With Italy establishing a colony in Somaliland
and France expanding its Saharan Empire, Britain had to protect its
own African empire from foreign encroachment and prevent territories such as Kenya and Uganda being cut off from Egypt.

Kitchener also sought to avenge the death of General Gordon in
1885 at the hands of the self-proclaimed Mahdi, Mohammed Ahmed.
Ahmed was a militant Islamic leader who led a fierce resistance to
Egyptian occupation in the Sudan a decade earlier. He was to confront the Mahdi's successor, Abdullah al-Taashi (the Khalifa) with his
nearly fifty thousand followers, or Dervishes.

Lord Kitchener initially vetoed Churchill's application to take
part in the Sudan campaign, scared of what he might write as a
newspaper correspondent. It was only his mother's entreaties to
Prime Minister Salisbury, as well as the death of another soldier, that
changed Kitchener's mind. The War Office telegram advising him
of his attachment to the 21st Lancers was hardly welcoming: 'You
will proceed at your own expense and ... in the event of your being
killed or wounded ... no charge of any kind will fall on British Army
funds.'[46]

Winston saw action at the vital moments of the campaign. He
arrived at the city of Omdurman, near Khartoum, late in August. On
September 1st the Khalifa's army lined up on a five-mile front and
the following day they advanced against Kitchener's troops. But the
Dervishes, for all their vigour, were no match for the British army,
who mowed them down with machine guns and a mass of artillery.
The Dervishes, armed with spears and rifles, fell in great numbers,
but Kitchener decided not to stop there. Fearful that they would
retreat to Khartoum, Kitchener ordered the 310 men of the 21st
Lancers to finish off the remnants of the Dervishes on the field of
battle. Churchill advanced, armed with a Mauser pistol and, according to the account he wrote later, shot a number of the Dervishes,
killing at least three for certain.

As well as participating in the fighting, Churchill had journalistic
responsibilities. Prior to this departure for Sudan, he had struck a
deal with *The Morning Post* to pay him £15 per column, a considerable
sum in those days. Thus, during the campaigns of the River War,
Churchill wrote fifteen long dispatches in the form of unsigned
letters (except the last) and these later formed the basis of a two-

volume account, *The River War*. Given his colossal ambition for military glory and his staunch defence of British imperialism, one might have expected the young Churchill to fully endorse British actions in Sudan, but this was far from the case. His writing was 'poles apart from the conventional jingoistic British journalism of the period'.47

Controversially, he paid tribute to the courage and fighting spirit of the Dervishes. They were, he wrote, 'as brave men as ever walked the earth ... their claim beyond the grave in respect of a valiant death was as good as that which any of our countrymen could make.' The Dervish warriors were 'valiant', 'confident in their strength, in the justice of their cause, in the support of their religion' but were now 'scattered and destroyed'.48 Already Churchill was displaying an unconventional attitude with this unrestrained accolade to the enemy. He was also generous to Mohammed Ahmed, describing him as 'the most remarkable Mohammedan of modern times' and a 'man of considerable nobility of character'.49

Churchill also criticised the decision not to spare the lives of wounded Dervish soldiers. For this, he laid the blame squarely on the shoulders of Kitchener, writing that 'there was a very general impression that the fewer the prisoners, the greater would be the satisfaction of the commander'. Later he would write to his mother that 'the victory at Omdurman was disgraced by the inhuman slaughter of the wounded and that Kitchener was responsible for this'.50 After 'atrocious' acts of cruelty by British soldiers, Omdurman became a tarnished event in which individual soldiers would 'carry from the field only a very transient satisfaction'.51

It was not just the lack of humanity that rankled with Churchill, but also the strategic incompetence of the campaign. The British failed to catch the Mahdi's successor, and once again Kitchener was singled out for opprobrium: 'On whom does the responsibility lie? Not on the troopers ... not on the cavalry leaders ... but upon the Sirdar, and on him alone.'52

But the event that most greatly aroused Churchill's indignation happened after the battle itself. On Kitchener's orders, the tomb of the Mahdi in Khartoum had been desecrated and the Mahdi's body disinterred. The corpse's head had then been removed for 'future disposal'. Churchill launched an outspoken attack on this action:

> If the people of the Sudan cared no more for the Mahdi, then it was an act of vandalism and folly to destroy the only fine building which

might attract the traveller and interest the historian ... If, on the other hand, the people of the Sudan still venerated the memory of the Mahdi ... then I shall not hesitate to declare that to destroy what was sacred and holy to them was a wicked act, of which the true Christian, no less than the philosopher, must express his abhorrence.[53]

For Churchill, the desecration of the Mahdi's tomb and the removal of his body was a 'wretched business'.[54] It was an act of barbarity that in his view could not be justified, no matter how treacherous the nature of the Dervish enemy. Much as he supported the decision to reconquer the Sudan, he could not acquiesce in such a blatant disregard for civilised morality. But, more significantly, Churchill's account challenged the view that war was always a chivalrous episode bringing out its combatants' noblest instincts. Far from 'gilding war', he had unearthed its darker side and, in the process, offered some remarkably prescient observations about the coming century.

Why did Churchill achieve world fame during the Boer War?

...in that fervid and picturesque imagination there are always great deeds afoot with himself cast by destiny in the Agamemnon role.[55]

THE SECOND Anglo-Boer War (1899-1902) resulted from a long-standing quarrel between the British and the Boers, the fiercely independent Dutch settlers in South Africa, at the end of the nineteenth century. When Britain occupied the Cape of Good Hope in 1806, the Boer settlers who lived there refused to submit to colonial control and started the Great Trek northwards in the 1830s. For the next six decades the Boers fought for independence, first against the Zulus in 1838, and then against the British in 1881. They settled in two independent republics, the Orange Free State and the Transvaal.

The discovery of gold and diamond fields in the Transvaal transformed the status of the territory, and overnight thousands of mainly British prospectors (Uitlanders) streamed into the country. Fearing that the Uitlanders would become a majority, the Boers denied them voting rights while also imposing taxes on the gold industry. In response, there was pressure from the Uitlanders and the British mine owners to overthrow the Boer government, pressure which led to the ill-planned and abortive Jameson Raid of 1895. The Boers now began to arm their militias while several key British colonial leaders favoured the outright annexation of the Boer republics. By September 1899 the failure to secure improved conditions for the Uitlanders made war between the two sides inevitable.

In his first thoughts on the subject, Churchill wrote supportively of the war against the Dutch settlers. In an unpublished memorandum, he talked of the need 'to redress the wrongs of the Outlanders' while curbing 'the insolence of the Boers'. For him, this fight was thoroughly consistent with maintaining the interests of the British Empire.[56] But, while he relished the prospect of a showdown, Churchill did not underestimate the strength of his opponents. Some people believed that the Boers would be rapidly defeated, but Churchill was more circumspect. In a letter to his mother, he wrote: 'We have greatly underestimated the military strength of the Boers. I vy much doubt whether one Army Corps will be enough to overcome their resistance – at any rate a fierce and bloody struggle is before us in which at least ten or twelve thousand lives will be sacrificed...'[57] His foreboding was to prove remarkably accurate.

It was a measure of Churchill's previous journalistic successes that he became the highest paid war correspondent in South Africa. After receiving an offer to write for *The Daily Mail*, Churchill agreed to be a correspondent for *The Morning Star* for the sum of £250 a month, an extremely lucrative deal at the time. Considering that Churchill faced competition from such household names as Rudyard Kipling, Arthur Conan Doyle and H.G. Wells, this was a formidable achievement in itself.[58] As a result of his dual role as reporter and soldier in Sudan and India, a new rule was devised that prevented officers doubling as war correspondents, though this rule could sometimes be circumvented. Churchill's chances of military glory seemed slight, but events were to prove otherwise.

Within a fortnight of arriving, Churchill was to take part in one of the most celebrated incidents of the entire war. Together with 117 men from the Durban Light Infantry and Dublin Fusiliers, he boarded an armoured train on a reconnaissance mission to reconnoiter the Boer troops who were besieging the town of Ladysmith. He later wrote: 'Nothing looks more formidable and impressive than an armoured train; but nothing is in fact more vulnerable and helpless. It was only necessary to blow up a bridge or culvert to leave the monster stranded, far from home and help, at the mercy of the enemy.'[59]

Unbeknown to those on board the train, the Boers had sabotaged the track by placing a large boulder on the line. Halfway through its mission, the train was derailed and then came under sustained Boer gunfire. With the engine driver injured by a bullet, Churchill now took control of events. Facing a barrage of Boer artillery, he led the effort to free the train while also taking injured soldiers on board.

There are ample testimonials to his gallantry on the armoured train. In one letter: 'The railway men who accompanied the armoured train this morning ask me to convey to you their admiration of the coolness and pluck displayed by Mr. Winston Churchill.' Captain Anthony Weldon wrote to Field Marshal Lord Wolseley, Commander in Chief of the British Army: 'I had a talk with the engine driver of the train ... and also with a platelayer who had accompanied it ... they both told me nothing could exceed Churchill's pluck and coolness during the whole affair.' The *Natal Advertiser* carried an account from a Captain Wylie, who had been wounded in the attack. Wylie described Churchill's conduct as 'that of as brave a man as could be found'. Even the burghers who were firing on the train 'gave glowing details about Winston Churchill's gallantry'.[60]

When the train had been freed and started to move away, Churchill noticed that some infantrymen had been left stranded. He then dismounted, insisting that he could not 'leave those poor beggars to their fate'.[61] Sadly he arrived too late, for the men had already surrendered to the Boers. Winston was suddenly shot at by two Boer soldiers who were near him on the railway track, and he ran, ducking bullets as he went. As he attempted to escape, he found himself confronted by a mounted Boer who began waving and shouting at him. Realising he was now unarmed (he had left his pistol on the train) and with no one to help, he had little choice but to surrender. He became a prisoner of war at the States Model School.

Churchill would later describe being taken prisoner as 'his greatest indignity'. There is no doubt that, as a non-combatant, he particularly resented his loss of freedom and he made numerous pleas to the authorities to release him on these grounds. But the event that would make Churchill a household name in Britain was his escape from the States Model School after nearly a month of captivity. The daring escape was originally planned by Captain Aylmer Haldane, a friend of Churchill's from their days in India who had been ordered to take the armoured train on a reconnaissance.

Though Haldane was reluctant to include Churchill in the escape, anxious lest he jeopardise their chances of getting away, he could hardly refuse the hero from the armoured train. The plan was to escape via a badly lit latrine that was situated against a fence at the back of the school. A sentry who was standing by the spot usually moved at dinner time, creating an opportunity for that unguarded section of the fence to be scaled. However, on the night that they planned to escape, the sentry stood by the latrine without moving and the escape had to be postponed for twenty-four hours.

The next evening Haldane went to the same spot and saw a sentry standing near the latrine. Judging that it was too hazardous to escape, he returned to his companions, but Churchill had already decided to take his chances. He went to the latrine and, when the sentry momentarily turned away, climbed over the prison wall and into an adjoining garden. There he stayed for up to an hour, waiting patiently for the other two would-be escapees. Eventually he communicated with Haldane through chinks in the wall, whereupon he was told to go on ahead on his own as an escape by the others would be impossible. Churchill strolled out of the prison on his own, without a compass, map or money.[62]

He decided to head to the Portuguese port of Lourenço Marques but knew he would stand little chance of succeeding on foot. Reaching the railway line, he clambered aboard a goods train that was heading eastwards. The following day, he left the wagon and waited near the railway track. He was near the coal mining village of Witbank, sixty miles from Pretoria. That night the tired and hungry Churchill walked away from the railway line towards lights in the distance which came from a coal mine. As he approached, he was fearful lest the owner be a Boer who might turn him in. It turned out that the coal mine owner was an Englishman called John Howard. 'Thank God you have come here,' Howard said. 'It is the only house for twenty miles where you would not have been handed over, but we are all British here and we will see you through.'

For three days, Winston hid at the bottom of a mine shaft and was then put on to a rail truck loaded with wool that was travelling into Portuguese Mozambique. His difficulties were still not over for he had to survive several train stops before he arrived safely in Lourenço Marques. From there he sailed by ship to Durban, where he was met by a jubilant crowd anxious to celebrate the feats of a new-found hero. His exploits were all the more welcome as they coincided with a series of demoralising British defeats at Magersfontein, Stormberg and Colenso. The public were entranced by the tale of this English 'David' outwitting the Boer 'Goliath' through sheer pluck and endurance. It helped to make him a household name in Britain.[63]

The armoured train incident and his escape from captivity were by no means the end of Churchill's adventures in South Africa. Instead of returning home, he rejoined General Redvers Buller's army on its march to relieve Ladysmith and take Pretoria. Although he continued as a war correspondent, Churchill was able to gain a commission in the South African Light Horse Regiment and was one of the first British troops into Ladysmith and Pretoria.

He subsequently published two books on the Boer War, *London to Ladysmith via Pretoria* and *Ian Hamilton's March*, which were published in May and October respectively. But it was the earlier incidents that solidified his reputation for bravery and gallant conduct. At this point Churchill could have pursued a successful career in the military, buoyed up by his courageous actions in Sudan and South Africa. But, while seeking to emulate the Duke of Marlborough, he also sought to exploit his battlefield success in order to build a career at Westminster. In 1900 his dream became a reality when he was elected MP for Oldham.

NOTES

1 WSC Bio 1, p.15.
2 C. Higham, *Dark Lady*, p.3.
3 W. Churchill, *My Early Life*, pp.4-5.
4 W. Churchill, *Thoughts and Adventures*, pp.31-2.
5 WSC Bio 1, p.45.
6 *Ibid.*, p.82.
7 *Ibid.*, p.90.
8 *Ibid.*, p.125.
9 *Ibid.*, pp.160-1.
10 C. Sandys, *From Winston with Love and Kisses*, p.76.
11 W. Churchill, *My Early Life*, p.62.
12 WSC Bio 1, p.97.
13 K. Aldritt, *Churchill the Writer*, p.2.

14 Companion I (i), p.439.
15 *Ibid.*, pp.390-1.
16 G. Rubin, *Forty Ways to Look at Winston Churchill*, p.106.
17 J. Keegan, *Churchill*, p.20.
18 Companion II (i), p.13. Those who listened to the speech noted similarities between father and son. A correspondent for the *Glasgow Herald* noted that 'there were tones and inflections of voice which forcibly recalled his father', though he felt that the son 'did not show much trace of his parent's brilliancy in debate' (*ibid.*, p.15). Another correspondent for the *Yorkshire Post* noted that he was 'not an orator any more than his father was' (*ibid.*, p.16), while the *Westminster Gazette* noted that, 'members last night thought they could detect some suggestion of Lord Randolph Churchill in the young member's pose' (*ibid.*, p.19).
19 W. Churchill, *The Life of Lord Randolph Churchill*, Preface.
20 W. Churchill, *My Early Life*, pp.15-16.
21 WSC Bio 1, p.107.
22 W. Churchill, *My Early Life*, p.16.
23 WSC Bio 1, p.107.
24 W. Churchill, *My Early Life*, p.15.
25 WSC Bio 1, p.115.
26 E. Chaplin (ed), *Winston Churchill and Harrow*, p.28.
27 *Ibid.*, p.34.
28 W. Churchill, *My Early Life*, pp.11, 23.
29 Companion I (i), p.90.
30 C. Sandys, *With Love and Kisses*, p.58.
31 *Ibid.*, p.94.
32 C. Eade (ed), *Churchill by His Contemporaries*, p.19.
33 Companion I (i), p.91.
34 *Ibid.*, p.95.
35 *Ibid.*, p.144.
36 C. Sandys, *With Love and Kisses*, p.68.
37 E. Chaplin (ed), *WSC and Harrow*, p.34.
38 *Ibid.*, p.17.
39 *Ibid.*, p.34.
40 W. Churchill, *My Early Life*, p.17.
41 E. Chaplin, *WSC and Harrow*, p.28.
42 *Ibid.*, p.17.
43 S. Haffner, *Churchill*, p.13.
44 WSC Bio 1, p.184.
45 W. Churchill, *The River War II*, p.221.
46 WSC Bio 1, p.394.
47 F. Woods, *Artillery of Words*, p.41.
48 *Morning Post*, October 6th 1898.
49 W. Churchill, *The River War I*, p.115; II, p.212.
50 WSC Bio 1, p.424.
51 W. Churchill, *The River War II*, p.195.
52 *Ibid.*, pp.193-4.
53 M. Gilbert, *Churchill: A Life*, pp.99-100.

54 Speeches I, p.31.
55 D. Jablonsky, *Churchill: The Great Game and Total War*, p.18.
56 C. Sandys, *Churchill: Wanted Dead or Alive*, p.10.
57 Companion I (ii), p.1058.
58 C. Sandys, *Churchill: Wanted Dead or Alive*, p.13.
59 W. Churchill, *My Early Life*, p.241.
60 C. Sandys, *Churchill: Wanted Dead or Alive*, p.65.
61 *Ibid.*, p.53.
62 Haldane would later bitterly accuse Churchill of recklessly jeopardising the
    escape plan by going ahead on his own. However, this accusation has been
    effectively countered by Celia Sandys in *Churchill: Wanted Dead or Alive*,
    pp.112-13.
63 The popular limerick went:

>   You've heard of Winston Churchill.
>   This is all I need to say:
>   He's the latest and the greatest
>   Correspondent of the day.

CHAPTER TWO
Political Firebrand

CHURCHILL DID NOT last long as a Conservative MP. Almost immediately he took a stand against Tory proposals for higher army spending, while his remarks about the fighting qualities of the Boers provoked further controversy. In 1903 Joseph Chamberlain split the Tories with his call for imperial protectionist tariffs and, as an ardent champion of free trade, Churchill found himself at loggerheads with his party.

After a long campaign against Chamberlain, Churchill 'crossed the floor' in 1904 to become a Liberal MP. In 1906 the Liberals seized power under Henry Campbell-Bannerman, after two decades of Conservative dominance, leading to charges that Churchill had opportunistically jumped ship to advance his career. This charge was to recur throughout his life. He was subsequently appointed Under-secretary of State for the Colonies and, in this position, played a leading role in reaching a lasting and magnanimous settlement in South Africa.

In 1908 he was appointed President of the Board of Trade and helped to spearhead an ambitious programme of social reform. He introduced labour exchanges, which helped the unemployed, while the Trade Boards Act established the minimum wage in a number of professions. He also played a leading role in the National Insurance Bill which was subsequently introduced in 1911 by the Chancellor, David Lloyd George. Together, Churchill and Lloyd George were the leading voices calling for progressive legislation to help society's most vulnerable members.

At the time of the 1909 budget, Churchill was a relentless critic of the House of Lords and advocated fundamental reform, or even abolition, of the second chamber. His progressive attitudes were also evident in his rejection of the Aliens Act, a piece of legislation which was designed to limit the entry of (mainly Jewish) immigrants to Britain.

In 1910 Churchill became Home Secretary at the age of 35. He reduced the amount of time prisoners could spend in solitary confinement and advocated special treatment for political prisoners. He also exercised clemency in a number of cases where prisoners faced the death penalty. His belief in the humane treatment of workers led him to introduce the Mines Eight Hours Bill, which introduced baths in pit heads and reduced hours for workers.

During the period 1910-11, industrial militancy blighted much of Britain and Churchill tried, where possible, to limit military intervention. He held troops on standby in the Tonypandy riots and insisted that police deal with rioters first, before the army was used. But in the following year soldiers were sent to Merseyside and other towns to protect the rail network. In all these cases, Churchill showed that, where the social order was threatened, the use of force was justified.

Why did Churchill switch parties in 1904?

LIKE HIS FATHER before him, Churchill was accused by his detractors of putting power before principle. He had entered the world of Westminster politics with a growing reputation for egotism and insatiable ambition, earning him distrust from many of his Conservative colleagues. Some had him marked out as an unstable maverick who would seize any opportunity for self-promotion at the expense of his party. In 1904 he confirmed their fears by switching from the Conservative to the Liberal Party. He had 'ratted' on the Tories and they were never to forget it.

Undoubtedly there was some truth in the Tory complaints. As a 'young man in a hurry', with little prospect of immediate advancement, Churchill was impatient for high office. As Sebastian Haffner wrote: 'He undoubtedly resented the fact that his party leaders had left him languishing on the back-benches for three long years. He yearned for office and power (less so for status); he craved it with every fibre of his being, and soon found it unbearable to lead the life of a back-bencher who could do nothing but deliver speeches and file obediently past the tellers when the House divided.'[1]

Observers also felt that Churchill showed little attachment to party. Like Lord Randolph with his call for a 'Fourth Party', Churchill called for a 'middle or coalition party' in British politics in which consensus could be more amicably reached on the issues of the day. Bourke Cockran gave Churchill a wise warning about how his decision to 'rat' (switch parties) would be viewed by uncharitable observers. They would assume that in order to fuel his ambition, 'party success or party prospects would be sacrificed without scruple or hesitation' and that he was 'actuated by the very basest desires and ambitions'.[2]

But it would also be wrong to suggest that his switch of parties was devoid of political principle. It had a great deal to do with rumblings within the Conservative Party, with the political machinations of Joseph Chamberlain and with an argument over free trade.

The big issue that had split the Conservative Party was protection, the rallying cry of Colonial Secretary Joseph Chamberlain. Chamberlain had previously called for the creation of a customs union, modelled on the German Zollverein, that would embrace the whole empire and involve the imposition of tariffs on all non-Empire goods. The arguments for tariffs could be expressed simply enough. Foreign countries were subsidising some of their producers whose cheap goods were then flooding into Britain. These foreign goods were undercutting British manufactured products through 'unfair' competition, leading to the decline of domestic industries. A tariff wall would bring greater economic prosperity to Britain and *keep out* unwanted foreign goods. For British industry, ending unwanted competition would lead to a revival of prosperity, while for the working classes the benefits would come in the form of important measures of social reform.

At the turn of the century, the economic reach of the state was relatively limited. Income tax was largely raised from the middle classes and those earning less than £160 annually were exempt. Other revenue was obtained indirectly from customs and excise duties. The Boer War had led to increases in the tax burden and, as the decade advanced, calls for higher military expenditure led to calls for higher taxation, something strongly resisted by free traders. As early as 1901, Churchill had argued that (free) trade was vital to Britain and that 'all taxation' was 'a drag on trade'.[3] He also described himself as a 'sober admirer of Free Trade principles', and he defended them as regularly as he could. Why this zealous defence of free trade when the arguments for economic protectionism seemed compelling?

The most persuasive argument for free trade (and against protection) was that a population ought to have unfettered choice in obtaining the varied goods of the world. In Churchill's words, a population should be 'free to purchase its supplies of food wherever it chooses and whenever it chooses in the open markets of the world'.4 An Englishman, he said, 'has a right to purchase what he lacks whenever and wherever he chooses, without let or hindrance or discouragement by the State'.5 Free trade would allow the 'good and varied merchandise' of the world to flow freely into Britain, goods that were more interesting than many found in the British Empire. By contrast protection would mean that the British Empire was shut in a 'ringed fence' and closed off from the rest of the world.6

Churchill also believed that a protectionist scheme would be accompanied by an unprecedented scale of corruption. He argued that, under this system, every trade in the country would lobby politicians for protection; MPs would be besieged by 'touts and concession hunters', who in turn would bring with them 'rivers of money' that would flow into the pockets of those prepared to 'protect certain great, important, well organised and progressive trades'.7 Protectionism, he said, would also hit the working classes hardest. Cheap imports provided inexpensive foodstuffs for the poor and the imposition of tariffs would lead to higher prices for bread and other commodities, thus leading to increased industrial costs.

In addition, free trade tended to correlate with better foreign relations, while tariffs frequently led to aggressive competitiveness and the souring of international relations. A tariff wall round the colonies would lead to a self-contained Empire and it was preferable, he wrote, that 'the great nations of the world should be interdependent one upon the other than that they should be independent of each other'.8 He thought it would be disastrous to see the Empire 'degenerate into a sullen confederacy, walled off, like a mediaeval town ... containing within the circle of its battlements all that is necessary for war'.9

The wording of this last sentence suggests that there was an intrinsic connection between free trade and the peace of Europe. Indeed Churchill was also thinking along these lines. As he wrote in 1903, 'it is chiefly through the cause of the great traffic of one great nation with another during the last twenty-five years, that the peace of Europe has been preserved through so many crises'.10 There was an argument for 'retaliatory' tariffs against countries that were dumping subsidised goods on other markets and, while Churchill could support this in selective cases, he was more a believer in free than fair trade.

Chamberlain responded to the growing unease over tariffs with a speech on May 15th 1903 in which he proclaimed his total conversion to a scheme of imperial preference. He also proposed retaliation against any nation which practised unfair trade and competition. Churchill responded by calling for a league to resist Chamberlain's protectionist proposals. 'Without organisation', he said, 'we are bound first to be silenced and secondly to be destroyed'.[11] The Unionist Free Food League was then set up, supported by many figures and institutions of the establishment, and with Churchill one of its young prominent members.

Unfortunately for Churchill, most back-bench Conservative MPs supported Chamberlain and his Tariff Reform League, while in Churchill's own constituency there was anger at the tactics of their recalcitrant young member. He was not helped by the vacillations of Prime Minister Balfour. Balfour tried to steer between the Scylla of undiluted free trade and the Charybdis of protection by sacking his free trade Chancellor and the protectionist Chamberlain, then announcing that, while he was not in favour of food taxes, he would support retaliation. The compromise failed to convince Churchill.

Contrary to those who see in Churchill an opportunist seeking the first chance to change party, Churchill's instinct was to call for a middle or coalition party. Free trade would be the one issue to unite such a coalition. However the three men on whom Churchill depended to bring about such a coalition, principally the former Liberal Prime Minister, the Earl of Roseberry, failed to take any decisive action.

Churchill's alienation from his own party was now complete. In October 1903 he described himself as 'an English Liberal' and added: 'I hate the Tory party, their men, their words and their methods ... It is therefore my intention that before Parliament meets my separation from the Tory party and the government shall be complete & irrevocable.'[12] In November he was barred from entering a Tory working men's club in his constituency and the following month his constituency passed a resolution of no confidence in their young member. Churchill was unable to entice Unionist (Conservative) free traders to secede from the party as the majority saw themselves as Tories first and free traders second.

From February 1904 he was voting with the Liberals and his Unionist whip was withdrawn. The final breach came in a dramatic scene in the House of Commons in March 1904. Churchill was speaking in the Commons, demanding to know what Prime Minister Balfour thought about the protection issue. While he was speaking, Balfour and his Conservative Cabinet promptly walked out of the Commons, followed by eighty or more Conservative MPs. It was only a matter of time before Churchill joined the Liberals. A suitable constituency was duly found for him in Manchester. On May 31st 1904, he entered the Commons, bowed to the Speaker, and took his seat on the Liberal benches next to David Lloyd George.

It is sometimes argued that Churchill showed little interest in economic questions. Haffner argued that Churchill 'displayed a cavalier indifference to economic problems throughout his life' and concluded, as we saw earlier, that the switch of parties in 1904 was about opportunism, not principle.[13] Against the first charge, it is worth noting that Churchill read a number of important economic treatises, such as Smith's *Wealth of Nations*, and was briefed by the enormously knowledgeable Permanent Secretary to the Treasury, Sir Francis Mowatt.

Against the charge of opportunism is Churchill's consistent support for free trade, even after 1904. After he became a Liberal minister in 1906, he wrote a manifesto expressing his firm belief in free trade principles.[14] As late as 1929 he wrote to Lord Beaverbrook rejecting the Empire Free Trade campaign. He argued that 'farmers would scorn a protective duty on foreign food which left them exposed to the equally unbearable competition of Canada and Australia'.[15]

However, in 1931 Churchill staged what Paul Addison has called a 'dignified retreat' from the classical doctrine of free trade by supporting tariffs.[16] In the 1931 budget debate he went out of his way to advertise his Damascene conversion: 'The tariff ... must become the agency by which the growing importance of the home market must be recognised.'[17] But this was an unprecedented national crisis and free trade was 'too expensive a luxury'. It was important to limit the import of foreign goods for, without some measure of protection, Britain's balance of payments crisis would not be corrected. The Conservative Party was also moving in the direction of tariffs and Churchill could hardly abandon a party for the third time. In fairness, many other lifelong liberal supporters of free trade (such as Simon and Keynes) expressed doubts about their free trade convictions given Britain's perilous economic position. But at heart, and under the right circumstances, he was an ardent champion of free trade.

Churchill's split from the Tories was, however, about more than free trade. During the previous two years, he had been busy writing a hagiographical biography of his father, a man who had arguably been betrayed by his fellow Conservatives in 1886. These same men were now Winston's political colleagues in the House of Commons. His resentment of the Tories for their alleged shabby treatment of his father certainly grated on him, adding to his hostility.[18]

Crossing the floor was a high-risk move for Churchill, saddling him with the sustained wrath of former allies and the potential mistrust of new ones. The bold gesture also left him open to the charge of inconsistency. But, while prepared to acknowledge an inconsistency in changing parties, Churchill did not think it was the worst form of inconsistency in politics. He wrote:

> A change of party is usually considered a much more serious breach of consistency than a change of view. In fact as long as a man works with a Party he will rarely find himself accused of inconsistency, no matter how widely his opinions at one time on any subject can be shown to have altered. Yet Parties are subject to changes and inconsistencies not less glaring than those of individuals.

What mattered more was that Churchill possessed 'a sincere conviction, in harmony with the needs of the time', for this would 'override all other factors'.[19]

Did Churchill oppose the entry of asylum seekers into Britain at the turn of the twentieth century?

DURING THE 1950s, Churchill expressed anxious concern about the number of black immigrants arriving in Britain. He told the Cabinet in 1954 that the 'continuing increase in the number of coloured people coming to this country and their presence here would sooner or later come to be resented by large sections of the British people'.[20] He asked for details of the number of 'coloured' immigrants in Britain and where they lived, and enquired whether the Post Office was employing too many coloured workers. 'He is alas very anti black', wrote Violet Bonham-Carter in one of her diary entries.[21]

Churchill's views on immigration reflected growing public concerns about what the *Sunday Times* called 'a serious colour problem' with the influx of immigrants from Commonwealth countries fuelling a deep level of public anxiety.[22] These views have cast him as a bigoted opponent of immigrants and asylum seekers. But this was far from being his attitude in the early 1900s during a period of increased Jewish immigration, when an anti-alien scare was sweeping much of southern England.

The last two decades of the nineteenth century witnessed a mass exodus of Jews from Eastern Europe. More than one million Jews from Russia, Russian Poland and Romania arrived in the West, the majority travelling to the United States, the remainder settling in Western Europe, including Britain. They were seeking refuge from ferocious Tsarist pogroms as well as a desperate economic downturn. Nearly a hundred thousand immigrants arrived in Britain over the course of a decade, and of this figure between forty and sixty thousand settled in the area of the East End known as Spitalfields, which had been a point of settlement for Jews since their re-admission in 1656.

The historian Anne Kershen writes: 'The visible concentration of so many outsiders in such a small space, their foreign appearance, their Yiddish dialect, the smell of their food – particularly fried fish – and their reportedly unsanitary style of living, only served to excite native feelings of hostility.'[23] This native hostility must be seen in the context of growing racial animosity and concerns about the state of the British economy.

In the last quarter of the nineteenth century, there were emerging signs of anti-Semitic prejudice in sections of British society. The Eastern Crisis of the late 1870s, in which Disraeli chose to support the Ottoman Turks despite their massacres of Bulgarian Christians, triggered off a spate of anti-Semitism. There were suggestions that Jews were not 'properly' British and that their attachment to the nation was tenuous at best. Disraeli was accused of having a 'foreign' mentality which was contrary to the country's interests. Towards the end of the nineteenth century, there were overtones of conspiratorial anti-Semitism when Jewish capitalists were accused of engineering the Boer War in South Africa to advance their own economic interests.

In addition, Britain experienced the twists and turns of economic flux during the late nineteenth century. There was a loss of confidence in the British economy as a result of the 1873-96 'Long Depression'.

The enormous mid-Victorian boom had given way to a cycle of slumps, with contemporaries suggesting that both industry and agriculture were in a process of terminal decline. In the face of foreign competition from the USA and Germany, profits from trade had fallen sharply. Between 1870 and 1900 the percentage of British exports going to the United States and Germany declined from 41 to 30 per cent. British industry found it more difficult to hold its own with major competitors in their home markets. Periodic unemployment resulted, the worst affected workers being those in seasonal, casual industries, including clothing and shoe-making. These were precisely the trades in which the newly arrived semi-skilled and unskilled Jewish immigrants most frequently sought and found work.[24]

After 1900, there was growing agitation against further immigration from some groups in Britain, most noticeably the British Brothers League founded by Major William Evans-Gordon.[25] As a result of this agitation, a Royal Commission on alien legislation was appointed in 1902 to investigate the issue. Specifically, they were to 'inquire into and to report upon the character and extent of the evils which are attributed to the unrestricted immigration of aliens especially in the Metropolis.'

After the commission concluded that 'the immigration of certain classes of aliens be subjected to State control', a bill was introduced in 1904 by the Home Secretary which intended 'to exclude various categories of alien: those convicted of an extraditable crime, those without means of financial support and those of notorious bad character.'

While he abstained from voting on the first two readings of the bill, Churchill soon made his views known on this legislative proposal. In a letter to Nathan Laski, the President of the Old Hebrew Congregation in Manchester, he wrote: 'To judge by the talk there has been, one would have imagined we were being overrun by a swarming invasion and "ousted" from our island through neglect of precautions which every foreign nation has adopted.' Quoting figures from the Board of Trade, Churchill declared that the immigrants constituted less than a 'one-hundred-and-fortieth part of the total population' and that they were 'increasing only 7,000 a year on the average'.

Having dismissed the scaremongering tactics of the anti-immigration bodies, Churchill went on to say that he could see no reason 'for departing from the old tolerant and generous practice of free entry and asylum to which this country has so long adhered and from which it has so often greatly gained'. He believed that it would be a mistake to grant the police or customs officers the power to refuse entry to immigrants as it could lead to 'bullying and blackmail', and in the hands of an anti-Semitic Home Secretary it would become 'an instrument of oppression'.[26]

In response to this letter, Nathan Laski wrote to Churchill saying that he had 'won the gratitude of the whole Jewish community'.[27] For its part, the *Jewish Chronicle* wrote that 'the community at large, Jewish and Christian alike, owe a debt of gratitude to Sir Kenelm Digby [another of the bill's critics] and Mr. Winston Churchill for their searching and outspoken criticism of the Restriction Bill'.[28]

When the bill was in Grand Committee, Churchill was one of its central opponents, fighting tirelessly for a number of important amendments. After seven days of deliberation, only a small fraction of the bill had been discussed, causing its abandonment. Those who supported restrictions on immigration accused Churchill of deliberately setting out to wreck the bill. But Churchill was adamant that the bill had to be opposed: 'Shut out the alien; if diseased, always; if immoral, when you can find out; if criminal, after you have convicted; but do not shut out persons merely because they are poor, and do not thrust upon police and Customs House officers duties which they cannot properly discharge.'[29]

Despite some initial reservations, Churchill campaigned tirelessly against the proposed legislation when a second bill was introduced in 1905. This new bill introduced a means test to differentiate the relatively poor immigrant, who could receive entry, from the destitute one, who would be excluded. Churchill made it clear that he was not soft hearted on the question of expulsion, for it was necessary to banish those 'who abuse the hospitality of this country' or who are 'considered a nuisance or a burden in the country'.

Churchill further considered that the denigration of the character of Jewish immigrants was unwarranted, for the 'crime, prostitution and disease' brought into Britain was 'not due to Jewish immigrants'. Churchill was certainly against banning people from entering Britain on grounds of poverty. 'I am of opinion that a man's own personal strength, his own bodily vigour as a man, is in itself an asset to us'.[30] He was opposed to a high naturalisation fee for immigrants because he felt this detracted from the really important criteria for entry: the character of an immigrant and whether that person strove to uphold the values of British society.

When the 1905 act was eventually passed, effective from 1906, Churchill's reaction was one of contempt. The act, he screamed, was 'a sham with lunacy superimposed upon it'. It contained 'absurdities which would make a deaf mute roar with laughter'. As for the means test, he believed it was always wrong to base decisions for immigrant entry on purely financial means. 'A few shillings made the difference between desirability and undesirability', he declared, something that would 'inflict hardship and vexation upon many deserving people who seek a refuge on our shores'.[31]

Churchill stressed that citizenship was not an automatic right and had to depend on accepting the British way of life. Citizenship, he wrote, 'ought never to be a mere formality', adding that it consisted of 'the solemn acceptance of duties and dignities'.[32] He also made no secret of the fact that the bill was intended to pander to crude anti-Semitic feeling. In 1904 he wrote that it was 'expected to appeal to insular prejudice against foreigners, to racial prejudice against Jews, and to labour prejudice against competition'.[33]

He also said that he had been subject to 'the foulest abuse and gross insults' for taking a tough stance on the Aliens Bill. He may have been thinking of an incident in Grand Committee when he was accused of having been 'bought by Rothschild'.[34] When he did mention Rothschild, it was to congratulate him for striving 'earnestly' to 'preserve a free asylum in England for [his] co-religionists' who were being 'driven out from foreign countries by religious persecution'. He added that this was an 'honourable act in thorough accordance with the traditions of the Jewish people'.[35]

While this bill was being debated, Churchill was anxious to uphold British traditions of liberty and hospitality against the clamour of xenophobic prejudice. At the same time his constituency, North-West Manchester, contained over seven hundred Jewish constituents and there is little doubt that political calculation entered his thinking during his opposition to the Aliens Bill. But, if so, this was arguably a legitimate case of merging self-interest with personal principle. This would become a consistent theme throughout Churchill's career.

Did Churchill want to abolish
the House of Lords?

AT THE START of his political career, Churchill was an ardent champion of the British Constitution and, in particular, the hereditary
House of Lords. In 1899 he had denounced the Liberals for their
hostility to the Lords, and he later described the peers as a 'bulwark
of the English Constitution'.[36] In 1906, while lauding Tory democracy, he made it clear that the British Constitution, far from need-
ing radical alteration, was a means by which to guide social progress.
In his first few years as an MP, he made no attempt to advocate
lasting constitutional change, which fitted well with his strong
aristocratic connections and Conservative viewpoint.

However, the Conservative inclinations of the Lords grated
with Churchill as a Liberal MP. In 1905 he mocked that 'the check
established by the House of Lords ... if it operated at all, operated
only when one political party was in power'.[37] His words would
prove prescient. The great shock for the Lords was the landslide
Liberal victory in 1906 that swept away twenty years of Conservative
predominance in English politics. Balfour, the Conservative leader
in the Lords, had declared that 'the great Unionist party should
still control, whether in power or in opposition, the destinies of this
great Empire'. Between 1906 and 1909, the Lords proceeded to
wreck or veto many pieces of reforming legislation, leading the
Chancellor David Lloyd George to remark that the Lords had
become 'not the watchdog of the Constitution, but Mr. Balfour's
poodle'. Lloyd George was already established as a fiery critic of
privilege and class, but from 1907, Churchill would join him in his
radical harangues.

Denouncing the House of Lords in 1907 as a 'fortress of negation
and reaction', Churchill condemned the way that a man could
acquire legislative functions 'simply through his virtue in being born'.
He wrote that, instead of acting as an 'impartial chamber of review',
the Lords had become an 'irresponsible body' and a 'spoke in the
wheel'; above all, they were the 'champions of one interest', namely
the 'landed interest'. There were some who favoured sending bills to
the Lords in the hope that they would be rejected, leading to a growing sense of public outrage which could be exploited in a general
election. But Churchill believed this approach to be somewhat des-

perate, amounting to 'the policy of bowling lobs for the House of Lords to sky in the hope that the spectators will take pity on the bowlers'.[38]

In a debate on constitutional reform later in 1908, he set himself up as a champion of parliamentary liberty against the encroachment of the peers and their landed interest. He was unsparing in his contempt for the Lords, describing them as a 'one-sided hereditary, unpurged, unrepresentative, irresponsible absentee' and 'obedient henchmen' of the Tories'.[39] The House of Lords was filled with 'old doddering peers, cute financial magnates, clever wirepullers, big brewers with bulbous noses ... weaklings, sleek, smug, comfortable self-important individuals'.[40] His desire was to 'wrest from the hands of privilege and wealth the evil and ugly and sinister weapon of the Peers' veto'.[41]

This violent outburst would have been unsurprising from Lloyd George, with his fiery brand of Welsh non-conformism; but, coming from the grandson of a Duke, raised in a privileged, aristocratic setting, it was truly shocking. Not surprisingly, Churchill was denounced by many as a traitor to his class.

The opportunity for a grave constitutional showdown came in 1909. The Liberals presented their budget for the year which included increases in naval expenditure, an old age pensions bill and a programme of social reform. To fund these measures, the government raised taxes on higher incomes, increased death duties and added a new 'super tax' on very high incomes.

However the most contentious idea in the budget, the one that really exercised the Lords, was the novel suggestion of a tax on land values. It was the brainchild of the American political economist, Henry George. George had argued, in his influential book *Progress and Poverty*, that poverty was caused by an unjust distribution of wealth which, far from being part of the natural condition, was the product of human laws.

For George, the maldistribution of wealth was inextricably linked to the unjust ownership and monopolisation of land. He argued that, as a town's population increased in size, so too did the value of land in and around that community. As the population expanded, new infrastructure (i.e. roads, railways, streets) was required, the cost of which was borne by the community, not the landlord. When the landlord came to sell the land, he could do so at enormous 'unearned' profit. George believed that the concentration of unearned wealth in the hands of land monopolists, which resulted in higher rents and thus reduced purchasing power for the working man, was the root cause of poverty.

To remedy this injustice, George sought a 'rental' tax on the annual value of privately owned land. This tax would be on the site value of the land, rather than on any man-made improvements or buildings. In this way, landowners would pay rent to the government, in effect returning some value to the community which was responsible for increasing the land value in the first place. In George's words, 'We would simply take for the community what belongs to the community.'[42] He argued that, with this new system of taxation in place, a government could abolish taxes on incomes and goods, both of which were harmful to the functioning of any dynamic economy. Land taxes would directly tackle the cause of poverty rather than mitigate its worst symptoms.[43]

Churchill came to be one of the most outspoken advocates for George's land taxes. Indeed, it was his support for Georgist thinking that most clearly marked him out as a liberal 'firebrand'. In 1906 he told Liberal MP Josiah Wedgwood that he had been reading George's *Progress and Poverty* and could 'see no answer to him'.[44] In April 1907 he told a crowd at the Drury Lane Theatre that land taxes would 'prevent any class from steadily absorbing under the shelter of the law the wealth in the creation of which they had borne no share – wealth which belonged not to them but to the community'.[45] 'Every form of enterprise,' he wrote later, 'is only undertaken after the land monopolist has skimmed the cream off for himself.'[46]

He also shared George's conviction that taxation was socially harmful, describing it in 1908 as 'a gross and unredeemable evil' which could not 'fail to diminish' the 'consuming and productive energies of the people'.[47] Nonetheless, by 1909 Lloyd George, under Cabinet pressure, had watered down Henry George's original proposal for a land tax. First there was to be a 20 per cent tax on 'unearned increment' from land, but only when the land was sold or passed on after death. There was also a small duty on undeveloped land in the budget.

But, despite this dilution of George's original proposals, the Lords still vehemently rejected land taxes. For months they examined the Finance Bill in meticulous detail, their central objections confined to the land taxes. While some of his Cabinet colleagues hoped that the Lords would pass the budget, Churchill clearly relished the prospect of a showdown. 'We shall send them up such a budget in June as shall terrify them'.[48]

He was aware that, if the Lords vetoed this bill, it would be tantamount to a non-elected chamber deciding which government was in power, in turn making the Lords 'the main source and origin of all political power under the Crown'. Control over finance was, after all, the 'keystone' of the Constitution. In his most caustic speech on the issue, Churchill denounced 'the small fry of the Tory party splashing actively about in their proper puddles'. He had little sympathy for the nation's Dukes, who were no more than 'ornamental creatures' blundering 'on every hook they seek'.[49] The forthcoming struggle over the budget was between 'a representative assembly elected by six or seven millions ... and a miserable minority of titled persons who represent nobody, who are responsible to nobody and who only scurry up to London to vote in their party interests, their class interests and in their own interests'.[50]

As Churchill expected, the Lords duly rejected the budget on November 30th 1909. Following the announcement of a general election for January 1910, Churchill condemned the Lords as 'a lingering relic of the feudal order'. When Curzon declared that 'all civilisation has been the work of aristocracies', Churchill responded, 'it would be much more true to say the upkeep of the aristocracy has been the hard work of all civilisations'.[51]

Churchill was rare among politicians in that his tone could be more vituperative in public than in private. In a memorandum in 1909, he presented a reasoned case for reform that accepted the need for a 'revising' second chamber. He seemed to agree with the Ripon Plan which advocated a hundred peers sitting and voting with all MPs when differences between the two houses arose. On November 9th he accepted the need for a second chamber to impose a check on the executive and thought joint sessions would 'be productive of debates of the highest value' while also providing 'an entirely fresh opportunity of conciliatory settlements'.[52]

He argued that peers should be chosen from different political parties, though other figures in public office, such as military officers and civil service figures, could be included. There would be a power of delay effective for one year with a joint session called when a disagreement arose between the two houses. Interestingly, Churchill did not call for the overthrow of the hereditary principle or the voting rights of peers. In short, there would be 'no break in the historical continuity of our constitutional development'.[53] He also accepted the principle that peers could renounce their peerages to take a seat in the Commons.

In January 1910 a general election was held. The Liberals won but with a massively reduced majority of two, leaving them in the difficult position of relying on the support of the Labour Party and the Irish Nationalists. Churchill believed that the government now had a mandate for Lords reform, but thus far his proposals had been limited to the modification of the powers of the second chamber. However, in 1910 he sent Asquith a memorandum in which he proposed something far more radical. 'The time has come', he declared, 'for the total abolition of the House of Lords.'[54]

He came to believe that, as long as the Lords remained, the Tory Party would find ways of controlling it. However, if the Lords were to be abolished, he would need to find something to replace it. He advocated a second chamber which would be wholly subordinate to the elected Commons, smaller than the Commons and elected from very large constituencies. This new second chamber would be unable to reject budgets, and thus would lack 'power to make or unmake governments'.[55]

Its ability to revise legislation and to 'interpose the potent safeguard of delay' was also paramount.[56] He envisaged a second chamber with 150 members, two thirds of whom would be elected from fifty major constituencies, sitting for eight-year terms, and the members chosen from 'a panel of public service'. The second chamber would be unable to reject a money bill but would possess a suspensory veto for three years, after which an issue would be decided by a majority vote in a joint session of the two houses. Instead of Law Lords, he advocated a 'Supreme Court of Appeal for the British Empire'. However, few other Cabinet members shared Churchill's enthusiasm for such a radical constitutional transformation, preferring a sustained attack on the Lords' powers of veto. Nonetheless, his notion of a Supreme Court of Appeal sounds uncannily similar to the body that has replaced the Law Lords in 2009.[57]

The Asquith government now introduced resolutions to limit the power of the Lords, which later formed the basis of the 1911 Parliament Act. The provisions of this act marked a milestone in relations between the two houses. Firstly, the Lords were denied the power to veto a money bill, the issue that had created the crisis in the first place. Secondly, it stipulated that any bill that had been passed by the Commons in three successive sessions, but rejected by the Lords in those sessions, would become law. It also included an amendment to the Septennial Act whereby the life of a parliament was reduced from seven down to five years.

Asquith knew that, without the assent of the intransigent Lords, this act would never become law. He therefore asked Edward VII whether he would be prepared to create 250 new Liberal peers in the event that the Lords rejected it. The King agreed, on condition that the Prime Minister call another election to seek a public mandate for his policy. Edward VII died in May 1910, but when George V came to the throne he also agreed to the constitutional changes only after an election. Following the January 1911 general election, the Liberals returned with a virtually unchanged majority but a clear mandate for the Parliament Act. With full knowledge of the royal threat looming over them, the Lords duly passed the Parliament Act by 131 votes to 114.

Churchill's role in 1911 should be noted. Far from wanting party bickering, he called for a cross-party approach to the future composition of the Lords. As he said: 'We should state at the proper time that after the veto has been restricted we shall be quite ready to discuss the future composition of the Lords with the Conservative leaders.' The government should pursue '*une politique d'apaisement*' (a policy of appeasement) which would partly consist in 'a liberal grant of Honours' to leading Conservatives as well as 'Tory peers and baronets'.[58]

In the Commons he spoke of his hope that the passage of the bill would 'mark a new era' in politics, an 'era not of strife but of settlement'.[59] Nonetheless, he remained unhappy with this bill as it gave considerable revising powers to the Lords which, he argued, could wreck the last two years of a government. In later life he came to accept much of the 1911 act, even to the point of rejecting the modification made in 1949 whereby the suspensory veto of the Lords would last only one year. He also supported a motion for members of the Lords to be able to renounce their titles and stand for election to the Commons.

Churchill was born into aristocratic surroundings but he never let that fact dictate his perspective. Accused of class disloyalty, he showed vigour and imagination in trying to reach an agreeable and workable constitutional settlement. Much as he admired features of the British Constitution, he could not accept the muzzling of the Commons by a hereditary chamber. In this sense, his reverence for parliamentary democracy remained paramount.

How did Churchill help to found Britain's welfare state?

'THE MINISTER who will apply to this country the successful experiences of Germany in social organisation may or may not be supported at the polls, but he will at least have left a memorial which time will not deface of his administration.'[60]

Between 1908 and 1911, a small step was taken towards creating the fully fledged welfare state we recognise today. The Liberal government under Asquith introduced a pensions system, social and health insurance for workers, a minimum wage in some of the sweated trades and labour exchanges. It was a limited form of social security but it represented an important advance in state intervention. As President of the Board of Trade from 1908 to 1910, Churchill was deeply involved in these measures. Between these years he gave numerous speeches highlighting the need to alleviate poverty and unemployment and campaigned for the People's Budget of 1909. He pioneered National Health Insurance and labour exchanges as well as important measures to improve working conditions in shops and factories.

But Churchill's role in these developments remains contentious among historians. For his official biographer, Sir Martin Gilbert, Churchill was 'a believer in the need for the State to take an active part, both by legislation and finance, in ensuring minimum standards of life, labour and social well-being for its citizens'.[61] However for Frances Lloyd George, Churchill 'had no interest in social reform',[62] while Beatrice Webb, commenting in her diary in 1904 after a conversation with Churchill, wrote simply: 'He has no sympathy with suffering.'[63]

Nevertheless, Violet Bonham-Carter believed that Churchill fully endorsed the Liberal government's desire to eradicate poverty and redress the wrongs of industrial life: 'It is to Winston Churchill's signal credit that he embraced these aims and worked and fought with all his heart and might to realise them.'[64] What becomes clear is that the Liberal Party introduced reforms for a mixture of moral and political reasons, giving their radicalism an air of moral authority *and* calculated self-interest. Churchill shared this mixture of motives to the full.

Churchill's interest in social reform predated the start of his political career. As a believer in Tory democracy, he stated as early as 1899 that 'the improvement of the British breed' was the main goal of his political life.[65] There was a link to be established here between domestic and foreign policy. 'To keep our Empire,' he declared in 1898, 'we must have a free people, an educated people and well fed people.'[66] Churchill recognised that a properly maintained and effectively run Empire required an improvement in the physical and social condition of the British electorate and, at the turn of the century, he had good grounds for questioning the 'health of the nation'.

In 1901 he read Seebohm Rowntree's work *Poverty*, which deeply impressed him. Rowntree had carried out a study of poverty in York and concluded that nearly one third of the population lived below the poverty line. To Churchill, that was a 'terrible and shocking thing'. His concern was partly based on the fear that, left unchecked, British workers would soon lose their competitive edge to Britain's (emerging) industrial rivals. 'It is quite evident from the figures which he adduces that the American labourer is a stronger, larger, healthier, better fed, and consequently more efficient animal than a large proportion of our population ... I see little glory in an Empire which can rule the waves and is unable to flush its sewers.'[67] That Churchill had the Empire in mind is made clear in a review of Rowntree's book that he wrote in 1902. He talked of a common people 'so stunted and deformed in body as to be unfit to fill the ranks the army corps may lack'.[68] Morality and pragmatism would jointly underpin any social reform programme.

However, in the first two years of his political career, he believed that reductions in government expenditure and free trade would provide benefits to the working man. His calls for domestic economy in the aftermath of the expensive Boer War did not sit well with a vigourous programme of social reform. Even in 1904, after his defection to the Liberals, Churchill showed little appetite for a reform agenda. Beatrice Webb wrote in her diary for June 1904: 'I tried the "national minimum" on him but he was evidently unaware of the most elementary objections to unrestricted competition.'[69] While evidently sympathetic to working-class distress, he had no plan to alleviate it.

In 1906 the Liberals swept to power but, as Paul Addison notes, this was supposed to be a victory for the old fashioned liberal principles of *laissez-faire* and free trade. In reality, 1906 marked a watershed between the old fashioned Gladstonian liberalism of *laissez-faire* and the 'new liberalism' of state intervention and collectivism. Churchill bought into the new liberalism while being aware that, in electoral terms, it would remove some of Labour's appeal to the working man. As he explained to the Scottish Liberal whip, he wanted to 'isolate the wreckers who vilify the Liberal Party and hand over its seats to the Tories'.[70] The ever-ambitious Churchill sensed an opportunity for personal promotion by tapping into this current of progressive thought.

In 1906 Churchill could look forward to 'the universal establishment of minimum standards of life and labour'. He believed the state could play a positive role in helping millions of the most unfortunate in society, those he termed 'the left out millions'. In a speech that same year, he talked of how the state could embark on 'various novel and adventurous experiments' without impairing 'the vigour of competition'. The idea was not to dampen the competitive spirit of capitalism but to protect the most unfortunate in society: 'We want to draw a line below which we will not allow persons to live and labour yet above which they may compete with all the strength of their manhood.'[71]

In 1908 he expanded on this theme, telling Sir Arthur Fox that there was a 'residue' of poor people for whom there was no social security provision in any form and who therefore required 'the aid of the state'. This meant 'competition upwards but not downwards'.[72]

Churchill had the opportunity to translate these ideals into reality in April 1908 when he was appointed President of the Board of Trade. One of his tasks was to deal with the changing fortunes of the labour market, which had been a recurrent problem throughout the latter stages of the nineteenth century. The Poor Law, designed to prevent the unemployed from starving, was under fierce attack. In 1905 a downturn in the labour market, with a consequent rise in unemployment, created pressure on the Liberals from both left and right to take a novel approach. In a speech in Dundee in 1908, Churchill lamented the lack of 'any central organisation of industry' and paid heed to the vicious condition of the plight of the casual unskilled labourer. These problems required 'scientific provision against the fluctuations and set-backs which are inevitable in world commerce and national industry'.73

In order to provide the appropriate scientific provision, Churchill consulted the journalist William Beveridge, who recommended the introduction of labour exchanges and a system of social insurance. In July 1908 Churchill told his Cabinet colleagues that he intended to adopt voluntary labour exchanges and a comprehensive scheme of compulsory unemployment insurance.

The idea behind the national insurance scheme was that the working people would be insured against the perils of sickness, premature infirmity or unemployment, all of which naturally exacerbated poverty. Prior to 1912, workers could subscribe to a voluntary society or trade union that would make regular payments to the ill or unemployed. But not all workers could afford such provision, and many relied on charity or their families for support. Churchill wanted a system of 'state-aided insurance' where the burden was 'shared by the individual and the State'.74 The inspiration for this measure, at least in part, was Bismarck's great scheme of social insurance created in the late nineteenth century. The German model, however, did not cover unemployment.

Churchill was no soft touch on the benefits system. He wanted to see excluded from the scheme those people who were persistently unemployed, which was considered 'proof of demerit'. But Churchill's thinking on this issue was more often progressive and based on a sympathetic regard for the underdog. He argued against William Beveridge that it was wrong to deny benefits to drunks. A drunkard, he argued, had paid his contribution under his scheme, thus insuring himself against unemployment, and it would be wrong to withhold benefits whatever the cause of dismissal.

He added: 'Suppose a man has a row with his employer, perhaps a person only one step higher than himself socially, or that there is ill temper on both sides; hot words pass, the employer swears at the man, or the man at the employer; the man is dismissed and the employer refuses a discharge note and answers all inquiries in an unfavourable manner: is the Insurance Office going to accept the employer's version of what has occurred?'75 Churchill deplored the way that moral criteria might be used to exclude claimants, arguing for a more scientific approach; nonetheless he lost this particular argument to Beveridge. Social insurance had to wait until it could be combined with Lloyd George's Health Insurance in

1911, but when the measures were introduced, Churchill welcomed them.

Social insurance measures were inextricably linked to labour exchanges. These exchanges, later called job centres, were designed to meet the needs of employers and the unemployed and served as 'the Intelligence department of labour'. Employers could register vacancies with the exchanges while the unemployed could find work in their local areas.[76] They were designed to provide 'exact and detailed information as to the labour market' and, by 1910, more than eighty exchanges had been set up across the country.

The third important landmark in Churchill's administration of the Board of Trade was the Trade Boards Act of 1910, which dealt with problems in the sweated industries. The sweated trades, which included tailoring, sewing and dressmaking, were characterised by long hours of work, very low wages and highly insanitary working conditions. When machinery was introduced into the industries, there was an excessive supply of unskilled workers who were accused of keeping down the standard of wages for more regular workers. Reformers such as Sir Charles Dilke had advocated a minimum wage rate for such workers on the model of Australian legislation. When the Wages Boards Bill was introduced in 1908 there was cross-party support, but the Home Secretary, whose job it was to regulate factories and jobs, declined to support it.

After a favourable report from a parliamentary select committee, Churchill took over responsibility for preparing the bill when he became Home Secretary. It covered only four trades: ready-made tailoring, paper-box making, machine-lace making, and chain making and about two hundred thousand people were affected. For each of these trades there was a trade board, which consisted of representatives of the employers and workers, whose job it was to establish a minimum wage. For Churchill this was an essentially conservative measure, designed to alleviate conditions in particular cases where wages were very low and where conditions were 'prejudicial to physical and social welfare'. He insisted that the principles behind this legislation could not be allowed to become 'the normal basis of industry'.[77]

Certainly Churchill did not initiate these measures and much of the impetus came from his hard-working officials. Nonetheless, he brought determination, drive and imagination to the Board of Trade and the resulting legislation provided 'a striking illustration of how much the personality of the minister in a few critical months' [could] change the course of social legislation'.[78] Churchill championed social reform for many reasons but one was purely paternalistic: a concern to improve the quality of life for the more vulnerable members of society. In a fundamental sense, Churchill anticipated the need for, to use twenty-first-century jargon, a 'work-life balance'. In 1908, while championing the Eight Hours Bill, he told the Commons:

> The general march of industrial democracy is not towards inadequate hours of work but towards sufficient hours of leisure. That is the movement among the working people all over the country. They are not content that their lives should remain mere alternatives between bed and the factory. They demand time to look about them, time to see their homes by daylight, to see their children, time to think and read and cultivate their gardens – time, in short, to live ... No one is to be pitied for having to work hard, but nature has contrived a special reward for the man who works hard ... This reward, so precious in itself, is snatched away from the man who has won it if the hours of his labour are too long ... to leave any time for him to enjoy the reward he has won.[79]

Churchill's paternalistic concern for the workers surfaced again in the 1909 debate on daylight saving time. Churchill argued that an extra hour of daylight would be a 'great boon to the working classes', for with these extra hours the working man would have 'opportunities of visiting parks and cultivating gardens to an extent which they are now unable to do'.[80] With these extra hours, there would be opportunities 'for the pursuit of health and pleasure and happiness' which could prolong 'the lives of millions of the people who live in this country'.[81]

Churchill's drive for social reform was genuinely meant, but it also represented a form of benevolent paternalism. Churchill the aristocrat remained wedded to a conservative view of society in which a ruling class dutifully protected its less fortunate members, so long as they did not threaten its ordered and hierarchical structure. Charles Masterman reflected that Churchill 'desired in England a state of things where a benign upper class dispensed benefits to an industrious, *bien pensant*, and grateful working class'. For Herbert Morrison, Churchill was a 'benevolent Tory squire, who does all he can for the people – provided always that they are good obedient people and loyally recognise his position, and theirs'.[82] As long as the people knew their place, all would be well.

But, if it was benevolent paternalism, it fitted the Churchillian conception that the best way to improve society was through gradual modification, not socialist transformation. As Robert Rhodes James has noted, the administration headed by Asquith from 1906 to 1914 was 'deeply committed to the economic status quo and, in fact, elected to defend it'.[83] This was precisely how Churchill envisaged the programme of welfare reform. 'The idea is to increase the stability of our institutions', he declared, 'by giving the mass of industrial workers a direct interest in maintaining them. With a 'stake in the country' in the form of insurance against evil days, these workers will pay no attention to the vague promises of revolutionary socialism'.[84]

In electoral terms, the welfare reforms would help to out-manouevre the Labour Party and attract working-class people to the Liberal fold. Winston had wanted to 'isolate the wreckers who vilify the Liberal Party and hand over its seats to the Tories'.[85] But this does not mean that the welfare legislation was simply a matter of political self-interest. Churchill pursued these reforms both because they suited his moral agenda and because they would advance his career as a Liberal. On this issue, as with so many others, self-interest and political cause went hand in hand.

Was Churchill a reforming Home Secretary?

CHURCHILL BECAME Home Secretary in February 1910, in the midst of the constitutional crisis with the Lords. He was the youngest person to hold the post since Sir Robert Peel and by the time he took over was already established as a leading light within the Liberal Party. The Home Secretary had a wide and demanding remit which included the maintenance of law and order, the efficient running of the Metropolitan Police and probation service, the control of prisons and the treatment of offenders, the regulation of the immigration service, and the passage of legislation on the criminal justice system. He also wrote to the King each day with a report of proceedings in the House of Commons.

Before 1910 Churchill had been at the forefront of the Liberal government's programme of social legislation. Now, as Home Secretary, he wanted to continue his programme of reform, extended into the field of law and order. In the space of eighteen months he would leave his radical stamp on the Home Office in important ways.

Churchill was ideally suited to a humane overview of the prison system. In *My Early Life* he had written of his loathing for incarceration:

> I certainly hated every minute of my captivity more than I have ever hated any other period in my whole life ... Looking back on those days, I have always felt the keenest pity for prisoners and captives. What it must mean for any man, especially an educated man, to be confined for years in a modern convict prison strains my imagination.[86]

As a former POW, he well remembered his own brief loss of liberty and therefore possessed a special affinity with prison inmates. For this reason, Paul Addison has written that Churchill, 'more than any other Home Secretary of the twentieth century ... was the prisoner's friend'.[87]

The biggest problem facing the prison service at the time was the sheer number of people being incarcerated. While he did not advocate leniency for its own sake, he sought to limit these prison numbers without harming wider society. As he put it, the 'first real principle which should guide anyone trying to establish a good system of prisons should be to prevent as many people as possible getting there at all'.[88] In a sense, this was an Edwardian formula for being 'tough on crime and tough on the causes of crime'.

In September 1910 he wrote to Asquith that 205,000 people had been committed in the previous year. But what startled Churchill was that over 60 per cent of these (125,000) had gone to prison for a fortnight or less. Churchill regarded this as a 'terrible and purposeless waste of public money and human character', given that it imposed a 'great strain on the prison staff'. He added: 'A few days' imprisonment to a workman does him as much harm as a much longer sentence, & in the great majority of cases may cause him to lose his job.' Neither was a short sentence an 'effective deterrent'.[89] This was particularly troubling if prison rules applied to those 'whose general character is good and whose offences, however reprehensible, do not involve personal dishonour'.[90] Many of these short sentences were for non-payment of fines. Churchill condemned the 'vicious system of credit' that trapped many working-class people with consequences 'injurious both to thrift and honesty'.[91]

He therefore proposed to extend the period during which people could pay fines prior to their imprisonment for non-payment, suggesting one week's grace to someone with a fine less than ten shillings and two weeks' grace if the fine was above ten shillings.[92] Finally, he proposed that all sentences of a month or less would be suspended. In 1914 the Criminal Justice Amendment Bill, introduced by Reginald McKenna, incorporated Churchill's proposal for an extension of time to pay fines. Sadly this was left at the discretion of magistrates in individual cases.

Churchill also reduced the amount of time that prisoners could spend in solitary confinement at the beginning of their sentences. A period of to up to nine months was reduced to one month for the majority of prisoners and three months for recidivists (repeat offenders). Churchill was spurred on in this decision by seeing John Galsworthy's play *Justice*, the central protagonist in which was imprisoned, humiliated and eventually destroyed by his experience of solitary confinement.[93] Finally, he insisted on the provision of concerts and lectures within prisons and improved the help given to prisoners after their release.

Churchill's humane concern for penal reform reflected his wider anxiety that the law was inherently biased against the working class. Churchill declared it a disaster to send young offenders aged 16 to 21 to jail, adding that it was an 'evil' that befell only 'the sons of the working classes'. The law, he said, was 'open to the grave reproach of partiality as between rich and poor' where only 'workpeople are sent to prison for not paying their debts'.[94] Churchill had good reason to be vexated by class bias. At the turn of the twentieth century, most prisoners came from the ranks of the poor, with vagrants, paupers, and the unemployed disproportionately represented. When he decided to release some young offenders from Pentonville prison, he gave the following justification:

> I must confess I was very glad of the opportunity of recommending the use of the prerogative in these cases, because I wanted to draw the attention of the country by means of cases perfectly legitimate in themselves to the evil ... by which 7,000 or 8,000 lads of the poorer classes are sent to goal every year for offences which, if the noble Lord [Earl Winterton] had committed them, at college, he would not have been subjected to the slightest degree of inconvenience.[95]

In later years Churchill would be condemned as an inveterate foe of the working class. In reality, he highlighted the way that the justice system was loaded against this class.

He also advocated the humane treatment of political prisoners, an idea he reached independently though it had also been proposed by his predecessor, Herbert Gladstone. Under his radical proposal, there was to be a new category of 'political prisoner' who would receive special benefits not accorded to other inmates. Political prisoners could purchase food from outside prison and wear their own clothes, while wardens could not impose compulsory work or interfere with their normal habits.[96]

While arguing that it was wrong to imprison petty offenders, Churchill was not an advocate of excessive leniency. He was in favour of flogging prisoners as a means of enforcing discipline. Further, he argued that those found guilty of rowdyism, gambling or stone-throwing, who refused to pay the fine imposed on them, should be ordered to perform up to 28 days defaulters' drill. This was not the same as military drill but it would involve severe training and vigorous physical activity in order to instill the much-needed correction and self-discipline they needed. Most of the Chief Constables, whose opinions were sought, favoured Churchill's suggestion.

The Home Secretary also exercised the royal prerogative of mercy in criminal cases. This meant that he could vary a sentence handed down by a judge or magistrate when he felt it was disproportionate to the crime committed. Churchill's sympathy for the underdog was reflected in some humane decisions. One of his interventions came in the case of Charles Bulbeck, a 12-year-old found guilty of stealing a piece of cod worth 5d. Bulbeck was sentenced to be birched and to spend seven years at a reformatory, but after the Home Secretary's intervention he was sent home to his parents.[97]

The case of the Dartmoor Shepherd caused some adverse publicity. The Dartmoor Shepherd (real name David Davies) was a habitual offender who had been imprisoned ten times since 1870 for theft. On a visit to Dartmoor in 1910, Churchill discovered that, under the system of preventive detention, Davies had been sentenced the previous year to three years penal servitude and ten years preventive detention for stealing money from a church offertory.[98] Churchill remitted most of this sentence and Davies was released in 1910. Rather embarrassingly, Davies was imprisoned the following year for housebreaking and Churchill had to face taunts from the opposition that he was soft-headed. Nonetheless, this case made Churchill determined to limit preventive detention except for 'the worst class of professional criminals' and its use declined from 1911 onwards.[99]

Perhaps the most daunting task that faced Churchill was to decide whether convicted murderers who had been sentenced to death should live or die. Although Churchill was a convinced advocate of capital punishment, believing that a 'life sentence is worse than a death sentence', in nearly half of the cases brought to him for careful and lengthy analysis he offered a reprieve.

Churchill's view of prison was that it should be 'corrective' rather than 'vindictive' in nature. 'No lad between 16 & 21,' he wrote, 'ought to be sent to prison for mere punishment. Every sentence should be conceived with the object of pulling him together & bracing him for the world: it should be in fact disciplinary & educative rather than penal...' Even in prison, he proposed that there should be either a concert or a lecture as the prisoners 'must have something to think about, & to break the long monotony'. It constituted an important 'immunising influence' which could not be neglected.[100] In a speech to the House of Commons in July 1910 he offered an outline of his penal philosophy:

> The mood and temper of the public in regard to the treatment of crime and criminals is one of the unfailing tests of the civilisation of any country. A calm and dispassionate recognition of the rights of the accused against the State, and even of convicted criminals against the State, a constant heart searching by all charged with the duty of punishment, a desire and eagerness to rehabilitate in the world of industry all those who have paid their dues in the hard coinage of punishment, tireless efforts towards the discovery of curative and regenerating processes, and an unalterable faith that there is a treasure ... in the heart of every man – these are the symbols which in the treatment of crime and criminals mark and measure the stored up strength of a nation, and are the sign and proof of the living virtue in it.[101]

In modern times, at least one Chief Inspector of Prisons has found inspiration in these words.[102]

Since Victorian times, the Home Office had also been involved in regulating social conditions and enforcing laws that governed working conditions in factories and shops. The Shops Bill was introduced to the Commons in 1910 and proposed a number of measures: shop assistants would work no more than sixty hours per week and no more than three evenings per week; they would receive a guaranteed half day off each week and there would also be restrictions on Sunday trading. The bill excluded self-employed shopkeepers and Jewish traders from many of these restrictions. Designed to benefit small family businesses and the self-employed, the bill was described as a 'non-controversial measure',[103] but sadly for Churchill the measure proved to be highly controversial, with hordes of tradesmen complaining of unfair competition. Before the bill was finally passed in 1912 it had to be emasculated, but the act did contain Churchill's original plan for a half-day holiday and provision for mealtimes.

Not all of Churchill's proposals as Home Secretary were enlightened by twenty-first century standards. He was interested in the control of antisocial minorities and proposed labour colonies for 'tramps and wastrels'. He also expressed an interest in eugenics. Eugenicists advocated the improvement of human hereditary traits through various forms of intervention that were intended to create healthier and more intelligent people and breed out groups that were seen as undesirable or unfit. The eugenicists painted an alarming portrait of a British race under siege from a class of poor people who were reproducing at a faster rate than the middle classes.

In 1904 a Royal Commission on the care and control of the feeble minded was set up to investigate how to deal with people who could not 'take part in the struggle of life owing to mental defect'.[104] The commission recommended a programme of compulsory detention for some classes of the mentally inadequate. The decision on whether to proceed was then shelved until Churchill became Home Secretary, but he clearly took the Commission's conclusions seriously. In a letter to Asquith he wrote: 'The unnatural and increasingly rapid growth of the feeble minded and insane classes, coupled as it is with a steady restriction among all the thrifty, energetic and superior stocks, constitutes a national and race danger which it is impossible to exaggerate.' Accepting the Commission's diagnosis of the problem, he then offered this cure: 'I feel that the source from which the stream of madness is fed should be cut off and sealed up before another year has passed.'[105]

What he meant by 'cutting off' the source of madness became clearer in July 1910 when he received a deputation on mental welfare which included the President of the Eugenics Society, one Montague Crackanthorpe. Crackanthorpe urged on the Home Secretary the need to forcibly segregate Britain's 'feeble minded'. Churchill talked of 'immense difficulties' in such a course of action but said that, if the feeble minded were segregated 'so that their curse dies with them', it would be beneficial for the rest of society. Then in

September Churchill revealed his interest in 'compulsory sterilisation' in a memorandum for his officials:

> I think there must be a considerable class among the feeble minded who might be allowed to live outside special institutions if only one could be sure that they did not continue to multiply in the next generation the evils from which we suffer so greatly in our own ... A very large proportion of criminals are abnormal only in the weakness of their faculty of self control. Surely that weakness is definitely traceable in a great number of cases to parentage ...

He went on to say that the class of people whose intelligence was so defective 'as to deprive them of the average restraining power' should be sterilised. Sterilisation was considered preferable to incarceration on grounds of avoiding cruelty. He went on:

> For my part I think it is cruel to shut up numbers of people in institutions, to them at any rate little better than prisons, for their whole lives, if by a simple surgical operation they could be permitted to live freely in the world without causing much inconvenience to others.[106]

While Churchill did not countenance one loss of liberty for these unfortunates, he was prepared to deprive them of another. Part of the reason for this flash of illiberalism was a concern about the differential breeding rates of sections of the community.

That Churchill took these ideas seriously is indicated in a diary entry from 1912 written by one of his contemporaries, William Scawen Blunt:

> Winston is also a strong eugenicist. He told us he had himself drafted the Bill which is to give power to shutting up people of weak intellects and so prevent their breeding ... many would ask to be sterilised as a condition of having their liberty restored ... without something of the sort the race must decay. It is decaying rapidly, but would be stopped by some such means.[107]

The notion of forcible sterilisation or incarceration for the 'unfit' is certainly anathema to modern liberal sensibilities, but Churchill was only one of a number of influential thinkers advocating such extreme measures as a way to 'improve' society. One might almost say that eugenics was part of the *Zeitgeist* for Britain's intelligentsia at the time. W.B. Yeats was concerned at the rapid growth of ill-educated people at the expense of those who were better bred. He warned that, since the start of the twentieth century, 'the better stocks have not been replacing their numbers, while the stupider and less healthy have been more than replacing theirs ... Sooner or later we must limit the families of the unintelligent classes.'[108]

H.G. Wells, in his book *Anticipations*, dreamt of a scientific utopia in which a ruthless but super-efficient world state, dominated by white English-speaking people, ruled over vast numbers of non-white peoples who were ripe for extermination. Wells envisaged a forcible system of birth control in which 'base and servile types' were gradually eliminated in every country, together with the globe's unwanted races.[109]

Sidney and Beatrice Webb were interested in eugenics and introduced Wells to their friends in the Fabian Society, the think-tank for the British Labour Party. The Webbs themselves called for the concentration of vagrants into penal camps, an idea to which Churchill seems to have warmed. As John Carey has observed, numerous British intellectuals in the early twentieth century took these ideas to extremes, advocating elitist solutions in which the masses would be gradually bred out of existence.[110]

Churchill was clearly not the only public figure interested in eugenics. While it would therefore be wrong to pass anachronistic value judgements on him, it is worth remembering that what passes for progressive politics can vary greatly from one age to the next. But, in most respects, his tenure as Home Secretary was enlightened even by modern standards.

Did Churchill order troops to fire on strikers in Tonypandy?

DURING THE PERIOD 1909-11, there was an upsurge in industrial unrest and militancy across Britain. Trade union membership surged, while small numbers of syndicalists, advocating the revolutionary overthrow of capitalism, became a more prominent influence. As Home Secretary, Churchill was charged with maintaining law and order. While he warmed to the demands of moderate labour, he feared the influence of more subversive elements and was ready to adopt strong-armed and, for contemporaries, highly illiberal tactics. At no time did he shrink from confronting a genuine challenge to the social order. However, part of the canon of Churchill mythology is that he ordered troops to fire at strikers in Tonypandy in the riots of 1910. This allegation is without foundation, though his attitude towards industrial unrest was more complex than some of his more generous supporters have alleged.

The background to the Tonypandy dispute was the wave of industrial unrest that started in 1909 and which would end with the outbreak of war in 1914. Strikes broke out in the railway, coal and shipbuilding industries and, as Addison has pointed out, the cause was economic: 'a decline in the purchasing power of wages, coinciding with a tightening of the labour market'.[111]

The main reason for the miners' disputes of 1910-11 was the change in the wage system that the owners, the Naval Colliery Company, were trying to introduce at the Ely Pit in Penygraig. When they opened a new seam at the pit, they asked miners to do a test extraction to determine the length of time involved. As wages were linked to the amount of coal produced, this would allow the owners to determine the wages 'per ton of coal' extracted. They accused the miners of working too slowly, so as to increase their wages 'per ton' and gain additional allowances, though this was disputed by the workers. Worried about having to pay high wages, the owners began to refuse to pay allowances and took the drastic step of locking out eight hundred workers. This led to a strike of twelve thousand miners in November 1910 and an outbreak of violence and rioting outside the Glamorgan colliery at Llwynypia, near Tonypandy.

The Chief Constable of Glamorgan, fearing that the local police would be overpowered, duly requisitioned four hundred local cavalry and infantry, informing Churchill and the Secretary for War the following morning. After consultations with the Glamorgan Chief Constable, Churchill decided that it would be better to use police instead of the military to quell the disturbances. While two hundred Metropolitan Police were sent to Wales, the infantry were detained at Swindon and the cavalry at Cardiff, pending further instructions. Churchill said that the troops would stay in the district but would be called upon only if the police were unable to contain the riots. The troops stayed in the background and intervened only on one or two occasions during the rioting, thus avoiding widespread bloodshed.

According to General Macready, who commanded the troops,

> It was entirely due to Mr. Churchill's forethought in sending a strong force of Metropolitan Police directly he was made aware of the state

of affairs in the valleys that bloodshed was avoided, for had the police not been in strength sufficient to cope with the rioters there would have been no alternative but to bring the military into action.[112]

Contemporary proof of Churchill's restraint can be found in a critical leader in *The Times*:

> The Home Secretary took upon himself a grave responsibility in interfering with the arrangements demanded by the Chief Constable and acceded to by the military authorities ... The Chief Constable knows the local conditions and the character of the men with whom he has to deal ... If he asked for troops it was no doubt because he was convinced that they were needed.

The Times hinted at the reason for the 'rosewater of conciliation' shown by the Home Secretary. No doubt, they said 'the motive for countermanding the arrangement [to send for troops] was the fear that the presence of the military would exasperate the strikers'.[113]

On the following day, *The Manchester Guardian* shared this view:

> One can imagine what would have happened if the soldiers instead of the policemen had come on the rioters while they were pillaging. Bayonets would have been used instead of truncheons; the clumsier methods of the soldiers would have exasperated the crowds, and instead of a score of cases for the hospital there might have been as many for the mortuary.

They added that Churchill 'never wavered in his determination not to employ the troops unless the disorders passed beyond the control of the police'.[114]

In their own way, both papers reveal that Churchill did all he could to avoid a confrontation between miners and troops. After attacks on him by the Conservative press, Churchill justified this decision, telling the Commons: 'For soldiers to fire on the people would be a catastrophe in our national life. Alone among the nations, or almost alone, we have avoided for a great many years that melancholy and unnatural experience.'[115] The myth of Churchill ordering troops to fire on the strikers of Tonypandy should be laid to rest for good.

In June 1911 a new wave of industrial unrest broke out in the ports and docks, from Southampton to London to Liverpool. Soon the railwaymen joined in sympathetically and threatened to turn a localised grievance into a nationally organised form of industrial militancy.

The government was suddenly faced with the prospect of a standstill in the import and distribution of food supplies. Churchill initially argued that troops 'should not be called on except as a last resource' but, after requests from the local authorities, he decided to send troops to Hull and to Liverpool.[116] *HMS Antrim* was dispatched to Merseyside while troops were sent into London and thirty-two other towns to protect the rail network. On the day that the strike was brought to an end, Churchill had told army commanders to use their own discretion as to whether they intervened in a riot.[117] As Norman Rose points out in his biography of Churchill, this action 'tilted the civil-military balance dangerously in favour of the army' – a far cry from the restraint of Tonypandy a year earlier.

Churchill, according to some contemporaries, clearly relished a militant confrontation with the forces of organised labour. According to Charles Masterman, Churchill had a 'rather whiff-of-grapeshot attitude towards these matters; and he enjoyed intensely mapping the country and directing the movements of troops'. When he heard that the strike had been settled, he is said to have telephoned Lloyd George and said: 'I am very sorry to hear it. It would have been better to have gone on and given these men a good thrashing.'[118]

This may be taken as a sign of intemperate bellicosity but it is essential to remember the context. The Lord Mayor of Liverpool said that a 'revolution was in progress', while Lord Derby told Churchill that the city was in a 'state of siege', with the hospitals having but two days' supplies and all poor people facing imminent starvation.[119] The Mayor of Birkenhead told the Home Office that, if military and naval support was not forthcoming, he could not 'answer for the safety of life or property'.[120] Under these circumstances, any responsible Home Secretary would have felt the urgent necessity of sending troops or countermanding the King's Regulations.

Churchill envisaged a protracted nightmare if the strikes continued, one in which the great mass of the nation would slowly suffer economic starvation. In his own words, the strike, if continued, would 'have produced a swift and certain degeneration of all the means ... on which the life of the people depends'. What was at stake was 'maintaining the vital service of the food supply and the scarcely less vital service of transport of the goods indispensable to the industrial population'.[121]

Much later Churchill justified his earlier use of troops in 1911:

To use soldiers or sailors ... to take sides with the employer in an ordinary trade dispute ... would be a monstrous invasion of the liberty of the subject, and I do say without hesitation that it would be a very unfair, if not an illegal, order to give to the soldier. But the case is different where vital services affecting the health, life and safety of large cities or great concentrations of people are concerned. Light, water, electric power, transport, the distribution of food, all these are indispensable ... If any of these commodities or facilities are suddenly cut off, the State must intervene and come to the rescue of the population.[122]

Churchill's handling of the strikes of 1911 has unfairly cast him as a zealous foe of organised labour. But more often than not he was a conciliator in industrial disputes and often took the side of workers against their more intransigent employers. As President of the Board of Trade, Churchill was asked to intervene in the shipbuilding and engineering strikes of 1908 and, in each case, a settlement was reached between employers and unions. Despite his willingness to send troops to the port strikes of 1911, Churchill allowed negotiations to proceed to solve the dispute. Accordingly, G.R. Askwith, the chief Industrial Conciliator at the Board of Trade, was given time for mediation and a settlement was duly reached on August 18th.

Askwith paid tribute to Churchill's refusal to bow to pressure: 'He refused to listen to the clamour of class hatred; he saved the country from a national transport stoppage becoming a riot and incipient revolution.'[123] Furthermore, Churchill recognised that deeply felt grievances underlay industrial unrest and sought to deal with these sympathetically. In the 1908 dispute in which cotton spinners decided to reduce wages by 5 per cent due to the economic difficulties of the time, Churchill made proposals to both sides of the industry to introduce a 'sliding scale scheme that would take into account the varying conditions of trade to supplement the existing conciliation machinery'.[124]

He also believed there should be a 'more formal and permanent machinery' for industrial conciliation. Since 1896 the Board of Trade had been empowered to conciliate in trade disputes at the request of both parties. It had intervened in dozens of cases and provided satisfactory settlements for the majority. In view of the scale of disputes, he proposed a Standing Court of Arbitration with two representatives for labour, two for the employers and a Chairman. The reason for this composition was to remove 'the reproach which workmen [had] sometimes brought against individual Conciliators and Arbitrators'.[125] This idea was put into practice in 1909 and was used to settle a number of grievances, including a dispute of boot and shoe operatives, coal miners, iron workers, carters and iron moulders. He was therefore prepared to support legislation which met the grievances of workers and which included a 48-hour week, higher wages and better housing conditions.[126]

Moreover, Churchill never wavered in his vigorous defence of the right to strike. 'It is most important for the British working classes that they should be able if necessary to strike – although nobody likes strikes – in order to put pressure upon the employers for a greater share of the wealth of the world or for the removal of hard and onerous conditions.' As long as the social order was not threatened, Churchill was prepared to accept the rights of organised labour.

The unions were 'safeguards and checks' to the vigorous competition of men in a highly capitalist society.[127] He gave his support to the Trade Union Bill of 1911, declaring in the same year that 'every workman [was] well advised to join a trade union'.[128] Even in 1919, when 'a spirit of rebellion was passing through Britain', Churchill would still lament that there 'was not enough of it' (trade unionism), for 'with a powerful trade union, peace or war could be made'.[129]

In case he was accused of supporting socialism, he went on to say that the trade unions were the very antithesis of socialism, 'for in the socialist state no strike would be tolerated'.[130] The contrast with 'socialism' was further pronounced in 1908 when he said that the unions were 'undoubtedly individualistic organisations, more in the character of the old Guilds and much more in the character of the individual, than they are in that of the smooth and bloodless uniformity of the masses'.[131]

Overall, Churchill can justifiably be described as a liberal insofar as he recognised, and sought to alleviate, the legitimate grievances of workers. But, when he sensed an imminent threat to the socio-economic order, he had no hesitation in using force to maintain law and order, revealing his conservative instincts.

NOTES

1 S. Haffner, *Churchill*, pp.31-2.
2 Companion II (i), p.394.
3 *Ibid.*, p.72.
4 V. Bonham-Carter, *Winston Churchill as I Knew Him*, p.120.
5 Speeches I, p.221.
6 Companion II (i), p.174.
7 P. Addison, *Churchill on the Home Front*, p.27.
8 WSC Bio 2, p.57.
9 Speeches I, p.441.
10 WSC Bio 2, p.57.
11 P. Addison, *Churchill on the Home Front*, p.29.
12 Companion II (i), p.243.
13 S. Haffner, *Churchill*, p.31.
14 Companion II (i), p.422.
15 WSC Bio 5, p.336.
16 P. Addison, *Churchill*, p.131.
17 Speeches V, p.5023.
18 K. Aldritt, *Churchill the Writer*, p.42.
19 W. Churchill, *Thoughts and Adventures*, p.29.
20 C. Ponting, *Churchill*, p.760.
21 V. Bonham-Carter, *Daring to Hope*, p.224.
22 A. Seldon, *Churchill's Indian Summer*, p.126.
23 *History Today*, March 2005, Volume 55, Issue 3, pp.13-19.
24 For more on the context for British *fin de siècle* anti-Semitism, see the masterly study by Colin Holmes, *Anti-Semitism in British Society, 1876-1939*.
25 He painted an alarming picture of a flood of immigrants, among whom were 'criminals, anarchists and immoral persons'. The immigrants were believed to have inundated the labour market with cheap labour, thus depressing wages and causing overcrowding in parts of London.
26 Companion II (i), pp.354-5.
27 *Ibid.*, p.356.
28 O. Rabinowicz, *Winston Churchill on Jewish problems*, p.53.
29 *Ibid.*, p.67.
30 *Ibid.*, p.73-4.
31 Speeches I, p.501.
32 Companion II (i), p.604.
33 *Ibid.*, p.356.
34 O. Rabinowicz, *Winston Churchill on Jewish Problems*, p.165.
35 Companion II (i), p.358.
36 Speeches I, p.44.
37 *Ibid.*, p.486.
38 *Ibid.*, pp.713-18.
39 *Ibid.*, p.807.
40 WSC Bio 2, p.263.
41 Speeches I, p.812.
42 J. Stewart, *Standing for Justice*, p.xx.

43 Proposals for land value taxation increasingly won support in Parliament. In 1905, 400 MPs presented the Liberal Prime Minister, Henry Campbell-Bannerman, with a petition for the same policy. Campbell Bannerman supported the measure, believing that its introduction was essential in eradicating Britain's endemic poverty.

44 M. Hill, *Churchill: His Radical Decade*, p.34.

45 Speeches I, p.782.

46 W. Churchill, *The People's Rights*, p.121.

47 M. Hill, *Churchill: His Radical Decade*, p.65.

48 K. Theakston, *Winston Churchill and the British Constitution*, p.30.

49 Speeches II, pp.1314-15.

50 *Ibid.*, p.1324.

51 *Ibid.*, p.1424.

52 K. Theakston, *Winston Churchill and the British Constitution*, p.33.

53 *Ibid.*, p.34.

54 Companion II (ii), p.968.

55 WSC Bio 2, p.336.

56 K. Theakston, *Winston Churchill and the British Constitution*, p.37.

57 Under the terms of the *Constitutional Reform Act* (2005), the Law Lords will be replaced by a British 'Supreme Court' modelled on the American body.

58 Companion II (ii), pp.1031-2.

59 WSC Bio 2, p.360.

60 Companion II (ii), p.863.

61 M. Gilbert, *Churchill: A Life*, p.xix.

62 F. Lloyd George, *The Years that are Past*, p.60.

63 P. Addison, *Churchill on the Home Front*, p.45.

64 V. Bonham-Carter, *Winston Churchill as I Knew Him*, p.135.

65 Companion II (i), p.xxvii.

66 Speeches I, p.30.

67 Companion II (i), p.104.

68 *Ibid*, p.111.

69 Blake/Louis, *Churchill*, p.59.

70 *Ibid.*, p.60.

71 Speeches I, p.676.

72 Companion II (ii), p.759.

73 Speeches II, p.1094.

74 Companion II (ii), p.895.

75 P. Addison, *Churchill on the Home Front*, p.76.

76 Companion II (ii), p.852.

77 *Ibid.*, pp.879-80.

78 W. Beveridge, *Power and Influence*, p.87.

79 Speeches II, p.1066.

80 *Ibid.*, p.1186.

81 *Ibid.*, p.1187.

82 Blake/Louis, *Churchill*, p.77.

83 R.R. James, *Churchill: A study in Failure*, p.36.

84 Blake/Louis, *Churchill*, p.62.

85 *Ibid.*, p.60.

86 W. Churchill, *My Early Life*, pp.256-7.
87 P. Addison, *Churchill*, p.51.
88 Speeches II, p.1591.
89 Companion II (ii), p.1199.
90 Speeches II, p.1511.
91 P. Addison, *Churchill on the Home Front*, p.116.
92 Companion II (ii), p.1201.
93 K. Aldritt, *Churchill the Writer*, pp.62-3.
94 Companion II (ii), p.1200.
95 Speeches II, p.1690.
96 WSC Bio 2, p.387.
97 P. Addison, *Churchill on the Home Front*, p.118.
98 The system of preventive detention allowed the courts, in the case of habitual offenders, to impose a sentence of five to ten years over and above the basic sentence.
99 P. Addison, *Churchill on the Home Front*, p.119.
100 Companion II (ii), pp.1189-90.
101 Speeches II, pp.1589-97.
102 Read Lord Ramsbotham's *Prisongate*.
103 P. Addison, *Churchill on the Home Front*, p.121.
104 C. Ponting, *Churchill*, p.101.
105 *Ibid.*, p.102.
106 P. Addison, *Churchill on the Home Front*, p.125.
107 A. Roberts, *Eminent Churchillians*, p.212.
108 J. Carey, *The Intellectuals and the Masses*, p.14.
109 *Ibid.*, p.125.
110 See John Carey, *The Intellectuals and the Masses*.
111 P. Addison, *Churchill on the Home Front*, p.140.
112 V. Bonham-Carter, *Winston Churchill as I Knew Him*, p.222.
113 WSC Bio 2, p.376.
114 *Ibid.*, p.377.
115 Speeches II, p.1677.
116 However, he urged the authorities there until August 17th to make maximum use of the police before making a request for military intervention (WSC Bio 2, p.383).
117 The King's Regulations stipulated that the military could not act unless help was requested by the civil power.
118 N. Rose, *An Unruly Life*, p.78-9.
119 WSC Bio 2, p.382.
120 *Ibid.*, p.384.
121 Speeches II, pp.1872-3.
122 Speeches IV, p.2788.
123 P. Addison, *Churchill on the Home Front*, p.149.
124 WSC Bio 2, pp.286-7.
125 Companion II (ii), p.837.
126 P. Addison, *Churchill on the Home Front*, pp.206-7.
127 Speeches I, p.873.
128 Speeches II, p.1825.

129 P. Addison, *Churchill on the Home Front*, p.206.
130 Speeches I, p.384.
131 *Ibid.* p.1030.

CHAPTER THREE

The Challenge of Total War

IN 1911 CHURCHILL was appointed First Lord of the Admiralty. He made some far-reaching decisions, including the creation of a Fast Division of ships which would run on oil, not coal. To this end, he purchased for the British government a 51 per cent share in the profits of the Anglo-Persian Oil Company (later BP), which ensured adequate oil supplies for the navy. He also introduced the Royal Naval Air Service which was later to merge with the Royal Flying Corps to form the Royal Air Force.

During his time at the Admiralty, Churchill became aware of the growing hostility between Britain and Germany. Seeking to avoid an Anglo-German confrontation, he called for a naval holiday that would involve a one-year suspension of naval rearmament in both countries. The Germans rejected the plan and tension continued to build up, especially in the Balkans.

When war broke out in August 1914, Churchill oversaw the dispatch of the British Expeditionary Force to France and ensured that the fleet was in maximum readiness for hostilities. As battles raged on the Western Front, he became a leading advocate for alternative strategies and methods for conducting the war, including the use of a new weapon, the tank.

He also pushed ahead with a plan to knock Turkey out of the war. This involved sending a fleet through the Straits of the Dardanelles to capture Constantinople, Turkey's capital. The policy won the support of the War Cabinet and the First Sea Lord, Admiral John (Jackie) Fisher; but the naval operation failed to achieve its initial objectives and, when Fisher resigned over a strategic disagreement, Herbert Asquith's government collapsed. A new coalition government was formed and Churchill was forced to resign in the face of mounting Tory pressure. He accepted the sinecure of Chancellor of the Duchy of Lancaster, but within months he had resigned, frustrated that he was no longer involved in the running of the war.

In 1916 Churchill became a battalion commander in France with the Royal Scots Fusiliers and saw at first hand the conditions men were facing in the trenches. Far from being aloof, he led his men by example and chose to share their dangers where possible. He returned to London to resume his parliamentary duties, railing at the tactics employed on the Western Front. He condemned the strategy of attrition, exemplified by the battles of Verdun and the Somme, but undermined his case when he called for the return of Admiral Fisher. He received ministerial office again, under Lloyd George, when he was appointed Minister of Munitions, a position he retained until the end of the war.

What changes did Churchill introduce at the Admiralty?

WHEN HE WAS offered the post of First Lord of the Admiralty in 1911, Churchill was in a state of euphoria. His close friend Violet Bonham-Carter recalled that, from that moment, 'his whole life was invested with a new significance'. She claimed that she had never seen him 'more completely and profoundly happy', while Churchill described the job in these glowing terms: 'This is the biggest thing that has ever come my way – the chance I should have chosen before all others.'[1]

Since childhood he had yearned to emulate the feats of his illustrious ancestor, the Duke of Marlborough. Now, in this new department, he would have a taste of naval glory, albeit from a civilian perspective. Though the years at the Admiralty were tainted by his acrimonious fall from power in 1915, he was to impose himself on his new department and produce significant and welcome innovations.

Churchill's stewardship of the Admiralty was marked by a hands-on approach to administration. He regularly paid visits to nearly every naval port and ship, witnessed tactical exercises, attended launches, inspected dockyards and thoroughly immersed himself in the complicated detail of naval administration. In short, he wasted no opportunity to meet the people under his control. Following a visit to a submarine in June 1912, the *Daily Express* wrote: 'He had a yarn with nearly all the lower deck men of the ship's company, asking why, wherefore, and how everything was done. All the sailors "go the bundle" on him, because he makes no fuss and takes them by surprise. He is here, there, and everywhere.'[2]

Churchill's concern for justice and his sympathy for the underdog were reflected in his reform of naval discipline. He set up a committee to review naval justice and its recommendations included changes in the imposition of summary punishments and improvements in the internal administration of ships. Naval offenders were sent to naval detention quarters instead of civilian prisons. A successful scheme was introduced whereby petty and warrant officers could be given educational training ashore and then sent to sea as officers, while the fees at Osborne and Dartmouth were halved. He observed:

> ... there is a deep and widespread sense of injustice and discontent throughout all ranks and ratings of the Navy. This discontent and the grievances which produce it are fanned and advertised in Parliament and the press. It is rendered more dangerous by every successful strike for higher wages which takes place on shore ... We have had great mutinies in the past in the British Navy, and we ought not to continue to bear the responsibility of refusing all redress to grievances so obvious and so harsh.[3]

Naval morale was also raised when Churchill suggested pay increases for the lower deck as well as recreational facilities on shore. After visiting Harwich, he sought funds for a canteen, a football pitch, billiard tables and bowling alleys. Even though it would take several years to pass, he pressed for pensions for the wives of sailors who died in the service. Not surprisingly, these measures proved to be highly popular with the sailors on the lower deck.

Churchill's achievements at the Admiralty went beyond improving the sailors' morale. He helped to push through some warships with 15-inch guns rather than the 12-and-a-half-inch guns developed by Lord Fisher. He also wanted to improve the speed of Britain's warships for, as he observed, 'Smashing up the tail of an enemy's Fleet ... is not comparable to smashing up his head.'[4] This led to the creation of the so called Fast Division, a fleet of ships able to travel at 25 knots, a speed at which the navy could outmanoeuvre their German opponents. In order to produce this speed, the faster ships would need to be powered by oil instead of coal. As Norman Rose points out, this was a brave decision for, while Britain had ample supplies of coal, she had no oil.

In order to obtain the necessary oil supplies, Churchill entered into negotiations with the Anglo-Persian Oil Company, which would later be known by its more familiar name, BP.5 After lengthy talks, Churchill negotiated a deal whereby the British government purchased a 51 per cent share in the profits of all oil produced by the company, and the first use of all oil produced at the company's wells. This deal ensured an adequate supply for the Royal Navy to maintain its warships.

Another innovation was the introduction of the Royal Naval Air Service (RNAS). In 1911 the aeroplane was in its infancy and the Royal Navy possessed only six, all manned by pilots from the Royal Flying Corps. Churchill's imagination was fired up by the military potential of aircraft and as early as 1909 he had urged the government to come into contact with Orville Wright.6 He built up the RNAS, whose main responsibilities included fleet reconnaissance, the protection of harbours and naval installations, and, later during war, patrolling coasts for enemy vessels and attacking enemy coastal territory. In April 1918, after months of discussions, the Royal Naval Air Service merged with the British Army's Royal Flying Corps (RFC) to form the Royal Air Force.

Churchill's involvement with aircraft went even further than this. As First Lord he had set up an inter-departmental committee to examine the establishment of air routes and landing grounds. In one of his minutes he had suggested that the Ordnance Survey prepare a 'regular flying map' to assist the creation of such routes and that flags and other conspicuous aviation landmarks be erected along the main aerial routes 'like lighthouses at sea'.7

Nothing better illustrates Churchill's hands-on approach to the Admiralty than his decision to learn to fly. It was highly unusual for a civilian, especially one aged over 30, to undertake such dangers, but Churchill approached the task with his usual relish and determination. Over many weekends, he took lessons in flying and proved to be an avid learner.

The introduction of the RNAS and oil-driven ships reveals the extent of Churchill's inventiveness. Inventive, too, was his pursuit of simple language and rejection of jargon. As a result of his forceful interventions, 'aeroplane' was shortened to 'plane', 'destroyer' replaced the unwieldy 'search and destroy vessel' and the term 'business as usual', attributed to Churchill, was used to describe a state of continuing normality in an emergency situation. In 1913 Churchill proposed a 'naval holiday' in the Anglo-German arms race, coining a term that would later enter the diplomatic vocabulary.[8]

These changes reflected Churchill's stubborn refusal to accept the status quo, and his unconventional and inventive approach to solving problems. But his interference was not always appreciated. John Jellicoe thought that Churchill's fatal error was that he did not recognise that he was a layman 'quite ignorant of naval affairs'. Sir Francis Hopwood accused him of 'foolishly' travelling around the country, holding reviews and inspections without considering naval opinion and custom. Indeed a quarrel on one of the ships he visited nearly led to the resignation of the four Sea Lords in 1913. Nonetheless, for Sir Roger Keyes, Churchill possessed a 'quick brain and vivid imagination', and 'in the majority of cases' his interventions were 'in the best interests of the Services'.[9]

One cannot evaluate Churchill's achievements at the Admiralty without mentioning his preparations on the eve of war. Towards the end of the July Crisis of 1914, Churchill made certain that the navy was prepared for battle if Britain were to declare war. He ensured that all ammunition, oil supplies and coastal lights were safeguarded from attack; he collected aircraft to defend against Zeppelin raids and he reinforced the British naval squadron in the Far East. Most importantly, he ordered the First Fleet to sail into the North Sea to guard against invasion. By the end of July 1914, the navy was ready to repel any German attack on the east coast. His crowning achievement was to oversee the successful transportation of the British Expeditionary Force to France without loss of ship or life. As Kitchener would tell Churchill later: 'One thing they can't take away from you: the Fleet was ready.'

Did Churchill try to prevent the First World War?

CHURCHILL HAD ALWAYS greeted the prospect of European war with ambivalence. In a speech in 1901 he had warned that such a conflict would be 'a cruel, heartrending struggle' which would demand 'the whole manhood of the nation, the entire suspension of peaceful industries, and the concentrating to one end of every vital energy in the community'. 'The wars of people,' he warned, would be 'more terrible than those of kings.'[10] In 1909 he told his wife that, while war fascinated him, he could not help feeling that it was 'vile & wicked folly & barbarism.'[11]

Churchill's foreboding about the length and cost of conflict co-existed with a visceral fascination for military action. After he was offered the Admiralty in 1911, Violet Asquith recalled that 'His whole life was invested with a new significance.' Certainly Churchill believed he was ideally suited to this post, and wrote to Morley, 'I have always been especially attracted to naval and military subjects. I have read much more about war than about anything.'[12] Such assertions make it easy to cast him as a warmonger, intent on pursuing a ruthless and egotistical quest for military glory. He was seen by others, as he often saw himself, as a modern Napoleon. Yet, in reality, this 'warmonger' made repeated and strenuous efforts to prevent war from breaking out in 1914.

From 1898 the German Emperor, Kaiser Wilhelm II, had embarked on a policy of *Weltpolitik* (world policy) which also had the support of two key political figures, the Chancellor von Bulow and the naval minister, von Tirpitz. The Kaiser looked with envy at the huge British and French empires, with their colonies scattered across the globe, and dreamt of Germany matching them in power. He was desperate for his country to have 'a place in the sun'. Colonial expansion could only be sustained by the possession of a fleet, meaning that *Weltpolitik* was inextricably linked to a policy of naval expansion. But, as Germany expanded her navy, there were ripples of suspicion and mistrust in London and, before long, a confrontational Anglo-German naval arms race was underway. This would be accompanied by howls of jingoistic protest in the national press of both nations.

In the first few years of the Asquith government, Churchill was often derided for being a pro-German appeaser. Prior to 1911, he thought an Anglo-German war highly unlikely, given the deterrent strength of Britain's navy. He was also one of a number of Liberal figures who, from 1908, advocated direct negotiations between Britain and Germany to reduce mistrust and prevent an escalating arms race. This seemed logical at the time as naval estimates would have to be reduced to fund the Liberal Party's social reforms. In a speech in 1908, Churchill said: 'It is greatly to be deprecated that persons should try to spread the belief that war between Great Britain and Germany is inevitable.' Germany, he went on, was one of Britain's 'very best customers' and there was 'no collision of primary interests' between the two nations. Any conflict between Britain and

Germany would produce a 'disaster of a most appalling and idiotic character'.[13] During this period he was most interested in securing measures of social reform, requiring financial arrangements that presupposed European stability.

In 1909, at the height of a scare about possible German invasion, Churchill was calling for a reduction in naval expenditure while remaining skeptical about the danger of the European situation. He even met the German ambassador in London for talks in order to establish 'a spirit of real trust and confidence between the two countries'.[14] Top secret Anglo-German negotiations in 1909-10, however, failed to achieve a breakthrough owing to the German demand for British neutrality in the event of a European war.

The Agadir Crisis of 1911 was a turning point in European relations. The crisis, precipitated by the potentially threatening dispatch of a German gunboat to the French-controlled Moroccan port of Agadir, nearly brought about an Anglo-German war and led to an acceleration of the naval arms race. From that moment onwards, Churchill became more suspicious of the German government. He urged his government to 'use pretty plain language to Germany and to tell her if she thinks that Morocco can be divided up without John Bull, she is jolly well mistaken'.[15] He also thoroughly approved of Lloyd George's 1911 Mansion House speech in which Germany was warned not to provoke the French or the result would be a war with Britain. The Agadir Crisis resulted in closer military ties between Britain and France, with their army commands agreeing a joint strategy in the event of a war with Germany.

In 1911 Churchill was appointed First Lord of the Admiralty. He was determined to prepare the navy for a possible war with Germany and, in order to do so, he insisted on maintaining Britain's naval superiority while matching Germany's high naval expenditure if necessary. Now his language became a little more alarmist as he confronted a potentially menacing naval rival.

> With regard to Germany we have to face a steady, remorseless development year by year of an immense naval force, created with the very latest science and all the efficiency of one of the most efficient peoples in the world, concentrated and kept concentrated within easy striking distance of our shores.

The German fleet was, he said, 'designed for aggressive and offensive action'.[16] He later declared, much to German displeasure, that a great navy was a luxury for the German nation, not a necessity.[17] The years 1912-14 would see the height of Anglo-German tension and the concurrent naval arms race; but during these years, and despite his gloomy predictions for the future, Churchill tried his best to avert a war between Britain and Germany.

He told his friend Sir Ernest Cassel that he deplored the Anglo-German rift, claiming that he had 'never had any but friendly feelings towards that great nation & her illustrious Sovereign'. He suggested to Cassel that he visit Germany, where he would be 'honoured' to 'discuss the great matters wh hang in the balance'. He expressed a degree of skepticism about whether Germany would drop her naval challenge, though 'any slackening on her part wd produce an immediate *détente* with much good will from all England'.[18] Cassel would say later that Churchill regarded as 'senseless' the growing 'estrangement' between the two countries'; Churchill 'would do anything in his power to establish friendly relations' towards Germany.[19]

It was amid this growing estrangement that, on March 18th 1912, Churchill put forward his idea for a 'naval holiday'. This was essentially a plan to freeze the arms race on the basis of the status quo. The idea was that both countries would suspend the building of dreadnoughts (battleships) for one year so that any reduction in German construction would be followed in Britain.[20]

Some might accuse Churchill of appeasing a fairly autocratic regime in the hope of future reward. However, his suggestion represented a policy of 'appeasement from strength' rather than craven submission, for he had first declared that Britain would adhere to its aim of maintaining a 60 per cent margin of naval superiority over Germany. Thus, for every three German dreadnoughts, Britain would build five. But the German government declined Churchill's offer, fearful that any cancellation of shipping orders would lead to unrest. Nonetheless, his firm but conciliatory approach won Churchill some friends. According to the *Western Daily Mercury*: 'His eyes are fixed upon Germany as he speaks. He tells Germany so, neither in arrogant nor aggressive terms, but with firm courtesy which befits one strong nation talking to another strong nation.'[21]

Churchill renewed his proposal for a naval holiday in a speech in October 1913 in Manchester. This time the response was negative in Britain as well as in Germany, the British Foreign Office suspecting that Churchill would end up driving a wedge between Britain and her

Entente Allies, France and Russia. In order to achieve such a naval holiday, France and Russia would have had to participate by reducing their armaments, a policy that would have proved deeply unpopular. Once again, the German government rejected the idea with sections of the German press calling for Churchill to take a holiday from making speeches.

Finally, in May 1914 Churchill suggested to Asquith and Grey, the Foreign Secretary, that direct talks between himself and his German counterpart, Admiral von Tirpitz, might lessen the misunderstanding between the two countries.[22] In words that would later echo his calls for a Cold War summit conference, he wrote: 'Personally I should like to meet von Tirpitz, and I think a noncommittal, friendly conversation, if it arose naturally and freely, might do good, and could not possibly do harm.'[23] He wished to discuss the 'good faith and sound reasons' on which his naval holiday proposal was based, limiting the size of capital ships and encouraging a reciprocal dispatch of ships to foreign ports in order to reduce 'the unwholesome concentration of fleets in Home Waters'.

He had no idea what results would be achieved by these discussions, nor did he have a strict agenda; but he did not believe that high level talks would worsen an already tense relationship. Churchill quoted this letter in his war memoirs as proof that, before the war started, he was anxious to 'mitigate asperity between the British and German Empires'.[24] However, as he was anxious to deprecate any suggestion that Britain was acting from alarm or desperation, he made it clear that Britain had to wait for an invitation from the Germans. No invitation was forthcoming, partly because of a lack of interest from von Tirpitz but also because of the overriding objections from Foreign Secretary Sir Edward Grey.[25]

On July 28th 1914, with the mighty European armies ranged against each other, Churchill revealed once again his ambivalence towards a European war:

> Everything tends towards catastrophe & collapse. I am interested, geared up & happy. Is it not horrible to be built like that? The preparations have a hideous fascination for me. I pray to God to forgive me for such fearful moods of levity. Yet I would do my best for peace, & nothing wd induce me wrongfully to strike the blow. I cannot feel that we in this island are in any serious degree responsible for the wave of madness wh has swept the mind of Christendom. No one can measure the consequences.[26]

Churchill's activities and statements in the period 1908-14 strongly detract from the view that he was a warmonger itching for a European conflict. Instead he realised that European stability, rather than an uncontrollable arms race, would enhance Britain's prestige and power.

Did Churchill invent the tank?

BY THE END of 1914, Europe's great mass armies were in a state of deadlock on the Western Front having dug themselves in lines of opposing trenches. The British and French armies had suffered one million casualties and neither side had a decisive means of breaking German defences. Amid the despair, a number of individuals started to think about a mechanical device that might break through the barbed wire of the trenches.[27] One such person was war correspondent Major Ernest Swinton.

In November 1914, Swinton put forward his idea of a 'machine gun destroyer' to the War Office. At the same time Churchill became interested in proposals for a mechanical trench-crosser. At Christmas 1914 he wrote to Asquith with a suggestion for a collective metal shield which could be 'pushed along either on a wheel or still better on a Caterpillar', and behind which 'several men could hide while crossing no man's land'.[28] In December 1914 he read a memorandum from Maurice Hankey outlining Swinton's ideas. He was immediately won over and wrote to Asquith:

> It would be quite easy in a short time to fit up a number of steam tractors with small armoured shelters, in which men and machine guns could be placed, which would be bullet proof. Used at night, they would not be affected by artillery fire to any extent. The caterpillar system would enable trenches to be crossed quite easily, and the weight of the machine would destroy all wire entanglements.[29]

This letter reveals that Churchill was full of boyish enthusiasm for the idea. He was already envisaging the potential of this weapon and the decisive advantages it could give to the Entente powers. His enthusiasm for the project led to the formation of the Landships Committee, a mini-cabinet whose function was to oversee the design and construction of the 'landship'. One of the key members of the committee was the Admiralty's leading naval architect, Captain

Eustace D'Eyncourt. Churchill asked D'Eyncourt to design a 'land-ship' and, together with a number of other individuals, D'Eyncourt began to investigate a caterpillar form of propulsion. An order for the first landships was placed with a firm of agricultural engineers, Foster and Company in Lincoln, who suggested modelling the vehicles on the tractor. Churchill then provided the necessary financial support by giving £70,000 of Admiralty funds in order to construct eighteen prototypes.[30] On March 9th Churchill was shown the first designs and gave his approval. 'Press on,' he minuted.

Initially the weapons were called 'landships' but, to add secrecy to the operation, they were dubbed 'water carriers for Russia'. It was put about that they were going to be a new type of water container that would be shipped to British troops in Mesopotamia. To prevent them being dubbed 'wcs for Russia,' the name was changed to 'water tanks', then later to 'tanks'.[31]

Churchill's advocacy of this weapon was brave considering the scepticism of many in the Admiralty; privately the tank was dubbed 'Winston's folly'. Among the skeptics were Douglas Haig and Sir Henry Wilson. Haig was an advocate of infantry and artillery attacks while Wilson believed that the Germans would use land mines to destroy tanks. Aware of the danger of mines, Churchill's fertile mind went into action. He suggested that tanks should be fitted with 'a large steel hammer' extending in front of them which 'could strike the ground heavy blows sufficient to spring off the shell'. He also suggested that the gun on the tank might be lowered so as to destroy the mine, and finally thought that some tanks could be fitted with an armoured undercarriage that could resist inevitable explosions. These were, he admitted, 'crude ideas', but Churchill was never afraid of ruffling feathers or forcing others to rethink.[32]

In a memorandum in 1916, Churchill further developed these ideas. Tanks and other armoured vehicles, he argued, could glide over the rough terrain of no man's land like a ship over a rough sea. In their wake there could be a pattern of 'paths and grooves', cut deeply into the surface of the ground, which would allow easy movement for the attackers. In the same paper he recommended the establishment of an anti-tank committee which could 'study the methods by which tanks can be defeated'. He wrote that the body 'should work in the closest harmony with those concerned in the production and design of tanks, each striving to defeat the other, exchanging information and perfecting their methods'.[33] This was vital because Churchill believed that the Germans could themselves develop the weapon, nullifying the British advantage.

This was by no means the last intervention that Churchill made. Sensing that tanks would only be effective if they involved an element of surprise, he pressed the government not to use them in small numbers in the Battle of the Somme. As he had put it in a memorandum in 1915, 'None should be used until all can be used at once'.34 Despite his objections, thirty-five tanks were used in September 1916, but to very little effect. 'My poor "land battleships" have been let off prematurely and on a petty scale,' he wrote.35 It was not till the Battle of Cambrai in November 1917 that tanks were used *en masse* and the decisive edge they gave the British army vindicated Churchill's earlier scepticism.

From then on the tank became one of the driving forces that enabled the Entente powers to defeat Germany in late 1918. Towards the end of the war, Churchill also urged Major-General Seely to produce a thousand light steel 'dummy tanks' that could 'create alarm and panic among the enemy' and 'divert and distract fire from the real Tanks'.36

Throughout the war Churchill remained convinced that mechanical weaponry could save lives and avoid the slaughter of attritional warfare, but he was not the tank's sole inventor as some have claimed. Indeed, in *The World Crisis* he acknowledged: 'There never was a person about whom it could be said "this man invented the tank".'37

Nonetheless, his indomitable energy and imagination were crucial to the development of this weapon. Lloyd George said in the Commons in 1916 that, while others made suggestions for the tank,

> these suggestions would never have fructified had it not been for the fact that Mr Churchill ... gave practical effect to them by making the necessary experiments, setting up committees for carrying the suggestions into effect, and for putting the whole of his energy and strength towards materialising the hopes of those who had been looking forward to an attempt of this kind.38

The Royal Commission on Awards to Inventors duly agreed. It was, they said, primarily due to Churchill's 'receptivity, courage and driving force' that the idea of the tank as a war-winning weapon was 'converted into a practical form'.39

Was Churchill responsible for
the Gallipoli disaster?

IN 1915 CHURCHILL embarked on one of the most controversial policies of his career: an attack by Allied ships on the straits of the Dardanelles in Turkey. The idea was to force Turkey out of the war, open a new front in the East from which to attack Germany, and bring the war to a speedy conclusion. All seemed well on paper but by the end of 1915 the operation had been abandoned in ignominy after the loss of more than a hundred thousand men. Churchill lost his job at the Admiralty and was shunted into a minor non-military office from which he had no say in the running of the war. He had been the leading advocate of the Dardanelles operation and it was understandable that he should take the fall when it failed.

Many people at the time shared Lloyd George's scathing verdict on Churchill: 'When the war came he saw in it the chance of glory for himself, and ... accordingly [he] entered on a risky campaign without caring a straw for the misery and hardship it would bring to thousands'.[40] For Clive Ponting the Dardanelles represented the height of 'naval and military ignominy' and it was entirely 'reasonable' for Churchill to be the scapegoat for the failure.[41] Nigel Knight offered an even more scathing verdict in his *Churchill: The Greatest Briton Unmasked*, where he blamed Churchill for ruining the military reputation of Lord Kitchener and helping to destroy the Liberal Party.[42] However, a dispassionate review of events reveals that Churchill was not primarily responsible for the disaster at Gallipoli.

By the end of 1914 the Western Front was deadlocked with a 500 kilometre line of front-line trenches separating Germany from the Entente powers. The great armies of Germany, France and Britain stared at each other across no man's land, with neither side possessing a decisive technical or strategic advantage. Already Allied casualties on the Western Front had reached nearly one million since August 1914 and the idea that the war would be won through the protracted agony of 'attrition' repulsed many politicians. In Churchill's words, soldiers were being sent to the Western Front 'to chew barbed wire'.[43] While 'Westerners' advocated the continuation of war on the Western Front, 'Easterners' such as Churchill looked for imaginative alternatives in other theatres of war.

One of these alternatives involved an attack on Turkey, which appeared to offer untold strategic advantages. At the start of war, Turkey was officially neutral but, on September 29th 1914, the Turks closed the straits of the Dardanelles and mined the entrance, a clear breach of neutrality. One of the Easterners' plans was to send ships up the Dardanelles Straits, knocking out its forts in the process and then going on to capture Constantinople, a plan which would ensure the defeat of Turkey. This would enable the Allies to send food supplies to Russia, giving the Russians access to a warm-water port and opening an Eastern Front against Germany. In addition, neutral Balkan states such as Greece would be compelled to join the Entente powers, which would have a considerable political impact in the war. That was the theory, and the hope.

By the middle of January 1915 the War Council had approved the Dardanelles operation, but some important points must be borne in mind. Firstly, Churchill did not originate the plan; indeed he advocated attacks elsewhere in Europe. Maurice Hankey, for one, circulated a memorandum towards the end of 1914 in which he outlined a plan for knocking the Turks out of the war and creating a powerful Balkan League. By December 1914 Churchill was calling for the seizure of the island of Borkum, so that it could be used as a base to attack Schleswig-Holstein, and then other parts of Germany via the Kiel Canal. 'The Baltic,' he had written to Lord Fisher, 'is the only theatre in wh naval action can appreciably shorten the war'.44 Even as late as January 8th, while plans for an attack on the Dard-anelles were being discussed, Churchill was considering applying pressure to bring Holland into the war, while he had not ruled out the Borkum plan.

Secondly, the Russians played an important role in deciding whether an operation against Turkey should take place. The War Cabinet had received a report from Britain's military attaché in Petrograd warning of the dire state of Russia's military forces and, in particular, its lack of adequate supplies. As a result, the Cabinet was haunted by the prospect of Russia's imminent collapse.

Then, on December 30th 1914, the Grand Duke of the Russian army made an urgent appeal for help against the Turks who, he claimed, were threatening the Caucasus. Lord Kitchener was asked 'to arrange for a demonstration of some kind against the Turk else-where, either naval or military ... and thus ease position of Russia'.45 The Russian appeal galvanised the War Cabinet, Kitchener in particular. It was he who suggested to Churchill that, 'The only place that a demonstration might have some effect in stopping reinforcements going East would be the Dardanelles.'[46] At this stage it was Kitchener who provided the impetus for a 'purely naval' operation at the Dardanelles.[47]

Thirdly, in response to Kitchener's request, Churchill was skeptical about a purely naval operation, favouring instead a combined naval and military assault. On January 3rd 1915, and with the express permission of the First Sea Lord, Admiral Jackie Fisher, he asked the Commander of the blockading squadron, Vice Admiral Carden, whether the Dardanelles could be forced 'with ships alone'. It was a crucial question and Carden's response would turn out to have immense repercussions. Nine days after he received the telegram, Carden replied that the Straits could be forced 'by ships alone' through a slow and methodical penetration. He then proceeded to outline a detailed plan of action and the vessels he would need to accomplish the task. Several days earlier, Lord Fisher had also warmed to the Dardanelles plan, telling Balfour of his belief in 'the peculiar merit of Hankey's Turkey plan'.[48] As a result of his warm endorsement, he ordered the dispatch of the *Queen Elizabeth* to the Straits. Without Fisher's assent, the plan would have been doomed. Without a positive memorandum from Carden, the expert on the spot, it is doubtful whether even an obstinate Churchill could have won over an ambivalent War Council.

On January 13th 1915 the War Council met to discuss the plan further. Churchill advised them that a total of fifteen battleships would be used, first to destroy the forts, then to sweep the minefields of the Dardanelles, which would allow the fleet to sail up towards Constantinople and capture the city. According to Hankey's memoirs, the idea of a sudden naval action had an immediate appeal: 'The War Council turned eagerly from the dreary vista of a "slogging match" on the Western Front to brighter prospects, as they seemed, in the Mediterranean.'[49] Fisher was present at those meetings but was silent, as were others in the Cabinet. As Violet Bonham-Carter wrote: 'Their silence could only be interpreted as assent, for the Carden plan had been approved at the highest level in the Admiralty.'[50]

It is therefore incorrect to suggest that Churchill forced this plan on a reluctant Council or Admiralty. As even the skeptical Tuvia Ben Moshe asserts: 'Most of the senior politicians on the War Council were themselves attracted to the plan ... Churchill exercised his not inconsiderable powers of persuasion on persons who were ready to be persuaded.'[51] Nonetheless, some doubts were being raised at this early stage by senior officers in the Admiralty. Admiral Jackson pointed out that, once the ships had entered the Sea of Marmora, the fleet's supply lines could not be ensured. Sir Henry Jackson and Sir Arthur Wilson also expressed doubts, but for Churchill, Fisher's assent was decisive.

One other crucial decision was taken at the War Council meetings of January 5th and 8th, with fateful consequences. Kitchener made it plain that 150,000 troops would be enough to capture the Peninsula, but no troops were available to accompany the naval operation. He also said that if the bombardment was not effective, it could be abandoned, which was the view of Vice Admiral Carden.[52]

Then, all of a sudden, Lord Fisher began to express doubts about the operation. On January 20th he argued that French ships should lead the operation and urged the recall of the British flotilla. However Fisher was overruled, not by Churchill, but by the War Council. A day later he wrote negatively of the operation and how it would fail unless the navy was supplemented by 200,000 troops. However Kitchener had already ruled out using spare troops and Fisher had hardly expressed any concerns at the crucial War Council meetings at which he was present. Later, Fisher's request to have his objections sent to the Council was overruled by Asquith, himself a supporter of the operation. On January 28th, by Fisher's own later admission, he gave his assent to the operation, '*totus porcus*'.[53]

Crucial issues arose on February 15th. Sir Henry Jackson, Captain Richmond and Lord Fisher all called for military reinforcements to join the ships as a naval expedition alone would not succeed. Churchill did not ignore these criticisms from senior Admiralty figures: he asked Kitchener for troops, reflecting the concerns he had expressed back in January. Kitchener now agreed that the 29th Division, together with ANZAC troops then in Egypt, should be available 'in case of necessity to support the naval attack on the Dardanelles'.[54]

Churchill insisted that the troops be available at three days' notice, to seize the Gallipoli peninsula and to occupy Constantinople. On February 19th, however, Kitchener reneged on this agreement and, much to Churchill's consternation, vetoed the dispatch of the 29th Division. The reason for the refusal was Kitchener's fear that the Germans were about to launch a huge attack on the Western Front, which would require the 29th Division to repulse.

Instead of the 29th Division, Kitchener offered 39,000 ANZAC [55] troops that were stationed in Egypt. In vain Churchill argued for the inclusion of the 29th Division and was ably supported by Lloyd George, Hankey and Asquith. But Kitchener was insistent that no further troops were needed. He argued that, as soon as the Dardanelles' forts were destroyed, the Turks would put up little resistance and seek refuge in Asia. Kitchener was adamant that a naval force alone would see Turkey's surrender, but this was to prove a fatal underestimation of Turkish resolve. Churchill was to remark that, 'If a disaster occurred in Turkey owing to the insufficiency of troops, he must disclaim all responsibility.' Churchill had certainly committed a volte-face, having previously advocated a purely naval action, but the advice he had received appeared to warrant this.

Kitchener's veto proved crucial and, despite his reservations, Churchill agreed to a naval operation without the 29th Division. In so doing, he helped to sow the seeds of his later downfall. By refusing the additional troops, Kitchener failed to meet one of his own conditions for the attack: the possibility of a speedy withdrawal if it went wrong. To complicate matters further, Kitchener then changed his mind again on March 10th, announcing that, after all, the 29th Division would be available for the Dardanelles operation. In his defence, Churchill would later claim that, had he known in January that additional troops were available, he would have delayed proposing a purely naval assault.[56]

As it was, the naval operation which started on March 18th might have succeeded.[57] At 10.45a.m twelve ships entered the Dardanelles Straits and bombarded the intermediate Turkish guns. Despite a successful bombardment, three British battleships were sunk by mines before the minefields could be swept, but the British casualties were minimal. De Robeck (Churchill called him 'De Row back') was 'mystified, disturbed and disconcerted by these losses'[58] and duly telegraphed to London that the attack would not be renewed until the arrival of the 29th Division, which had been promised on March 10th. Churchill, supported by Asquith and Kitchener, urged immediate action, arguing that the loss of up to twelve battleships was to be expected.

Churchill was also enthused by intercepted German telegrams which suggested that the Turks were running very low on heavy ammunition and might be unable to sustain gunfire for another full day. But De Robeck had second thoughts and by March 23rd he had informed General Hamilton that the Straits could not be forced without troops. He argued that, unless the army took the Gallipoli peninsula, his naval supply lines would be endangered once the ships entered the Sea of Marmora. While Kitchener, Balfour and Asquith supported Churchill in urging De Robeck to renew the attack, they could not force their view on the Admiralty. Fisher and two other senior Admiralty figures concurred with De Robeck's decision to delay, and Asquith could do little to overrule them.

De Robeck's decision meant a lengthy delay in the operation; it was not until April 25th that troops were landed in the region. On that day 35,000 men under Lieutenant General Hunter Weston landed at Cape Helles and 17,000 ANZAC troops landed at 'Anzac Cove'. They were later supported by reinforcements and, for the next nine months, struggled to defeat the Turkish forces. However, the operation was abandoned by the start of 1916 after nearly a hundred thousand Allied deaths.

From the moment that the army became involved, none of the military disasters were Churchill's responsibility. Kitchener now controlled the military initiatives at the Dardanelles and, in the next nine months of fighting, never tried to break through into the Narrows or the Sea of Marmara. Every decision for action subsequently taken at Gallipoli was approved by the War Office or by Hamilton and it would therefore be wrong to blame Churchill for the *subsequent* deaths in the Gallipoli landings from April onwards.

Fisher would later claim in a War Cabinet meeting on May 14th that he had been against the operation from the start, an outburst that was 'received in silence'.[59] Lloyd George later reminded Fisher that 'he had never expressed any dissent from the policy or the plans of the expedition' and that he had 'not heard one word of protest from him'.[60] Yet the First Sea Lord was prone to fits of melodrama; on several occasions he had announced his resignation, only to be talked out of it by Lloyd George or Churchill. By mid-May he had finally made up his mind to resign his position, citing his strategic disagreements with Churchill.[61]

Fisher's resignation in May 1915, combined with the shock announcement of a shell shortage on the Western Front, brought down Asquith's Liberal administration and paved the way for a coalition government. One of the conditions laid down by Conservative leader Bonar Law was that Churchill, with whom he had had acrimonious relations, be excluded from government. In the midst of a personal crisis, Asquith lacked the stomach for a battle and meekly acquiesced. Thus, by the middle of May 1915, Churchill's career had come crashing down around him.

So, to what extent should Churchill take the blame for the disaster? We have already seen that the massive casualties associated with the Gallipoli landings cannot be blamed on him. From the moment that he ceased to be First Lord of the Admiralty, he 'no longer possessed operational responsibility for the continuation of the Gallipoli campaign' and therefore there 'exists no direct link between him and the military operations, moves and failures that happened after his resignation'.[62] The blame for the fiasco from April 25th onwards cannot reasonably be pinned on Churchill.

Up to January 1915, the Western Front had been deadlocked with neither side possessing a decisive technological or strategic advantage. With casualties mounting in this stalemate situation, an imaginative alternative was surely worth pursuing. Secondly, in looking at any operation, the price of failure has to be measured against the price of success. In this case, the cost of Churchill's failure was a small number of obsolete battleships and very light casualties (dwarfed by those on the Western Front). Looked at in this light, the Dardanelles operation in March 1915 can hardly be termed an expensive failure.

Churchill's key conviction, shared by Keyes, that the minesweepers should have continued up the Narrows on March 18th, appears to have been vindicated. The Turks were short of mines by that date, so much so that they had been forced to collect some that the Russians had been floating down the Bosphorus from the Black Sea. According to Enver Pasha, 'If the English had only the courage to rush more ships through the Dardanelles they could have got to Constantinople but their delay enabled us thoroughly to fortify the Peninsula and in six weeks' time we had taken there over two hundred Skoda guns.'[63] Later Ismet Inonu, who had been Ataturk's lieutenant at the Dardanelles, would also vindicate Churchill's claim that De Robeck should have continued the naval assault after the initial setback of March 18th.[64] The opinion of military experts is, however, a little more divided.

Nonetheless, one can question some of the assumptions behind this operation. The military historian Michael Howard has asked whether the defeat of Turkey and the provision of supplies to Russia would have turned the scales on the Eastern Front. In his view, 'the problems of the Russian imperial regime were too deep-rooted to be solved by short term material or financial help'.[65] In addition, there were problems with the idea of a united Balkan League. The Balkan states were riven by internal dissent, while Bulgaria and Greece were strongly opposed to Russian control of Constantinople.

Churchill made much of the massive armies of a Balkan League which could join forces with the Entente powers, but these troops lacked an 'organisational infrastructure and modern military equipment' and would therefore have been dependent on the 'massive logistic support of Britain and France'.[66] At the time, these two countries would have found it difficult to supply equipment and ammunition for the region. The assumption that Turkey's defeat would have led to the downfall of Austria-Hungary and the rallying of the Balkan countries has been questioned.

In retrospect, it would have been better to have planned a joint naval and military operation, something that Fisher himself began to urge in January 1915. But Churchill cannot take sole responsibility for this failure, or for his hurriedness in starting the purely naval operation. The responsibility lies partly with Admiral Carden, whose initial positive assessment gave Churchill the spur he needed. The fault also lies with the War Cabinet itself. In 1915 the war was under civilian direction and the military members of the Cabinet said very little. Kitchener was in overall strategic command; 'he neutralised the General Staff, and concentrated most power in his own hands'. This meant that there was 'an unnatural imbalance' between 'statesmen and soldiers'.[67] Not enough questions were asked at the early stages of planning and not enough doubts were raised about whether the Admiralty was fully behind a purely naval operation.

As a subordinate in the War Cabinet, Churchill was answerable to Kitchener, who called the shots as far as troops were concerned. Churchill later argued that his greatest mistake was 'seeking to attempt an initiative without being sure that all the means & powers to make it successful were at [his] disposal'.[68] Whether or not success could have been achieved, Churchill seriously underestimated his own political weakness at the time.

One matter about which there is little doubt is the devastating effect the disaster had on Churchill. Violet Bonham-Carter recalled that he looked 'like Napoleon at St. Helena'[69] while his wife

Clementine believed that her husband 'would die of grief' after losing office. In later years, however, he would be more philosophical. Leo Amery recalled Churchill saying that the only consolation from the failure of the Dardanelles campaign 'was that God wished things to be prolonged in order to sicken mankind of war, and that therefore He had interfered with a project that would have brought the war to a speedier conclusion'.[70] It was perhaps a comforting thought.

Was Churchill an effective battalion commander?

IN MAY 1915 Churchill was forced out of the Admiralty when it became clear that the Tories would not countenance his presence in a coalition government. Churchill was offered the relatively insignificant role of Chancellor of the Duchy of Lancaster, which gave him no say over grand strategy and the direction of the war. Reeling from his new-found impotence, he resigned from the government and decided to experience the grim conditions of war on the Western Front. For several months in 1916 he was a battalion commander in charge of about a thousand men. One might have expected a clash between the haughty politician and the working men under his command, but class differences were to prove a surmountable barrier. Churchill would win over his men, at the same time proving his considerable bravery and adroitness as a military commander.

Before taking charge of the battalion, Churchill asked to experience trench life and to see for himself the conditions faced by ordinary men on the Western Front. To this end, he was attached to the 2nd Battalion, Grenadier Guards for five days and saw at first hand the dismal conditions experienced by the men. In one letter to his wife he painted a rather morbid picture of trench life:

> Filth and rubbish everywhere, graves built into the defences & scattered about promiscuously, feet & clothing breaking through the soil, water & muck on all sides; & about this scene in the dazzling moonlight troops of enormous bats creep & glide, to the unceasing accompaniment of rifle & machine guns & the venomous whining & whirring of the bullets wh pass over head.[71]

When he subsequently criticised the government's conduct of the war in the Commons, he was speaking from personal experience.

On January 1st 1916 Churchill found out that he was to command the 6th Royal Scots Fusiliers, a battalion in the 9th Division. The battalion, consisting of 700 men and 30 officers, had already seen action at the Battle of Loos the previous year. Despite some reservations, Churchill was optimistic, telling his wife that he would succeed in his endeavours and find an outlet for his energies. The reaction of the men to news of Churchill's arrival was one of dismay and anger, as Captain Gibb recalled: 'When the news spread, a mutinous spirit grew... Why could not Churchill have gone to the Argylls if he must have a Scottish regiment!'[72] The officers, too, believed that they 'were in for a pretty rotten time'.[73]

Churchill knew that he would have to win over his men and he set about doing this from the start. According to one of the Scots Fusiliers:

> After a very brief period he had accelerated the morale of officers and men to an almost unbelievable degree ... He had a unique approach which did wonders to us. He let everyone under his command see that he was responsible, from the very moment he arrived, that they understood not only what they were supposed to do, but why they had to do it ...[74]

Being aloof was clearly not Churchill's style of man management, neither was it in his nature to be a strict disciplinarian. He was aware that the 6th Royal Scots Fusiliers had incurred dreadful losses at Loos and he imagined the torment experienced by those who were left. When any miscreant was brought before him for disciplinary treatment, the first question he would ask was, 'Were you in the battle of Loos?' If the man replied, 'Yes,' then the charge against him was dismissed. The rather unfortunate consequence was that all the men then said they had been involved in the battle.[75]

On another occasion Churchill wrote to his wife: 'I keep watch during part of the night so that others may sleep. Last night I found a sentry asleep on his post. I frightened him dreadfully but did not charge him with the crime. He was only a lad ... the penalty is death or at least 2 years.'[76]

Churchill was also minded to give second chances to men who were guilty of indiscipline and insubordination for he considered that 'no man would wittingly incur the serious penalties inevitable in such a case'. Not surprisingly, this generous approach to indiscipline appalled the officers. As Gibb wrote: 'I am afraid the men began to realise that they might at least once indulge themselves in the luxury of telling their sergeants to go to hell!'77 Churchill clearly did possess 'an instinctive sympathy for the rank and file, whether soldiers in the army or sailors at sea'.78

Churchill was also concerned for the comfort of his men. On his first day with the battalion, he announced to the officers: 'Gentlemen, we are now going to make war – on the lice.' As an essential part of delousing, the men were given baths and a generous supply of new clothes and steel helmets. Morale was improved through a greater emphasis on relaxation and recreation. Churchill oversaw an improvement in the men's rations, encouraged football matches (which he attended) and even arranged a concert. Weeks later, Churchill could write to his wife about how the Corps Commander 'expressed himself astonished at the improvement in the battalion since he last saw it five weeks ago'.79

Churchill believed in leading by example. He experienced the dangers of trench life at first hand and refused to be separated from his men when they were in danger. 'I have seen him stand on the fire step in broad daylight to encourage the Jocks, and to prove to the man on the fire step how little danger there was of being hit.'80 He also frequently accompanied his men into no man's land, where they came under enemy machine gun fire. According to one recollection: 'He never fell when a shell went off; he never ducked when a bullet went past with its loud crack.' These were examples of personal bravery, but it was bravery for a purpose. He knew that leading by example and sharing danger would raise morale and encourage his men to trust him.

Even when he was out of the trenches, Churchill did not lose his concern for the battalion. In a critical speech to the House of Commons in 1916, he expressed anger at the delay in introducing steel helmets in the trenches. With such helmets, he pointed out, 'Many men might have been alive to-day who have perished, and many men would have had slight injuries who to-day are gravely wounded...'81

He was also concerned that men were finding it harder to be promoted if they were in danger than if they were at home out of harm's way. It was, he said, 'a very anomalous state of affairs that one man should be a year or a year and a half in the trenches, in continual danger, and should actually make slower progress up the military ladder than his brother who has joined a Home service battalion and has not been ordered to the front.'82 On the same theme, he argued that honours and awards should be given to those who were facing the greatest dangers, rather than to men in the highest ranks. 'Honours should go where death and danger go, and these are the men who pay all the penalties in the terrible business which is now proceeding.'[83]

But above all, Churchill expressed grave concerns about the attritional strategy being advanced on the Western Front. As early as December 29th 1914 he was skeptical about the British army achieving a breakthrough on the Western Front. 'I think it quite possible that neither side will have the strength to penetrate the other's lines in the Western theatre,' he wrote to Asquith. He added rather cynically that, 'the position of both armies is not likely to undergo any decisive change – although no doubt several hundred thousand men will be spent to satisfy the military mind on the point ... Are there not other alternatives than sending our armies to chew barbed wire in Flanders.'[84]

This deeply rooted skepticism was only intensified by the deadly offensives of 1916. Churchill wrote that the attritional bloodbath at Verdun, in which, after four months, 650,000 French and German soldiers had been killed, appeared 'to vindicate all I have ever said or written about the offensives by either side in the West'.[85] The clear lesson to learn from the horror of Verdun was that a premature offensive would achieve little but cost many lives. Despairing of 'the unwisdom, with wh our affairs are conducted', he wrote to his wife: 'Do you think we should succeed in an offensive, if the Germans cannot do it at Verdun with all their skill & science'.[86]

When he returned from the front line Churchill addressed the House several times, warning of the futility of a war of attrition: 'I say to myself every day, What is going on while we sit here, while we go away to dinner, or home to bed? Nearly 1,000 men – Englishmen, Britishers, men of our own race – are knocked into bundles of bloody rags every twenty-four hours, and carried away to hasty graves or to field ambulances ...'[87] Attrition involved 'dismal processes of waste and slaughter'.[88] Throughout the war, Churchill believed the great offensives on the Western Front were wasteful and futile exercises. He thought instead that it would have been better for Britain and France to wait on the defensive, building up a numerical advantage in tanks, aircraft and artillery before launching attacks on the German positions.

To those who were disinterested in these calls, Churchill offered the following observation: 'I do not believe that people in this country have any comprehension of what the men in the trenches and those who are engaging in battles are doing or what their sufferings and achievements are'.[89] Churchill's empathy and humane approach came from direct personal experience, a factor that gave him an inestimable advantage over his contemporaries.

NOTES

1 V. Bonham-Carter, *Winston Churchill as I Knew Him*, p.237.
2 WSC Bio 2, p.576.
3 P. Addison, *Churchill on the Home Front*, p.156.
4 WSC Bio 2, p.610.
5 The Anglo-Persian Oil Company was founded in 1909, following the discovery of a large oil field in Iran.
6 Companion II (iii), p.1874.
7 *Ibid.*, pp.1910-11.
8 J. Humes, *Churchill: Speaker of the Century*, p.135.
9 N. Rose, *An Unruly Life*, p.99.
10 Speeches I, p.82.
11 Companion II (ii), p.912.
12 M. Gilbert, *Churchill: A Life*, p.239.
13 Speeches II, p.1085.
14 K. Larres, *Churchill's Cold War*, p.8.
15 WSC Bio 2, p.522.
16 Speeches II, p.1972.
17 *Ibid.*, p.1910.
18 Companion II (iii), p.1492.
19 K. Larres, *Churchill's Cold War*, p.15.
20 Speeches II, p.2072.
21 WSC Bio 2, p.600.
22 He hoped that he would receive authorisation to travel to Germany to see the annual celebratory review of the German fleet.
23 K. Larres, *Churchill's Cold War*, pp.27.
24 W. Churchill, *World Crisis I*, p.144.
25 K. Larres, *Churchill's Cold War*, pp.28-9.
26 M. Soames (ed), *Speaking for Themselves*, p.96.
27 Günther Burstyn, an Austrian army officer, is credited by many with inventing the tank. In 1911 he designed a small tracked vehicle, a *Motorgeschütz* (motor-gun), with a swivelling turret. Though discredited by the German authorities at the time, he later received recognition for his invention.
28 W. Manchester, *The Last Lion I*, p.509.
29 Companion III (i), pp.377-8.
30 P. Addison, *Churchill*, p.75.
31 M. Gilbert, *Churchill: A Life*, p.298.

32 WSC Bio 4, p.74.

33 Companion IV (i), p.30.

34 Companion III (ii), p.1304.

35 W. Manchester, *The Last Lion I*, p.565.

36 Companion IV (i), pp.400-1.

37 D. Jablonsky, *Churchill: The Great Game and Total War*, p.62.

38 WSC Bio 3, p.810-11.

39 M. Gilbert, *Churchill: A Life*, p.299.

40 A.J.P. Taylor (ed), *Lloyd George: A Diary by Frances Stevenson*, p.50.

41 C. Ponting, *Churchill*, p.178.

42 N. Knight, *Churchill: The Greatest Briton Unmasked*, Chapter 1.

43 WSC Bio 3, p.226.

44 Companion III (i), p.326.

45 *Ibid.*, p.360.

46 *Ibid.*, p.361.

47 Ben Moshe rightly says (*Churchill: Strategy and History*, p.62) that the emergency situation in Russia had passed by the end of January, meaning there was no need for urgent action at the Dardanelles. However, blame cannot be solely attached to Churchill for this.

48 WSC Bio 3, p.237.

49 *Ibid.*, p.252.

50 V. Bonham-Carter, *Winston Churchill as I Knew Him*, p.353.

51 T. Ben Moshe, *Churchill: Strategy and History*, p.48.

52 It is true, as Ben Moshe points out, that these discussions left out some crucial questions. One was how the Gallipoli peninsula was to be captured without troops. Another problem was how the fleet's supply lines would be ensured once they had entered the Sea of Marmora, given that troops were unavailable to seize the shores of the Straits. These plans lay in the future.

53 WSC Bio 3, p.273.

54 Companion III (i), p.516.

55 This is an acronym for the 'Australian and New Zealand Army Corps'.

56 There are suggestions that Churchill ought to have postponed the naval bombardment, which started on February 19th, on hearing that the 29th Division was not going to arrive in March, and then postpone it again when hearing on March 10th that they would be sent after all; however the initial hesitation came from Kitchener, when he ruled out sending them in January, in the absence of which it is unlikely that Churchill would have called for a naval only operation. In addition, the longer the delay, the more supplies the Turks would be able to amass. Churchill also believed that, in the absence of haste, the Balkan countries might be that much less inclined to come over to the Entente.

57 At the last minute, Vice Admiral Carden had gone on the sick list and been replaced by the number two in command, John De Robeck who concurred fully with the operational plans.

58 V. Bonham-Carter, *Winston Churchill as I Knew Him*, p.371.

59 *Ibid.*, p.431.

60 *Ibid.*, p.439.

61 Birkenhead, *FE*, p.278.

62 T. Ben Moshe, *Churchill: Strategy and History*, p.57.
63 V. Bonham-Carter, *Winston Churchill as I Knew Him*, p.372.
64 M. Gilbert, *In Search of Churchill*, pp.57-8.
65 M. Howard, 'Churchill and the First World War', in R. Blake and W. Louis (eds), *Churchill*, p.143.
66 T. Ben Moshe, *Churchill: Strategy and History*, p.67.
67 *Ibid.*, p.48.
68 WSC Bio 3, p.488.
69 Bonham-Carter, *Champion Redoubtable*, p.52.
70 M. Gilbert, *In Search of Churchill*, p.227.
71 Companion III (ii), p.1286.
72 WSC Bio 3, p.630.
73 *Ibid.*, p.632.
74 *Ibid.*, p.635.
75 M. Gilbert, *In Search of Churchill*, p.92.
76 W. Manchester, *The Last Lion I*, p.579.
77 WSC Bio 3, p.638.
78 M. Gilbert, *In Search of Churchill*, p.93.
79 WSC Bio 3, p.646.
80 *Ibid.*, p.657.
81 Speeches III, p.2471.
82 *Ibid.*, p.2468.
83 *Ibid.*, p.2466.
84 Companion III (i), p.344.
85 WSC Bio 3, p.754.
86 Companion III (ii), p.1488.
87 Speeches III, p.2439.
88 *Ibid.*, p.2522.
89 *Ibid.*, p.2469.

CHAPTER FOUR

Rebuilding a Shattered World

As MINISTER FOR War and Air, one of Churchill's first tasks was to demobilise the British army. He achieved this task with some skill and managed to avoid a damaging confrontation with the forces of labour. He also established the Ten Year Rule: that military spending should follow the assumption that Britain (and the Empire) would not face an enemy within the next decade.

In 1919 the world's leading statesmen met at Versailles to determine the contours of post-war Europe. Churchill rejected a vindictive peace but believed that Germany could not escape the consequences of her actions. One reason for his magnanimity was that he believed a strong Germany was needed as a bulwark against the new Russian Bolshevik regime, which he detested.

Churchill supported the White anti-Bolshevik armies in their attempt to destroy Leninism, providing them with various forms of assistance. He also played a leading role in bringing about a settlement in Ireland, negotiating with IRA leaders in the build-up to the 1921 Anglo-Irish agreement. Later, as Colonial Secretary, he helped to carve out the new unitary nation of Iraq from the Mesopotamian remnants of the Ottoman Empire.

In 1922 the Lloyd George coalition government fell and Churchill lost his seat at Dundee. For two years he sought a return to Westminster, losing a number of by-elections; he eventually returned to Parliament in 1924 as a Conservative. He was appointed Chancellor of the Exchequer and one of his first decisions was to restore Britain to the Gold Standard. However sterling was overvalued in 1925 and the consequence was to increase the cost of British exports, with serious ramifications for industry. The following year the government's subsidy to the coal industry came to an end and, in order to prevent paralyzing strike action, the government began talks with the Trades Union Congress.

When talks broke down and the General Strike ensued, Churchill adopted an uncompromising and bellicose attitude towards it. Arguing that the strike had to be defeated, he oversaw the publication of a government newspaper, the *British Gazette*. However, when the TUC called off the strike, Churchill played a leading role in negotiating a fair settlement within the coal industry.

Nonetheless, as Chancellor, Churchill sought to pursue a traditional, free-trade approach through his policy of de-rating. He rejected a loan-financed scheme of public works and cut spending by the armed forces. His decision to abolish the duty on tea was to prove highly popular. In 1929 the government fell and Churchill resigned as Chancellor of the Exchequer.

Did Churchill support a punitive peace after the First World War?

I know that it is not always a fashionable opinion, but the facts repudiate the idea that a Carthaginian peace was in fact imposed upon Germany.[1]

THROUGHOUT THE WAR Churchill had advocated no let-up in the struggle against Germany, denouncing those who advocated a compromise peace. In response to Lord Landsdowne, the former Foreign Secretary, who called for a negotiated end to the war, he declared: 'To set out to redress an intolerable wrong, to grapple with a cruel butcher, and then after a bit to find him so warlike that upon the whole it is better to treat him as a good hearted fellow and sit down and see if we can't be friends after all, may conceivably be a form of prudence but that is the very best that can be said for it.'[2] Using uncompromising language in 1918, he described the conflict with Germany as a fight between 'Christian civilisation and scientific barbarism' and stated categorically that 'Germany must be beaten'.[3] At no time did he question the commitment to the total and unmitigated defeat of the German war machine.

However, he had also promised during the war that any peace settlement would leave intact the independence, customs and language of the German people. 'Their rights as citizens and freemen', he declared, would 'never be assailed by us'.[4] He hinted that any future settlement had to revolve around 'the reorganisation of Europe according to the sentiments of nationality',5 echoing the calls for self-determination that were to be found in Woodrow Wilson's fourteen points. One month before the end of hostilities he again stressed that he did not seek to 'trample these millions of people, misguided, in the dust' and merely sought 'effective guarantees against the repetition of the injuries and the miseries to which we have been exposed'.6

In the aftermath of victory, public sentiment was unsurprisingly hostile to Germany. There was widespread support for 'hanging the Kaiser' and for imposing a punitive peace settlement on Germany. Strangely, Churchill did not share these sentiments. Indeed, on the evening of November 11th 1918, hours after the signing of the armistice, he seemed more concerned about supplying Germany with adequate provisions following years of food shortages. He suggested that Britain rush 'a dozen great ships crammed with provisions' into Hamburg to stave off mass starvation. He did not share the widespread desire for retribution. Sir Henry Wilson wrote in his diary, 'LG wants to shoot the Kaiser ... Winston does not.'7 While war had to be fought with resolution, victory could only be achieved magnanimously and this largely coloured his views in the coming months.

Churchill was not one of the key participants at the peace conference in 1919, apart from one unsuccessful mission to encourage a united front against Bolshevik Russia. Nonetheless, as soon as the war had finished, his thoughts turned to a future peace settlement with Germany. He accepted the principle (later enshrined in War Guilt Clause 231) that the Germans had ultimate responsibility for the war. As he put it, 'Practically the whole German nation was guilty of the crime of aggressive war conducted by brutal and bestial means ... They were all in it and they must all suffer for it.'8 He supported 'stern justice' for the Kaiser and welcomed the principle of reparations against the Germans 'to the uttermost farthing they are capable of paying'.9

But, despite this tough talk, Churchill advocated a sensible and moderate peace. He was aware that the French in particular feared a resurgent Germany, and that Germany would need to compensate other countries for their war debts. Nevertheless, he urged the victors to 'proceed with great care and vigilance' so that any new German government would be 'strong enough to shoulder the burden of reparation and yet not capable of renewing the war'. He admitted the difficulties inherent in this moderate approach but insisted that the victors not get 'drawn into extravagances by the fullness of their victory'.[10]

In terms of reparations, he supported the principle that Germany pay for much of the damage caused by the war. He felt that the wartime harm to British trade was as real as the 'material damage to France and Belgium' and that Germany ought to take over British debts to the USA.[11] As late as 1922 he argued that Germany ought to 'make a genuine contribution towards repairing the injuries and suffering she has caused.'[12]

But he also believed it would be physically impossible for the mass of German workers and families to pay the full costs of war. The consequences of a draconian reparations bill would be suffering for the German people: they would be reduced temporarily 'to a condition of sweated labour and servitude'. He also realised that, as Germany had been a major pre-war trading partner of Britain, any German economic deterioration would hinder Britain's own survival.[13] As he explained in the *Illustrated Sunday Herald* in November 1919, 'The reconstruction of the economic life of Germany is essential to our own peace and prosperity.' Like Lloyd George in his 1919 Fontainebleau Memorandum, Churchill was concerned that high reparations would have a negative impact on British trade with Germany.

He also perceived a fundamental link between poverty and war: 'We do not want a land of broken, scheming, disbanded armies, putting their hands to the sword because they cannot find the spade or the hammer.'[14] It would later become a central staple of *bien pensant* opinion that one of the main reasons for the Nazis' electoral success was the bitterness felt by Germans towards the Treaty of Versailles.

In his memoirs of the Second World War, Churchill would come to share this analysis:

> The economic clauses were malignant and silly to an extent that made them obviously futile. Germany was condemned to pay reparations on a fabulous scale. These dictates gave expression to the anger of the victors, and to the failure of their peoples to understand that no defeated nation or community can ever pay tribute on a scale which would meet the cost of modern war.[15]

But it seems that he objected more to the actual reparations sum imposed on Germany than the principle itself.

Churchill was also not in favour of the victors forcibly annexing German territory, leaving Germans under foreign domination.

Indeed, he had anticipated this point before the war ended. In an interview published in *The Times* he pointed out that the war was designed to 'reform the geography of Europe according to national principles'. There was a strong case 'for settling generally on ethnographic principles'.[16]

In 1918, in response to a leading Liberal in Dundee who advocated treating Germany along the lines of the Prussian settlement of 1871 by which French territory was seized, Churchill responded: 'If we were now to take provinces of Germany inhabited by Germans who wished to stay with Germany, and held them down under a foreign government, should we not run the risk of committing the same crime as the Germans committed in 1871 and bringing about the same train of evil consequences?'[17] In December 1918 he urged that the new frontiers of Europe be drawn 'in broad conformity with the groupings of the populations'.[18] In other words, he, like President Wilson, wanted where possible to extend the principle of national self determination to Germans.

In general, he wanted Germany to be treated 'humanely and adequately fed, and her industries restarted' and deprecated the 'cranks of various kinds who denied that Germany suffered any privations at all'.[19] He was aware that the popular press was baying for 'the most extreme terms upon the vanquished enemy...' but he questioned the logic of applying a vindictive peace. The consequences for the victorious army of occupation could be severe, for any such army would be 'holding down starving populations, living in houses with famished women and children, and firing on miners and working people maddened with despair'. He warned: 'Disaster of the most terrible kind lies on that road.'[20] He thus warned the French war minister in 1920 that Britain 'would have nothing to do with a policy of crushing Germany'.[21] Nonetheless, he wanted Britain to be sympathetic to the French, to win over Clemenceau to his anti-Bolshevik policy and also to persuade the French to adopt 'a merciful policy towards Germany'.[22]

Churchill was no advocate of leniency for its own sake. He believed in a moderate peace negotiated from a position of political and military strength. He therefore proposed that, during the peace negotiations, the Allies send an army of occupation of 900,000 men into parts of Germany, and that this army should not be disbanded until its leaders had agreed peace terms. This army was necessary to exact from Germany 'the just terms' the Allies would demand.[23] He would later plead for 'the maintenance in these times of trouble of a strong armed Power, to be used with sober and far-sighted moderation in the common good'; as a result, there would emerge the desired combination of 'power and mercy'.[24]

Finally, he disliked the fact that the terms of the treaty were imposed on Germany without any redress, believing that, if the Germans had a chance to modify the treaty, it might produce 'a genuine German acceptance of a defeated peace'.[25] In this he was probably being naïve. The German masses were persuaded that they had not suffered a military defeat and that their country did not have sole responsibility for starting the war. They were led to believe that war was the collective responsibility of all Europe's great powers and their representatives would have found it hard to accept any peace settlement which did not accept that view. It is unlikely that Germany could have played a meaningful role in deciding her own fate at Versailles.

In the early 1920s Churchill pressed for an improvement in the German situation. Writing to Lloyd George in 1920, he feared 'universal collapse and anarchy' in Europe and Asia and suggested a defensive alliance with France against Germany if France altered its hostile approach towards Germany and accepted British help for the reconstruction of her country. This would rally 'all that [was] good and stable in the German nation to their own redemption.'[26]

Churchill's central fear was that Bolshevik Russia, rather than Germany, constituted the principal threat to European civilisation. Russia, therefore, had to be confronted by a united European power bloc. Later that year he proposed a 'binding alliance' of 'Great Britain, France and Germany' which could 'defend the Western Front in the event of an unprovoked attack by Russia'.[27] In return, Britain would demand that France and Germany work towards a reconstruction of the Continent.

Above all else, Churchill desired the pacification of the Continent and the 'appeasement of the fearful hatreds and antagonisms' blighting Europe, something that presupposed a just settlement between France and Germany. Naturally any such alliances and commitments necessitated 'a profound revision of the Treaty of Versailles' and the restoration of Germany as 'an equal partner in the future guidance of Europe'.[28]

As late as 1933 he denied that Versailles had been a 'Carthaginian peace'. He believed it had been founded upon self-determination, 'the strongest principle in the world', and that it had achieved much of the 'great work of conciliation and appeasement' in Europe up to that point. Furthermore, he denied that Germany had suffered brutal treatment as 'no division was made of the great masses of the German people'.[29] He also pondered the likely fate of the Allied nations if the Germans had won instead, citing the harsh terms that Germany imposed on Russia at the Treaty of Brest Litovsk.[30]

For Churchill, war required maximum force to defeat a determined enemy but peace required an equally strong measure of goodwill.

Why did Churchill want to strangle the Bolshevik Revolution at its birth?

IN NOVEMBER 1917 a small group of zealous ideologues seized power in Russia and changed the course of history. Vladimir Lenin and Leon Trotsky led the October (Bolshevik) Revolution which overthrew Russia's provisional government and imposed communist rule on the country. In the following months the secret police arrested and executed class enemies while targeting counter-revolutionaries across the country. Instead of preserving religious freedom, the Bolsheviks ruthlessly attacked the Church and the monasteries, following the Marxist dictum that religion was the opium of the masses. Disregarding the notion of inviolable property rights, the Bolshevik state seized swathes of noble and Church land for the purpose of forcible redistribution, while war imposed terrible burdens on the peasants. As a utopian experiment in socio-economic relations, the Revolution was a direct challenge to the values of the liberal, enlightened West.

From the outset, Churchill recognised the uncompromising character of Bolshevism and condemned it in the harshest terms possible. 'Of all tyrannies in history,' he said in 1919, 'the Bolshevik tyranny is the worst, the most destructive, and the most degrading.'[31] He considered the Bolsheviks to be 'the enemies of the human race' who had to be 'put down at any cost'.[32] Having faced up to the danger of German militarism, he now considered the Bolshevik danger to be 'the most formidable which has ever threatened civilisation'. In somewhat prophetic tone, he issued this chilling statement: 'It is a movement which will deluge in blood every country to which it spreads, and if it triumphed it would extinguish, perhaps for long centuries, the whole prosperity and genius of mankind.'[33]

The Bolsheviks were likened to a destructive virus. Bolshevism was 'a hateful and sub-human barbarism',[34] the Bolsheviks were 'foul, filthy butchers' trying to establish 'germ cells' in overseas regiments to disseminate their 'vile doctrine'.[35] Lenin had been sent to Russia in the same way that 'you might send a phial containing a culture of typhoid or of cholera to be poured into the water supply of a great city'.[36] Moscow was a 'dark, sinister, evil power' run by a 'plaguish band of conspirators' which was aiming to 'overthrow all civilised countries and reduce every nation to the level of misery to which they have plunged the great people of Russia'.[37] This was intemperate language that reflected a visceral loathing of everything the Bolsheviks stood for.

But they were not words for words' sake. As Minister for War and Air in 1919-20, Churchill was an irreconcilable adversary of the Bolshevik regime. In 1919 he travelled to the Paris Peace Conference and called for an 'Allied Council for Russian affairs', the military section of which could consider the prospect of overthrowing the Bolsheviks altogether. Much to Churchill's chagrin, Lloyd George and the Americans jointly rejected the proposal. Realising that a war against the Bolsheviks was impossible with Allied armies, he supported the anti-Bolshevik Whites who were struggling to overthrow the new Bolshevik regime, supplying their leader, Denikin, with food and equipment, and sending a military mission which manned tanks and planes in the front line. But Churchill's hopes for an early end to the Bolshevik regime were dashed as the White armies fell back in the face of a determined Bolshevik counter-attack. By the end of 1919 the White leaders had been captured and any prospect of reversing the Revolution had been lost by the following year.

Churchill accepted this result with equanimity but his hatred for the Bolsheviks remained: 'I do not of course believe that any real harmony is possible between Bolshevism and present civilisation,' he said.[38] Indeed he even argued that recognition of the Bolsheviks was tantamount to legalising sodomy.[39] What exactly was the source of such deep-seated animosity?

As already noted, Churchill rejected any notion of a compromise peace in the First World War and believed that nothing should stand in the way of total victory. It was not surprising, then, that he began to loathe the Bolsheviks after they had made the decision to remove

Russia from the war. The Treaty of Brest-Litovsk in March 1918 not only weakened Russia but destroyed at a stroke the Eastern Front against Germany that had been in place since August 1914. Churchill firmly believed that this decision would delay an Allied victory and cause untold death and suffering on the Western Front.

This view was reinforced in a speech made in 1918 in which he dwelt on what he regarded as Russia's wartime act of betrayal. 'Every British and French soldier killed last year was really done to death by Lenin and Trotsky,' he said. This was the result of their 'treacherous desertion of an ally without parallel in the history of the world'. Even the Germans, for all their crimes, 'stuck to their allies', he added.[40] Indeed Churchill was prepared to recognise the Revolution as long as the Bolsheviks re-committed Russia to the war.

In a speech he gave in 1920 he reflected further on the consequences of the Bolshevik Revolution:

> They broke the pact which Russia had made with Britain and France to fight the war, for better or for worse, till victory over Germany was won. By so doing they liberated, during the winter of 1917, more than a million Germans to come over from the east and attack the British armies and their French comrades in France. And by this treacherous desertion they inflicted upon us the most frightful losses of the whole war and very nearly robbed us of victory.[41]

Towards the end of the war he was equally outraged by the assassination of Captain Cromie at the hands of Bolsheviks. Cromie, a British naval attaché in Russia, was shot outside the British Embassy in Petrograd in 1918 by the Bolshevik secret police. Churchill demanded that the government pursue the perpetrators of this crime, writing: 'The exertions which a nation is prepared to make to protect its individual representatives or citizens from outrage is one of the truest measures of its greatness as an organised state.'[42]

Nonetheless, during the Russian Civil War Churchill deprecated the use of excessive force. 'Wholesale executions are unpardonable in policy,' he wrote.[43] Instead of the 'indiscriminate shooting' of Bolshevik suspects, he urged 'a fair public trial of all culprits and stringent orders against terrorism'.[44] The need for justice was a guiding principle for, as he put it: 'Even the worst criminals are entitled to a trial.'[45]

To understand the longevity of his fierce anti-communism, one must appreciate his intense ideological opposition to Bolshevism.

Churchill repeatedly expressed his contempt for the ideology of Lenin and Trotsky, which he saw as the antithesis of classical liberalism, given that it denied the sacrosanct right of individual liberty. In the Bolshevik philosophy, individuals were subservient to the wider community with no economic, social or religious freedoms beyond those which the community's rulers deemed permissible. As he put it, 'The Communist theme aims at universal standardisation. The individual becomes a function ... No one is to think of himself as an immortal spirit, clothed in the flesh, but sovereign, unique, indestructible.' Such a society, Churchill wrote, was modelled on the ant.[46] For a man who interpreted the history of the world as mainly 'the tale of exceptional human beings' and their 'thoughts, actions, qualities, virtues, triumphs, weaknesses and crimes', the denial of individuality was galling.

The political differences between European Liberalism and Bolshevism were also spelt out:

> We believe in Parliamentary Government exercised in accordance with the will of the majority of the electors constitutionally and freely ascertained. They seek to overthrow Parliament by direct action or other violent means ... and then to rule the mass of the nation in accordance with their theories, which have never yet been applied successfully...[47]

He also condemned the Bolsheviks' economic ideology. Addressing an audience in 1920, he surveyed Russia, a once prosperous country, which had been 'one of the great granaries of the world' but which had been 'reduced to famine of the most terrible kind'. This was due not to a lack of food but to an abundance of poor ideology. Famine had taken hold because Leninist and Trotskyite theory had 'fatally ... ruptured the means of intercourse between man and man, between workman and peasant, between town and country ... because they have raised class against class and race against race in fratricidal war'.[48] Thus he railed against a Marxist economic doctrine that he thought senseless and destructive.

But an ideological disagreement over doctrine was not enough to unsettle Churchill's mind, or leave him, in Lloyd George's words, 'obsessed' with Russia. One clue to the intensity of his hatred can be found in a speech given in 1920:

> ...my hatred of Bolshevism and Bolsheviks is not founded on their silly system of economics, or their absurd doctrine of an impossible

equality. It arises from the bloody and devastating terrorism which they practice in every land into which they have broken, and by which alone their criminal regime can be maintained.49

Churchill did not believe that Bolshevism was just a misguided utopian philosophy that could be sensibly discussed and debated. For him it was an inherently subversive ideology whose implementation required an extraordinary level of terror and violence. The Bolshevist could not promote his ideas through the rational means of 'argument or example'. It was dictated 'by the bullet or the bomb', and 'propagated and maintained by violence'.50 Churchill was convinced that the Bolshevik utopia required the overthrow of all the things he held dear: monarchy, aristocracy, parliamentary democracy, private property, free speech and free religious practice. In short, it required a war against the very idea of civilisation itself in an attempt to create a utopian 'year zero'. As he wrote in 1919: 'They seek as the first condition of their being the overthrow and destruction of all existing institutions and of every state and Government now standing in the world.'51

Churchill came to these views by being an astute observer of Russia in the years after the Revolution. The Cheka had been arresting, imprisoning and executing 'class enemies' since 1917. It also helped orchestrate the 'Red Terror', a campaign of mass arrests and deportations targeting counter-revolutionaries during the Russian Civil War. This campaign marked the beginning of the Gulag: 70,000 were imprisoned by September 1921. Lenin's 'Decree on Land' also forcibly redistributed the landed estates of the nobility, the monasteries and Church among the peasantry. The implementation of Bolshevism required 'in every country a civil war of the most merciless kind between the discontented, criminal and mutinous classes on the one hand and the contented or law abiding on the other'. 'Bolshevism,' he added, 'means war of the most ruthless character, the slaughter of men, women and children, the burning of homes, and the inviting in of tyranny, pestilence and famine.'52

As Churchill saw it, Bolshevism was objectionable because it allowed one man to decide the fate of a nation regardless of the needs and desires of its inhabitants. In this sense he saw Lenin as the ultimate tyrant, a tyrant being one who 'wrecks the lives of millions for the satisfaction of his own conceptions'.53

Churchill's greatest concern was a rapprochement between a militaristic Russia and a resentful Germany. Acting together, these pariah nations would unsettle Europe's balance of power and confront the Allied victors with a formidable power bloc. During the Versailles treaty negotiations, Churchill sought to persuade Lloyd George that Germany and Russia had 'miseries and ambitions in common' and that, if a rejuvenated Russia joined hands with Germany and Japan, they would form a powerful triumvirate that would 'constitute a menace for Britain, France and the United States'.54

It was for this reason that he was prepared to keep Germany strong after 1919, reducing the burden of reparations and restoring Germany to a position of international respectability. Both measures would maintain goodwill and a rejuvenated Germany would act as a bulwark against Russian aggression. His immediate post-war motto was 'Kill the Bolshie, kiss the Hun'. He feared that an economically weak Germany would embrace Bolshevism and seek a *rapprochement* with her Russian neighbour, much to the detriment of the Western Allies.55

Churchill's concept of Bolshevik war was not confined to the march of the Russian army. He was haunted by the prospect of Bolshevik ideas spreading, like a virus, among peasants, workers and soldiers, undermining the social order that he held so dear. The march of Bolshevism required, not an army or weapons, but insidious propaganda, which could be spread in peace or war. As he put it: 'The Bolshevik aim of world revolution can be pursued equally in peace or war. In fact a Bolshevist peace is only another form of war.'56 If the Bolsheviks could not work purely by military means they would 'employ every device of propaganda in their neighbours' territories' to ensure those countries were 'poisoned internally'.57

Churchill's fears of Bolshevik-inspired subversion were fully exposed during the Zinoviev affair. This centred on a letter allegedly sent by Grigori Zinoviev of the Executive Committee of the Communist International (Comintern) to the Central Committee of the Communist Party of Great Britain. It called for intensified communist agitation in Britain, especially among the armed forces. The letter, which was almost certainly a forgery, was intercepted and leaked to the *Daily Mail* and then used by critics to imply that a strong relationship existed between the Labour Party and Moscow. Published just four days before the 1924 general election, it contributed to Labour's defeat.

It took little to persuade Churchill of this link, leading him to accuse the Labour leader, Ramsey MacDonald, of 'a sense of comradeship with these foul, filthy butchers of Moscow'. He believed that the Bolsheviks were seeking to forment 'bloody revolt' and 'civil war' throughout Britain, with 'flames and carnage to disturb and defile our streets'.[58] Two years later he would come to view the General Strike through the same red-tinted spectacles. Churchill's relations with the Soviet Union would alter over time as a result of changing historical circumstances and his own pragmatic mindset, but he would never lose his revulsion for Bolshevism.

How did Churchill rebuild modern Ireland?

CHURCHILL IS OFTEN remembered with bitterness in both Northern and Southern Ireland. For many Protestants he is the 'great betrayer' of Ulster, prepared to spill blood during the Curragh mutiny; for Catholics he is a modern Cromwell, the man who unleashed the 'Black and Tans' on innocent civilians. There is some truth in each of these views but what they overlook are the years of magnanimous statesmanship that characterised Churchill's approach to Irish politics.

Churchill's father had been an implacable opponent of Home Rule.[59] He had fiercely believed in the union between Britain and Ireland and was happy to play 'the Orange Card' when Gladstone announced his conversion to Home Rule. In 1886 Randolph made a daring trip to Ulster Hall and urged Protestants to resist the measure, if need be with force. His subsequent motto, 'Ulster will fight, Ulster will be right,' neatly encapsulated his belligerent stance. Randolph then overplayed his hand and resigned as Chancellor of the Exchequer, but his stance was not lost on the adoring son. Writing to his mother in 1897, Winston declared that: 'Were it not for Home Rule – to which I will never consent – I would enter Parliament as a Liberal.'[60]

Even as a Liberal in 1904, he had described Home Rule as unworkable, adding, 'I remain of the opinion that the creation of a separate Parliament for Ireland would be dangerous and impracticable.'[61] In 1906 he told the voters: 'I am myself not prepared to support any legislation which, in my opinion, will affect or injure the integrity of the United Kingdom.'[62]

Nonetheless, there were signs of a more conciliatory attitude. He spoke of the need for administrative reforms in the Irish government, saying he would 'gladly see the Irish people accorded the power to manage their own expenditure, their own education and their own public works according to Irish ideas'.[63] It was not lost on Churchill that his moderate stand would be warmly welcomed by Irish voters in his Manchester constituency. Two years later his views had matured to the point where he welcomed 'some great national settlement which will make [Ireland] really a partner in the grandeur and freedom of the British Empire, and set free the native genius of her people to develop their own land'.[64]

Churchill's later support for Home Rule was based on a perception of British national and imperial interests. As Colonial Secretary he had overseen a generous and conciliatory settlement in South Africa which had strengthened that country's ties to Britain. He believed that Home Rule would similarly bind Ireland to Britain, strengthening imperial relations in the process and winning sympathy in the 'republic across the water'. Churchill's shrewd appreciation of America's growing power was evident. As Home Secretary, he gave his full support to Asquith's Home Rule Bill but the domestic political situation counted against success. The Conservatives were implacable opponents of Home Rule, much as Lord Randolph had been, urging the Unionists to forcefully defy the government. Not surprisingly Home Rule also went down badly with Ulster's Protestant majority who fervently rejected 'Rome rule' from the Catholic South.

Churchill understood the concerns of Ulstermen and therefore proposed two alternative formulas. One plan was for Irish Home Rule with Ulster excluded so that the Protestant counties could have 'a moratorium of several years before acceding to an Irish Parliament'.[65] The second was to have a series of regional parliaments in the British Isles, one each for England, Wales, Scotland and Ireland, with an imperial Parliament in London (predominantly English) overseeing them. This plan for devolved Parliaments was typically Churchillian in its radicalism but it won few prominent supporters.

Churchill had long believed in a bipartisan political approach to politics that involved coalition and compromise. In order to reach compromise on the Irish issue, he conducted talks in 1913-14 with the most diehard opponents of Home Rule in the opposition parties. The Conservatives would be hard to win over, especially as they had rather unconstitutionally approached the King, urging him to dissolve Parliament rather than accede to Home Rule. The staunch unionist Edward Carson was in open revolt, threatening to set up a provisional government in the North while the Irish Nationalists were unhappy with the break-up of the country.[66] Hopes of a breakthrough had failed by the beginning of 1914 as none of the parties involved could agree on a compromise formula over the exclusion of Ulster. But Churchill's hopes of achieving a 'grand compromise' were also shattered by the 'Ulster Plot' of 1914.

On March 9th 1914 Asquith had announced an amendment to the Home Rule Bill, whereby a county (he had Ulster in mind) could opt out of Home Rule for six years. While the Ulster Unionists and Conservatives rejected this settlement out of hand, Churchill was convinced the government was in the right and was determined to see the policy carried out. The government was worried by reports suggesting that the hundred-thousand-strong Ulster Volunteers were planning to seize depots, police barracks, railways and post offices. In response, they decided to send eight hundred soldiers to Ulster to enforce the act and to resupply depots in the province. Meanwhile Churchill authorised the dispatch of the Third Battle Squadron of eight battleships to Lamlash, seventy miles from Belfast, with Asquith's full knowledge. The orders were later countermanded as the army's movements in Ireland had not met serious opposition from the Ulster Volunteers.

Nonetheless, Churchill's move convinced many in Ulster that the government intended to repress the North, using highly draconian methods. He was a figurehead of the administration and his fiercest critics accused him of seeking to coerce the Ulster Volunteers through a harsh military crackdown. Typical was Carson, who labelled Churchill 'the Belfast Butcher', while Lord Charles Beresford described him as an 'egomaniac whose one absorbing thought was personal vindictiveness towards Ulster'.[67]

In reality there was no 'Ulster Plot', even though the government was considering what measures might be needed if the Ulster Volunteers did break into open revolt. And, while Churchill did often use intemperate language, such as his comment that 'there are worse things than bloodshed', the notion that he was central to a planned pogrom in Northern Ireland has little basis in reality.

Thus far Churchill had proved he was willing to reach a settlement while being prepared to use force if necessary. The Great War put the Irish issue on the back-burner for four years, but a crisis was inevitable once the guns had stopped firing on the Western Front.

Churchill's controversial involvement in Irish affairs reached its height in 1920-1. In the previous year, Sinn Fein ('Ourselves Alone') had become Ireland's dominant political party, winning 76 of the 105 parliamentary seats. They rejected the Nationalist claim that Ireland's future was bound up with that of Britain and dismissed Home Rule altogether. They demanded independence for Ireland, with or without the consent of the Protestants in the North, and accordingly set up their own parliament, the Dail. The Irish Volunteers (later the Irish Republican Army or IRA) started a guerilla campaign targeting policemen and police barracks, most of which belonged to the Royal Irish Constabulary (RIC).

Alarmed at the breakdown of order and the mounting anti-British violence, the Viceroy, Lord French, called for British ex-servicemen to join the RIC as recruits. Because of their khaki uniforms and black and green caps, they were later nicknamed the Black and Tans. Churchill, though not involved in the recruitment decision, welcomed taking the fight to Sinn Fein. As he put it in June 1920, 'no course is open to the government but to take every possible measure to break the murder campaign and to enforce the authority of the law'.[68]

Despite this apparently hard-line attitude, he was critical of Sir Henry Wilson's call for all-out war against Sinn Fein. While acknowledging the seriousness of the Catholic revolt, Churchill did not think it would be beaten 'by the kind of methods the Prussians adopted in Belgium'.[69] Nonetheless, among the plans Churchill produced was one that involved bombing the IRA from the air, though the aim was to 'scatter and stampede them' rather than carry out a mass killing.[70]

Churchill supported the Black and Tans in their policy of unofficial reprisals against Sinn Fein members and welcomed the arrival of the Auxiliary Division (the Auxis) to bolster the RIC. His rhetoric suggests that he relished the confrontation. At one point he proposed sending a force of thirty thousand Ulstermen to 'uphold the authority of the Crown throughout Ireland'. He believed that a policy of firmness, even ruthlessness, was necessary to break the murderous gangs, but also held out hope for better times in Ireland. As he put it in December 1920, 'No one desires more than I do a cessation of the conditions of strife which are ruining the happiness and the prosperity of the Irish people.'[71] What he could not accept was the negotiation of a settlement while members of the police and military were being murdered.

In retrospect, Churchill's support for the Black and Tans was scarcely justifiable. The men he regarded as 'honourable and gallant officers' meted out brutal reprisals against many innocent people.[72] Perhaps the most notorious example was on November 21st 1920 when a group of Black and Tans fired into a packed football ground, murdering twelve people. This strategy of meeting terror with terror was hardly likely to win over moderates or lead to a cessation of violence. In fairness, though, Churchill's views were widely shared by his political colleagues.

In May 1921 the British Cabinet discussed the possibility of a truce with Sinn Fein. Churchill was in a minority supporting such a move. Crucially he felt a truce would not be interpreted as a sign of weakness and that a continuation of the war would alienate opinion in the United States.[73] While Churchill was overruled on this occasion, Lloyd George swung round to a more conciliatory view and hostilities ceased on July 11th. Shortly after, dominion status was offered to the twenty-six counties of Southern Ireland and the path to a negotiated settlement was open.

The Anglo-Irish Conference was duly convened in October 1921, with Churchill as one of the British representatives and Arthur Griffiths and Michael Collins heading the Irish delegation. Tensions between the sides were understandable and during the negotiations two main stumbling blocks emerged. The first was the question of naval defence. Both Lloyd George and Churchill insisted that Britain control the Irish coastal ports (later known as treaty ports) which were seen as essential to Britain's own defence during wartime. There were also acrimonious discussions about the exact relationship between the twenty-six counties and Britain. For the British delegation, it was essential that Southern Ireland remained connected to the British Empire but it was the depth of that tie that was contentious for the Irish Nationalists.

The resulting treaty was able to resolve these problems to the satisfaction of the majority. It oversaw the creation, not of an Irish Republic, but an Irish Free State which was a dominion of the British Empire. Officials of the new Irish Free State were required to swear allegiance to the Crown and, according to the sixth and seventh clauses of the treaty, the Royal Navy would have the right to patrol the coastal waters of the Free State and maintain naval bases at three coastal ports. This meant that the Irish Free State could not meaningfully claim neutrality if Britain was at war. Churchill strongly defended these naval clauses, claiming that while the Royal Navy would not need to patrol Southern Ireland's coasts in peacetime, it would be necessary in wartime to enable 'the control of coastal waters, the defence of these islands, and the sea routes by which our food is brought to this country'.74 At no point was any attempt made to coerce Ulster into joining with Southern Ireland.

It fell to Churchill to defend the Anglo-Irish Treaty in Parliament. In one of his classic speeches, he dismissed out of hand those dissidents who regarded the treaty as an unmitigated sell-out, offering some telling words which reverberate today:

> Are we not getting a little tired of all this? These absolutely sincere, consistent, unswerving gentlemen, faithful in all circumstances to their implacable quarrels, seek to mount their respective national war horses, in person or by proxy, and to drive at full tilt at one another, shattering and splintering down the lists, to the indescribable misery of the common people ...75

On January 7th 1922 the Dail narrowly ratified the Anglo-Irish Treaty and, shortly afterwards, a provisional government, headed by Michael Collins and Arthur Griffith, was set up. The aim was to transfer power from Britain to the Irish Free State and this included the establishment of a national army to replace the IRA. In June 1922 Churchill helped Collins to devise a constitution for the South. The Irish Free State would be a co-equal member of the Commonwealth, would be responsible for revenue and would have the right to declare war. The rights of Protestants in the South would be protected. Shortly after this, Collins' pro-treaty party won a majority in his country's general election, easily defeating De Valera's anti-treaty Republicans.

The issue, however, split Irish Nationalists and the IRA into pro-treaty and anti-treaty factions. When the provisional government tried to assert its authority over well-armed anti-treaty IRA units around the country, fighting was inevitable. In April 1922, IRA militants occupied the Four Courts in Dublin, resulting in a dramatic stand-off. Under pressure from Churchill, Collins was forced to end the stand-off by bombarding the Four Courts garrison into surrender. With the Free State Government in control of Dublin, the anti-treaty forces dispersed around the country, mainly to the south and west. Eight months of intermittent civil war followed, marked by political assassinations and executions, before the fighting came to an end. Collins was himself assasinated in an ambush near his home in County Cork in August 1922.[76]

As Colonial Secretary, Churchill was responsible for affairs in both Northern and Southern Ireland and made some decisive contributions to peace. Firstly, it was his job to ensure the passage of the Treaty through Parliament. In speech after speech, he sought to persuade the diehards of the need for legislative change. He talked of how the Irish sectarian feud had convulsed and disfigured British politics and of how delaying the bill would lead Ireland to 'degenerate into a meaningless welter of lawless chaos and confusion'.[77] His tireless endeavours and oratorical skills helped to produce an impressive parliamentary majority when the bill was passed in March 1922.

Churchill was also a firm believer in the reconciliation of enemies. In 1922 he invited the President of Northern Ireland, Sir James Craig, and the Southern Irish Prime Minister, Michael Collins, to meet at the Colonial Office. Shortly after this meeting, a free-trade agreement between the two countries replaced the South's economic blockade of Ulster. An amnesty was also given to all British soldiers, sailors and policemen who had committed 'acts of hostility against the Irish people', and this was followed by the release of thirteen Sinn Fein prisoners. In the wake of a series of brutal murders on both sides in March 1922, Churchill again summoned the two leaders to a conference in London. Condemning the 'cold blooded, inhuman, cannibal vengeance' taking place on both sides, Churchill said he would do all he could to shake the Irish from 'this convulsion and spasm'.[78]

A day after this speech, he helped to draft an agreement, signed by Craig and Collins, which would end the hostilities. Among its provisions was an agreement on the boundary between North and South, and a new Belfast police force with equal numbers of Catholics and Protestants, while Collins agreed to end border attacks by the IRA. In the Commons, Joseph Devlin praised Churchill's 'superb tact and ability' in conducting the talks.[79] Churchill had not been a sudden convert to Home Rule after the Great War, but once he had become convinced of the case for it he worked hard to reach a compromise that would satisfy all sides in the conflict. He worked tirelessly as Colonial Secretary to end the bloodshed, while believing that peace was in Britain's imperial interests.

Churchill never flagged from insisting that the fledging Irish state remain a dominion of the Empire. Sadly events were to undo this achievement. Eamon De Valera, who with other Republicans rejected the 1921 agreement and boycotted the Dail, had by 1937 become the democratically elected Taoiseach.[80] He helped to write a new constitution for the Catholic Republic of Eire. With the repudiation of the 1922 Treaty, the Royal Navy was denied the right to use Ireland's treaty ports and links with the British monarchy were severed.[81]

But none of this could have been foreseen in the early 1920s. Churchill had striven to bring about a settlement which, though imperfect, appeared to offer the best compromise for all sides. No one acknowledged his heroic efforts more than Michael Collins. Shortly before his death, Collins told a friend: 'Tell Winston we could never have done anything without him.' It was a fitting tribute.

How did Churchill help create modern Iraq in the 1920s?

DURING THE First World War, the Ottoman Empire, Europe's 'sick man', was allied to Germany. From 1915 onwards, Britain sought to encourage an Arab revolt against Ottoman rule that would ultimately lead to the defeat of Turkey and precipitate Germany's collapse. To that end Britain promised Sherif Hussein, the spiritual guardian of Mecca, that it would support the creation of an independent Arab state in Ottoman lands in return for an Arab revolt. In the following year, T.E. Lawrence (Lawrence of Arabia), together with Feisal, Sherif Hussein's son, conducted a campaign of guerilla warfare against the Ottoman Turkish authorities.

But in the same year Britain and France signed the Sykes-Picot Agreement setting out their post-war spheres of influence in the Middle East, with France claiming Syria and Britain Mesopotamia (modern Iraq). To complicate matters, the Balfour Declaration of 1917 provided British support for the creation of a Jewish homeland in Palestine. After the war, at the San Remo Conference, the Ottoman Empire was dissolved: Britain was awarded the mandate for Iraq and France the mandate for Syria. As Secretary of State for War, and Colonial Secretary between 1919 and 1921, Churchill was intimately involved in these affairs and helped to make decisions the consequences of which reverberate to this day.

As Secretary for War and Air, Churchill's central aim – one might call it an obsession – was to save money by cutting the costs of imperial rule. He wanted Britain to be 'empire lite'. This would be accomplished by ruthlessly slashing defence expenditure and reducing the number of Britain's potential enemies. From an economic perspective, this made perfect sense. After the First World War, Britain had gone from being a creditor to a debtor nation. The massive financial costs of war burdened a government which had to pay war widows' pensions as well as alleviate a soaring national debt. In the face of mounting public anger, and the need for economy, the army had been demobilised, leaving the country's overseas military resources rather thin on the ground.

The problem was that Churchill's desire for economy ran up against the costs of Britain's post-war liabilities. Not only was the British Empire globally scattered but, after 1919, there were nationalist uprisings in Egypt, India and Ireland that compounded this 'imperial overstretch'. Churchill was also deeply concerned that Bolshevik Russia would threaten the British Empire and welcomed any potential bulwark against Russian expansion. Turkey had always been seen as a barrier to Russian ambitions in the Mediterranean, while, as a Muslim power, it had great influence over the inhabitants of Egypt and India. As a result, Churchill repeatedly urged Lloyd George to support Turkey and stop 'estranging the Mohammedan world'.[82]

As Colonial Secretary, Churchill was still desperate to reduce the costs of imperial administration, but he did not favour a withdrawal from Mesopotamia, which he feared would irreparably stain Britain's reputation. The country was still strategically important, for it formed part of the overland route to India; it was also a major oil producer. Churchill would need to engineer a solution that gave Britain informal control at relatively little expense.

At the Cairo Conference convened in 1921, the decision was made to turn Mesopotamia, which had largely consisted of the three *vilayets*, or regions, of Mosul, Baghdad and Basra, into a unitary state called Iraq. This was, and remains, a hugely controversial decision, for Iraq was an ethnically disunited state. To the north were the Kurds, who were non-Arab Sunni Muslims; Sunni Arab Muslims lived in the centre of the country, while in the south the Shia Muslims were dominant. As one commentator put it: 'The result was not so much a country as an imperial convenience.'[83]

To his credit, Churchill favoured independence for the Kurds and expressed concern over how an unsympathetic ruler might treat them. For such a ruler, 'while outwardly accepting constitutional procedures and forming a Parliament, [might] at the same time despise democratic and constitutional methods ... [and] with the power of an Arab army behind him ... ignore Kurdish sentiment and oppress the Kurdish minority'.[84] He stressed to Sir Percy Cox[85] the importance of 'the principle of not putting Arabs over Kurds'.[86] Sadly this concern did not inform policy: the Kurds ended up being part of a unitary state.

The biggest challenge for this ethnically divided and potentially troublesome state was how it would be governed. Churchill decided that the most cost-effective option for controlling Iraq was indirect rule through a pro-British Arab government. In other words, Iraq would become a classic example of a client state run on the cheap. Sir Percy Cox suggested that Feisal Hussein, recently kicked out of Syria by the French, would make a suitable ruler. Churchill was impressed with Feisal and thought his credentials as a Sharifian Hashemite made him suitable. Feisal's brother, Abdullah Hussein,[87] had been installed on the Jordanian throne and 'keeping it in the family' would be practicable as well as cost-effective politics. But in selecting Feisal Churchill became aware that he was selecting a Sunni Muslim to rule a predominantly Shia country. This 'legitimacy gap' is one which would haunt most Iraqis until the fall of Saddam Hussein in 2003.

The decision to select Feisal was a classic case of imperial bribery. Britain was already paying a subsidy to Feisal's father, Sherif Hussein of Mecca, while his brother Abdullah was Britain's client king in Transjordan. The reasoning was simple: Feisal would toe the British line as ruler of Iraq, knowing that, if he did not, Britain would end his father's subsidy and any support for Abdullah.

This Sharifian solution (having Hashemite pro-British client rulers) was colonial rule on the cheap, rather like in India; crucially it was a solution that would not require the expense of maintaining a powerful British military presence. Churchill believed that he would be able to withdraw British troops from Iraq, leaving only Arab troops and the RAF to carry out essential policing. Independence would be granted, but it would be more apparent than real. Britain would keep control, albeit from a distance.

Churchill and his adviser T.E. Lawrence believed that a British-appointed ruler, rather than a local figure, would best control potentially recalcitrant 'natives'. Lawrence's comments about the appointment of Abdullah are applicable to Feisal as well: 'by reason of his position and lineage, [he] possessed very considerable power for good or harm over the tribesmen.' Churchill's overriding concern, as always, was that the policy should be cost-effective. As he told Lloyd George, 'I have no doubt personally [that] Feisal offers far away [the] best chance of saving our money.'[88] Whether a client ruler would also serve Arab interests was not a major consideration. This much was clear from a memo written in January 1921, when Churchill was considering the appointment of a ruler: 'Western political methods are not necessarily applicable to the East and basis of election should be framed.'[89]

After a referendum in August 1921, Feisal was appointed King by the British. Once in power, fearing he would be seen as a stooge by his people, Feisal started to assert his independence by making anti-British statements.[90] He claimed that he no longer saw the restrictions imposed on him by the League of Nations mandate as valid and wanted a new treaty that granted him sovereign powers. Churchill believed that, as long as Britain paid the piper, she should be 'consulted as to the tune', and that Iraq was becoming a 'burdensome charge'.[91] He told Lloyd George that the British were 'paying eight millions a year for the privilege of living on an ungrateful volcano out of which we are in no circumstances to get anything worth having'.[92] Churchill would come to regret Feisal's manner of 'ingratitude' but, unlike the French, the British had little stomach for removing him, knowing that the human and financial costs of this action would be very high. In retrospect, it was understandable that Feisal should want to assert his independence from Britain. He knew that he was seen as the tool of a colonialist power and that he lacked credibility as a result.

If the key to Iraq's future was the 'relief of military commitments', how was Iraq to be controlled? The decision was made to use the RAF, an option with the advantage that it would lead to the scaling down and withdrawal of British troops. Using air power would avoid 'long and vulnerable lines of communication', allowing small garrisons to be 'fed or reinforced or relieved by aeroplanes from Baghdad at any time'.[93] The RAF could also provide a cost-effective means of dealing with any uprising against British troops: in 1920 insurgent action in the country had been put down by the RAF. To Sir Hugh Trenchard Churchill made the following, now notorious, suggestion: 'I think you should certainly proceed with the experimental work on gas bombs, especially mustard gas, which would inflict punishment upon recalcitrant natives without inflicting grave injury upon them.'[94]

This was not the first time that Churchill had advocated the use of such a weapon. In May 1915, at the height of the Gallipoli crisis, he had told Kitchener to send a gas-making outfit to the Dardanelles as 'the use of gas on either side might be decisive'.[95] In October 1915 he told his political colleagues that mustard gas could be devastatingly effective in reaching a breakthrough in Gallipoli and hoped that 'the unreasonable prejudice against the use by us of gas upon the Turks will cease'. He added that the winter season with its southwesterly gales 'would afford a perfect opportunity for the employment of gas'.[96] In 1918 Churchill wrote that he was 'in favour of the greatest possible development of gas-warfare' and, as Munitions Minister, he oversaw an increase in the production of gas shells for the Western Front.[97] He welcomed the use of mustard gas, 'this hellish poison,' against the Germans.[98] In the light of Saddam Hussein's decision to use gas against the Kurds at Halabja in 1988, Churchill's memo may seem ruthless to posterity.

In Churchill's defence, however, he did not intend to carry out a mass killing of native people, unlike the Iraqi dictator. He believed that poison gas would merely punish natives rather than inflict grave injury on them. As he put it, the gas that was used would 'cause great inconvenience and would spread a lively terror and yet would leave no serious permanent affect on most of those affected.'[99] Gas, he said, was 'a more merciful weapon than high explosive shell'[100] and it was 'sheer affectation' to 'lacerate a man with the poisonous fragment of a bursting shell and to boggle at making his eyes water by means of lachrymatory gas'.[101] As Addison notes, the gas that Churchill had in mind was more akin to tear gas than poison gas. He certainly recoiled from the deliberate targeting of civilians in imperial conflicts and condemned General Dyer's massacre of Indians at Amritsar.

Churchill's legacy, in sum, was a politically unified but ethnically divided Sunni-dominated country. The Sunnis constituted a religious minority, no more than a quarter of the population; over the next eight decades, Iraq's Shia Muslims would have little say in how their country was ruled. Worse, the Kurdish minority in the north remained stateless, despite Churchill's best efforts to redress this.[102]

By 1921 Churchill had come to regret the expense and trouble of the new Iraq. To the occupiers, the country had become an 'ungrateful volcano' and scarcely one newspaper in Britain was supportive of the continuing occupation. Even before he had been appointed Colonial Secretary, Churchill had characterised the conflict in Iraq as 'this miserable, wasteful, sporadic warfare, marked from time to time certainly by minor disasters and cuttings off of troops and agents, and very possibly attended by some very grave occurrence.' He added: 'We have not got a single friend in the press upon the subject, and there is no point of which they make more effective use to injure the Government.'[103] These are words that would become very familiar in the following century.

Why did Churchill cross the floor for a second time in 1924?

IN 1922 CHURCHILL was a Liberal serving in Lloyd George's coalition government. After the fall of the government, Churchill lost the seat at Dundee which he had held since 1908. For the next two years he embarked on the first of his two periods in the political wilderness, writing his war memoirs and refining his skill as a painter in the sunny climes of southern France. By 1924 he had made a triumphant return to British politics, not as a Liberal but as a Conservative. It seemed incredible that the man who had deserted the Tories in 1904 was now reunited with them. Despite Lloyd George's warning that, 'A rat could desert a sinking ship but it couldn't climb back on board if the ship didn't sink after all',[104] Churchill was just that type of 'rat'. He had not just ratted but re-ratted.

There was to be a worse shock for the Conservatives. Not only was Churchill back in the Tory fold but he was now a member of the Conservative government, and an important one at that – he was now Chancellor of the Exchequer. But why did he decide to change party for a second time? Was it due to his insatiable Napoleonic ambition and a perception that the dwindling Liberal Party would never afford him an opportunity for power?

As evidence that his move was unprincipled we can quote from a letter that Churchill wrote to Sir Robert Horne: 'Force of circumstance has compelled me to serve with another party, but my views have never changed, and I should be glad to give effect to them by rejoining the Conservatives.'[105] Ponting cites this letter as evidence that Churchill was itching to rejoin the Conservatives 'as the best way of becoming a minister again'. His only problem was how 'to manage the transition as smoothly as possible'. Ponting adds that the explanation for the move was that 'it was difficult to see how he could advance further in the Liberal party'.[106]

Ponting suggests that Churchill's second defection was devoid of political principle and that he was simply bidding to join the party that offered him the greatest prospect of power. Sebastian Haffner commented that Churchill's defection may have had something to do with a 'lifelong horror of wasting away in idle, impotent opposition'.[107] It is true that in the general election in October 1924 the Liberals were eliminated as a force in British politics, retaining only 40 seats out of their original 158. The Conservatives in 1924, just like the Liberals of 1904, were very much the party of the moment and Churchill did not want to absent himself from this 'wind of change'.

But restless political ambition is not sufficient to explain his behaviour. His move back to the Conservatives can be seen as part of a longer process of conversion. He had left the Tories because of their premature conversion to protectionism, but his readiness to use force in order to preserve law and order was fully in accord with Conservative thinking. According to Charles Masterman, writing in 1910, there was an 'aboriginal and unchangeable Tory' in him.[108]

External circumstances also explain why Churchill felt the need to switch parties again. From 1922 he perceived the rise of Bolshevik Russia as the portent of a new dark age. He was concerned that the doctrine would spread like a virus to neighbouring states and destroy the social order. At the same time he began viewing the emerging Labour movement as the Bolsheviks' 'would-be imitators in this country'.[109] He saw the Labour Party as unfitted for the responsibility of government and later referred to it unapologetically as a subversive cause. It was perceived as 'a great, vehement, deliberate attack upon the foundations of society'; a socialist government would 'cast a dark and blighting shadow on every form of national life and confidence';[110] it would be a 'monstrosity'.[111] The socialist movement as a whole had 'subversive and ruinous aims' and a 'retrograde character'.[112]

The party, he argued, had embroiled the nation in 'calamitous strikes' and its moderate leaders had been unable to 'control their extremists'. Thus its accession to power would 'utterly destroy the commercial credit and confidence upon which our hopes of economic revival can alone be based'.[113] Though the party would prove it was not beholden to Moscow, Churchill took its commitment to expropriation and nationalisation as a serious threat to the social and economic order. Labour ministers, once in power, would 'sit high above the masses, ruling their lives, and appointing their toil as if they were gods in heaven'.[114] They would, Churchill said, rig elections to maintain their authority and eventually put their tyrannical rule on a hereditary basis.

At the start of his political career, these attacks would scarcely have mattered as Labour was a politically insignificant force. By 1918, however, this had all changed. Labour was now the second force in British politics and Churchill's antipathy to socialism was allied to that of the Conservative Party. Thus he could write to Baldwin of the 'cause we have at heart', and of the two men being 'able to work together in the national interest'. What was needed was 'the strongest combination of forces against the oncoming attack'.[115] He favoured a Liberal-Conservative coalition against Labour.

Churchill's anti-socialism merged more easily with the Conservatives as a result of decisions made in 1923 by the Conservative leader Stanley Baldwin. The rise of Labour led to a period of three-party politics and considerable political instability. In order to unite his own Conservative Party in 1923, Baldwin had campaigned on a theme of protectionism which re-opened old wounds left by Joseph Chamberlain's campaign in 1903. This led to a general election in which the Conservatives lost their majority of 73 seats.

The House of Commons now had no party with a clear majority. After the December 1923 election, the Conservatives had 258 seats, Labour had 191 and the Liberals, who held the balance of power, 158. When Baldwin sought a vote of approval in the Commons, Asquith informed him that the Liberals would support the Labour Party. In the ensuing vote, the combined forces of Labour and the Liberals meant a 328 to 256 defeat for the Tories. In due course, Ramsey McDonald became Britain's first Labour Prime Minister, albeit of a minority government. This was enough to persuade Churchill that British politics would now be polarised between the Conservatives and the Labour Party, thus ending his career as a Liberal MP.

Churchill was alarmed at the prospect of a Labour government. On January 18th 1924, in a letter to *The Times*, he declared: 'The enthronement in office of a socialist government will be a serious national misfortune such as has usually befallen great States only on the morrow of defeat in war.'[116] Later that year he wrote that the socialist movement would 'diminish the productivity of this island', which would lead to a 'frightful and irreparable catastrophe'.[117]

Asquith's political positioning led to Churchill's final break with the Liberals. When a by-election presented itself in the Abbey division of Westminster, Churchill decided to stand as an Independent, with Conservative support. Though he narrowly lost to the official Conservative candidate, he had ensured that the Asquithian Liberal was humiliated. After some negotiating, a safe seat was found in Epping and, in October 1924, Churchill spoke there for the first time, launching a bitter attack on the Labour Party. Though he stood as a Constitutionalist, his local constituency saw him as a Conservative, as did Tory Central Office. His anti-Bolshevik language was vehement enough to put him on the right of the party, so there were few doubts about his political position.

But it would be a mistake to think that Churchill's motives in switching parties were purely ideological. Ever the astute politician, he was sensitive to the changing fortunes of political parties and realised that the Liberals were a spent force by 1924. If he was to satisfy his thirst for office and avoid languishing in opposition, he would need to leave the Liberals and rejoin his old party. This was not power for its own sake but power for the sake of pursuing the causes he held dear, none more so than defeating socialism. As always for Churchill, 'ego' and 'cause' went hand in hand.

Was Churchill a free-trading Chancellor?

SINCE THE BEGINNING of his career, Churchill had longed to emulate his father by becoming Chancellor of the Exchequer. In 1924 his ambition was satisfied when Stanley Baldwin offered him the post, and he duly became the second most powerful person in British politics. During his five-year chancellorship he practised a form of Gladstonian liberalism which was based largely on free trade and economy in public expenditure. This reflected a consistently held political philosophy which centred on 'the operation of self regulating markets' and a minimum of state intervention in the economy.[118]

His belief in free trade was central to his most important decision as Chancellor: the reintroduction of the Gold Standard. The Gold Standard was a monetary system in which participating countries agreed to fix the prices of their domestic currencies in terms of a precise amount of gold. National currencies could all be freely converted into gold at the fixed price and, as the Gold Standard was international, with participating countries maintaining a fixed price for gold, rates of exchange between currencies were fixed. The system broke down under the financial strains of the First World War as participating countries resorted to inflationary increases in the money supply to pay their way through the conflict.

Free trade was premised upon the notion of a self-righting and flexible free market, allowing the Treasury to be non-interventionist (*laissez-faire*) in economic matters. The Gold Standard would underpin free trade by regulating the level of prices through the bank rate. Churchill pointed out in 1925 that the working classes wanted, above all else, stability of prices which would guarantee them an affordable food supply.[119] He had, according to his parliamentary private secretary, a 'hankering to be orthodox'.[120] In 1925 the financial free-trading orthodoxy dictated a return to the Gold Standard, and when Churchill took over as Chancellor he came under enormous pressure to restore it.

However, when the decision was made to restore the Gold Standard, the pound had been significantly overvalued by 10 per cent. This was because Churchill had restored the pre-war parity of $4.86 to the pound, a fact that was noted by economist John Maynard Keynes in *The Economic Consequences of Mr. Churchill*. The decision to artificially enhance the value of sterling meant that British exports became more expensive, hence uncompetitive in foreign markets. This added to the strain on British industry and the most immediate consequence was the need to cut costs by reducing wages.[121]

The coal industry was worst hit by the higher pound, which exacerbated the problem of its already declining exports and forced mine owners to propose drastic wage cuts. The result one year later was the General Strike.

Most historians agree that the return to the Gold Standard was an error with harmful consequences, and Churchill himself would later admit that the decision was the worst of his chancellorship. But, if his judgement had gone astray, it was only because he was swept along by a prevailing tide of opinion. In the mid-1920s nearly every section of the economic and political establishment, both in Britain and elsewhere, argued for the reintroduction of the Gold Standard. Previous governments had committed themselves to returning to gold and Churchill's predecessor at the Treasury, Philip Snowden, accepted this advice.[122]

The Governor of the Bank of England, Montagu Norman, stated that he was in favour of a return to gold in 1925 and told Churchill that, in the opinion of 'educated and reasonable men', there was no sensible alternative. Financial expert Sir Otto Niemeyer advised that a decision not to return to the Gold Standard would lead to a 'considerable withdrawal of balances and investment (both foreign and British) from London'. In America the Governor of the Federal Bank unhesitatingly supported a return to gold, and other experts that Churchill consulted concurred with this view.

Churchill admitted that he had 'little comprehension of these extremely technical matters' and thus consulted as widely as he could before reaching a decision.[123] In March 1925 he brought together two leading advocates of the reinstatement of gold, Bradbury and Niemeyer, and two critics, former Chancellor McKenna and Keynes, to a round-table dinner conference to thrash out the issue. After hours of intense discussion, Keynes emerged as the sole critic and thus the argument had been effectively settled. In *The Economic Consequences of Mr. Churchill*, Keynes would later declare that the Chancellor had been 'deafened by the clamorous voices of conventional finance' and that he had been 'gravely misled by his experts'.[124] Nonetheless, Churchill can hardly be absolved from blame for the damaging consequences of what was, ultimately, his own decision.

As Chancellor, Churchill robustly defended the principle of free trade, refusing a safeguard for the steel industry. As he put it to Baldwin, steel was 'one of the fundamental basic raw materials of British industry' which affected, in one way or another, 'all the greatest trades in the country'; any safeguard for steel would open the floodgates to other dependent trades that were suffering from international competition. He threatened resignation unless he got his way, and he duly won his case.[125]

However, Churchill was unable to resist a nine-month subsidy for the coal industry in 1925. Partially as a consequence of the Gold Standard, coal owners were threatening to reduce wages unless the miners were prepared to work longer hours for the same pay. When the miners rejected this demand, the real prospect of a protracted coal dispute opened up before the government and a £10-million subsidy appeared the cheaper option.

The belief in a liberal economy based on free trade was reflected in Churchill's most imaginative economic scheme: de-rating. He proposed to abolish rates on industry and agriculture, which would transfer costs from producers to consumers, who would then pay increased taxes. Producers would repay a quarter of their gains in a new profit tax, while a petrol tax would be introduced which would boost the railways and coal industry. Churchill thought that depressed areas, which had the highest rates and lowest profits, would benefit substantially from de-rating. The scheme was designed to thwart protectionist plans, and Churchill also believed it would prove to be popular with voters. He won the Cabinet round to his plan and de-rating became a major plank of the 1928 Budget. From October 1929, agriculture was to be excluded from rates, with a 75 per cent relief for industry. Local authorities would receive grants from the Exchequer, paid for by the new petrol tax.

Churchill showed respect for orthodox financial opinion by rejecting a loan-financed system of public works on the Keynesian model or any large-scale increase in income tax to finance public projects. As he told a deputation of the Federation of British Industries, 'Every form of borrowing impaired the national credit.'[126] When it came to raising money, Churchill chose to tinker round the edges rather than produce imaginative schemes of financial reconstruction. He raised money to balance his budgets by emptying the Road Fund over two years, raising a betting tax and increasing taxes on luxury goods and petrol. Throughout the period, however, he was forced to cut funding for the armed services in an effort to reduce overall expenditure.

He was highly progressive in his attitude towards taxation. In his first budget, he proposed a reduction in income tax of sixpence to four shillings in the pound but called for a shift in the tax burden from active to passive wealth. There was to be a reduction in Super Tax but an increase in Death Duties to compensate for this. Relief would be given to 'professional men, small merchants and business men – superior brain workers of every kind ... The doctor, engineer and lawyer earning 3 or 4 thousands a year and with no capital will get the greatest relief; the possessor of unearned income derived from a capital estate of 2 or 3 hundred thousand pounds, the smallest relief.' The philosophical assumptions underlying this decision were also spelt out: 'The process of the creation of new wealth is beneficial to the whole community. The process of squatting on old wealth though valuable is a far less lively agent.'[127]

However, he was open to some limited forms of protectionism where revenue could be made. He reinstated the 'McKenna Duties' which covered an eclectic range of items, principally clocks, films, motor cars and musical instruments. Churchill explained to the House that they would bring in £3 million in a full year. In subsequent budgets he added duties on silk, hops, sugar, pottery, buttons and motor tyres. This protectionist activity was condemned by *The Economist*, which declared that, 'Mr Churchill seems determined to maintain his record as the most consistent imposer of Protectionist duties that we have had in Britain for a hundred years.'[128]

His decision in 1929 to rescind the duty on tea, at a cost of £6 million to the Exchequer, proved to be very popular. However, cutting import duties meant that the government received less revenue to finance its social reform projects, including the Widows and Old Age Pensions Act (1925) and the National Health Insurance Act. This naturally led to cutbacks elsewhere, such as reducing the budgets of Britain's armed forces.

Churchill largely adhered to the financial orthodoxy by refusing to increase public debt and spending, and supporting free trade where possible. He was later criticised for failing to prevent Britain from falling into a protracted economic slump in the 1930s, albeit one that was less severe than the American Great Depression, but it is difficult to see how any alternative approach in the preceding decade could have worked any better.

What was Churchill's attitude in the General Strike?

IF ANY ONE EVENT has solidified Churchill's image as a reactionary, it is the General Strike of 1926. The Left have alleged that Churchill was a dangerous extremist, advocating violence in order to teach the miners 'a lesson' while, for more sober-minded historians, Churchill's mood during the strike expressed the 'utmost bellicosity'.[129] According to one contemporary, J.C.C. Davidson, Churchill was 'absolutely mad' during the strike and his suggestions for dealing with the crisis were 'poppycock and rot'.[130] When Baldwin allegedly remarked, at the beginning of the strike, that he was 'terrified of what Winston [was] going to be like',[131] he was expressing the fears of many political colleagues. Churchill certainly saw the strike as a grave threat to the social order, and believed that a battle had to be won against the forces of reactionary socialism. But, while his language was intemperate and bellicose during the strike, his attempt to produce a magnanimous settlement afterwards is often overlooked.

The causes of the General Strike were several and complex. After the First World War, the staple industries (coal, steel and textiles), which prior to 1914 had accounted for half of Britain's industrial output, went into a slow decline. They became increasingly inefficient and little was done to modernise their outdated production techniques. As they became less competitive in the face of international competition, there was a growing tendency to blame the inefficiency on high wages, leading to rifts between owners and workers. Coal, which was Britain's leading industrial export, suffered from declining productivity after 1918.[132]

When, in 1925, Churchill reintroduced the Gold Standard, the pound was overvalued so that British exports became increasingly uncompetitive in foreign markets. Coal exports were accordingly reduced, piling further problems on an already beleaguered industry. In 1925 the mine owners proposed an increase in hours and a reduction in wages in order to increase the efficiency of the industry.

The General Council of the TUC responded by promising to support the miners in any dispute with their employers. To avoid tension, Baldwin's government paid a nine-month subsidy (supported by Churchill) to maintain miners' wages while establishing a Royal Commission to look into the problems of the mining industry. Nine months later, the commission reached the conclusion that the subsidy should end, allowing mine owners to impose temporary wage cuts until the industry had introduced more efficiency in the mines. It also recommended that there should be no extension of the seven-hour day.

The mine owners rejected this solution and imposed a unilateral wage cut, telling the miners that they would be locked out of the pits unless they accepted new terms of employment. On May 1st 1926 a conference of the TUC announced that a General Strike 'in defence of miners' wages and hours' would begin two days later. Talks between the TUC and the government to avert a strike started almost immediately. Late on May 2nd Baldwin discovered that printers at the *Daily Mail* had refused to run a scathing editorial ('For King and Country') which condemned the General Strike and immediately he called off negotiations with the TUC. From the next day, until the TUC called off the strike on May 12th, millions of workers came out in solidarity with the miners.

One myth that should be laid to rest is that, in the days leading up to the General Strike, Churchill persuaded an otherwise pacific Prime Minister to end negotiations with the mine owners. According to Ernest Bevin, 'The two sides were in another room getting almost to the last clauses to hand to the Prime Minister, when Mr. Churchill walked in and upset the Cabinet, and we had the ultimatum.'[133] The story was also propagated by the *New Statesman*, which alleged that Churchill threatened resignation if talks with the TUC continued, and believed that a little 'blood letting' would be worthwhile. For Mackenzie King, Churchill was an 'evil genius' whose machinations led to the General Strike.[134] Yet Churchill had taken no part in the negotiations with the miners and the TUC before the strike started. More to the point, Baldwin was the 'unchallenged arbiter of industrial policy' and it was down to him alone to negotiate a settlement or break off talks with the TUC.[135]

So, how belligerent was Churchill during the General Strike itself? There is no doubt that he viewed the strike through the red-tinted spectacles of Bolshevik Revolution. Since 1918 he had become convinced that the Bolsheviks were seeking to spread their subversive doctrines in other countries, particularly among the forces of organised labour. Shortly before the strike started, Neville Chamberlain told his wife that Churchill was 'getting frantic with excitement and eagerness to begin the battle'.[136] On May 4th Sir Samuel Hoare wrote in his diary: 'Visit to Max. Winston there. Blood and iron.'[137]

Once the strike had started, Churchill's line was intransigent: war had been declared by the unions and the strike had to be broken at all costs. Chamberlain wrote to his wife: 'He simply revels in this affair, which he *will* continually treat and talk of as if it were 1914.'[138] On the fourth day of the strike, there were some calls for a moderate tone that would split the union leadership. Jones went to see Churchill to enlist his support and remembered what happened: 'I then hurried to see Winston and had one of the fiercest and hottest interviews in my life ... he overwhelmed me with a cataract of boiling eloquence, impossible to reproduce. "We were at war ... We must go through with it." '[139]

Churchill also supported actions that were likely to inflame the situation. On May 7th he called for the Territorial Army to combat the strike but Cabinet colleagues overruled him. When the government organised a food convoy from the London docks to bring much-needed supplies into the country, Churchill suggested that it should be accompanied by an escort of tanks and armoured cars to deter the strikers. 'Winston was all for a tremendous display of force,' one contemporary recalled, but Churchill was rebuffed again. At one point he even called for outright control of the nominally independent BBC in order to demonstrate the government's authority. According to J.C.C. Davidson: 'The Prime Minister played a very skilful game in postponing a decision by the Cabinet, on the question, repeatedly raised by Winston and F.E. of taking over the BBC and running a governmental propaganda agency. Winston was very strong in his insistence that the Government ought to assume complete possession.'[140]

When the strike was announced, Churchill was behind the establishment of a government newspaper, *The British Gazette*. He played a leading role in its propagation and, by the time the last edition was published, nearly 2,200,000 copies were in circulation. Churchill's idea was that it would consist mainly of news and speeches and, without being violently partisan, would convey sentiments that were 'agreeable to the great majority'. Among these sentiments was 'the hope for peace'.[141] However, he left his readers in no doubt about what consequences the restoration of peace may entail: 'Should the efforts of the Government and its volunteers to preserve the vital services in any large area of the country be frustrated, a great and terrible disaster will occur and the lives of very large numbers of people will be in jeopardy.'[142]

Talking of the *Gazette*, Davidson said: 'The result was, I think quite good, and the energy and vitality of Winston were very largely responsible for it. He is the sort of man, whom, if I wanted a mountain to be moved, I should send for at once.'[143] Churchill wrote articles for *Gazette* which were unsigned but which betrayed his obdurate stance. There could be 'no question of compromise of any kind', he wrote.[144] As Davidson recalled, 'A good deal of Winston's pugnacious spirit penetrated the *Gazette* and brought storms of questions in the House of Commons.'[145]

In fairness, Churchill's aggressive tone was mirrored by Baldwin. According to Davidson, 'Baldwin took an extremely simple but very stubborn line', namely that 'the General Strike was an attempt at political revolution – the destruction of the Constitution – and the perpetrator must surrender before conversations were possible.'[146] Nonetheless, Churchill consistently maintained that the strike was tantamount to an act of war and that it had to be met with an equally belligerent response. As he put it, 'Any section of citizens, however powerful or well organised, who set themselves against the common-wealth must be made to surrender unconditionally.'[147]

However, this is not a full and fair picture of Churchill's role in the strike. In the House of Commons on May 3rd, Churchill tried to strike a balanced note, defending the government's right to protect the social order while holding out the hope of future negotiation. 'We are seeking peace, we are defending ourselves, we are bound to defend ourselves from the terrible menace which is levied upon us from tomorrow morning,' he said, but added: 'There is no question of there being a gulf across which no negotiator can pass ... it is our duty to parley with them.'[148]

While he was not prepared to back down during the strike, Churchill was a leading advocate of magnanimity once it was over. He differentiated between the General Strike, which he saw as a threat to the Constitution, and a specific trade dispute over which he was prepared to 'take the utmost pains to reach a settlement in a con-ciliatory spirit'.[149] In an effort to reach a compromise, Baldwin allowed Churchill to take charge of negotiations between the miners and the mine owners; and, to the surprise of many, the Chancellor took the side of the miners. When the owners initially demanded a reduction in miners' wages, Churchill said this had to be met with a reduction in the owners' profits. He sided with the mine leaders' desire for a national settlement based on a minimum wage which could not be undercut by the owners. However, when he put this to the owners at a secret meeting at Chartwell, they refused to accept, leaving Churchill to describe them as 'recalcitrant and unreasonable'.

When he sought to incorporate the minimum wage in a govern-ment bill in September 1926, to pressurise the owners, the Cabinet dissented, further frustrating the chances of a settlement. Finally, Churchill proposed setting up an independent National Tribunal which would examine regional wage settlements with the miners, and ensure fair settlements were reached in every case. The miners refused to accept this and Churchill's Cabinet colleagues were not in the mood for further government interference. After four months of pressure and negotiations, Churchill's tireless efforts came to nothing. By the end of November 1926 most miners had been forced back to work, but those that were employed were forced to accept longer hours and lower wages. The following year the government passed the Trade Disputes and Trade Union Act which made all sympathetic strikes illegal.

Churchill's attitude to the General Strike reflected his earlier handling of industrial militancy. Where there was a political grievance, he was prepared for dialogue and conciliation because of his genuine sympathy for the workers. But, where he sensed a wider challenge to the social and economic order, he was intractable and warlike. Once the General Strike had started, all meaningful dialogue was suspended until order had been restored. As he put it so succinctly during the crisis, 'tonight surrender, tomorrow magnanimity'.[150]

NOTES

1 M. Gilbert, *The Wilderness Years*, p 61.
2 Companion IV (i), p.364.
3 Speeches III, p.2615.
4 *Ibid.*, p.2339.
5 *Ibid.*, p.2575.
6 *Ibid.*, p.2634.
7 Companion IV (i), p.412.
8 Speeches III, p.2643.
9 *Ibid.*, p.2646.
10 WSC Bio 4, p.168.
11 Companion IV (i), p.553.
12 Companion IV (iii), p.2081.
13 Companion IV (i), p.424.
14 *Illustrated Sunday Herald*, November 23rd 1919.
15 W. Churchill, *The History of the Second World War 1*, p.7.
16 WSC Bio 3, p.202.
17 Companion IV (i), p.423.
18 WSC Bio 4, p.174.
19 Companion IV (i), p.557.
20 *Ibid.*, pp.656-7.
21 M. Soames (ed), *Speaking for Themselves*, p.222.
22 Companion IV (i), p.557.
23 *Ibid.*, p.464.

24 Speeches III, p.2685.
25 Companion IV (i), p.657.
26 Companion IV (ii), p.1054.
27 *Ibid.*, p.1193.
28 WSC Bio 4, p.427.
29 Speeches V, pp.5260-1.
30 Under the terms of this treaty, Russia lost many of the Baltic States, half her industry and a third of her population.
31 Speeches III, p.2771.
32 Companion IV (i), p.531.
33 Companion IV (ii), p.1024.
34 Speeches IV, p.4305.
35 *Ibid.*, p.3498.
36 Speeches III, p.2870.
37 Speeches IV, p.3809.
38 Companion IV (ii), p.1054.
39 Companion IV (i), p.479.
40 Speeches III, p.2771.
41 Companion IV (ii), p.1203.
42 Companion IV (i), p.383.
43 *Ibid.*, p.673.
44 *Ibid.*, p.677.
45 Companion IV (ii), p.934.
46 W. Churchill, *Thoughts and Adventures*, p.195.
47 Speeches III, p.2919.
48 *Ibid*, pp.2919-20.
49 *Ibid.*, p.3011.
50 WSC Bio 4, p.375.
51 *Ibid.*, p.903.
52 *Ibid.*, p.305.
53 *Illustrated Sunday Herald*, January 25th 1920.
54 Companion IV (i), p.550.
55 *Ibid.*, p.640.
56 *Evening News* July 28th 1920.
57 Companion IV (ii), p.1099.
58 D. Carlton, *Churchill and the Soviet Union*, p.34.
59 Home Rule was a political demand for national self-determination and self-governance for Ireland, with the country remaining part of the UK.
60 Companion I (ii), p.751.
61 Companion II (i), p.337.
62 Speeches I, p.531.
63 WSC Bio 2, p.443.
64 Speeches I, p.1006.
65 WSC Bio 2, p.470.
66 *Ibid.*, p.474.
67 WSC Bio 1, p.501.
68 WSC Bio 4, p.454.
69 *Ibid.*, p.455.

70 Companion IV (ii), p.1135.
71 *Ibid.*, p.1265.
72 *Ibid.*, p.1195.
73 WSC Bio 4, p.664.
74 *Ibid.*, p.678.
75 Speeches III, p.3154.
76 Churchill's support (including military) for Collins came at a price, for there is evidence that the former IRA man was supporting an IRA offensive in the North and seeking to destabilise the new state. For reasons of expediency, Churchill chose to ignore this evidence (D. Stafford, *Churchill and Secret Service*, p.160).
77 Speeches III, p.3195.
78 *Ibid.*, pp.3288-9.
79 WSC Bio 4, p.701.
80 Prime Minister of Ireland.
81 J. Ramsden, *Man of the Century*, pp.242-3.
82 Companion IV, p.1249.
83 Ben Macintyre, 'Invasion, bombs, gas – we've been here before', *The Times*, February 15th 2003.
84 WSC Bio 4, p.549.
85 The British High Commissioner for Iraq, appointed in 1920.
86 Companion IV (iii), p.1548.
87 Abdullah was the first ruler of the Hashemite Kingdom of Jordan. His grandson, Hussein bin Talal, was the King of Jordan from 1952 until his death in 1999.
88 Companion IV (ii), p.1389.
89 *Ibid.*, p.1300.
90 Sir Percy Cox understood this, telling Churchill: 'If impression is given that he is to be merely a puppet in hands of British his influence will be weak and he will not be able to recover it' (WSC Bio 4, p.806).
91 Companion IV (iii), pp.1602, 1869.
92 *Ibid.* p 1974.
93 Companion IV (ii), pp.1079-82.
94 *Ibid.*, p.1190.
95 Companion III (ii), p.947.
96 *Ibid.*, p.1230.
97 Companion IV (i), p.301.
98 M. Soames (ed), *Speaking for Themselves*, p.214.
99 Companion IV (i), p.649.
100 *Ibid.*, p.661.
101 *Ibid.*, p.649.
102 It would, however, be utterly ahistorical and false to blame Churchill for the subsequent toppling of the pro-British monarchy in 1958 and the rise of the fascistic Baath party. This is a mistake made in Knight's *Churchill: The Greatest Briton Unmasked* (pp.43-4).
103 Companion IV (ii), p.1199.
104 S. Haffner, *Churchill*, p.63.
105 Companion V (i), p.48.

106 C. Ponting, *Churchill*, p.276.
107 S. Haffner, *Churchill*, p.64.
108 N. Rose, *Churchill: An Unruly Life*, p.69.
109 Speeches III, p.2920.
110 C. Ponting, *Churchill*, p.280.
111 Companion V (i), p.94.
112 *Ibid.*, p.142.
113 Companion IV (iii), p.1721.
114 Speeches IV, p.3307.
115 R.R. James, *Churchill: A Study in Failure*, p.152.
116 Companion V (i), p.94.
117 Speeches IV, p.3491.
118 P. Addison, *Churchill on the Home Front*, p.235.
119 *Ibid.*, p.250.
120 P. Neville, *Churchill: Statesman or Opportunist*, p.49.
121 Blake/Louis, *Churchill*, p.88.
122 WSC Bio 5, p.93.
123 *Ibid.*, pp.94-5.
124 Blake/Louis, *Churchill*, p.81.
125 P. Addison, *Churchill on the Home Front*, p.251.
126 Speeches IV, p.4151.
127 P. Addison, *Churchill on the Home Front*, p.239.
128 *Ibid.*, p.274.
129 R. Jenkins, *The Chancellors*, pp.317-18.
130 R.R. James (ed), *Memoirs of a Conservative*, p.242.
131 D. Carlton, *Churchill and the Soviet Union*, p.36.
132 Output per man had fallen to just 199 tons in 1920–4, from 247 tons in the four years before the war.
133 P. Addison, *Churchill on the Home Front*, p.261.
134 P. Addison, *Churchill*, p.120.
135 P. Addison, *Churchill on the Home Front*, p.261.
136 C. Ponting, *Churchill*, p.308.
137 Companion V (i), p.702.
138 C. Ponting, *Churchill*, p.311.
139 WSC Bio 5, p.163.
140 *Ibid.*, p.162.
141 Companion V (i), p.697.
142 *Ibid.*, p.711.
143 WSC Bio 5, p.173.
144 *Ibid.*, p.159.
145 R.R. James (ed), *Memoirs of a Conservative*, p.242.
146 *Ibid.*, p.232.
147 Companion V (i), p.881.
148 Speeches IV, p.3952.
149 P. Addison, *Churchill on the Home Front*, p.265.
150 WSC Bio 5, p.171.

CHAPTER FIVE

Gathering Storm

THE 1930S IS A PERIOD often described as Churchill's 'wilderness years'. During this decade he was to become alienated from his party over a number of key issues, mostly related to foreign affairs. He vehemently rejected the Irwin Declaration granting India dominion status, arguing that it would lead to inter-communal violence and a gross diminution of British power. He broke with the Conservative leadership and became the leader of the 'Diehards', a group opposed to government policy in India.

He was also a thorn in the side of the Conservatives over German rearmament. In 1933 President Hindenburg appointed Adolf Hitler Chancellor of Germany. Churchill immediately recognised the danger of this racist, reactionary regime and condemned proposals for general disarmament in the absence of a political settlement. He also called on the government to remedy the deficiencies of Britain's air forces, and was helped by receiving information from contacts such as Desmond Morton, a government official.

Though he equivocated on the threat from Italy and Japan, praising Mussolini on various occasions in the 1930s, he remained a consistent critic of Nazi policy. Churchill became a founder member of Focus, a non-partisan group which sought to defend 'freedom and peace', and gave a number of speeches in defence of democratic principles. He also wrote the multi-volume biography of his ancestor Marlborough.

In 1936 he played a leading part in the Abdication Crisis. The new King Edward VIII made it clear that he intended to marry the divorcee, Wallis Simpson, something that was unacceptable to Baldwin's government. Churchill urged Baldwin to give the King time to reconsider, hoping that Edward would see the error of his ways. However, his support for Edward was widely seen as an opportunistic bid to topple Baldwin and replace him with a King's government. The affair did much to cement Tory mistrust of Churchill.

In 1938 Hitler occupied Austria in the *Anschluss* and declared his intention of making Czechoslovakia his next target. Churchill criticised 'appeasement from weakness' and urged the creation of a European anti-fascist 'Grand Alliance'. Chamberlain rejected these overtures and visited Hitler in Germany, intent on facilitating a negotiated settlement over the Sudetenland. Churchill was to describe the subsequent Anglo-German Munich Agreement as a 'black day in history'. When war was declared in September 1939, following the German invasion of Poland, Churchill was returned to his former role as First Lord of the Admiralty.

Why did Churchill oppose Indian self-rule in the 1930s?

DURING THE First World War it became increasingly obvious that the status quo in British-ruled India[1] would have to change at the end of hostilities. The Indian nationalist movement, which had been weakened by pre-war divisions, received a boost with the 1916 Lucknow Agreement and was further emboldened by the severe strains of war.[2] In 1917 the Secretary of State for India, Edwin Montagu, promised 'the gradual development of self-governing institutions with a view to the progressive realisation of responsible government in India'.

The 1919 Government of India Act gave Indians a greater say in local government while also creating a democratically elected lower chamber for central government. However, Britain (represented by the Viceroy) controlled defence, law and order and taxation. A statutory commission was to be established within a decade to examine the effectiveness of these reforms and consider ways to make the Indian states 'increasingly representative of and responsible to the people of all of them'.[3] In 1927 the Simon Commission, chaired by an ardent supporter of British rule in India, Sir John Simon, recommended a scheme of provincial self-government, with British control firmly at the centre of Indian life.

But this recommendation was not accepted by the Labour government. In 1929 Lord Irwin, Labour's Viceroy, issued a declaration that the aim of British Rule in India was for the country to achieve dominion status. This would allow for an all India federation with

Indian self government at the provincial as well as the national level. The Viceroy would retain control over defence, taxation and foreign affairs. Instead of opposing the government, Baldwin, the leader of the opposition, endorsed the Declaration fully and enforced this view on his party. Churchill was 'demented with fury' at this decision, but worse would follow. After a campaign of civil disobedience, the Labour government was persuaded to convene a Round Table Conference with representatives from Britain and India to discuss issues of constitutional reform.

In 1931 Gandhi and other Congress politicians were released from prison and allowed to attend the Round Table Conference. Churchill resigned from the Shadow Cabinet, horrified that Gandhi, an implacable opponent of British imperial rule, was being privileged in this way. As early as 1920 he had fulminated against Gandhi, arguing that he should be 'trampled on by an enormous elephant with the new Viceroy seated on its back'.4 He later declared: 'It is alarming and also nauseating to see Mr. Gandhi, a seditious Middle Temple lawyer, now posing as a fakir of a type well known in the East, striding half naked up the steps of the Vice-regal palace, while he is still organising and conducting a campaign of civil disobedience, to parley on equal terms with the representative of the King-Emperor.'5 Given this strikingly immoderate language, one has to ask why Churchill was so hostile to the India Bill.

One school of thought ascribes Churchill's venom to an opportunistic bid for the leadership of the Tory Party. It is alleged that Churchill sought to replace Baldwin as leader and used this issue as the vehicle for his ambitions. Clive Ponting interprets Churchill's position in this way: 'He was convinced opinion was moving away from Baldwin and as long as a general election was not called he expected to be successful in bringing him down as party Leader.'6 Samuel Hoare would have agreed. In 1933 he wrote to Lord Willingdon: 'I believe that at the back of his mind he thinks that he will ... smash the government'.7

Certainly there were many Conservative MPs who were unhappy with Baldwin's position on India, and Churchill enjoyed the editorial support of Lords Rothermere and Beaverbrook. It is also true that, during 1931, Baldwin's position was somewhat precarious. But, as the years went on, Churchill became ever more marginalised within the party and came to be seen as the representative of a politically anachronistic fringe group. As J.C.C. Davidson recalled, 'In opposition to the Government of India Bill there were really two groups; there was the Tory Opposition and the Churchill Opposition ... the diehard Tories who opposed us over India never regarded Churchill as a Conservative at all.'[8] Political ambition alone cannot explain Churchill's long campaign over India.

Churchill had always been a staunch defender of Britain's mission in India. As he wrote, 'The rescue of India from ages of barbarism, tyranny and internecine war, and its slow but ceaseless forward march to civilisation constitute upon the whole the finest achievement of our history.' British rule had also 'gripped and controlled' famine, bestowed impartial justice 'equal between race and race', and generously imparted to Indians the many benefits of Western science. For Churchill British rule was beneficent and enlightened, enabling India to progress beyond primitive ethnic violence into an era of civilisation and tranquillity. These were typical Victorian sentiments, reflecting a powerful belief in Britain's civilising mission in the world.

The Empire, on this reading, was less about imparting power or wealth to Britain and more about serving the less fortunate indigenous peoples of the colonies. It was a mission that bestowed duties and responsibilities, rather than privileges, on the ruling class. Thus he wrote in 1931 that many lives had been lost on Indian fields and far more lives were 'given and consumed in faithful and devoted service to the Indian people themselves'.[9]

Undoubtedly his Victorian racial assumptions influenced the way he thought about India. In 1922 he argued that it was wrong to grant 'democratic institution to backward races which had no capacity for self government'.[10] Only a 'fraction' of the Indians 'are interested in politics and Western ideas', he said in 1931, adding that they were 'dependent for their livelihood and for the happiness and peace of their humble homes upon the rule of a very small number of white officials who have no personal interests of their own to serve'.[11] He had a highly derogatory view of the Hindus, whom he described as 'a foul race protected by their pollution from the doom that is their due'.[12] Later, in 1937, he added:

> I do not admit, for instance, that a great wrong has been done to the Red Indians of America, or the black people of Australia. I do not admit that a wrong has been done to these people by the fact that a stronger race, a higher grade race, or at any rate, a more worldly wise race ... has come in and taken their place.[13]

As much as Churchill justified British rule because of perceived cultural superiority, he also believed that it benefited the indigenous community. He thought that colonial rule was a force for racial harmony and that the grant of dominion status would open up the country to all manner of simmering racial hatreds. In 1931 he painted a grim picture of post-imperial rule, describing how the end of British authority would lead to a fatal decline in India's legal, medical and administrative apparatus. He foresaw the rise of political corruption, nepotism and profiteering as 'handmaidens' of a 'Brahmin' domination. But, most importantly, he believed that, without strong British rule, India would fall pray to the very worst state of religious and ethnic strife. 'Left to herself,' he said, 'India would rapidly degenerate to the condition of China at the cost of measureless suffering among three hundred and fifty million people.'[14] Thus any retreat from India would reduce the country to 'the deepest depths of Oriental tyranny and despotism'.[15]

He was also deeply concerned for India's sixty million so-called 'untouchables', for whom he predicted continual persecution under Hindu rule. In 1935 Churchill told one of Gandhi's friends that Gandhi had gone up in his estimation because he championed the rights of the untouchables.[16] Following the riots at Cawnpore in 1931, which left hundreds of Muslims and Hindus dead, Churchill felt his warnings had been vindicated and that the bloodshed, 'a hideous primordial massacre', provided a grim foretaste of what would follow self-rule.[17]

Churchill believed that this violence would not just affect the native population. In his first speech in the House of Commons, he stressed that an All India Parliament would be dominated by a nationalistic Congress which was bound to come into conflict with the Viceroy. If the Viceroy wished to assert his power with repressive measures, he would incur a great deal of popular displeasure while the All India Parliament would become dominated by forces that were intent on driving Britain out of the country. This in turn could lead, Churchill thought, to a repressive crackdown or, even worse, another Amritsar massacre.

Churchill knew that imperial rule in India conferred distinct economic benefits on Britain and believed that these benefits would be squandered if India achieved self-rule. Addressing the House of Commons in May 1931, Churchill said that, if India achieved dominion status, she would likely claim the same right as other dominions to embargo or prohibit British goods or give preferential treatment to foreign over British goods.[18] He was greatly concerned at the commercial consequences of losing India, and warned that the cost of cotton imports for the Lancashire cotton industry would rise.

His concern for Britain's possible economic dislocation sounded alarmist, but in the midst of the 1930s Depression, with millions unemployed, these sentiments were understandable. He talked of how 'the loss of our external connections' and 'shrinkage in foreign trade and shipping' had brought 'the surplus population of Britain within measurable distance of utter ruin'. The future would be a 'struggle for self preservation' to industrial areas which would be based on the retention of India and a 'stronger assertion of commercial rights'.[19]

Churchill linked these economic fears to a haunting perception that Britain's international standing was in decline. He believed that the keys to British greatness were her role in the international trading system, her superior navy and the strength of her imperial mission. Indian self-rule would undoubtedly undermine the last of these and, unchecked, Britain would soon be reduced 'to the degree of states like Holland and Portugal, which nursed valiant races and held great possessions, but were stripped of them in the crush and competition of the world'.[20]

His fears were exacerbated by the instability and uncertainty of global politics in the 1930s. The totalitarian dictators in Italy, Germany and Japan had overturned parliamentary democracy and the liberal tradition of Churchill's youth. Spurred on by recurrent economic crises, they were pursuing a militant form of nationalism that involved the forcible conquest of foreign territory and the enslavement of indigenous peoples. For Churchill, these dictators represented an imminent threat to the British Empire, that pillar of stability and prestige that was central to the maintenance of British power. In these circumstances, Churchill was desperate to cling on to the certainties of his youth and one of these was British pre-eminence in the Asian subcontinent.

However, Churchill did not simply want to acquiesce in the status quo. He was prepared to grant self-government to each of the Indian provinces, which were 'great states and separate nations comparable in magnitude and in numbers with the leading powers in Europe'. Provincial government would open up 'an immense and fertile field for Indian self government'[21] provided that Britain retained full control at the centre of India. Only a strong central British power, he argued, would act impartially between all the conflicting races and creeds in India. In 1933 he proposed that a trial period of provincial autonomy should precede any plan for federal self-government. This trial period would determine how loyal Indian politicians were to the Crown and how justly they treated their religious minorities.

The government rejected this plan and pressed on, winning key votes at Conservative Conferences and in the House of Commons. In 1935 Churchill was gracious enough to concede defeat when the Government of India Act was finally passed. He invited one of Gandhi's supporters, G.D. Birla, to lunch at Chartwell, where they discussed India's prospects for the future. Birla asked Churchill what his criterion of success would be for India. Churchill replied, 'My test is improvement in the lot of the masses, morally as well as materially.'[22]

His fears of intra-ethnic violence never left him. During the Second World War he spoke about India's future with American officials: 'I warn you that if I open the door a crack there will be the greatest bloodbath in all history.'[23] In 1946 he told the Commons that, 'all the facts and all the omens point to a revival, in an acute and violent form, of the internal hatreds and quarrels which have long lain dormant under the mild incompetence of liberal minded British control'.[24] During and after partition in 1947-8, when hundreds of thousands of Hindus, Muslims and Sikhs died in terrible massacres, Churchill felt sadly vindicated.

Did Churchill admire Mussolini?

IN 1927 CHURCHILL toured Italy and had personal glimpses of life under the new fascist regime. He wrote to his wife: 'This country gives the impression of discipline, order, goodwill, smiling faces. A happy, strict school – no talking among the pupils ... The Fascisti have been saluting in their impressive manner all over the place.'[25] He was clearly struck by the appearance of martial discipline and order in the country.

During his stay in Rome he met the Italian ruler, Benito Mussolini. His comments to the press afterwards suggest that he strongly fell under the dictator's charm, speaking of his 'friendly and simple attitude' and his 'calm and serene manner' while commenting that

Mussolini's sole thought was 'the lasting well being of the Italian people'. He told them that he had said, 'If I had been an Italian I am sure I should have been entirely with you from the beginning to the end of your victorious struggle against the bestial appetites and passions of Leninism.'

Churchill was grateful that the Italian revolution, unlike other revolutions, was not a 'movement to the left' but a bulwark against the agitation of revolutionary socialism, but he was quick to add that this type of undemocratic regime was unsuitable to Britain. 'We have our own particular method of doing things.'[26] Not surprisingly, the Italian press was delighted with the respect that Churchill lavished on the regime. Interestingly, Clementine Churchill, who had visited Mussolini a year earlier, echoed her husband's lavish praise, telling him that Mussolini 'fills you with a sort of pleasurable awe'.[27] In response Winston declared that he had no doubt Mussolini was 'one of the most wonderful men of our time'.[28]

If these sentiments seem strange in the light of Churchill's later battle against fascism, it must be remembered that, in the 1920s, he still believed that Bolshevism represented the greatest threat to world peace. During the previous year the General Strike had crippled Britain for ten days and Churchill was not alone in seeing a Soviet hand at work. Churchill had Bolshevism in mind when he had an audience with the Pope in Rome. According to Randolph Churchill, the main topic of conversation was the Bolsheviks and 'what they thought of them'.[29] Nonetheless, his words represented 'the most extreme endorsement of right wing dictatorship that he was ever to utter'.[30]

For much of the 1930s Churchill refused to temper his admiration for the dictator. In 1933 he was invited to speak at the Anti-Socialist and Anti-Communist Union. Shortly before, the Oxford Union had passed the motion, 'That this House refuses in any circumstances to fight for King and country'. Condemning this action as an 'abject, squalid, shameless avowal', Churchill looked 'across the narrow waters of the Channel' where the youth of other countries was imbued with a fierce patriotic spirit. He was clearly thinking of Germany and Italy. He praised Mussolini as 'the Roman genius' and 'the greatest lawgiver among living men'. Ponting believes this passage provides clear evidence of Churchill's unbounded admiration for the fascist regime but he ignores his other comments. In 1927 Churchill had rejected fascism as a model for British politics. 'It is not a sign post which would direct us here,' he said, 'for I firmly believe that our long experienced democracy will be able to preserve a parliamentary system of government with whatever modifications may be necessary from both extremes of arbitrary rule.'[31]

In 1935 it became clear that Italy would invade Abyssinia. The reaction of the British government was to issue a clear warning that, if an invasion took place, Britain would uphold the Covenant of the League of Nations. Churchill argued that it was important to uphold the spirit of the League of Nations and supported the idea of an Anglo-French alliance to act against Mussolini.[32] But in private he was sceptical about the Government's attitude towards Italy. He had argued since 1933 that Germany represented the greater threat to European security and began to think that a harsh anti-Italian line would compromise plans for an anti-Nazi Grand Alliance. He told Austen Chamberlain that it 'would be a terrible deed to smash up Italy, and it will cost us dear'.[33]

In truth, Churchill was torn between a strong League line, that might have alienated Mussolini and driven him into the arms of Hitler, and a weak League line, that would have undermined the instrument of collective security. However, Germany's invasion of the Rhineland in 1936, an action in contravention of the Treaty of Versailles, caused Churchill to abandon support for sanctions. Following Churchill's speech, Mussolini cabled the Italian ambassador in London, Dino Grandi, a personal message for Churchill: 'On your attitude and from your speech the future of Anglo-Italian relations depends, and on my part I desire them to be close and fruitful.'[34]

As late as 1937, two years after the Italian invasion of Abyssinia, Churchill could write in *The News of the World* that: 'It would be dangerous folly for the British people to underrate the enduring position in world-history which Mussolini will hold, or the amazing qualities of courage, comprehension, self-control and perseverance which he exemplifies.'[35] The need for close Anglo-Italian ties as a deterrent to Hitler's expansionism was at the forefront of Churchill's mind. But by 1938 Mussolini had changed tack, allowing Hitler the *Anschluss*[36] he had originally planned in 1934 and moving further away from Britain and France. On the subject of recognising Italy's Abyssinian conquest, Churchill was adamant that 'we should never recognise ... it would be the depth of humiliation'.[37]

In peacetime Churchill courted Mussolini because the Italian leader was viewed as a potential bulwark to Bolshevik and German expansionism. But at no time did he ever endorse the dictator's brand of fascist ideology or believe that such a radical political experiment was viable in Britain. Nor was Churchill alone in being seduced by an authoritarian regime with its promise of economic and social rejuvenation. Many on the British Left, who condemned Churchill's views on Mussolini, openly praised Stalin's regime yet were rarely censured by contemporary mainstream opinion. Ultimately, Stalinism would prove to be more brutal than Italian fascism.

What was Churchill's role during the Abdication Crisis?

ON FEBRUARY 2nd 1936 Churchill wrote to his new sovereign, Edward VIII, offering him heartfelt wishes for what he hoped would be a lengthy and successful reign. He ended his letter with the following hope: 'in the long swing of events Your Majesty's name will shine in history as the bravest and best beloved of all the sovereigns who have worn the island Crown'.[38] Ever the monarchist, Churchill anticipated a lengthy reign that would usher in a period of peace and tranquillity.

But he was also aware that the King's reign might not be quite so long-lasting. Rumours had circulated that the King intended to marry his lover, Mrs Wallis Warfield Simpson, who had been twice married and was looking to divorce her second husband. Many British people strongly objected to their sovereign, the head of the Church of England, marrying a divorcee, and hoped that the government would intervene to prevent an act of constitutional impropriety. Nonetheless, in October 1936 Wallis obtained her second divorce and, on November 16th, Edward duly informed Prime Minister Baldwin of his intention to marry Wallis. Baldwin and the Cabinet strenuously opposed the marriage.

No one was more sensitive to constitutional issues than Churchill himself. Sensing that an improper royal wedding would damage the monarchy, he believed that the King had to abandon plans to marry Wallis if he was to retain the throne. However, he gave his consent to a plan for a morganatic marriage between the couple. Under this arrangement, Wallis, as Edward's wife, would remain a private citizen with an honorary title, such as the Duchess of Cornwall. Another stipulation was that any children would be excluded from the succession. Baldwin, however, was far less receptive to this idea.39

On November 25th Churchill assured Baldwin that he would support a firm line from the government; but Churchill also felt a sense of duty and loyalty to the King and believed that Edward needed adequate time to see the folly of his ways. On December 2nd he pleaded with the government not to take an 'irrevocable step' before consulting Parliament, thus ensuring that the King would not make a reckless decision. Two days later Churchill met the King at the latter's request at Fort Belvedere.

According to the King's memoirs, Churchill showed his deep reverence for the monarchy. He told the King that 'the hereditary principle must not be left to the mercy of politicians trimming their doctrines to the varying hour'. But this did not mean that Churchill was secretly supporting the King's right to marry Mrs Simpson, or undermining the government. He felt aggrieved only that the King was being rushed into making a decision of grave importance to the country. Afterwards he wrote to the King: 'No pistol to be held at the King's head. No doubt that this request for time will be granted. Therefore no final decision or Bill till after Christmas – probably February or March.'40

Churchill was optimistic that Baldwin would not unduly pressurise Edward and that the King would prioritise duty over personal interest. On December 6th in Parliament Churchill again 'pleaded for time and patience', stressing that, while King and Parliament were not at loggerheads, the issue was whether the King was to abdicate 'upon the advice of the Ministry of the day'. He went on: 'The King has been for many weeks under the greatest strain, moral and mental, that can fall upon a man. Not only has he been inevitably subjected to the extreme stress of his public duty, but also to the agony of his own personal feelings. Surely if he asks for time to consider the advice of his Ministers ... he should not be denied.'41 In taking this position, Churchill believed that the relationship with Wallis Simpson would not last for, as he told Mrs Belloc Lowndes, 'He falls constantly in and out of love. His present attachment will follow the course of all the others.'42

For Churchill the most important issue was the future of the monarchy itself. He often described the institution in reverential tones and regarded it as a true symbol of Britain's enduring greatness. He sensed that an enforced abdication would cause irreparable harm to the monarchy 'irrespective of the existing occupant of the throne'.43 But his repeated calls for delay were unrealistic on at least two counts. Not only did he fail to appreciate how urgently Baldwin wanted a solution but he was also blind to the King's own loss of resolve. Edward was determined to marry Wallis and thus his room for flexibility was very narrow. Lord Beaverbrook summed it up when he told Henry Channon in early December: 'Our cock would be all right if only he would fight but at the moment he will not even crow.'44

Churchill also appeared blind to the mood in the Commons, where MPs were increasingly supportive of Baldwin. When, a few days later, Churchill again demanded that 'no irrevocable step be taken before the House had received a full statement', he was greeted with howls of derision. In Amery's words, the House reacted with 'unanimous hostility' while Lord Winterton recorded that the House exploded with 'one of the angriest manifestations I have ever heard directed against any man in the House of Commons'.45 Churchill was forced to leave the Commons in demented fury. As he was leaving he shouted to Baldwin: 'You won't be satisfied until you've broken him, will you?'

In a meeting on December 8th at Fort Belvedere, Baldwin realised that the King was resolved to marry Wallis, even though Wallis herself offered to withdraw her divorce petition to prevent an abdication. Two days later the King signed a formal Deed of Abdication, an outcome which Churchill was forced to accept with sadness and equanimity. In the Commons he paid tribute to the King's 'sacrifices for the peace and strength of his realm'. He also tried to defend his earlier position, claiming that, as a personal friend of the King, he had merely tried to 'cast about for every lawful means ... to keep him on the throne of his fathers'.46 From all accounts, his words were accepted graciously by MPs. His final task on December 11th was to help Edward write a broadcast to the British people.

It was widely believed at the time that, in supporting the King, Churchill was playing a mischievous game of power politics, seeking to oust Baldwin in order to form his own administration. According to Boothby, several of Churchill's supporters believed that he was playing for his 'own hand' while Baldwin described Churchill as 'the most suspicious man I know'.47 Such suspicions had lingered from earlier in the crisis. On November 25th, when Churchill had met Baldwin and the opposition leaders, Chamberlain had believed that

Churchill was 'moving mysteriously in the background and ... expressing willingness to form a government if there should be any refusal on our part to agree'.[48] Lord Zetland wrote that the King had been 'encouraged to believe that Winston Churchill would ... be prepared to form an alternative government'.[49] Another of Churchill's contemporaries believed he was simply maneuvering to form a 'King's Party' to replace Baldwin's administration.[50]

Certainly Churchill did not help his cause by so misjudging the mood of the House of the Commons and the British establishment in general. His association with Lord Beaverbrook aroused suspicions that he was seeking to embarrass the government. According to Lockhart, Beaverbrook was trying to use 'the King issue to beat Baldwin with'.[51] Moreover, his antipathy to Baldwin, the Prime Minister who kept Churchill out of office in the mid-1930s, was well known.[52]

However, it is possible to look at Churchill's motives in a less cynical light. Churchill had been on personal terms with Edward for more than a quarter of a century. He fondly recalled the investiture ceremony at Carnarvon Castle in 1911 when Edward became Prince of Wales, and during the 1920s the two men exchanged letters and played polo together. Churchill also helped the prince with some of his speeches and sent him copies of his First World War memoir, *The World Crisis*. He felt genuine affection for Edward as well as a deep sense of loyalty.

But his reverence for the institution of monarchy was greater still. 'You are monarchical no. 1,' his wife once told him. He regarded the hereditary principle as inviolable and felt that nothing should stop Edward remaining King, barring a grave offence against the state. For, as he asked Duff Cooper: 'What crime ... had the King committed? Had we not sworn allegiance to him? Were we not bound to that oath?'[53] Churchill believed that the King's abdication would represent a grave constitutional crisis which would do untold harm to the institution of monarchy and, for this reason, sought time and patience until Parliament could find a 'happier solution'.[54] In adopting this position, Churchill fatally misjudged Baldwin's resolve, as well as the strength of the King's love for Wallis.

How did Churchill react to
the Nazi revolution?

CHURCHILL'S LASTING REPUTATION rests on his long battle against Nazism and Adolf Hitler. Throughout the 1930s, while he was out of office and confined to the back-benches, he consistently warned of the growing Nazi threat and predicted that appeasement from weakness would be futile. This campaign established his reputation as the most fearsome public critic of the pre-war government and helped to bring him back into government in 1939.

From early on, Churchill grasped the *revolutionary* nature of the Nazi movement. He saw that the Nazis were committed, not just to rearming, but to territorial expansion and racial conquest, and therefore posed a real and growing danger to European civilisation. He viewed Nazism and Bolshevism as two sides of the same coin.

While the Nazis were a small, fringe party with barely 3 per cent of the German vote, Churchill wrote about the 'enormous contingents of German youth growing to military manhood year by year' who were 'inspired by the fiercest sentiments'. 'The soul of Germany', he continued, dreamt of a 'War of Liberation or revenge'.[55] It is remarkable that these highly prescient words were written during a period of relative European tranquillity in the Weimar years.

As early as 1930 Churchill was convinced that Hitler would resort to armed force 'at the first available opportunity' and, speaking at the German Embassy in London, he expressed his anxiety about the Nazi leader.[56] His words were judged important enough to be relayed back to Germany. In 1932 he could write of Hitler that he was 'the moving impulse below the German government and may be more than that soon.'[57] Shortly before the Nazis came to power, he reflected on what their aims really were:

> All these bands of sturdy Teutonic youths, marching through the streets and roads of Germany, with the light of desire in their eyes to suffer for their Fatherland, are not looking for status. They are looking for weapons, and, when they have the weapons, believe me they will then ask for the return of lost territories and lost colonies.[58]

These were the same youth that Churchill predicted would 'never accept the conditions and implications of the Treaty of Versailles'.[59]

Following Hitler's appointment as Chancellor on January 30th

1933, the Nazi revolution began in earnest with the suspension of civil liberties, the establishment of concentration camps, the banning of political parties and the ruthless persecution of Jews and political dissidents. Churchill viewed these developments with alarm, describing the new regime in April 1933 as a 'grim dictatorship' that was characterised by 'militarism, appeals to every form of fighting spirit ... and this persecution of the Jews'.[60] Aware of Hitler's oft expressed desire to smash the Treaty of Versailles, Churchill told his constituents in August 1933 that there was 'grave reason' to believe that Germany was arming herself 'contrary to the solemn treaties exacted from her in her hour of defeat'. Not surprisingly, he went on, Europe's more vulnerable nations such as Austria, Belgium and Denmark were now feeling 'a deep disquietude'.[61] He later described Nazi ideology as 'a philosophy of blood lust' being inculcated into German youth 'in a manner unparalleled since the days of barbarism'.[62]

Churchill perceived the Nazi revolution to be the very antithesis of liberal parliamentary democracy. As an ardent champion of individual freedom and liberal values, he wrote to Bernard Shaw in 1934 that 'freedom for the individual to succeed or fail, in spite of all the resulting irregularities, gives the best climate for culture, happiness and material well being'.

By contrast, in Nazi Germany there existed all 'the monstrosity of the totalitarian state'. In this system, all had to think alike, and to dissent from the regime was 'heresy and treason'. Churchill was appalled that so many eminent figures of culture and learning were being forced out of the country or being persecuted by the Nazis. This deculturation was affecting 'venerable pastors, upright magistrates, world famous scientists and philosophers [and] capable statesmen.'[63]

The extreme anti-Semitism of the Nazis also repelled him. In 1932 Churchill and his son Randolph were touring Munich in order to do some research for the forthcoming biography of Marlborough. During the visit, Randolph tried to arrange a meeting between his father and Hitler. Churchill dined with Hitler's press secretary, Ernst Hanfstaengl, and gave him a message for the Nazi leader. 'Tell your boss from me,' he said, 'that anti-Semitism may be a good starter, but it is a bad sticker.'[64] Hitler put off meeting Churchill, though not entirely as a result of these remarks, and thus denied history one of its greatest encounters.

During the ferocious onslaught against the Jews in Nazi Germany, Churchill offered unmitigated condemnation. He wrote in 1933: 'These men and women have a right to live in the world where they are born, and have a right to pursue a livelihood which has hitherto been guaranteed them under the public laws of the land of their birth.'[65] In a newspaper article in 1934, he condemned the situation whereby Jews were being baited 'for being born Jews' and had to be 'insulated by regulation and routine on particular days of the week or month and made to feel the ignominy of the state of life to which the Creator has called them.'[66]

In 1935 he condemned the 'ferocious' doctrine that had seen the German Jewish population 'stripped of all power, driven from every position in public and social life, expelled from the professions, silenced in the press, and declared a foul and odious race'.[67] Clement Attlee once recalled a conversation with Churchill regarding the Jews in Germany. He remembered 'tears pouring down his cheeks one day before the war in the House of Commons, when he was telling me what was being done to the Jews in Germany'.[68] In an article for the *Evening Standard* in 1937, Churchill appealed to Hitler to end his persecution of the Jews as well as other persecuted minorities. The appeal was in vain.

Some critics allege that his opposition to Nazism was based on a much wider Germanophobia. Churchill was certainly aware of the frequent criticisms of him that appeared in the German press. As early as 1932 they seized on his anti-Nazi comments, accusing him of 'imprudence', while in 1935 one of his election speeches that attacked Nazism generally received a 'hostile reception'.[69]

In Germany, Churchill was condemned for articulating an insult to Hitler that was 'hardly to be exceeded for odiousness'.[70] In response to these criticisms he pointed out the actions he had taken to avert an Anglo-German war in 1914, and to mitigate the effects of Germany's subsequent defeat in that war. He had opposed the French invasion of the Ruhr in 1923 and welcomed the Franco-German peace at Locarno. 'No one,' he said, 'has a right to describe me as the enemy of Germany except in wartime.'[71]

Churchill also recognised that Germany had legitimate grievances over the Treaty of Versailles and consistently urged the government to redress them. Crucially he believed that these grievances had to be addressed while the victors were in a position of military strength. Thus he issued his call for Germany to be dealt with by 'a Concert of

Europe'.[72] He condemned as 'folly' the attempts by the British government and the International Disarmament Conference to bring about 'equality of arms' between Britain, France and Germany. 'The removal of the just grievances of the vanquished ought to precede the disarmament of the victors,' he said. To allow Germany equality of arms with the victors would be 'almost to appoint the day for another European war – to fix it as if it were a prize-fight'.[73]

Churchill, then, was no Germanophobe, but he vehemently rejected the ideological basis of Nazism, which was violently illiberal, racist, militarist and anti-democratic. He recognised, before many of his contemporaries, that Nazism was a revolutionary movement which posed a grave threat to the European order. It remains one of the great ironies of history that it took a man as wicked as Hitler to cement Churchill's reputation for political genius.

Why did Churchill condemn the Munich Agreement?

THE MUNICH AGREEMENT of 1938 was the epitome of the Anglo-French policy of appeasement pursued in the inter-war years. It is usually a byword for cynical and short-sighted diplomatic surrender through the refusal to contemplate the use of force. For its critics, Munich is synonymous with betrayal and capitulation, a stab in the back by the Western powers against the interests of weaker and more vulnerable states. This criticism of appeasement, which has been echoed by world leaders ever since, was stated most eloquently by Churchill, both in the House of Commons and in his war memoirs. He regarded the Munich Agreement as a 'total and unmitigated defeat', an unwise and unrequited set of concessions which would provide only an illusion of peace amid growing international tension. His speeches and articles at that time contain separate but inter-related criticisms of British foreign policy.

The 1938 Munich Agreement was a settlement between Europe's major powers (Britain, Germany, France and Italy) regarding the Sudetenland, following a conference held in Munich. The Sudetenland was a part of Czechoslovakia that included over three million ethnic Germans. One of Hitler's foreign policy aims was to unite all Germans in one state and he argued that the acquisition of the Sudetenland was based on the legitimate rights of self-determination.

The main political group representing the Sudeten Germans was the *Sudeten Deutsche Partei* led by Konrad Henlein, who demanded the secession of the Sudetenland to Germany. On a visit to London, Henlein urged the British government to accept secession as the only viable path to peace.

The Czech government was prepared to consider some form of autonomy for the Sudeten Germans but it was not prepared to grant them independence, understandably believing that a successful secessionist claim by the German inhabitants could lead to irredentist[74] claims from other minority groups. In addition, the Sudetenland contained the important Skoda arms works and vital fortifications and was thus an important strategic barrier against German expansion. As the Czechs had a guarantee of security from both France and Russia, they felt confident that they could negotiate their case from a position of strength. However, tension rose in June and July 1938 as Hitler continued to threaten a violent invasion of Czechoslovakia unless his demands were met.

Contrary to the conventional wisdom, Churchill was not itching for a war in 1938. He gave his support to Lord Runciman's summer mission which aimed to broker a peace between the parties in the region. He also met Konrad Henlein, leader of the Sudeten Nazis, and accepted his formula for greater German self-determination in the Sudetenland. It was Hitler who rejected any hint of compromise during the summer of 1938.

By the end of August it had become clear to the British Prime Minister, Neville Chamberlain, that the crisis over the Sudetenland would not be resolved unless he personally intervened to bring about a lasting territorial settlement. During September 1938, with the approval of his Cabinet, he flew three times to see Hitler in order to discuss the Sudeten crisis. After the first meeting, Hitler told Chamberlain that he wanted the transfer to Germany of all districts of Czechoslovakia with a 50 per cent or more German-speaking population. Chamberlain gained the consent of his Cabinet. However, when they next met, on September 22nd, Hitler demanded an immediate occupation of the Sudetenland, including areas with a non-German majority. This demand became known as the 'Godesberg Memorandum'.

Chamberlain now faced a Cabinet mutiny, led by the Foreign Secretary, Lord Halifax, who made it clear that no such capitulation was acceptable. The Czechs unsurprisingly also rejected the

Godesberg Memorandum. The following week was one of unbearable international tension. On September 23rd the Czechs ordered a general mobilisation and the French started to marshal troops as well. On September 27th the Royal Navy was mobilised, gas masks were distributed and air raid shelters were dug in parks across Britain. Finally, on September 29th, when war seemed a certainty, Hitler accepted that troops would occupy only the agreed areas of Czechoslovakia, that a free plebiscite would be held in other areas and that Germany would guarantee the independence of the rest of Czechoslovakia.

To the relief of millions in Britain, Chamberlain signed the Munich Agreement and brought home – so he claimed – 'peace with honour'. Churchill was enraged by Chamberlain's decision; so much so that, on the evening of September 29th, he told Duff Cooper that he 'would speak on every socialist platform in the country against the Government'.[75]

Almost as soon as the ink was dry on the agreement, Churchill became the government's, and Chamberlain's, sternest critic. By signing the Munich Agreement Britain had suffered, in his words, 'a total and unmitigated defeat'.[76] Britain and France were in the 'presence of a disaster of the first magnitude',[77] which had weakened their own standing while leaving Czechoslovakia 'abandoned', 'broken' and 'mutilated'. Churchill used an arresting metaphor. Hitler had found that, 'instead of snatching his victuals from the table', they were 'served to him course by course'.[78] Quite simply, the country had 'suffered a defeat without a war'.

Churchill was certainly not the only critic of the government; the leaders of the opposition parties were equally scathing. Attlee condemned Munich as 'a victory for brute force' while Archibald Sinclair for the Liberals denounced a policy which imposed 'injustice on a small and weak nation'.[79] Duff Cooper spoke for many when he said that Hitler understood only 'the language of the mailed fist'.

But it was Churchill's speech that provided the most trenchant and memorable denunciation of Munich: his rhetoric and oratory were perfectly matched to the moment. From this and other speeches we can discern the reasons for his strenuous opposition.

A year before the Munich Agreement was signed, Churchill had argued that it would be 'wrong and cynical' for Britain and France 'to buy immunity' for themselves 'at the expense of the smaller countries of Central Europe'. He added: 'It would be contrary to the whole tide

of British and United States opinion for us to facilitate the spread of
Nazi tyranny over countries which now have a considerable measure
of democratic freedom'.[80]

The Munich Agreement subsequently cemented Germany's
position as the most powerful nation on the Continent. In March
1938 Austria had been incorporated into Germany through the
Anschluss and, by the end of the year, a valuable slice of the Czech
state had been added to the expanding Reich. The smaller nations of
Europe were now ripe for the picking, dependent for their existence
on the fluctuating whims of the German dictator. More importantly,
those nations were aware that they could not rely on Anglo-French
support in the face of the German threat.

It was this latter fact that exercised Churchill the most. Since 1938
he had sought to create a Grand Alliance of smaller nations, dominated by Britain, France and Russia, which would unite to deter
German aggression. As he put it, 'the maintenance of peace depends
upon the accumulation of deterrents against the aggressor coupled
with a sincere effort to redress grievances'.[81] He had warned that the
partition of Czechoslovakia was tantamount to 'a complete surrender by the Western democracies to the Nazi threat of force'.[82]

The Munich Agreement had dashed these hopes. He wrote after
the agreement: 'An injury has, however, been sustained by the
prestige and authority of both the Western democracies which must
woefully reduce their influence with small countries of all kinds'.
Countries like Poland, Yugoslavia and Romania, that might have
been brought into the Anglo-French orbit, would now feel compelled
to 'make the best terms possible with the one Power which is ready
to use brutal violence without scruple'.[83] Even the remainder of the
Czech state would be impossible to maintain as 'an independent
entity'. There would be 'a period of time which may be measured by
years, but may be measured only by months', when Czechoslovakia
would end up 'engulfed in the Nazi regime'.[84] Six months after
Munich, Nazi Germany, in collaboration with Slovakia, duly dissolved the Czech state.

Churchill did not believe, in 1938, that an Anglo-German war was
inevitable. But, amid the clamour for appeasing the dictators, he
believed the dilemma of British foreign policy had been wrongly
posed. It was not a question of war or peace but 'war now or war
later'. The problem with 'war later' was that it would prove more
costly than 'war now' though it would not seem that way at first.

Before Munich, Churchill had confided to a friend his growing fears for the future. 'We seem', he wrote, 'to be very near the bleak choice between War and Shame. My feeling is that we shall choose Shame, and then have war thrown in a little later on even more adverse terms than at present.'[85]

The Munich Agreement only vindicated his fears that the policy had been short-sighted and contrary to Britain's long-term national interests. As he told the Commons, 'This is only the beginning of the reckoning. This is only the first sip, the first foretaste of a bitter cup which will be proferred to us year by year...'[86] The reason why the cup would get increasingly bitter was that Germany's war power was set to grow 'faster than the British [could] complete their preparations for defence'.[87] The German army did indeed become more powerful in the following year, as did the German air force.

Allied to Churchill's belief that Germany would be weaker in 1938 than in 1939 was his optimistic assessment of the strength of German resistance. In his war memoirs, Churchill wrote that 'the [German] generals were repeatedly planning revolts' and that a stronger stand by the Allies at Munich might have forced Hitler out. As it was, the agreement left the generals 'abashed' while Hitler remained in a stronger position.[88] It is widely believed by historians that Churchill exaggerated the level of army resistance at the time.

Churchill's belief in the futility of appeasing Nazism was based on accurately assessing the demands of Hitlerism. He recognised one point very clearly from the outset: that Hitler's ideological goals far surpassed discrete territorial demands arising from the terms of the Treaty of Versailles. Instead, Hitler was a revolutionary whose abiding ideological mission was to replace European civilisation with a *Pax Germanica*. His ideal of a greater Germany could not be moderated by a peace agreement, negotiation or compromise.

To come to terms with Hitler meant accepting, at the very least, his overlordship of Central and Eastern Europe, and the permanent subjugation of entire nations and minorities. It meant 'the prostration of Europe before the Nazi power'.[89] Churchill understood that appeasement, far from satisfying the cravings of a determined foe, would only whet his appetite for further conquests. In the eyes of a powerful adversary, an appeaser who merely took the line of least resistance by ruling out the use of force would appear unwilling to defend his true interests, thus giving his opponent an insuperable advantage. Hitler appreciated the force of this argument better than anyone; in *Mein Kampf* he had written: 'History teaches us that nations which have once given way before the threat of arms without being forced to do so will accept the greatest humiliations and exactions rather than make a fresh appeal to force.'[90]

Churchill understood this too. Shortly after the Munich Agreement, he foresaw a time when the country would be 'confronted with demands' affecting 'the surrender of territory or the surrender of liberty'. These would entail 'restrictions upon the freedom of speech and debate in Parliament, on public platforms and discussions in the Press'. Appeasement could not, in Churchill's view, lead to peaceful Anglo-German relations. Instead, it would involve the end of the British Empire and acceptance of 'the Teutonic domination of Europe'.[91] In short, if Britain submitted to Hitler's demands, she would rapidly become a satellite state of Nazi Germany, forever subject to the grace and favour of its dictatorial leader.[92]

In any case, Churchill did not accept that the sacrifice of a small country like Czechoslovakia would give Britain any long-term security. 'The idea', he said, 'that safety can be purchased by throwing a small state to the wolves is a fatal delusion.' Hitler's appetite would remain and, with the Czechs 'neutralised', twenty-five German divisions would be liberated to 'threaten the western front'. Thus the annexation of the Sudetenland had wider regional implications. It was a menace not just to Czechoslovakia but 'to the cause of freedom and democracy in every country'.[93]

Churchill believed that the Czechs, left to their own devices, were in a powerful position to confront their German adversaries. As Chamberlain flew out to Munich for his first meeting with Hitler, Churchill paid tribute to the martial spirit of the 'resolute' Czechs. They possessed an 'absolute determination to fight for life and freedom' and their spirit was matched by a powerful army that was 'one of the best-equipped in the world ... with admirable tanks, anti-tank guns and anti-aircraft artillery'. He added that the Czechs, like the Spanish Republicans, would maintain their morale under air bombardment and the 'hideous slaughter' the Nazis would wreak on them. It is true that the Czechs possessed a powerful army and they were aided by the Skoda arms works in the Sudetenland.[94]

But Churchill was of the belief that the Czechs would have fared better if left alone by those who claimed to be defending them. As he put it in his Munich speech, 'I believe the Czechs, left to themselves and told they were going to get no help from the Western powers, would have been able to make better terms than they have got – they could hardly have worse.'95

Perhaps most galling of all for Churchill was that the Munich Agreement had irreparably stained Britain's reputation and prestige. On many occasions he used words like 'dishonour' and 'shame', and bemoaned the 'betrayal' of the Czechs. Take this quote from his Munich speech: 'there can never be friendship between the British democracy and the Nazi power, that power which spurns Christian ethics, which cheers its onward course by a barbarous paganism, which vaunts the spirit of aggression and conquest, which derives strength and perverted pleasure from persecution and uses ... with pitiless brutality the threat of murderous force.'96

Churchill felt that any deal with Hitler would be futile because it would neither satisfy the dictator's megalomaniac ambitions nor purchase a meaningful measure of security for the Western Allies. Appeasement from weakness was judged to be ineffective and morally bankrupt. As he put it, 'The idea that dictators can be appeased by kind words and minor concessions is doomed to disappointment.'97

How realistic were Churchill's alternatives to appeasement?

CHURCHILL OBJECTED to Chamberlain's appeasement at Munich not because the Prime Minister had negotiated with Hitler but because he had made a set of craven concessions from a position of weakness. Churchill felt this strategy was futile in the face of a determined and ruthless enemy who was intent on bullying weaker nations. But, as well as condemning government policy, Churchill proposed two alternative strategies for combating the Nazi threat: aerial rearmament and a Grand Alliance. Both were designed to bolster Britain's credibility in dealing with her enemies but, as it now turns out, neither policy would have been the panacea Churchill hoped for.

Grand Alliance
Churchill had often talked of building political and military alliances to deter national enemies. As early as 1911 he had urged an alliance between Britain, France and Russia to safeguard the Low Countries from hostile activity. After the Great War, he wanted to re-create an

alliance system, this time involving Germany, to defend Western Europe against Russia.[98] On both occasions he recognised the fundamental importance of creating alliances between nations in order to deter one other potentially aggressive power from dominating the Continent. In this way, the European balance of power would be preserved.

While Hitler was in the process of building up his personal dictatorship, Churchill talked increasingly about the strategic benefits of a grand European alliance. Citing Hitler's rearmament in violation of the Treaty of Versailles, he called for a revival of the Concert of Europe through the League of Nations so as to address Germany collectively. No better way existed to confront an aggressor than 'with the prospect of such a vast concentration of force, moral and material, that even the most reckless, even the most infuriated, leader would not attempt to challenge those great forces'.[99]

While the terms 'Concert of Europe' and 'concentration of force' suggested secret agreements and power politics, Churchill also implied that it was perfectly compatible with international laws and conventions. Throughout the 1930s the concept of the Grand Alliance would have a dual basis: effectiveness through powerful alliances and legitimacy through the language of the League of Nations.

This dual theme was apparent in 1936 when Churchill called for 'the assembly of overwhelming force, moral and physical, in support of international law'. He added: 'If the forces at the disposal of the League of Nations are four or five times as strong as those which the Aggressor can as yet command, the chances of a peaceful and friendly solution are very good.' The 'Constabulary of the world is at hand' he wrote, and, 'On every side of Geneva stand great nations, armed and ready, whose interests as well as whose obligations bind them to uphold, and in the last resort, enforce, the public law.'[100]

This idea was reiterated in 1937 when he said that the peace and future security of Europe would depend on 'the combination of many well-armed states, great and small, upon the basis of the Covenant of the League'. He also called this allied combination 'a League of mutual defence against unprovoked aggression'.[101] The League would have an 'immense and perhaps decisive part to play in the prevention of a brutal trial of strength'.[102] Peace, he said, could only be founded on 'preponderance': if 'there were eight or ten on one side, and only one or two upon the other, and if the collective armed forces of one side were three or four times as large as those of the other, then there will be no war'. The 'first stage' of this structure could be built by the League.[103]

By 1938 he was calling his doctrine 'arms *and* the covenant', allowing him to court influential opinion in both left-wing and centre groups. By 1938 his call for a Grand Alliance, following Hitler's *Anschluss*, had a greater urgency:

> If a number of states were assembled around Great Britain and France in a solemn treaty for mutual defence against aggression; if they had their forces marshaled in what you may call a Grand Alliance; if they had their Staff arrangements concerted; if all this rested, as it can honorably rest, upon the Covenant of the League of Nations, in pursuance of all the purposes and ideals of the League of Nations; if that were sustained, as it would be, by the moral sense of the world; and if that were done in the year 1938 – and, believe me, it may be the last chance there will be for doing it – then I say that you might even now arrest this approaching war.[104]

Churchill was ever happy to supply a historical argument for his case. In 1935 he advised Lord Rothermere that, if Britain acquiesced in the German domination of Europe, 'this would be contrary to the whole of our history'.[105] A year later, while denying to Lord Londonderry that he had an 'anti-German obsession', he wrote:

> British policy for four hundred years has been to oppose the strongest power in Europe by weaving together a combination of other countries strong enough to face the bully. Sometimes it is Spain, sometimes the French monarchy, sometimes the French Empire, sometimes Germany. I have no doubt who it is now... It is thus through the centuries we have kept our liberties and maintained our life and power.[106]

In calling for a Grand Alliance, Churchill was influenced by his illustrious forbear, the Duke of Marlborough. In the 1930s Churchill wrote a mammoth multi-volume biography of Marlborough in which he paid great attention to the Duke's creation of alliances against Louis XIV. As Ben Moshe rightly observes, these seventeenth- and eighteenth-century struggles waged during Marlborough's lifetime 'became the prism through which he observed Britain's political and military problems during the 1930s'.[107]

Clearly Churchill was advocating a traditional balance of power strategy, linking weaker states with Britain and France in an effort to

deter the strongest and most aggressive power, Hitler's Germany. All
these allied nations would act in the name of collective security, but
their actions would be legitimate in international law because they
invoked the League of Nations.

Contrary to the views of some, Churchill did not assert the immi-
nence of war, nor did he seek only a military angle on the 'German
problem'. He remained convinced that, if the Western Allies were in
a position of strength, they could adequately deal with any German
grievances left over from the Treaty of Versailles. These included the
question of lost colonies, German self-determination and any territorial changes. It was crucial for Churchill that no British Prime
Minister offer concessions from a position of weakness, but instead
should negotiate from a position of strength. He regarded a strategy
of arms reduction prior to peace talks as nothing short of a formula
for another European war.[108] Further, he did not even envisage the
diplomatic encirclement of Germany, for the Grand Alliance was
merely 'the largest possible forces combined against the aggressor,
whoever he may be'.[109]

How realistic was the Grand Alliance?
Looking at Churchill's idea of a Grand Alliance, Neville Chamberlain
commented that 'there was almost everything to be said for it until
you come to examine its practicability. From that moment its attraction vanishes.'[110]

It is not difficult to appreciate Chamberlain's view. Part of the
problem was the central role of the Soviet Union, which, as Stalin
never forgot, Churchill had tried to strangle at birth. Many of the
countries of Central and Eastern Europe rejected any alliance with
the USSR. The Poles in particular were highly suspicious of Russian
troops entering their territory and many believed that, if the Red
Army arrived, they would never leave. In view of the 45-year post-war
Soviet occupation, this fear was prescient.

There was also a very obvious geographical problem. Russia could
not help Czechoslovakia directly because they lacked a common
border, and neither of the two countries with direct access to
Czechoslovakia was likely to offer the Soviets any help. Furthermore,
on the military front there were very real doubts about the strength
of the Red Army. Throughout the 1930s a highly paranoid Stalin had
been busy purging its officers and senior staff, thus depleting his
country's armed forces at a vital moment in history.

The Foreign Office had also long ruled out help from France in a time of crisis. Ever since Britain had refused to back the French over their invasion of the Ruhr in 1923, the French had adopted a defensive strategy against Berlin. Instead of planning for offensive operations against Germany, they had invested time and money in building the seemingly impregnable Maginot line.[111] This created a bunker 'Maginot mentality' throughout the 1930s, which left the country badly prepared for offensive warfare.

Finally we come to the United States. In 1938 President Franklin D. Roosevelt offered to convene an international conference to explore the general basis of a peace settlement. In his memoirs of the war years, Churchill castigated Chamberlain for neglecting this offer, which he described as 'the last frail chance to save the world from tyranny otherwise than by war'.[112] He ignored his own thoughts at the time, for in 1939, despite hoping the USA would join a Grand Alliance, Churchill wrote, 'We may be certain that the United States will not intervene in any British or European quarrel.'[113] This skeptical sentiment aligned Churchill with the predominant opinion-makers in Whitehall and Westminster. As John Charmley also points out, no major American politician called for a US-led anti-fascist alliance while the country remained in the grip of isolationism. That left only Britain herself to make up the proposed alliance.

Nonetheless, by 1939 the government had adopted Churchill's suggestion of engaging with the USSR in an effort to halt German expansionism. A minor British official was sent to the Soviet Union by slow boat for talks on signing a possible Anglo-Soviet alliance. Despite the half-hearted and irresolute manner in which the British conducted these talks, there was some evidence of Churchillian influence in the months before the war.

Aerial rearmament

During the 1930s, the British government began to rearm significantly under the Baldwin and Chamberlain governments. The bulk of the increased defence spending was on the air force, with the navy and army receiving correspondingly less attention. Many politicians shared Baldwin's pessimistic prognosis that 'the bomber will always get through'. Churchill, too, shared this assumption and, from 1933 onwards, painted an alarming picture of Britain's military deficiencies, while urging greater spending on Britain's defences.

In response to a 1934 government White Paper, which restricted the British air force to five hundred aircraft, Churchill urged the government that the country's air force had to be 'at least as strong as that of any power that can get at us'.[114] Baldwin subsequently pledged that Britain would never lose parity with Europe's dominant air force.

In a debate in the Commons in July 1934, Churchill warned the government that Germany was playing a game of catch-up with its air force. He warned that, by 1936, the German air force would exceed Britain's in size and that Britain would be unable to catch up. He also warned that Germany's civil aviation force was several times larger than Britain's, with commercial planes being designed for conversion to military purposes. This information came directly to Churchill from Desmond Morton, head of the Industrial Intelligence Centre of the Committee of Imperial Defence and one of Churchill's closest confidants. Churchill was accused of being an alarmist warmonger, but the government was also aware of Germany's extensive rearmament and of the widespread unease that this was causing in political circles.

In November 1934 Churchill launched his most sustained assault on the government to increase aircraft production and work on anti-aircraft defences. Arguing that, by 1937, the German air force would be double the size of Britain's, he urged an acceleration of aircraft production so that Britain's air force would have the power to inflict as much damage on the enemy as the enemy themselves could inflict. It was the tardiness of Britain's rearmament that gravely concerned him.

In 1935 Churchill continued his vigorous campaign. Armed with information from two officials in the Foreign Office, Ralph Wigram and Michael Cresswell, that suggested Germany would be vastly superior in the air by 1936, Churchill once again warned of a 'period of peril': from being 'the least vulnerable of all nations, we have, through developments in the air, become the most vulnerable'. Worse, the government was not taking the measures that were necessary for the protection of the country. Churchill was accused of scaremongering but his fears were shared by senior figures in the Air Ministry and the Foreign Office.[115]

Throughout 1937 and 1938 he continued to argue for increased rearmament, especially in the air, while also calling for a 'Munitions Ministry'. Churchill believed that the country's industries had to be ready 'to turn from peace to war production at the pressing of a button' in order to catch up with German development, but the government did not heed this call until 1939.

How realistic was aerial rearmament as an alternative to appeasement?

Churchill's warnings about the dangers of Nazism were generally vindicated. He was aware that Germany was rearming at an astounding rate and that its air force would become numerically stronger than its British counterpart. The sluggish nature of Britain's rearmament programme alarmed him and he was surely right in calling for it to be speeded up. On March 14th 1939 Hitler broke the spirit of the Munich Agreement by invading Czechoslovakia and, in the following years, followed this up with the ruthless conquest of other European countries. In each case, the German air force provided essential support and cover for its troops in blitzkrieg campaigns. The question has naturally arisen: Would a more urgent rearmament of Britain's aerial power have prevented a European war? The consensus among recent military historians is that it would not have.

Firstly, Churchill exaggerated the likely effects of German aerial attacks. Typical is his comment in a speech on November 28th 1934:

> No one can doubt that a week or 10 days intensive bombing attack upon London would be a very serious matter indeed. One could hardly expect that less than 30,000 or 40,000 people would be killed or maimed ... We must expect that under the pressure of continuous air attack upon London at least 3,000,000 or 4,000,000 people would be driven out into the open country around the Metropolis.[116]

Yet it was an exaggeration shared by many at the time. Bombers were widely viewed as invincible super-weapons capable of laying waste to entire cities. It was believed that, in the first few days of war, hundreds of thousands of people would die in an assault by bombers, with millions being left homeless and starving. This obsessive fear of mass casualties was stoked up by the apocalyptic visions of H.G. Wells in *The Shape of Things to Come*. The bombing of Guernika on April 26th 1937 by the German Condor Legion,[117] which destroyed most of the town, convinced many of what would be in store for them if war broke out.

This alarmism, however, only induced a deeper pessimism among the British establishment about Britain's chances in an aerial war. On November 10th 1932 Stanley Baldwin declared:

I think it is well for the man on the street to realise that there is no
power on earth that can protect him from being bombed. Whatever
people may tell him, the bomber will always get through ... The only
defence is in offence, which means that you have to kill more women
and children more quickly than the enemy if you want to save
yourself.

This reinforced a belief that 'no effective defence against the
bomber existed, though one's own bomber force would be a deterrent against attack'.[118]

Not surprisingly, when it came to allocating money for the armed
services, the air force was given priority. This might not have been a
problem were the air force also *Hitler's* main priority. But it was not.
Crucially, what Churchill failed to concentrate on was the real and
growing danger from the German army. Throughout the 1930s he
bought into the inter-war doctrine of 'limited liability', believing that
the French army, rather than the British Expeditionary Force (BEF),
would contain German expansion in Western Europe. In this way,
he hoped that both powers could avoid a repeat of the protracted
horrors of the Western Front. Perhaps this was the reason why
Churchill was less interested in expanding the BEF which, in 1939,
was a mere four divisions in strength. In a visit to France in 1939, he
described the Maginot Line as a guarantee of 'absolute security
against the horrors of invasion'.[119]

Despite the important role of the *Luftwaffe* in spearheading
advances in 1939 and 1940, Germany's modernised and well-equipped
army was to play a more crucial role. Churchill also underestimated
the role that tanks and motorised armour were to play in the
blitzkrieg operations of the Second World War.[120] As Donald
Cameron Watt has observed, this meant that Churchill's campaign
'never focused on the issues that might have made an impact on
German military opinion – military arms production, conscription,
a Continental commitment'. But Churchill's flawed strategy was
shared by the Chiefs of Staff, as well as by Chamberlain.

Churchill also fell into the trap of assuming that the sole aim of
the *Luftwaffe* would be to inflict a knock-out blow against Britain. At
the time of the Munich crisis, the staff of the *Luftwaffe* admitted
that their planes could not reach Britain and were to be used as
an adjunct to any projected land campaign. Until 1939 the German
air force was no real threat to Britain.[121] In any case, Churchill chose
to downplay the rearmament policies pursued in the 1930s by the

Baldwin and Chamberlain governments. Much as he would regard these governments as committed solely to appeasement, they were, in reality, following a dual policy: appeasement and rearmament. The Spitfire and Hurricane, the twin fighters that proved so crucial in the Battle of Britain, flew in 1935 and 1936, during the Baldwin era, while radar stations were built under Neville Chamberlain.

Churchill was more than just a sniping critic of government policy for he offered alternative ways of dealing with the Nazi threat. But, contrary to the self-serving portrait offered in *The Gathering Storm*, his alternatives were fraught with difficulties and, even if implemented, might not have prevented a European war. Nonetheless, Churchill had an astonishing grasp of the core issue: that Hitlerism represented a grave threat to European peace and security and could not be tackled from a position of military weakness. Churchill possessed the intuitive sense, and the bravery, to interpret Hitler as a revolutionary ideologue rather than an aggrieved nationalist. For this reason, we can leave the last words to Churchill's close friend and colleague, Brendan Bracken. 'No public man in our time has shown more foresight,' he wrote, adding that Churchill's 'long, lonely struggle to expose the dangers of the dictatorships' might one day be seen as 'the best chapter in his crowded life'.[122]

Was Churchill completely in the wilderness in the 1930s?

THE 1930S HAVE often been called Churchill's 'wilderness years'. They mark a period of political isolation in which he was excluded from government and faced alienation from his party. It also happens to be the title of a popular mini-series about Churchill's life in the 1930s. In his war memoirs, the 'wilderness' image suited Churchill's purposes perfectly. He cast himself in the role of a lone Cassandra, whose prescient warnings were ignored by a misguided political elite. In this position, he could not be blamed for the follies of appeasement, while his image as a prophet of war remained unsullied. As he put it after the war, 'I saw it all coming and cried aloud to my own fellow-countrymen and to the world, but no one paid any attention ... One by one we were all sucked into the awful whirlpool.'[123]

But was the political wilderness less empty than Churchill liked to believe? Were the years of wilderness no more than a romantic, self-serving myth? As with much mythology, an element of truth has become intermingled with a heavy dose of fiction.

India

On the question of Indian self-rule, Churchill's concerns were shared by many lesser-known contemporaries. As early as 1929, when Baldwin announced his support for the Irwin Declaration, many Conservative MPs were deeply hostile and prepared to vote against their party. Lord Irwin was informed by the editor of *The Times*, a leading barometer of Conservative opinion, that the 'tide here is running pretty strongly against your ideas'.[124] In the debate in 1931, Baldwin's defence of the Indian bill was cheered by Labour MPs while there was an 'ominous silence' from fellow Conservatives.

As late as 1934 Hoare had to admit that there were 'not thirty' Conservative MPs who were 'keen to go on with the Bill', that those who actually supported it were 'very lukewarm' and 'that a very strong minority is actively hostile'. Nor was the India Defence League, of which Churchill was Vice-President, in any way an unpopular organisation. When it was launched in 1933, with the aim of campaigning against Indian self-rule, it had the support of nearly sixty MPs, 28 peers and a number of important privy councillors.[125]

Despite the vigorous campaign, on the second reading of the Government of India Bill, in 1935, the legislation was much the same as it had been in 1930. Nonetheless, despite a three-line whip, 84 Conservative MPs rebelled against the bill, the largest Tory rebellion on a three-line whip against any British bill in the twentieth century.[126] On the issue of Indian self-rule, Churchill's defiant stand was clearly not a lonely one.

Rearmament

Neither was Churchill isolated in calling for a vigorous increase in general rearmament. Many in the Conservative Party agreed with his condemnation of Labour's naval disarmament policy in 1930. In 1933, at the party conference, a motion from Churchill and Lord Lloyd calling for British rearmament was passed unanimously amid 'scenes of great enthusiasm'.[127] His call in 1934 for the creation of an air force larger than that of Germany was greeted, according to Frances Stevenson, with 'almost an ovation', while his line 'greatly pleased the Tory party'.[128]

In 1935, at the party conference at Bournemouth, Churchill's amendment stating that it was 'the duty of His Majesty's Government forthwith to repair the serious deficiencies in the defence forces' using 'any financial measures which may be necessary for the national safety' was again passed unanimously.[129] These calls for bolstering Britain's defences did not go down well with the party leadership, however. It was precisely because Churchill could powerfully appeal to the party caucus and the parliamentary party on this issue that Baldwin was anxious to exclude him from government after 1935.

Churchill's fears over Britain's sluggish rearmament, especially in the air, were shared by many fellow Conservatives, as well as the wider military establishment. We now know that Churchill was receiving secret information on the German air force from a variety of civil servants and senior military figures.

Two important figures in the foreign office provided Churchill with support and information. One was the permanent secretary, Sir Robert Vansittart, who had expressed deep misgivings about government policy towards Nazi Germany. The second was Ralph Wigram, who was the head of the Central Department of the Foreign Office. Wigram provided Churchill with secret Foreign Office documents that clearly showed the rapid expansion of the German air force. Like Vansittart, Wigram was deeply concerned about the inadequacies of Britain's defences and wanted the wider British public informed of the dangers. As Gilbert points out, Churchill 'was the instrument that Wigram chose to alert the British public to the reality of German air power'.[130]

Churchill's concerns about the Royal Air Force were shared by a number of serving officers, the most prominent being Torr Anderson. Anderson, who had served on the Western Front in the First World War and was later director of the RAF Training School, regularly informed Churchill about weaknesses in the service, hoping that the information he relayed would lead to drastic improvements. The inventor of radar, Robert Watson-Watt, also confided in Churchill that the Air Ministry had not taken 'emergency measures' to test his new invention.

Another vital contact was Desmond Morton, the head of the Industrial Centre of the Committee of Imperial Defence. He was involved in collecting information on German war industries and, until the outbreak of war, provided Churchill with information about

Germany's military preparedness. In many ways, Churchill was at the centre of an intelligence distribution process with far-reaching consequences for public policy.

But, in many respects, the 1930s was a period of political wilderness for Churchill. Even if his political views were widely shared, he was still a deeply mistrusted figure in political circles. Brigadier J.H. Morgan, who was a constitutional adviser to the 'India' diehards, recalled: '*All* of them distrusted Churchill: their attitude to him was summed up by Wolmer when, dining with me at the Reform one night, he said: "We don't want Winston with us, he has forced himself upon us ... He *discredits* us; *we* are acting from conviction but everybody knows that Winston has no convictions; he has only joined us for what he can get out of it."'[131]

The charge that Churchill lacked firm political convictions and acted opportunistically was made frequently, particularly during the Abdication Crisis. According to Boothby, several of Churchill's supporters believed that he was playing his 'own hand' while Baldwin described Churchill as 'the most suspicious man I know'.[132] If anything, his championing of the King was a distraction from the larger issue of European security, casting additional doubt on his judgement and sense of proportion. However, Churchill became more isolated in 1937 not so much because of the Abdication Crisis but because there was relatively more calm in Europe that year.

But what about the most important issue of all in the 1930s, the campaign against appeasement? There is no doubt that Churchill had been winning supporters in the Liberal and, to a lesser extent, the Labour camp with his vigorous opposition to appeasement. But his inconsistency in condemning fascism bred suspicion and alienated many potential supporters.

He equivocated on the Italian threat to the Mediterranean, staying away from Parliament during debates on the Hoare-Laval Pact;[133] overall his attendance record on the Abyssinia crisis was sporadic. He certainly argued that the Italian triumph in Abyssinia was a lamentable event, and said he felt sympathy for a 'feudal people' who were seeking to defend their freedom from a 'scientific invader'.[134] Nonetheless, he also claimed on more than one occasion that Abyssinia was the worst issue for the League to make a stand on, given that the country was 'a backward slave-owning state not fit for inclusion in the League of Nations'.[135] The Hoare-Laval Pact was, he said, 'a shrewd, far seeing agreement'.[136]

In the Spanish Civil War, Churchill seemed to show equal disdain for both sides, though he was at times more scathing of the communist forces.[137] Indeed, at an early stage of the fighting he said: 'I am thankful the Spanish Nationalists are making progress ... better for the safety of all if the Communists are crushed.'[138] Furthermore, he was occasionally sympathetic to Japan, describing her in 1933 as 'an ancient State, with the highest state sense of national honour and patriotism' and a nation that was confronted by the 'dark menace of Soviet Russia'.[139]

As James has pointed out, Churchill had an obsessive concern with the German threat in Europe – rightly as it turned out – while his concern for the behaviour of other totalitarian regimes was more limited. Talking of German rearmament, he said, 'There is the dominant factor; there is the factor which dwarfs all others.'[140] If at times he condemned the excesses of Franco's Nationalists or Mussolini's conquests, he did so without the crusading spirit of his anti-Nazism. By not joining the ideological dots on the European map that linked Spain, Italy and Germany (and, in a wider sense, Japan) he failed to win over many fervent anti-fascists who found these regimes equally abhorrent.

In 1938 there was a small constellation of Conservative MPs willing to criticise the government, but they coalesced around the younger figure of Anthony Eden, who resigned as Foreign Secretary. There was little co-operation between Eden and Churchill, and no organised party-within-a-party existed within which their grievances could be expressed. The small band of anti-appeasers, while united in their opposition to appeasement, did not form a united campaign group and few, other than Bracken and Boothby, were loyal to Churchill. Chamberlain, by contrast, had a huge, obedient majority in the Commons made up of Conservative or National members elected to support the Prime Minister. Dissenters realised that they risked losing their seats at the next election unless they secured a change in policy or in government personnel.

In the aftermath of Munich, during the winter of 1938-9, Churchill faced his worst period of isolation. In November 1938 he voted against the government after it rejected a Liberal motion calling for the creation of a Ministry of Supply. This was a cause dear to his heart and one for which he had campaigned for several years. Churchill's attempt to lead a back-bench rebellion of fifty MPs failed, however, and only two other MPs, Brendan Bracken and

Harold Macmillan, joined him in the opposition lobby. Resolutions were passed in his Epping constituency condemning him for 'continued disloyalty' to his party, and in March 1939 he survived a determined campaign to have him deselected.

By April 1939 his position was far more secure. By then Hitler's troops had marched into Czechoslovakia, destroying the promises made at Munich six months earlier. When war broke out in September 1939, Churchill returned to government as First Lord of the Admiralty, ending his period of political isolation. In part, Churchill's rehabilitation came courtesy of his greatest foe, a dictator who proved that the wayward English genius had been right all along.

NOTES

1 Until 1858, the British East India Company had ruled much of India, excluding the native Princely States. Following the Indian mutiny in 1857, control of India was transferred to the British Crown, and the Raj (British rule) was to last until partition created the independent states of India and Pakistan in 1947.

2 There was a heavy death toll among Indian soldiers serving in Europe, while the 1918 influenza pandemic claimed the lives of nearly three million Indians. High inflation also contributed to lower living standards among Indians.

3 G. Smith, *Burying Caesar*, p.144.

4 J. Norwich, *The Duff Cooper Diaries*, p.133.

5 Speeches V, p.4985.

6 Ponting, *Churchill*, p.342.

7 Companion V (ii), p.567.

8 R.R. James (ed), *Memoirs of a Conservative*, p.384.

9 Speeches V, p.4956.

10 P. Addison, *Churchill*, p.135.

11 Speeches V, p.4969.

12 J. Colville, *The Fringes of Power*, p.563.

13 P. Addison, *Churchill*, p.137.

14 Speeches V, p.4936.

15 *Ibid.*, p.4927.

16 WSC Bio 5, p.618.

17 Speeches V, p.5045.

18 *Ibid*, pp.5025-32.

19 Companion V (ii), p.595.

20 Speeches V, p.4990.

21 Speeches V, p.5006.

22 M. Gilbert, *Churchill's Political Philosophy*, p.87.
23 D. Stafford, *Roosevelt and Churchill*, p.220.
24 WSC Bio 8, p.293. He was speaking after ferocious massacres in Calcutta and Bihar in 1946 had claimed over ten thousand lives.
25 M. Soames (ed), *Speaking for Themselves*, p.303.
26 Speeches IV, p.4126. For an interesting first-hand account of the meeting, see *Churchill's Bodyguard*, p.53.
27 M. Soames (ed), *Speaking for Themselves*, p.295.
28 *Ibid.*, p.297.
29 WSC Bio 5, p.227, note 1.
30 D. Carlton, *Churchill and the Soviet Union*, p.38.
31 WSC Bio 5, p.456-7.
32 *Ibid.*, p.662.
33 *Ibid.*, pp.670-1.
34 R. Lamb, *Mussolini and the British*, p.165.
35 *News of the World*, October 10th 1937.
36 The union between Germany and Austria, which was banned under the terms of the Treaty of Versailles.
37 J. Norwich, *The Duff Cooper Diaries*, p.241.
38 Companion V (iii), pp.34-5.
39 S. Williams, *The People's King*, p.112.
40 Companion V (iii), p.455.
41 *Ibid.*, p.458.
42 Blake/Louis, *Churchill*, p.192.
43 Companion V (iii), p.458.
44 R.R. James (ed), *Chips*, p.92.
45 WSC Bio 5, p.822.
46 Speeches VI, p.5822.
47 WSC Bio 5, p.826.
48 *Ibid.*, p.812.
49 C. Ponting, *Churchill*, p.383.
50 R.R. James (ed), *Memoirs of a Conservative*, p.415.
51 J. Charmley, *Churchill: The End of Glory*, p.317.
52 R.R. James (ed), *Chips*, p.60.
53 J. Norwich, *The Duff Cooper Diaries*, p.234.
54 See Lascelles, p.414 for an account of a conversation between Jock Colville and Churchill in which the latter said that he would never have accepted Wallis Simpson as Queen.
55 WSC Bio 5, p.51.
56 *Ibid.*, p.407.
57 Lukacs, *Churchill: Visionary, Statesman, Historian*, p.6.
58 Speeches V, pp.5199-200.
59 WSC Bio 5, p.410.
60 Speeches V, p.5263.
61 *Ibid.*, p.5292.
62 *Ibid.*, p.5297.
63 M. Gilbert, *Churchill's Political Philosophy*, p.93.
64 WSC Bio 5, p.448.

65 Speeches V, p.5263.
66 M. Gilbert, *The Wilderness Years*, p.111.
67 WSC Bio 5, p.681.
68 P. Addison, *Churchill*, p.140.
69 M. Gilbert, *Wilderness Years*, p.140.
70 WSC Bio 5, p.682.
71 W. Churchill, *Step by Step*, p.155.
72 Speeches V, p.5298.
73 *Ibid.*, p.5204.
74 Irredentism: a movement that claims ownership of territories because of their ethnic make-up or because of a claim to historical ownership.
75 J. Norwich, *The Duff Cooper Diaries*, p.270.
76 Speeches VI, p.6004.
77 *Ibid.*, p.6009.
78 *Ibid.*, p.6005.
79 M. Gilbert, *Churchill: A Life*, p.598.
80 Companion V (iii), p.812.
81 Speeches VI, p.6006.
82 Companion V (iii), p.1171.
83 W. Churchill, *Step by Step*, p.274.
84 Speeches VI, p.6008.
85 J. Lukacs, *The Duel*, p.23.
86 Speeches VI, p.6013.
87 Companion V (iii), pp.1171-3.
88 D. Reynolds, *In Command of History*, p.96.
89 Speeches VI, p.6003.
90 W. Churchill, *Step by Step*, p.329.
91 M. Gilbert, *Wilderness Years*, p.117.
92 Speeches VI, p.6011.
93 *Ibid.*, p.6003.
94 W. Churchill, *Step by Step*, p.269.
95 Speeches VI, p.6005.
96 *Ibid.*, p.6011.
97 *Ibid.*, p.5978.
98 WSC Bio 4, p.427.
99 Speeches V, p.5378.
100 W. Churchill, *Step by Step*, pp.2-3.
101 *Ibid.*, p.93.
102 *Ibid.*, p.129.
103 WSC Bio 5, p.567.
104 Speeches VI, p.5927.
105 J. Lukacs, *The Duel*, p.48.
106 J. Littman and C. Sandys, *We Shall Not Fail*, p.92.
107 T. Ben Moshe, *Churchill: Strategy and History*, p.101.
108 WSC Bio 5, p.452. Churchill was certainly not alone in his advocacy of an alliance. A number of influential policymakers recognised the Nazi threat from the outset and sought to counter it in similar ways, among them the Soviet commissar for foreign affairs, Maxim M. Litvinov, Robert

Vansittart, and a variety of French politicians including Herriot, Mandel and Reynauld.

109 Companion V (iii), p.375.

110 *Ibid.*, p.953.

111 The Maginot Line, named after French minister of war Andre Maginot, was a vast fortification on the Franco-German border that was designed to impede any future attack on French soil.

112 D. Cannadine and R. Quinault, *Churchill in the Twenty First Century*, p.136.

113 W. Churchill, *Step by Step*, pp.337-8.

114 Speeches V, p.5325.

115 On April 9th 1935 the British ambassador in Berlin announced that Germany had between 800 and 850 aeroplanes, giving them 55 per cent superiority over Britain's air defences and making a mockery of Baldwin's parity pledge.

116 Speeches V, p.5441.

117 The attack was carried out by the *Luftwaffe*'s Condor Legion and Italy's *Aviazione Legionaria* during the Spanish Civil War.

118 E. Ranson, *British Defence Policy and Appeasement Between the Wars*, p.24.

119 J. Lukacs, *The Duel*, p.63.

120 T. Ben Moshe, *Churchill: Strategy and History*, p.116.

121 Churchill shared the assumptions of many in Britain's military establishment.

122 M. Gilbert, *The Wilderness Years*, p.253.

123 Speeches VII, pp.7292-3.

124 M. Gilbert, *The Wilderness Years*, p.29.

125 G. Smith, *Burying Caesar*, p.164.

126 *Ibid.*, p.188.

127 *Ibid.*, p.212.

128 A.J.P. Taylor (ed), *Lloyd George: A Diary*, p.294.

129 G. Smith, *Burying Caesar.*, p.217.

130 M. Gilbert, *In Search of Churchill*, pp.112-13.

131 P. Addison, *Churchill*, p.134.

132 WSC Bio 5, p.826.

133 A pact between the British and French foreign sectaries, Samuel Hoare and Pierre Laval, which proposed to give Mussolini two thirds of Abyssinia in an effort to end the Italian-Abyssinian war. When details were leaked to the press there was widespread condemnation and Hoare and Laval were forced to resign.

134 Speeches VI, p.5684.

135 Companion V (iii), p.308.

136 Speeches VI, p.5747.

137 W. Churchill, *Step by Step*, pp.83-5.

138 M. Soames (ed), *Speaking for Themselves*, pp.415-16.

139 Speeches V, p.5220.

140 Robert Rhodes James, *Churchill: A Study in Failure*, pp.328-9.

CHAPTER SIX

Saviour of the Free World

THE YEAR 1940 was pivotal in British history as the country survived the threat of invasion and won the Battle of Britain against Nazi Germany. Before his 'finest hour', Churchill was in charge of his country's only active instrument of war, the navy. As First Lord of the Admiralty, he was able to announce a significant victory at the Battle of the River Plate, which involved the sinking of the German battle-ship *Graf Spee*. By all accounts, his leadership of this department was marked by vigour and determination, and his oratory helped to stir the nation. But the failure of the Norway campaign, which involved stopping the flow of iron ore from Norway to Germany, undermined Prime Minister Neville Chamberlain's authority.

After a stormy debate in the House of Commons, Chamberlain survived a vote of no confidence but saw his authority fatally weakened by a loss of Conservative support. He thus turned to his Foreign Secretary, Lord Halifax, to succeed him, but Halifax turned down the premiership, ostensibly because of constitutional difficulties but more likely because he knew he was not suited to wartime leadership. Instead, Churchill became Prime Minister on May 10th 1940, on the same day that the Germans invaded France and the Low Countries.

He immediately formed a coalition government with Labour and Liberal leaders and made himself Minister of Defence. But, despite accruing significant powers, he sought the approval of the War Cabinet and Chiefs of Staff for any major decisions. He never once overruled his Chiefs of Staff. Over the next few weeks he tried to rally despondent leaders in Paris but, when it became clear that the French had lost the battle, he ordered the evacuation of British (and later French) troops from Dunkirk. He also established the Special Operations Executive to stir subversion among the occupied peoples of Europe.

At the same time, he was confronted by a potential rebellion among his five-man War Cabinet. The Foreign Secretary, Lord

Halifax, suggested that the government explore the possibility of a compromise peace with Germany, given Britain's parlous military situation. Churchill rejected the notion out of hand and called for a continuation of the war. Eventually he won over his War Cabinet, but not before some stormy discussions. Following the death of Neville Chamberlain in November 1940, Churchill became leader of the Conservative Party.

With the French out of the war and Britain facing the prospect of Nazi invasion, Churchill rallied Parliament and the nation with a series of inspiring speeches. He promised 'blood, toil, tears and sweat' and declared that Britain would 'never surrender' to the forces of tyranny. His messages of hope and defiance helped galvanise the nation throughout the Battle of Britain and the Blitz that followed. But he was also aware that, with the Royal Navy in the ascendant, Britain's chances of withstanding invasion were favourable.

Churchill knew that, without help from the United States, Britain's chances of victory were thin. Throughout 1940 he did all he could to convince Roosevelt that Britain would fight on regardless, though he also emphasised the nightmare consequences of the Royal Navy being defeated by Germany. In July he ordered the destruction of the French fleet at Oran, to stop it from falling into German hands, an action that won him limited American military support in the form of fifty destroyers. But Britain and her empire would fight on alone until June 1941.

Why did Churchill become Prime Minister in May 1940?

CHURCHILL LIKED to think of his rise to power in 1940 as the unfolding of a historic destiny. Throughout his life he believed that a 'lucky star' hovered over him, sparing him from disaster and saving him for a moment of supreme national importance. When he became Prime Minister on May 10th 1940, the very day that Hitler's armies invaded Western Europe, it seemed that fate was simply playing its hand. For Lord Hailsham,[1] the sudden emergence of Churchill as Prime Minister at a time of dire national emergency was final proof of the existence of God.[2]

Rather disappointingly for posterity, Churchill's ascent to the 'top of the greasy pole' has a more prosaic explanation. While his pre-war stand on appeasement and his dynamism at the Admiralty earned him respect and credibility, it took backstairs political intrigue and the support of the Labour Party to ensure his accession to No. 10.

In many ways, Churchill was the obvious choice for the premiership. His warnings about Nazi Germany had proved remarkably prescient and, from the moment that Hitler tore the Munich Agreement to shreds by invading Czechoslovakia, few could reasonably question Churchill's judgement in foreign affairs. Not only were his views well known to the public through his newspaper articles but, from 1936, he was involved in non-partisan anti-Nazi organisations such as 'Freedom and Peace'. This enabled him carefully to court opinion in liberal and left-wing circles and emerge as a truly national figure. Later on, Churchill's national appeal would make it all but impossible for Chamberlain to sack him in the early months of the war.

By contrast, Chamberlain was indelibly associated with the Munich Agreement and 'peace for our time'. If Hitler had not violated the Munich Agreement, had merely confined himself to minor 'irrendentist' claims, Churchill would probably have languished on the back-benches while a triumphant Chamberlain basked in the role of peacemaker. Events were to prove otherwise.

During the war Churchill became an indispensable member of Neville Chamberlain's War Cabinet. From all accounts, he was a dynamic and vigourous First Lord of the Admiralty who was constantly buzzing with ideas of how to defeat the enemy. According to his secretary, Kathleen Hill, 'When Winston was at the Admiralty, the place was buzzing with atmosphere, with electricity.'[3] It helped that he was in charge of the only military instrument, the navy, that was actively engaging the Germans during the 'Phoney War'. He was able to report to the Commons on some Admiralty successes, most notably the scuttling of the battleship *Graf Spee*, the defeat of the 'magnetic mine' and the rescue of sailors from the *Altmark*.[4] This enabled him to be the main news spokesman for the war effort and the man who was single-handedly raising national morale. Harold Nicolson recalled the electrifying effect of a Churchill speech in September 1939:

> One could feel the spirits of the House rising with every word. It was quite obvious afterwards that the Prime Minister's inadequacy and lack of inspiration had been demonstrated even to his warmest

supporters. In those twenty minutes Churchill brought himself nearer the post of Prime Minister than he has ever been before.[5]

As a war minister in two world wars, Churchill had long advocated an offensive strategy which would produce an outright victory over Germany. Early in the war Leo Amery noted 'that the present War Cabinet was, with the exception of Winston himself, entirely devoid of the offensive fighting spirit'.[6]

In September 1939 Churchill sought to widen the war, calling for an alliance with Balkan countries in order to relieve the pressure on Britain and France. Halifax believed this would merely hand Hitler a series of cheap victories, but Churchill countered that, 'if Yugoslavia and Turkey joined us in hostilities with Germany', Germany would have no cheap victories.[7] Later he probed other ideas for offensive actions, such as the mining of the Ruhr and the bombing of German industrial targets. But he was overruled by colleagues who feared that attacks by the RAF would invite unwanted reprisal raids by the *Luftwaffe* on Britain's industrial centres. In general, Churchill believed in offensive warfare, even if it was 'three or four times as hard as passively enduring from day to day'.[8]

In contrast, Chamberlain eschewed the idea of offensive warfare. He believed that the economic blockade imposed by the Allies would severely weaken an already strained German economy. Time, Chamberlain argued, was on the side of the Allies; soon enough Germany would be forced to seek terms to end the war. Much to Churchill's intense frustration, Chamberlain remained wedded to this limited defensive strategy, hopeful that he could soon return to the grind of domestic issues. As Chamberlain wrote to his sister in 1939, 'How I hate and loathe this war. I was never meant to be a war minister.'[9] This reliance on defensive warfare was viewed by some as a passive and lethargic means of running the war. It was neatly encapsulated in Chamberlain's complacent comment that 'Hitler had missed the bus.'

But Hitler had very much caught the bus. In April 1940 German troops invaded Norway. By May Hitler was consolidating this military triumph and it became obvious that British and French troops would be powerless to dislodge them. Ironically Churchill had been in charge of sending the troops to Norway in the first place, as part of the Narvik expedition. The plan was to send an Allied force to aid the Finnish army in its struggle against the Russians, combining this with a blow against the transport of iron ore from northern Sweden to Germany. The expedition was a humiliating failure, but by May it was Chamberlain's direction of the war, not Churchill's naval failure, that became the focus of political discontent.

On May 7th and 8th 1940 Parliament met to discuss the war situation in what would become one of the 'classic parliamentary occasions of the twentieth century'.[10] Ostensibly the discussion focused on the Norwegian campaign but attention soon switched to the government's overall handling of the war. A number of back-bench groups were known to be dissatisfied with the government. One, the Watching Committee, had been set up by Lord Salisbury to monitor government activity and hold it accountable to back-bench opinion.

All the back-bench dissenters wanted a change in the handling of war, though many were unprepared to oust Chamberlain. Instead, some looked to an all-party coalition government, with Chamberlain at its head but with the removal of some unpopular ministers. Even those who wished to see Chamberlain resign had little thought of who might succeed him.[11]

During the course of the debate, Chamberlain suffered badly as former colleagues and serving officers united to criticise his handling of the war. Labour's Clement Attlee accused Chamberlain of not waging the war 'with sufficient energy, intensity, drive and resolution'. To win, Britain needed 'different people at the helm'. Sir Archibald Sinclair, for the Liberals, contrasted the 'complacent and ... ill founded boastings of ministers' with the 'hard, swift blows of the German forces'. These harsh blows might have been expected from political rivals, but far worse was to come from political allies. Admiral of the Fleet and Conservative MP Sir Roger Keyes stood up in naval uniform and launched an attack on the Norwegian naval disaster, describing the operation as 'a shocking story of ineptitude', but, far from blaming Churchill, who had had overall control of the operation, Keyes said that Britain was 'looking to him to help win the war'.[12]

The most dramatic intervention came from Leo Amery, one of Chamberlain's former ministerial colleagues. Quoting from Cromwell's address to the Long Parliament in 1653, he told Chamberlain: ' "You have sat too long here for any good you have been doing. Depart, I say, and let us have done with you. In the name of God, go!"' The speech electrified the House and encouraged the motley collection of party rebels and former anti-appeasers to defy the government. By the end of May 7th, Chamberlain's government was reeling, but events were to take an even more dramatic turn the next day.

On May 8th Herbert Morrison for Labour demanded a division in the House so that members could 'broadly indicate whether they are content with the conduct of affairs or whether they are apprehensive about the conduct of affairs.' For the government, this meant a vote of no confidence, which Chamberlain, rather complacently, accepted. The result was ostensibly a success for the government: 281 for and 200 against, but it was a hollow victory. The government's majority had been slashed from around two hundred to 81, with forty Conservatives voting against Chamberlain and some thirty more abstaining. It was clear that Chamberlain had been fatally weakened and a successor would have to be found. Was Churchill's lucky star inevitably leading him to the pinnacle of political glory?

The answer, surprising to posterity, is that, while Churchill might have been the public's choice for the succession, he was not the favoured choice of the establishment. The man on whom the political elite were pinning their hopes was the Foreign Secretary, Lord Halifax. Halifax was an intellectually capable man, highly experienced and knowledgeable, a friend of the royal family and a man of high religious scruples whose integrity was unquestioned. Though he was indelibly associated with appeasement, he had played a pivotal role in the Cabinet revolt against Hitler's Godesberg Memorandum, insisting that Chamberlain fight for better terms. Halifax was also widely respected by all parties in Parliament, as well as the House of Lords and Whitehall. The King was also prepared for a Halifax-led government: in his diary he had written, 'I thought H. was the obvious man.'[13]

Later that afternoon on May 9th, Churchill, Halifax, Chamberlain and Margesson, the Chief Whip, met in the Cabinet Room. In front of the only two candidates for the job, Chamberlain asked who he should advise the King to send for in the event of his resignation. This is Churchill's account:

> As I remained silent a very long pause ensued. It certainly seemed longer than the two minutes one observes at the commemoration of Armistice Day. Then at length Halifax spoke. He said that he felt

that his position as a Peer out of the House of Commons would make it very difficult for him to discharge his duties as Prime Minister in a war like this. He spoke for some minutes in this sense and by the time he had finished it was clear that the duty would fall upon me – had in fact fallen upon me.[14]

This account may not be accurate, given that the length of the silence is described differently in Halifax's diary account. What is certain is that Halifax had decided not to accept the top job. The most glittering prize in British politics was there for the taking – but Halifax turned it down. Historians have long speculated on the reasons for this spectacular self-denying ordinance. In his diary, Halifax wrote the following explanation:

> I had no doubt at all in my own mind that for me to take it would create a quite impossible position. Quite apart from Winston's qualities as compared with my own at this particular juncture, what would in fact be my position? Winston would be running defence, and in this connection one could not but remember how rapidly the position had become impossible between Asquith and Lloyd George, and I should have no access to the House of Commons. The inevitable result would be that being outside both these vital points of contact I should speedily become a more or less honorary Prime Minister, living in a kind of twilight just outside the things that really mattered.[15]

Certainly no peer had been Prime Minister since Lord Balfour in 1902, but the constitutional difficulties were not insurmountable.

Halifax, like Chamberlain, was simply not cut out to be a wartime Prime Minister. As his biographer says, 'He had no illusions whatever as to his suitability for the role which a Prime Minister would have to play at this desperate moment in history ... he was lacking in the drive and ruthlessness which the situation demanded.' More important-antly, 'he knew that Churchill was pre-eminent in both'.[16] Halifax preferred to play a role behind the scenes, where he could more effectively restrain Churchill's reckless urges.

But there was another obstacle Churchill would have to overcome if he were to succeed Chamberlain. By May 9th it was clear that a National Government was needed on the model of Lloyd George's wartime coalition. Chamberlain now asked Labour if they were will-ing to serve in a coalition government with him as leader. The option was put to Labour's National Executive Committee at their party

conference at Bournemouth and their decision the next day was that
they would serve in a coalition government but not under Chamberlain. They would serve under Halifax or another Conservative figure:
while they had a veto on Chamberlain, they were unable to exercise
a choice for the position of Prime Minister. With Halifax rejecting
the post, it was clear that Chamberlain would have to recommend
Churchill to the King. Later, on May 10th, Churchill arrived at Buckingham Palace to kiss hands with his monarch, having, quite literally,
become Prime Minister 'by default'.[17]

Nonetheless, Churchill's appointment has to be seen in a longer-
term view. His tremendous drive and resolution, his supreme skills as
an orator, his immense political experience and, above all, his sheer
thirst for leadership at a moment of supreme crisis combined to
make him the man for the hour. In at least one sense, there was only
one real contender for the top job in May 1940.

Did Churchill betray the French in 1940?

WHEN HE BECAME Prime Minister in May 1940, Churchill faced
two strategic decisions of monumental importance. The first was
whether to provide the French with additional British fighter
squadrons to bolster their air defences. The second was whether to
withdraw the British Expeditionary Force from France in the event
of a French military collapse. As he was an ardent Francophile,
Churchill's gut instincts were to help the French, Britain's pivotal ally,
in their hour of need, but rational calculation and logic dictated
otherwise. Painful decisions had to be made in the British national
interest. Contrary to the romantic stereotype of a belligerent leader
defying the odds to win the war, Churchill's strategy was logical and
shrewdly took into account Britain's own chances of survival.[18]

From the outset, Churchill accepted the consensus view that
France was an impregnable fortress which could be relied on to contain the German threat. 'Thank God for the French army,' he often
declared.[19] This partly explains why Britain sent only a token force
there in 1939. The French, together with military figures in Britain,
believed that they could contain the Germans as they had done in
the First World War. French commanders like Gamelin adopted a
defensive strategy based on the premise that the Germans would try
to outflank the French on the Maginot Line by invading the Low

Countries. To counter this threat, Gamelin sent the best units of the French army (and much of the BEF) to defend the north of the country.

However, an intelligence lapse forced on Hitler a slight revision of strategy. The new invasion plan called for a German attack through the heavily wooded Ardennes region. The German army would attack the weak Allied forces in the centre of France, then march north in order to trap and encircle the Allied army, before going on to capture Paris. At the same time, the Germans would attack Belgium and the Netherlands in order to draw Allied forces east-wards into the developing encirclement.

The plan worked to perfection. On May 10th 1940 Hitler's forces invaded France, Belgium, Holland and Luxembourg, ending a six-month period of 'phoney war'. Hitler planned to eliminate these Western European nations before turning eastwards and attacking the Soviet Union. In this way he would avoid the dreaded perils of a two-front war.

The Allies reacted to the invasion by sending their forces north to combat what they believed was an updated version of the Schlieffen Plan. This committed the Allied troops to moving north, diminishing their fighting power and mobility through loss of fuel.

By May 15th French Prime Minister Paul Reynaud told Churchill that his country was 'defeated' and had 'lost the battle'. In an attempt to console his French counterpart, Churchill flew to Paris on May 16th. He quickly saw the gravity of the situation when he observed French officials hastily destroying their archives and preparing to evacuate the capital. In a sombre meeting with General Gamelin, Churchill demanded to know the location of the French strategic reserve that had saved Paris in the First World War. Gamelin replied, 'Aucune' ('None'), an incredible admission which Churchill later described as one of the most shocking moments in his life. When he asked how Gamelin would counter the Germans, the Frenchman simply replied 'inferiority of numbers, inferiority of equipment, inferiority of methods'.[20]

Despite a spirit of defeatism in the French government, Reynauld begged Churchill to supply France with several air squadrons. Initially, Churchill was dubious about denuding 'the heart of the Empire', a sentiment that was echoed by Newall and by Hugh Dowding, the head of Fighter Command. Dowding argued that Britain would survive provided that no more fighters were removed from her own air defence. If more fighters were sent to France, they would scarcely influence the course of the battle there while leaving Britain in a vulnerable position.

On May 16th, after receiving a message that the Germans had breached the Maginot Line, Churchill agreed to the dispatch of four air squadrons, rather than the six or ten that had been requested. He accepted that, despite the 'grave risk', it was necessary to 'bolster up the French'.[21] After a further meeting with French politicians, Churchill and the War Cabinet authorised the dispatch of six further squadrons, but only for limited periods of time. Churchill would later describe this as 'the gravest decision that a British Cabinet had ever had to take'.[22] He had to balance the need for continued French participation in the war with Britain's own survival.

By May 19th the Germans had driven a narrow salient between the British and French armies and threatened to trap British forces against the coast. It soon became clear that there was little chance of the BEF linking up again with the French, making an evacuation of the army seem the only feasible option. On May 25th Churchill told the Defence Committee that the BEF would have to be evacuated from Dunkirk, though this decision initially was kept from the French. Fears were expressed that no more than a tiny fraction of the army would be rescued and even Churchill expressed hopes for the safe return of only fifty thousand men. But, by the end of Operation Dynamo, more than 338,000 men had been safely withdrawn, more than a hundred thousand of them French. Almost all of their heavy armour and weapons had been left behind in France.

Despite the withdrawal of British and French forces, France still clung on in the war against Germany. Throughout early June 1940 the French made repeated requests for increased British fighter support. With his ally on the verge of collapse, Churchill faced a stark choice over the level of help to provide. If too much hardware (specifically fighter aircraft) was committed to France and they were subsequently defeated, it could gravely threaten British prospects of survival. If Britain maintained her forces, she would at least have a chance of final victory and be able to restore France to independence later on. John Colville noted comments made by Pug Ismay on June 6th which reflected a sense of military realism: 'We should be insane to send them all our fighters because if they were lost the country would be beaten in two days, whereas even if France surrenders we shall still win the war – provided our air defences are intact.'[23]

Churchill was forced to agree, and he began to see the war in France as less pivotal for the survival of the Western Alliance.[24] Churchill informed Reynauld accordingly, pointing out that additional fighters would provide only temporary relief, whereas the survival of Britain's air force would prolong the war for both countries. In France, British fighters would be outnumbered and destroyed in greater proportion to German fighters, whereas Hitler would lose any aerial confrontation over Britain.

Churchill continued to do all he could to keep the French in the war. Even though military aid was now at an end, he pinned his hopes for bolstering the French on eventual US participation. He drafted a number of messages to Roosevelt, urging an American declaration of war to provide 'moral support' to the French. When Roosevelt was unable to offer such firm support, Churchill raised the spectre of the French fleet being added to those of Germany, Italy and Japan, causing a 'revolution' in naval terms which would be injurious to American interests. Churchill did not call for the dispatch of an expeditionary force but felt that a US declaration of war would at least have a 'tremendous moral effect' in France.[25] Churchill was to be disappointed by Roosevelt's reply, which fell far short of a declaration of war. Nonetheless his attempts to woo the American President revealed an indomitable resolve and firm sense of moral purpose.

The most bizarre attempt to maintain French participation in the war was the hastily conceived plan for Anglo-French union. The idea appears to have been mooted first by Rene Pleven, a member of the French economic mission to Britain. Pleven conceived of a political union between Britain and France, with the two governments acting as one and the two countries' armies fighting as one unit. Citizens of each country would have citizenship in the other. Despite his keenness to stiffen French resolve, Churchill was initially wary of such a monumental constitutional alteration. But by June 16th, with France on the verge of collapse, he was won over by de Gaulle's concept of 'an indissoluble union of the French and British peoples'.

On the evening of June 16th, armed with the War Cabinet's approved text of the Anglo-French union, Churchill set out for France in a last-ditch attempt to keep his ally in the war. But, as his train was about to depart from Waterloo station, he was told that the meeting could not go ahead. Within hours, Reynaud had resigned and been replaced by Marshal Petain,[26] whose government duly sought an armistice from Germany. From this time on, Britain would fight on in Europe alone.

Continuing recriminations that 'perfidious Albion' abandoned the French in June 1940 are usually exaggerated. Churchill was prepared to provide as much support for the French as Britain's own meagre resources allowed, so long as it appeared that France would continue fighting the Germans. This was an act of rational calculation on Churchill's part. So long as the French were engaged in the fight, they were giving Britain time to prepare for their own imminent showdown with Germany. Churchill could hardly abandon an ally that was holding out against the Nazi onslaught. But, when it appeared that the French had succumbed to despair and defeatism, Churchill had little choice but to prevent the release of any further hardware.[27]

The minutes of the June War Council meetings show Churchill proposing a number of options for helping the French, limited naturally by the constraints of war. Yet there was little sign of anything constructive from the French, Churchill's proposals being met by a continual 'No.' It seemed that the French were edging closer to a compromise peace and there was little Churchill could do to forestall this. An increasingly Anglophobic French cabinet showed little enthusiasm for Anglo-French unity, with only four cabinet members giving it their full approval.[28] Reynaud finally lost his nerve and, facing divided ministers who were unsure whether to continue the war, announced the resignation of his cabinet late on June 16th.

There are other factors that must be taken into account when considering France's catastrophic defeat. Firstly, the French made some severe tactical errors. Their confidence in the Maginot Line had created a defensive 'Maginot' mentality which the Germans skilfully exploited. They wrongly assumed that the Germans would be unable to send a mechanised army quickly through the Ardennes forest, and thus they failed to extend the Maginot fortresses to that region. When battle commenced, General Gamelin sent the best trained and equipped troops to the northern part of France early in the battle. These troops were subsequently encircled and lost much of their heavy equipment. The Germans also had a superior command system that allowed local commanders to take the initiative in battle.

Secondly, the morale of many units in the French army was poor, as Gamelin was to admit in his memoirs: 'The regrettable instances of looting of which our troops have been guilty at numerous points on the front offer manifest proof of ... this indiscipline.' He spoke of an 'every man for himself attitude' among French soldiers, adding that a failure to act dutifully had been exploited by the enemy.[29] According to Sir Henry Pownall, the French 1st Army, far from being let down, had 'no spirit to continue the fight'.[30] Further proof of low morale can be found in the simple fact that, by the end of July 1940, no more than seven thousand French troops had rallied to the cause of the Free French. Of those troops who were sent back to France, only a small number opted to continue the battle against Germany. The spirit of defeatism spread quickly to the upper echelons of government, with Reynauld believing that the conflict was lost after only five days of battle.

Certainly there were problems of indiscipline, looting and low morale in the British army for which Churchill cannot reasonably be blamed. But one must remember that nearly 140,000 French soldiers were brought back to England from Dunkirk, and many were re-embarked to ports in western France so that they could continue the fight. Churchill established the principle that British and French soldiers should share available shipping even if this meant reducing the number of British fighting men who could be saved.

In retrospect, Churchill offered the French as much help as he could, consistent with upholding the British national interest. But he was also convinced that, if France fell, the war against Hitler could be carried on from Britain. As he told his Cabinet colleagues in June 1940: 'One thing was certain. If this country were defeated, the war would be lost for France no less than for ourselves, whereas, provided we were strong ourselves, we could win the war, and, in so doing, restore France to her position.'[31]

Did Churchill seek a compromise peace with the Nazis in 1940?

IN THE LAST WEEK of May 1940 a series of extraordinary meetings took place in London that helped to decide Britain's role in the Second World War. At centre stage were two of the titans of British politics, the Prime Minister Winston Churchill and his Foreign Secretary, Lord Halifax. Their discussions turned on whether Britain would continue fighting Germany or settle for a compromise peace to be negotiated by Mussolini. Had Churchill lost the argument to Halifax, the implications would have been immense, affecting Britain and the wider world for years to come.

During May 1940, the German army achieved a series of swift and devastating victories against Holland and Belgium, and their army looked set to defeat France. The imminent defeat of the French army, an institution regarded as 'the one firm rock on which everybody had been willing to build for the last two years', was an unmitigated strategic disaster. It appeared that the BEF would be encircled by the German army, and plans had already been drawn up to have them evacuated from northern France. With Germany controlling Western Europe and the channel ports, the threat of a German invasion loomed menacingly.

The military situation at home was also far from encouraging. By 1942, Britain was projected to have an army of fifty-five divisions of British and imperial troops, but this was no match for the mighty German army which had already established a dominant position in Central and Eastern Europe. In May 1940 Britain had to rely on French forces to hold the Germans back; in the event of a French collapse, she would need the assistance of the United States. But in May 1940, there was precious little sign of an imminent American entry into the war.

Furthermore, Britain's financial position appeared parlous. In February 1940 the Cabinet was told that, if all saleable British overseas assets were commandeered and sold at market value and one third of Britain's gold reserves sold as well, Britain would run up a balance of payments deficit of £250 million. The best prediction was that Britain's full gold and dollar reserves would last until February 1942, after which the British would have to buy goods from America. This option would lead to national bankruptcy.

This perilous situation formed the background to the first of a series of meetings of the War Cabinet in late May 1940. The discussion on May 26th centred on an Italian offer to mediate peace talks between Britain and Germany. Halifax, spurred on by an increasingly worried Reynauld, was in favour of exploring peace talks using the Italians as intermediaries. He felt at the very least that the Cabinet should inquire into Germany's peace terms and judge whether they safeguarded Britain's independence and military strength.

Churchill's initial response suggests that he was not unequivocally opposed to Halifax. He replied that 'he would be thankful to get out of our present difficulties on such terms provided we retained the essentials and the elements of our vital strength even at the cost of cession of territory.' According to Neville Chamberlain, Churchill had said that 'if we could get out of this jam by giving up Malta and Gibraltar and some African colonies, he would jump at it.'[32] However Churchill also believed that it was highly unlikely that Hitler would offer such terms and that it was crucial to show the German leader that 'he couldn't beat us'. Furthermore, he argued, such talks would undermine British resolve and lead to humiliating terms which would be hard to reject.

On May 27th, Halifax again raised the issue of negotiations, calling for the Cabinet to discover the terms that the Allies would be offered. Chamberlain, Lord President of the Council, appeared to back Halifax, saying that the French would be disappointed if 'we had been unwilling even to allow them the chance of negotiations with Italy'. Again, Churchill did not dismiss the idea out of hand, replying that, 'If Herr Hitler was prepared to make peace on the terms of the restoration of German colonies and the overlordship of Central Europe, that was one thing', though, once again, 'it was quite unlikely that he would make any such offer'. As a result, Churchill suggested 'that under no conditions would we contemplate any course except fighting to a finish'.[33]

Churchill warned Halifax that peace negotiations involved a slippery slope. The longer that peace terms were dangled before British eyes, the more likely that her resolve would be eroded. He thought that it was better to continue fighting for another few months and judge the military position in the future. Crucially for Churchill, the terms Hitler would offer would be no harsher if Britain suffered a military defeat than if she sought terms in May. This is one of the fundamental differences between the positions of these two statesmen. While Halifax believed that Britain would get better terms before France went out of the war, Churchill thought that the chances of 'decent terms' being offered to Britain 'were a thousand to one against'.[34]

Later, on May 28th, Churchill decided to settle the issue once and for all. He summoned the ministers in his Cabinet who were not part of the War Cabinet and told them that, whatever the fate of the BEF, Britain would fight on regardless. According to the recollections of Hugh Dalton, Churchill ended a peroration to the Cabinet with the following words: 'We shall go on and we shall fight it out, here or elsewhere, and if at the last the long story is to end, it were better it should end, not through surrender, but only when we are rolling senseless on the ground.'[35] He received a resounding ovation from those present.

For some historians, including revisionists like Clive Ponting, Churchill's conversations with Halifax provide evidence that, away from the public gaze, the war leader was not the indomitable figure of romantic legend. They point to the fact that he was objecting, not to negotiations per se, but to the terms that would be offered by the enemy. The implication is that, if the terms on offer had been more favourable, Churchill would have agreed to peace talks with the Nazis. Though less critical than Ponting, Reynolds argues that Churchill 'expressed acceptance, in principle, of the idea of an eventual negotiated settlement, on terms guaranteeing the independence of the British Isles'.[36]

But Churchill's apparent flexibility during the stormy War Cabinet debates does not necessarily imply that he was open to appeasing Hitler. To understand why, one has to appreciate the vulnerability of his political position in the first few weeks of his prime ministership.

In 1940 the majority of the Conservative Party would have preferred Halifax to succeed Chamberlain. According to the Chairman of the 1922 Committee, three quarters of back-benchers wanted Chamberlain back as Prime Minister soon after his dismissal.[37] Many Tories also privately distrusted Churchill, the man who had switched from Tory to Liberal and then back again to Tory. He was widely viewed by them as an unstable political adventurer, a man responsible for military blunders such as Gallipoli and Narvik and the figure who had repeatedly defied his own party over India, abdication and appeasement.

On May 13th Churchill delivered his first speech to the Commons as Prime Minister, where he promised 'blood, toil, tears and sweat'. His oration received cheers from the Labour back-benchers but was met with silence from the Tories. In the words of Henry Channon, 'he was not well received'.[38] When Chamberlain appeared, Tory MPs cheered and waved their order papers. Churchill sensed his vulnerability, which explains why he wrote to Neville Chamberlain shortly after becoming Prime Minister: 'I trust that I shall succeed ... To a very large extent I am in your hands.'[39] Until his death in November 1940, Chamberlain remained leader of the Conservative Party while Halifax was kept on as Foreign Secretary. This simply reflected the Conservatives' dominance of Parliament and the government.

Churchill knew that he could not afford a rupture between himself and these powerful figures. Their sudden resignation would have threatened the integrity of his government and sent shock waves through Parliament. Even the withdrawal of Halifax would have led MPs to question Churchill's judgement at a very early stage of his prime ministership. When he condemned the terms of a compromise peace rather than negotiations per se, it is likely he was trying to let Halifax down gently while winning Chamberlain over to his side. He could certainly not afford to isolate either man. As Smith puts it, 'Keeping them on board was the price that had to be paid in return for their giving him the legitimacy he needed with which to govern – a parliamentary majority.'[40]

Far from seeking to appease Hitler if only the price was right, he was half appeasing the appeasers out of sheer political necessity. When Churchill told Chamberlain on May 10th, having just been appointed Prime Minister, 'I am in your hands,' he was reflecting on his own political vulnerability. This vulnerability also explains why he refused to sack Rab Butler, one of Chamberlain's leading acolytes. By contrast, when Churchill told his wife on the night he became PM that 'only one man can turn me out and that is Hitler', he was offering a misleading account of the political situation.[41]

The revisionist argument ignores the fact that Churchill had rejected any notion of a compromise peace earlier in the war. During early September 1939 he had learnt of a conversation between Britain's ambassador in Rome, Sir Percy Loraine, and Count Ciano, the Italian foreign minister. Loraine had suggested that a German-Polish peace treaty might be enough to end the state of hostilities between Germany and Britain, given that it was the ostensible *casus belli* on September 3rd. Writing to Lord Halifax, Churchill declared that he intended 'to see the war through to a victorious end, whatever happens to Poland' and questioned whether Loraine could be 'rallied to a more robust mood'.[42]

Several weeks later he again dismissed suggestions of acquiescing in a Nazi peace offensive. 'It would seem our duty and policy', he told the Cabinet, 'to agree to nothing that will help [Hitler] out of his troubles.'[43] He believed that German peace offers were unlikely to be genuine and were merely aimed at causing division among British leaders.[44]

In similar vein, Churchill dismissed the suggestion made by the Australian High Commissioner, Stanley Bruce, for a peace settlement with Hitler with one word, 'Rot.'[45] On October 6th 1939 Hitler proposed a negotiated peace with Britain and France on condition that Germany's territorial domination of Central and Eastern Europe be recognised. Churchill's response was that no such offer should be accepted until Germany had paid reparation to the peoples that Hitler had 'wrongfully conquered'.[46]

The rationality of fighting on

It is frequently assumed that Churchill's decision to fight on in 1940 resulted from gut instinct and sentimentality rather than intellectual deliberation. In popular stereotype, Churchill bravely defied the odds to keep Britain in the war, despite the overwhelming likelihood of defeat at the hands of the Axis powers. Yet the notion that Churchill's war leadership was based on blind pugnacity is a romantic legend which overlooks his capacity for shrewdness and political calcultion. In May 1940 Churchill genuinely had grounds for thinking that Britain would survive, making his rejection of a compromise peace genuine, consistent and, above all, rational.

On May 19th the British Chiefs of Staff produced a document, 'British Strategy in a Certain Eventuality', which outlined a worst-case scenario for the immediate future. It involved Italian entry into the war, Axis control of Europe, a direct attack on the United Kingdom and the widening of the war to Egypt. The crux of the matter, they said, was 'air superiority' and how well Britain's personnel and civil population stood up to mass bombing. The Chiefs crucially argued that morale would be maintained and that it would 'counterbalance the numerical and material advantages Germany enjoys'.[47]

Churchill accepted that, if Britain were to survive in 1940, the RAF would be paramount, a factor that influenced his decision to limit the air commitment to France in June 1940. Behind the air force lay the supreme power of the Royal Navy, the only force capable of preventing a German overnight invasion of the British mainland. Derek Robinson has argued, in *Invasion, 1940*, that it was the deterrent power of the navy which finished off Operation Sealion[48] more than the RAF's victory. He writes: 'The RAF had proved that Nazi Germany was not invincible. Fighter Command had denied victory to the *Luftwaffe*. For that, it deserved all praise.

But it was also praised for what it could not do: preventing an invasion by sea – and that tribute belongs to the Royal Navy.'[49]

This is not to deny that the RAF played a key role in reversing the tide of Nazi fortunes in 1940; it is to acknowledge a counterfactual truth: that any invasion by sea would have been (and could only have been) repelled by the navy. With all the military options at his disposal, Churchill had pragmatic reasons for continuing the fight against Nazi Germany in the summer of 1940. Indeed, later in life he admitted this very fact to the historian Rowse. When asked whether Britain could have been invaded in 1940, he replied: 'No... We should have put everything into it: the whole of the Navy and Air Force. They couldn't have got across.' Rowse added: 'And he made the gesture familiar to us at the time, of their swimming in the Channel in vain.'[50]

Churchill also realised that any negotiated peace with Hitler would not have been in Britain's long-term political interests. To leave Hitler in control of Central and Eastern Europe unopposed would have violated a cardinal principle of British foreign policy, namely to ensure a balance of power by opposing a hegemonistic Continental power. Any peace deal would also have given Hitler effective carte blanche to attack Russia earlier than June 1941, bringing Operation Barbarossa forward by some months. Given the narrow margin between victory and defeat in that actual campaign, it is conceivable that Hitler might have emerged triumphant against Stalin, given the additional breathing space.

With Hitler being such an unreliable guarantor of British survival, a wartime British government would have existed in a permanent state of insecurity, entailing high defence expenditure, constant vigilance and extensive rearmament. Late in life Churchill articulated this very argument. According to the memoirs of his private secretary Anthony Montague-Brown, Churchill believed that, under any peace agreement, Britain 'would have been a German client state', adding, 'there's not much in that'.[51] For Churchill it was a matter of honour as well as national interest to fight on against Nazi Germany.

Why did Churchill order an attack on the French fleet in July 1940?

ONE ISSUE that caused British naval commanders tremendous anxiety in 1940 was the prospect of the mighty French navy being captured by Nazi Germany in the event of a French defeat. Admiral Darlan, Commander of the French fleet, had assured Churchill on June 12th that his country would never surrender her navy to Germany. For Darlan such an action was 'contrary to [French] naval tradition and honour'.[52] On June 16th Halifax told the French government that Britain would respect a French armistice on condition that her fleet was ordered to sail to British ports. The French did not agree to this request but made a promise that their ships would be scuttled rather than surrendered, a condition that Churchill accepted.

On June 16th 1940 the French signed an armistice agreement with Germany. The terms of the armistice confirmed Churchill's worst fears, for Article 8 stipulated that French warships were to be collected from various ports and 'disarmed under German or Italian control', with additional ships outside French territorial waters being 'recalled to France'. Among the ships to be handed over were the *Richelieu*, regarded as the most powerful battleship in the world at the time, and two enormous battle cruisers, the *Dunkerque* and the *Strasbourg*. These last two battleships were part of a powerful squadron based at the port of Mers-el-Kébir in French-controlled Algeria and under the control of Marshal Marcel Gensoul. Other vessels in the French fleet were at anchor in Portsmouth, Plymouth and Alexandria, out of reach of the enemy.

Churchill knew very well that an enlarged German navy, strengthened by the addition of these French super-weapons, would pose tremendous risks for British shipping. Convoys could be sunk, depleting the UK of vital food supplies and further reducing American confidence in the country's survival prospects. It was a direct challenge to British naval supremacy.

Darlan had given orders to the fleet to 'fight to a finish', appearing to honour his pledge to Churchill. The opinion of British naval liaison officers in North Africa was that the French would honour their agreement not to surrender the fleet and that any attempt to seize or destroy the French ships would be futile. However, Churchill could not be sure of this and warned that the situation was so 'vital to the safety of the whole British Empire' that the government 'could not afford to rely on the word of Admiral Darlan'.53

Churchill was further disturbed by an intelligence report which suggested that French crews in all the North African ports were suffering from declining morale and might withdraw from the battle ahead. The report ended with this alarming statement: 'Though diminishing minorities may wish to continue the struggle, it seems clear that senior officers will no longer do so.'54 The Chiefs of Staff drew the conclusion that the Germans would seek to use the French ships against Britain at the earliest opportunity.

Within this context, *Operation Catapult* was drawn up. French naval vessels would be seized or forcibly disarmed if the French had not surrendered them to Britain by July 3rd 1940. British Admiral James Somerville, based in Gibraltar, was told to deliver an ultimatum to Marcel Gensoul offering four choices. Firstly, the French ships could sail to Britain and continue fighting against the Germans. Secondly, they could sail with a reduced crew to a British port prior to the sailors being repatriated. Thirdly, the ships could sail with a reduced crew (to be later repatriated) but to a French port in the West Indies where the ships could be demilitarised. Fourthly, the French could sink their own ships. The ultimatum ended with a chilling warning: 'Finally, failing the above, I have the orders from His Majesty's Government to use whatever force may be necessary to prevent your ships from falling into German or Italian hands.'

On July 1st Admiral Somerville expressed doubts about the operation, stressing that the use of force 'should be avoided at all costs' in order not to alienate the French nation. The Admiralty, however, stood firm, insisting that, if Gensoul did not accept the conditions, the ships had to be destroyed.

But Darlan and the French Admiralty instructed the admiral on July 3rd to pay no attention to the British demands. This made a confrontation between the French and British fleets inevitable. At 5.55 pm on July 3rd, several French ships were attacked. The *Bretagne* sank with the loss of nearly a thousand men, while the *Dunkerque* and the *Provence* were badly damaged. The *Strasbourg* escaped and, several days later, the *Richelieu* was put out of action at Dakar. The French ships docked at Portsmouth had already been taken over without bloodshed on July 3rd, while a French submarine was also seized.

More than 1,250 French sailors lost their lives in the initial attacks at Mers el Kebir.

Richard Lamb has taken issue with Churchill's decision to sink the fleet at Oran. Lamb interpreted Clause 8 of the armistice to indicate that Hitler never intended to capture the fleet and that the word 'control' meant the same as in the control of a 'passport'.[55] But this is to trust in Hitler's good intentions and believe he was likely to honour an agreement, in contrast to all his behaviour until that date. But trust was in short measure in 1940, in regard to the German leader's intentions and also the French. The French government had already sent back to Germany four hundred captured German pilots, even though Reynauld had promised that they would be sent to Britain. Churchill regarded this breach of trust as 'particularly odious'.[56]

Given that intelligence reports suggested declining morale among French sailors, the Chiefs of Staff believed that they could 'no longer place any faith in French assurances', including that their ships would be rendered 'unserviceable' before reaching a French 'metropolitan port'. Lamb's statement that 'Darlan's orders to sink the ships rather than allow the Germans or Italians to seize them would always have been carried out' is therefore unconvincing.

While questions remain about the timing and morality of the Oran attacks, there is little dispute about their domestic and international repercussions. Churchill's ruthlessness in attacking a former ally demonstrated to the Americans the British determination to crush Nazism. As Derek Robinson put it, 'Americans discovered a fearlessness and a ferocity in Britain that dissolved all those stories of a nation on its knees, helpless before a looming invader.'[57] President Roosevelt had privately feared that Britain would surrender her fleet to the Germans in the event of defeat.[58]

For Churchill this international support was decisive. As he later recalled in a conversation with Montague-Brown, the attack 'spelled out to the world our determination to fight on *at whatever cost*'.[59] But domestic opinion was also critical for Churchill. The day after the attack at Mers el Kebir he gave a lengthy and moving speech in the House of Commons explaining his decision on July 3rd. From all accounts, the speech was tremendously received with an unprecedented outburst of cheering for the new Prime Minister. According to Harold Nicolson, the 'grand finale' received an 'ovation' which moved Churchill to tears.[60]

This was the first unanimous parliamentary approval Churchill had received. In his memoirs he wrote: 'Up till this moment the Conservative party had treated me with some reserve, and it was from the Labour benches that I received the warmest welcome when I entered the House or rose on serious occasions. But now all joined in solemn stentorian accord.'[61]

The attack on the French fleet was a vital turning point in Britain's international position during the Second World War. The ruthless but necessary action enhanced Churchill's domestic standing and revealed to the world, above all the United States, that Britain would fight on alone, 'whatever the cost'.

Did Churchill sacrifice Coventry during the Blitz?

ON NOVEMBER 14th 1940, German bombers struck at the heart of Coventry. During a raid code-named Operation Moonlight Sonata, more than sixty thousand buildings were destroyed or damaged and at least 380 civilians perished.[62] Coventry's historic cathedral was also struck, causing extensive damage. The city was selected because its armaments factories and industrial infrastructure were used to supply the British army and the RAF.[63] Without doubt, the raid was one of the most devastating episodes of the entire Blitz: a historic city crushed beneath the weight of German bombs.

The bombing has led to one of the most enduring and pernicious wartime myths, namely that, having discovered that Coventry was a target, Churchill did nothing to prevent an attack so as not to compromise British intelligence. In 1974 Group Captain Winterbotham was the first to make this startling claim in his book *The Ultra Secret*. Winterbotham wrote that the Coventry raid had been known about beforehand, owing to an inadvertent coup by Ultra, Britain's most important source of intelligence. However, Winterbotham claimed that Churchill decided against evacuating the city in order not to compromise Ultra, Britain's prize intelligence asset.

The claim was reiterated in *Bodyguard of Lies*, where Anthony Cave Brown wrote that Churchill and his advisers received at least forty-eight hours' warning of the raid and decided against an evacuation. Far from condemning the Prime Minister, both authors contended that he made the right decision. Faced with the agonising

choice of saving hundreds of civilians or protecting Britain's intelligence sources, they argued that it was better to do the latter. Most
recently a play by Alan Pollock, *One Night in November*, resurrected
the Coventry bombing myth in dramatic form. Risking the wrath of
'Churchill apologists', Pollock said: 'My strong feeling is that when
[Churchill] knew the target was Coventry, he made a spur-of-the-
minute decision that Coventry was expendable.'[64]

But the central assertion in these books and in the play was almost
certainly wrong. The evidence suggests that Churchill was never
faced with the stark choice of allowing Coventry to be destroyed or
compromising British intelligence.

In fact some intelligence did suggest that Coventry would be
targeted, but it was so vague as to be of little use to policy planners.
It came from the Directorate of Air Intelligence at the Air Ministry,
which at the time was collecting information about the *Luftwaffe's*
future raids.[65] On November 11th they decoded a message about an
impending raid which went under the code-name 'Moonlight Sonata'.
The decrypt specifically mentioned that Marshal Goering was
involved, an indication that it was a high-profile assault by the *Luftwaffe*. Also mentioned was a strange word, 'Corn', which was short
for Coventry, though this was not appreciated at the time. It was
assumed that the urban targets would be in the south of England, and
that London in particular would be hit.

At the same time, interrogators at the Air Ministry summarised a
conversation between a German POW and an *agent provocateur*, an
anti-Nazi German who had masqueraded as a fellow prisoner of war.
The German prisoner had mentioned that a massive raid was being
planned by the *Luftwaffe* for November 15th-20th and that the
target was Coventry, Birmingham or Wolverhampton. Reflecting on
the conversation, the AI memo said that the source of the information had to be 'treated with reserve' as he was 'untried', and that the
probable target for the attack was London or the Home Counties.
Quite understandably, no one connected Moonlight Sonata with this
new revelation.

For this reason, Air Intelligence planned on the assumption that
the forthcoming raid would indeed be on London. On November
14th Churchill was told that the likely targets were 'Central London,
Greater London, the area bounded by Farnborough-Maidenhead-
Reading and the area bounded by Rochester-Favisham-Isle of
Sheppey.'[66] The memo added that, if further information suggested

Coventry or Birmingham as the target, the information would hopefully be got out in time.

However, it became clear on November 14th that the *Luftwaffe* would target Coventry. Since October 1940 the Air Ministry had been intercepting a German technical system known as *Knickebein* which was being used to guide its pilots. It involved sending out a continuous dot-dash signal along a narrow beam which was designed to create a radio path for pilots to follow in the dark. When the RAF followed the navigational path of the beam, they were able to discover the *Luftwaffe*'s intended targets. They could then set to work jamming the beams so that they could be deflected, allowing any subsequent air raid to affect a much less heavily populated area. On November 14th beams were intercepted which indicated that the intended target was Coventry. The RAF's jammers set to work to counter the beams and were confident that no populated area would be hit. Sadly the wrong frequency was mistakenly given out and the beams were not subsequently deflected.[67]

In a letter to *The Times*, John Martin, one of Churchill's private secretaries, helped to dispel the myth that Churchill had foreknowledge of the raid. Martin recalled Churchill's movements on November 14th:

> In the late afternoon of the 14th we set out from No. 10 for Ditchley. Just before starting from the garden gate I handed the Prime Minister a box with a top secret message. A few minutes later he opened this and read the contents – which I subsequently understood were a report that the German 'beam' seemed to indicate a raid on London ... he immediately called to the driver to return to Downing Street.[68]

After sending his two young secretaries to a nearby underground shelter, Churchill went to the Air Ministry roof and waited there for the bombers which, of course, never came. Churchill fully expected the capital to come under attack and prepared himself accordingly, only to find that the target was deep in the Midlands.

'We were sold down the river,' says a character in the play *One Night in November*, implying that there was a terrible conspiracy behind the destruction of Coventry. Indeed there was, except that the conspiracy was hatched by Adolf Hitler and the *Luftwaffe*, not by Winston Churchill.

Was Churchill a reactionary
on the Home Front?

BETWEEN 1940 and 1945, Churchill's government was granted the most far-reaching extension of state powers in modern British history. Using emergency legislation, the government was able to intern people without trial, restrict freedom of speech, commandeer property – in fact exercise a draconian control over life, liberty and property. John Lukacs wrote of Churchill: 'He was a "dictator" in the ancient, original, Roman meaning of the word: a man entrusted with very great powers at a time of a great national emergency.'[69] Of course, the conditions of total war made this necessary and the Prime Minister was not slow to appreciate the extraordinary range of his powers. However, the image of Churchill as an unquestioning and unrepentant reactionary needs to be challenged.

In some respects, Churchill's behaviour did reveal a reactionary streak that appeared to be on a par with his crackdown on militant labour. On several occasions he was inflamed by media criticism that he believed would undermine civilian morale. When both the *Sunday Pictorial* and the *Daily Mirror* criticised the failure of the Dakar expedition in September 1940, Churchill suggested that they should be suppressed. He argued that the stance of both papers went beyond simple 'disgruntlement' as they were attempting 'to bring about a situation in which the country would be ready for a surrender peace'. The *Mirror*, he argued, was pursuing 'fifth column' tactics. However, he was dissuaded by his Cabinet colleagues from taking any such course.[70]

Owing to the left-wing bias of many of its writers and publicists, Churchill also denounced the BBC as 'an enemy within the gate'. He had been upset when, during the summer of 1940, J.B. Priestley had talked of post-war aims in some of his radio addresses and he even wrote to his Minister of Information, Duff Cooper, to ask if he had any control over Priestley's broadcasts.

During 1941 Churchill prevented the BBC from playing the *Internationale* for fear that it might rouse support for communist principles. He was forced to change this policy the following year due to Soviet intervention in the war effort. In 1942 Churchill's wrath was aroused by a cartoon by Philip Zec that appeared in the *Daily Mirror*, showing a shipwrecked seaman clinging to some wreckage in the water; above it appeared the caption: 'The price of petrol has been increased by one penny.' The message was that, in view of the increased dangers to seaman who were supplying the nation with petrol, there was a need to cut back on consumption. However, Churchill interpreted the cartoon as a subversive attack on profiteering and asked MI5 to investigate Zec. He even suggested closing the *Mirror* and conscripting its proprietor, but on this occasion, as on others, he was overruled by Cabinet colleagues.[71]

The cinema was another medium that received Churchill's highly critical attention. Early in the war he tried to prevent the release of the film *Ships with Wings* on the grounds that it would cause alarm and despondency. In the end he delegated the decision to Sir Dudley Pound, the First Sea Lord, who saw no reason to block its release. Churchill was similarly unhappy with *Next of Kin*, an Ealing production from 1942. The film was designed to show how careless talk was inadvertently helping the enemy and causing greater loss of life on military operations. In the film's opening sequence, a commando raid is carried out on a submarine base in Brittany. The raid's success is tempered by the fact that the Allies suffer an unexpectedly large number of casualties as a result of the enemy's eavesdropping on informal conversations in England. Churchill was unhappy with the depiction of army casualties, but his objections were assuaged after some prudent cuts were made.[72]

In 1942 Powell and Pressburger's unreleased film *The Life and Death of Colonel Blimp* came under scrutiny. This production traced the progress of a soldier from a responsible young recruit to an old-fashioned, rather incompetent 'Blimp' figure. Even though he came across as a rather lovable character, the film was seen as an attack on army life and Churchill sought to stop 'this foolish production' which he felt would be 'detrimental to the morale of the army.'[73] Fortunately for posterity, Churchill's objections did not prove decisive.

If these examples run counter to the idea of Churchill as a democrat, two points should be borne in mind. Firstly, he never imposed full-blown censorship of the cinema, unlike his counterparts in Germany and Russia. Secondly, his objections were part of a desperate attempt to maintain civilian morale during a difficult stage of the war. In 1942 the Battle of the Atlantic was raging and the Allied triumvirate could not be certain about the ultimate direction of the war. One thing that would have badly undermined the war effort was a downswing in the public mood and a lowering of morale.

Churchill is also well known for ordering the internment of thousands of foreign citizens during the early stages of the war. Following the German invasion of Holland on May 10th, which took British intelligence by surprise, he was alerted to the possibility that, during the attack, German agents and sympathisers had helped the Nazi attackers. There were widespread but unfounded rumours that a similar fifth column was operating in Britain and that it would actively assist an invasion attempt. In Cabinet Churchill called for 'a very large round-up of enemy aliens and suspect persons', arguing that, 'Internment would probably be much safer for all German speaking persons themselves'.[74] Among those considered for internment were 'British fascists' and communists. Then, on June 10th, following Italy's declaration of war, Churchill issued his famous 'Collar the lot' instruction.[75]

Churchill also told the Ministry of Information to launch a campaign against the spreading of false rumours. From July 1940 the 'Silent Column' was launched, involving a campaign by press and poster to silence rumour-mongers. The public became acquainted with 'Miss Leaky Mouth', 'Mr. Knowall' and 'Mr. Glumpot', all of whom were seen as a danger to morale. The public were instructed to report rumour-mongers to the police as a last resort, and some individuals were duly prosecuted for lowering morale and spreading despondency.[76] Unsurprisingly, many viewed this campaign as highly patronising and it was soon abandoned.

These examples aside, Churchill generally believed that national morale was best sustained by minimising interventions on the Home Front. In this he was influenced by a strong streak of libertarianism. While First Lord of the Admiralty in 1939, he had strenuously opposed the introduction of food rationing and other 'negative restrictions', arguing that the country would prefer 'positive action.'[77] He thought that public opinion was becoming 'critical of governmental control and interference with liberty of the individual'.[78]

Even when rationing was introduced, Churchill was positively irked by it. Writing to the Minister of Food, Lord Woolton, in July 1940, he wrote: 'The way to lose the war is to try to force the British public into a diet of milk, oatmeal, potatoes etc., washed down on gala occasions with a little lime juice.'[79] He argued that it was wrong to restrict the consumption of luxury foods in hotels. His reasoning revealed a contempt for bureaucratic restrictions: 'Is it worse for the country for a man to eat a little of three or four courses of food, daintily cooked out of scraps, or a good solid plate of roast beef? Is it more patriotic to avoid luxury by having the food, whatever it is, badly cooked? Is it wrong to eat up the luxury foods which are already in the country, or ought they to be wasted?' Churchill's concern was not just to buttress the stomachs of the rich. In the same letter he suggested that the army consume more fresh meat in order to 'liberate more frozen meat for the benefit of the poorer class of manual workers'.[80]

For Woolton, Churchill was 'benevolently hostile to everything that involved people not being fed like fighting cocks'.[81] Later in the war, Churchill would deprecate examples of 'silly bureaucracy', such as when he came across the case of a householder who had been fined one pound and two guineas costs for borrowing coal from a neighbour. He considered such cases to be 'typical of a vast amount of silly wrong doing by small officials and committees'.[82]

Despite his early enthusiasm for interning enemy 'aliens', Churchill came to regret this measure. Even when approving measures that were designed to intern enemy aliens, giving his own justification that this would place them out of harm's way, he argued that the government would have to assess individual cases and 'release those who were found to be well disposed to this country'.[83]

However, some 27,000 mostly innocent enemy aliens had been interned by July 1940. Many were fervent anti-Nazis. Following the sinking of the *Arandora Star*, which was carrying 1,200 German and Italian internees bound for Canada, there was a public outcry, forcing Churchill to order a retreat. In August 1940 he told two members of the Coldstream Guards how much he disliked the suspension of *habeas corpus*, and later in the war condemned as 'in the highest degree odious' the attempt by the executive to cast a man in jail without legal charge or a jury trial.[84] In a newspaper article published later in the war, Churchill again rejected the notion of keeping people in prison without trial as 'a frightful thing to anyone concerned about British liberties'.[85]

It is certainly instructive to compare the attitudes of Churchill and Roosevelt over this issue. While Churchill came to regret the suspension of *habeas corpus* as 'odious' and totalitarian, there was no such contrition from his American counterpart. In February 1942 Roosevelt signed Executive Order 9066 which led to the forcible relocation of 120,000 Japanese people (most were US citizens) living on the West Coast. They lost their homes, farms and livelihoods.

The policy remained in force until December 1944 and Roosevelt at no time expressed regret over this wholesale violation of civil liberties.[86]

Did an actor deliver some of Churchill's 1940 speeches?

MOST PEOPLE who idolise Churchill remember his stirring speeches and fighting rhetoric in 1940. In his first speech to Parliament on May 13th, he promised the nation 'blood, toil, tears and sweat'. His most famous peroration, on June 4th 1940, ended with a message of defiance and determination: 'We shall fight on the beaches, we shall fight on the landing grounds, we shall fight in the fields and in the streets, we shall fight in the hills, we shall never surrender.'

Later, on June 18th, he predicted that, 'if the British Commonwealth and its Empire last for a thousand years, men will still say, "This was our finest hour."' Churchill's soaring oratory galvanised a beleaguered nation at one of the defining moments in its history. Not only were his words uplifting but his voice also had a resonant quality that echoed throughout the free world. But were some of these magnificent orations delivered, not by Churchill, but by an actor?

This was the claim made by David Irving in his 1987 book, *Churchill's War*: that during the war an actor had agreed to mimic the Prime Minister before the microphone and read the iconic speeches mentioned above, thus duping the entire British nation. The actor in question was Norman Shelley, best known for his work on the BBC's *Children's Hour*. This allegation subsequently appeared in Clive Ponting's revisionist work, *1940: Myth and Reality*. Ponting wrote: 'the BBC asked Churchill to repeat [his June 4th speech] as a broadcast to the nation. Churchill refused and instead the BBC used an actor, Norman Shelley ... to imitate Churchill's voice while pretending to the public that it was Churchill speaking.'[87]

In an article in *Atlantic Online*, polemicist Christopher Hitchens wrote that Shelley 'ventriloquised Churchill for history and fooled millions of listeners', and added, 'Perhaps Churchill was too much incapacitated by drink to deliver the speeches himself.'[88] The allegation that Shelley was substituted for Churchill is also made by historian James Hayward, in a book that rather ironically sets out to expose the Second World War's 'myths and legends'.[89]

Under serious scrutiny, however, these allegations lack credibility. Firstly, Irving claimed to have interviewed Shelley in 1981, but the actor had actually died the year before. Secondly, the Dunkirk speech of June 4th ('We shall fight on the beaches'), which Churchill originally delivered in the House of Commons, was not broadcast on radio later that day, either by Churchill or by an actor. Instead, a BBC news reader read out selected extracts from the speech to the public. Later, some years after the war, Churchill made a recording of the speech at Chartwell.

Next, we have evidence that it *was* Churchill who read the 'finest hour' speech to the nation. On June 20th the Ministry of Information managed to persuade a reluctant and exhausted Prime Minister to deliver the oration on the wireless. According to Junior Minister Harold Nicolson, 'When we bullied him into speaking ... he just sulked and read his House of Commons speech over again.'[90] Churchill's trusted Private Secretary, John Colville, wrote this in his diaries: 'At 9.00 the P.M. spoke on the wireless, almost word for word what he had said in the House. It was too long and he sounded tired.'[91] Though they disliked the way it sounded on the wireless, we at least have first-hand evidence that it was Churchill who delivered the speech.

In 2000 Alexander Cockburn reported in *The Observer* that Shelley's son had found a 78rpm BBC recording dated September 7th 1942 and said that he had proof that some of Churchill's famous wartime radio speeches had been delivered by a stand-in performer. The Shelley recording, however, was not from 1940; it concerned events in North Africa in 1942 or 1943. Crucially, it did not relate to any events in Churchill's and Britain's finest hour.

As for the Dunkirk speech of June 4th, there is some evidence that Shelley did record the speech, but not in 1940, and not to the British public. According to Stephen Bungay, 'Churchill was asked by the British Council later in the war to make a recording for the US, and having rather a lot on his plate, he suggested they use an actor instead. Shelley did the recording, Churchill heard it, was much amused and gave his approval ... there is no evidence of its having been used in Britain.'[92] Further evidence supporting this claim comes from the testimony of Alexander Shelley, Norman's son, who said that, 'at the height of the war the British Council had asked his father to impersonate Churchill for broadcasts in America ... He did it secretly for Winston, who was his great hero.'[93]

Clearly it is possible that Shelley impersonated Churchill's voice during the war for a non-English audience, but there is no proof that he broadcast the iconic speeches of 1940 in Britain. In the absence of credible evidence, this allegation should be laid to rest.

NOTES

1 Quintin Hogg (1907-2001). Hogg was a judge and Tory politician, serving under Harold Macmillan in two ministries and as Lord Chancellor under Edward Heath.
2 A. Roberts, *Secrets of Leadership*, p.36.
3 *War Papers 1*, p.100.
4 G. Smith, *Burying Caesar*, p.392.
5 N. Nicolson (ed), *Harold Nicolson: Diaries and Letters, 1939-45 11*, p.37.
6 *War Papers 1*, p.30.
7 *Ibid.*, p.131.
8 *Ibid.*, p.493.
9 G. Smith, *Burying Caesar*, p.387.
10 P. Hennessey, *Never Again*, p.17.
11 G. Smith, *Burying Caesar*, p.407.
12 A. Roberts, *Secrets of Leadership*, pp.76-7.
13 *War Papers 1*, p.1282.
14 W. Churchill, *History of the Second World War 1*, p.524.
15 *War Papers 1*, p.1260.
16 Blake/Louis, *Churchill*, p.266.
17 G. Smith, *Burying Caesar*, p.421.
18 See R. Lamb, *Churchill: War Leader Right or Wrong*, p.46, and Lawlor, *Churchill and the Politics of War*, pp.50-1.
19 Speeches V, p.5236.
20 W. Churchill, *History of the Second World War 2*, pp.42-4.
21 *War Papers 2*, p.62.
22 *Ibid.*, p.66.
23 J. Colville, *The Fringes of Power*, p.150.
24 WSC Bio 6, pp.482-3.
25 *War Papers 2*, p.341.
26 Petain had been the hero of Verdun: his generalship had saved the French army at a vital time in 1916. His reputation was sullied when he became the leader of Vichy France.
27 S. Lawlor, *Churchill and the Politics of War*, pp.50-1.
28 J. Lukacs, *The Duel*, p.129.
29 J. Hayward (ed), *Myths and Legends of WW2*, p.161.
30 WSC Bio 6, p.431.
31 *War Papers 2*, p.269.

32 C. Ponting, *1940: Myth and Reality*, p.107.
33 R. Jenkins, *Churchill*, pp.605-6.
34 *Ibid.*, p.607.
35 *Ibid.*, p.608.
36 David Reynolds, 'Churchill and the British decision to fight on in 1940', *Diplomacy and Intelligence During the Second World War*, pp.15-16.
37 G. Smith, *Burying Caesar*, p.427.
38 R.R. James (ed), *Chips*, p.252.
39 K. Jeffreys, *Finest and Darkest Hours*, p.19.
40 G. Smith, *Burying Caesar*, p.421.
41 Lord Moran, *Churchill: The Struggle for Survival*, p.347.
42 *War Papers 1*, pp.64-5.
43 *Ibid.*, p.149.
44 *Ibid.*, p.208.
45 WSC Bio 6, p.436.
46 *War Papers 1*, p.226. There is evidence that many people in Britain desired a negotiated compromise peace with Germany (see Lamb, *War Leader*, pp.17-18). This makes Churchill's rallying of the nation later in 1940 that much more remarkable and important an achievement.
47 R. Callahan, *Retreat from Empire*, p.83.
48 The name given to Germany's plan to invade the UK in 1940.
49 D. Smith, *Invasion, 1940*, p.268.
50 Alfred Rowse, *Memories of Men and Women*, p.8.
51 A. Montague-Brown, *Long Sunset*, p.200.
52 WSC Bio 6, p.520.
53 *War Papers 2*, p.395.
54 WSC Bio 6, p.628.
55 R. Lamb, *Churchill as War Leader*, p.67.
56 Speeches VI, p.6242.
57 D. Robertson, *Invasion, 1940*, p.92.
58 In a conversation with Lord Lothian, Roosevelt had spelt out the imperative need to forcibly seize the French ships rather than let them fall into German hands (Gilbert 6, p.635, par 2).
59 A. Montague-Brown, *Long Sunset*, p.160.
60 N. Nicolson (ed), *Harold Nicolson: Diaries and Letters, 1939-45 II*, p.97.
61 W. Churchill, *The History of the Second World War 2*, p.211.
62 Dear, I. (ed), *The Oxford Companion to World War II*, p.213.
63 Among the companies were Dunlop, Hawker Siddeley, Vickers Armstrong, Armstrong Whitworth and Rolls-Royce.
64 Lyn Gardner, 'The ultimate sacrifice', *Guardian*, March 4th 2008.
65 N. West, *Unreliable Witness*, p.24.
66 *Ibid.*, pp.28-9.
67 Dear, I. (ed), *The Oxford Companion to World War II*, p.213.
68 J. Martin, *Downing Street: The War Years*, p.33.
69 J. Lukacs, *The Duel*, p.164.
70 P. Addison, *Churchill on the Home Front*, p.344.
71 S. Hylton, *Their Darkest Hour*, p.147.
72 M. Balcon, *A Lifetime of Films*, p.135.

73 N. Rattigan, *This is England*, p.223.

74 *War Papers 2*, p.40.

75 There was an outcry from Parliament at the policy of mass internment and internees were gradually released from August 1940 onwards. By the summer of 1941 only five thousand internees remained in detention.

76 S. Hylton, *Their Darkest Hour*, p.140.

77 WSC Bio 6, p.47.

78 *War Papers 1*, p.306.

79 *War Papers 2*, p.514.

80 P. Addison, *Churchill on the Home Front*, p.339.

81 *Ibid.*, p.340.

82 WSC Bio 7, p.780.

83 *War Papers 2*, p.286.

84 D. Stafford, *Churchill and Secret Service*, p.212.

85 D. Stafford, *Roosevelt and Churchill*, p.145.

86 *Ibid.*, p.148.

87 C. Ponting, *1940: Myth and Reality*, p.158.

88 C. Hitchens, 'The Medals of his Defeats', *Atlantic Online,* April 2002.

89 S. Hayward, *Churchill on Leadership*, p.10.

90 N. Nicolson (ed), *Harold Nicolson: Diaries and Letters, 1939-45 II*, pp.93-4.

91 J. Colville, *Fringes of Power*, p.165.

92 'Leading Churchill myths', *Finest Hour* (112), Autumn 2001.

93 Vanessa Thorpe, 'Finest hour for actor who was Churchill's radio voice', *Observer*, Sunday October 29th 2000.

CHAPTER SEVEN

Towards Triumph and Tragedy

THE YEAR 1941 was to be one of mixed fortunes for Churchill. General Wavell achieved success against Italian forces in North Africa and, by February, British troops had advanced five hundred miles and captured 130,000 prisoners. At the same time British forces under General Cunningham successfully attacked Mussolini's troops in Italian Somaliland, helping to bring to an end the dictator's dream of an African Empire. But, instead of consolidating Britain's position in North Africa, the government sent troops to Greece to help defend against a German invasion.

While the decision to help Greece was motivated by political considerations, it was not (as Churchill feared) the wisest strategic move. Rommel's panzers immediately attacked Egypt, undermining the gains that had been achieved by Britain in the previous few months. German troops then attacked Greece in April 1941, forcing the British and New Zealand forces to withdraw to Crete. But Crete itself fell to the Germans after paratroopers launched an effective airborne assault, causing yet more humiliation.

In June 1941 Germany carried out its long-planned invasion of the Soviet Union in Operation Barbarossa. Six months later the Japanese attacked the US Pacific Fleet at Pearl Harbor, triggering a German declaration of war against the United States. With America and the Soviet Union at war with Germany, Britain was now the junior member of a global tripartite alliance.

In 1942 Churchill and Roosevelt made a major decision to adopt a 'Germany first' strategy. This meant that both countries agreed to concentrate on the defeat of Germany, the most powerful of the Axis nations, before dealing with Japan. However, the American and British Chiefs of Staff were divided on strategy, the Americans calling for an early cross-Channel invasion and their British counterparts arguing that this was not logistically feasible. The British strategists won the day and it was decided to delay the invasion of Europe until at least the following year. As an alternative theatre of war was needed, Operation Torch was duly planned, involving an Anglo-American landing in North Africa.

In the spring of 1942 the global situation looked bleak for the Allies. Germany was in control of much of Europe, with her forces advancing towards oil-rich Baku and Stalingrad. German U-boats were inflicting damage on British merchant shipping in the Battle of the Atlantic, while Japan was busy demolishing Britain's Far East Empire, threatening Australia and India. The Middle East's oil reserves lay at the mercy of the Axis powers. But this was also a war of racial genocide. In January 1942 Nazi leaders and officials met at Wannsee in Berlin to execute the Final Solution, a systematic attempt to eliminate European Jewry through industrialised mass murder. By 1945, the Nazis had murdered six million Jews.

Before Torch was launched, the humiliating military defeats continued with the fall of Tobruk (in Libya) in June 1942. Churchill had to face two votes of confidence in his leadership, and Britain's former ambassador to Russia, Sir Stafford Cripps, emerged as his main rival for power. In the end, Montgomery's victory at El Alamein ensured that the Prime Minister's job was safe for the rest of the war.

Operation Torch commenced in November 1942 when Anglo-American forces landed along the coastline of Vichy-controlled Morocco and Algeria. Despite meeting initial resistance, the Allies were able to advance rapidly, thanks in part to skilful diplomatic initiatives with Vichy French leaders. At the same time, the Russians were launching their counter-offensive against the German army at Stalingrad, while the Japanese had already suffered a serious naval defeat at the Battle of Midway, losing all four of their aircraft carriers. Thus, by the end of 1942, the Allies were 'turning the tide' against the Axis powers.

At the beginning of 1943 Churchill met Roosevelt at the Casablanca Conference, where they made decisions of far-reaching importance. The two war leaders decided that, after defeating German troops in Tunisia, there should be an Anglo-American invasion of Sicily, followed by an invasion of Italy. In Churchill's words, the Allies would be attacking southern Europe via its 'soft underbelly'. Roosevelt also insisted that the Allies should seek the 'unconditional surrender' of the enemy. By May 1943 German troops had lost in Tunisia, and in July British and American forces invaded Sicily in Operation Husky. Later that month Mussolini was dismissed by

Victor Emmanuel and put under house arrest. He was rescued later by German forces and became the ruler of a puppet fascist state under German command. With the Germans in control of Italy, it would take the Allies until June 1944 to capture Rome.

In November 1943 the three Allied leaders, Churchill, Roosevelt and Stalin, met at the Teheran Conference. Here they took the decision to invade mainland Europe the following year in what became known as Operation Overlord. As the American military contingent predominated, it was natural that an American Commander-in-Chief should be appointed. General Dwight D. Eisenhower was the man selected for the task. The invasion of Europe began on June 6th 1944, with Churchill fearing a protracted bloodbath along the lines of First World War battles. In the event, British and American casualties were kept low, partly due to the Allies' massive aerial superiority but also because of an elaborate deception that persuaded Hitler to expect the main invasion in the Pas de Calais. Within a month of the Normandy landings, one million Allied troops had landed in France, facing 400,000 German soldiers.

Events were to move swiftly on the Eastern Front too. Having driven German troops from Russian soil, Stalin now went on the offensive. In the summer of 1944 Russian troops advanced across Poland and Romania, and the whole of Eastern Europe lay at the mercy of the Red Army. It was with fears of future Soviet domination that Churchill travelled to Moscow in October 1944 to agree spheres of influence with Stalin. In return for recognising Russian control in the Balkans, Churchill asked Stalin not to interfere in Greece, where a power struggle was soon to rage between royalists and communists. Stalin duly signed up to this 'percentages agreement'.

Despite facing stiff opposition from the occupying German army, the end of the war was in sight. Paris was liberated in August 1944 and Belgium the following month. In a final desperate gamble, Hitler's forces attacked the Allies in the Ardennes at the Battle of the Bulge in December 1944. After six weeks of heavy fighting, the Allies prevailed, inflicting a hundred thousand deaths on the *Wehrmacht*. The Allies met at Yalta in the Crimea, where they agreed to administer Germany (and Berlin) jointly, and allow the Russians a sphere of influence in Eastern Europe. They also decided to put on trial Nazi war criminals who had administered Hitler's Final Solution.

By April 1945 the Allies had swept through Germany and forces from East and West linked up on the Elbe on the 25th. Five days later

Hitler committed suicide in his bunker, and within a week the Germans had surrendered in Europe. On May 8th 1945 (VE Day) Churchill proclaimed that, in Britain's history, there had 'never been a greater day than this'.

How 'special' was the Churchill-Roosevelt partnership before Pearl Harbor?

CHURCHILL COINED the term 'special relationship' in 1946 to describe the closeness of Anglo-American relations during and after the war. It has since become a standard part of the international political lexicon. The term was also retrospectively applied to the Churchill-Roosevelt wartime relationship which lasted for nearly four years. During this time, the two men created a victorious alliance against the forces of German, Italian and Japanese militarism. They felt a shared abomination for fascism, while both saw their war against Hitler as a crusade against evil. They exchanged a vast number of telegrams during the war years and met on eleven separate occasions in different parts of the globe. As author Joseph Lash put it, this was truly a 'partnership to save the West'.

Underpinning this relationship was a genuine sense of mutual affection. As Elizabeth Nel, one of Churchill's private secretaries, put it, 'the sympathy and understanding, the knowledge of a common aim, which existed between these two leaders was a great force sustaining them both'.[1] Churchill declared: 'I felt the utmost confidence in his upright, inspiring character and outlook, and a personal regard – affection I must say – for him beyond my power to express today.'[2] Naturally the men clashed on many issues: the British Empire, the future of India and Stalin's intentions in Europe to name just three. That this relationship was maintained despite these fierce ideological disagreements is testament to their character.

But much of what we think we know about their wartime relationship comes from Churchill's war memoirs, which are, in their author's own words, a 'contribution to history'. In truth, there is still a great deal of romantic mythology attached to the Churchill-Roosevelt relationship which detracts from the notion of a 'special relationship'. This is especially so in the years 1939-41.

At different times in the 1930s Churchill had called for closer ties between America and Britain. During a lecture tour of the country in 1932 Churchill told an audience in New York that both England and America had 'the same outlook and no common discords', and that both should be 'the strong nucleus at the council board of the nations'.3 He took to Roosevelt after the latter won the 1932 election, and also expressed support for the New Deal, calling it the 'greatest crusade of modern times'.4 When he entertained James Roosevelt, the President's son at Chartwell in 1933, Churchill said that his greatest wish was to be a British Prime Minister working closely with the American President. 'There is', he said, 'nothing that we could not do if we were together.'5 On a more personal level, he admired the way that the President coped with his physical infirmity.6

During the Munich crisis of 1938 he again welcomed the idea of Anglo-American collaboration. He wrote that, 'These two great kindred powers, in collaboration, could prevent – or at least localise and limit – almost any quarrel that might break out among men.' He continued in the same vein: 'Collaboration of the English-speaking peoples threatens no one. It might safeguard all.'7 But Churchill was also aware of the strength of isolationist sentiment in America. He wisely counselled European leaders not to 'count upon the armed assistance of the United States even if his country were the victim of unprovoked aggression'.8

This lukewarm and rather skeptical view of American intentions was carried over into 1940. Churchill knew that many politicians, mostly Republican, did not share Roosevelt's Anglophile tendencies, while some groups, like America First, were positively hostile to ending isolationism. Roosevelt had already promised the American people, a week after Poland was invaded, that the nation would be kept 'on a peace basis'.9 To make matters worse, 1940 was an American election year. Nonetheless, Roosevelt did possess a powerful ideological distaste for totalitarian government and understood the threat that Nazism posed to American security. Perhaps sensing this, Churchill wrote to Roosevelt on May 15th 1940 with a special appeal for direct military aid. Britain, he said, would fight on regardless and, if necessary, alone; but without some material assistance from the United States, Roosevelt could 'have a completely subjugated Nazified Europe established with astonishing swiftness'.10

To remedy this, Churchill requested the loan of forty old destroyers, as well as hundreds of aircraft and anti-aircraft equipment. Roosevelt vetoed the request for the loan of destroyers, claiming that it would require authorisation from Congress. Privately, Roosevelt doubted whether Britain would survive beyond 1940. He was playing out his own nightmare scenario, whereby a defeated Britain was forced to surrender to Germany its vast navy, including any loaned US destroyers; a new super-navy, under German control, could threaten America's own safety.[11] It was precisely this fear that Churchill sought to exploit.

Having failed in his first request, Churchill now appealed to American self-interest directly. While promising that he 'would fight on to the end in this island', his administration would likely fall if matters went 'adversely'. If that were the case, a new administration, in an attempt to secure the best terms it could, might have to use Britain's 'sole remaining bargaining counter', namely the British fleet. He continued: 'If this country was left by the United States to its fate, no one would have the right to blame those then responsible if they made the best terms they could for the surviving inhabitants.'[12] In other words, a defeated 'Quisling' administration, starved of the weapons Churchill was requesting, might be forced to surrender the navy to Germany in order to secure the best deal for the country's inhabitants, something that would augment the enemy's strength.

Churchill was playing on American concerns about a 'super-enemy fleet', consisting of the combined navies of Germany, Japan and Britain, which would seek hegemonic control of the Atlantic. According to the Mackenzie King diaries, 'The President ... was doubtful if England would be able to bear up under attack' and was aware that Britain's bargaining chip was 'the turning over of the fleet to the Germans'. He went on: 'The President wanted me to line up the dominions to bring concerted pressure to bear on England not to yield to making of any soft peace even though it might mean destruction of England...'[13] Naturally, with the Americans so unsure of Britain's chances of survival, it was unlikely that additional weapons would be shipped across the Atlantic where they might eventually fall into German hands. Thus by early June Churchill was forced to concede that 'no practical help [had] been forthcoming from the United States as yet'.[14]

However, some help was forthcoming. In June 1940 Roosevelt authorised the dispatch of 900 field guns, 80,000 machine guns and half a million surplus rifles manufactured in the First World War. Churchill would later describe these sales as 'a supreme act of faith and leadership' by the United States. But they should be seen through the prism of national self-interest, not blind altruism. When

Roosevelt supplied Britain and France with ammunition, his aim was to make those countries America's shield. Though America was not actively engaged in the conflict, she was at least attacking the enemy by proxy. Nonetheless, and to Churchill's chagrin, Roosevelt rejected the second appeal for destroyers on June 4th.

Further disappointment was in store when Roosevelt refused to declare publicly that America would enter the war on the side of France. Churchill hoped that such a positive message would boost French morale and persuade their flagging leaders not to contemplate any separate peace with Hitler. The American refusal hit Churchill hard and even led him to fear that the US would 'issue an appeal to all belligerent governments to call the war off'.[15]

Roosevelt still held out on the loan of destroyers, and continued to worry about the consequences of a British defeat. Eventually, and after receiving more upbeat assessments of Britain's ability to survive, Roosevelt agreed to lend the ships, but this was scarcely an act of political altruism.[16] In return for 99 fairly poor quality destroyers, Roosevelt secured the use of British bases in Newfoundland and the Caribbean for a 99-year period. The Americans had driven a hard bargain.

On August 22nd 1940 the Chancellor of the Exchequer, Sir Kingsley Wood, gave Churchill a stark assessment of Britain's perilous financial situation. He told him that, since the beginning of 1940, Britain's gold reserves had been falling dramatically and predicted that her remaining reserves would last only for another three or four months. After this time Britain would quite simply no longer be able to continue the war by her own efforts and would have either to settle for a compromise peace or rely on open-ended American assistance. Naturally such assistance would be given on American terms and some fairly unpalatable ideas were discussed.

The Chancellor suggested requisitioning wedding rings, while others argued that the gold reserves in parts of the empire could be seized to pay for war material. Churchill even considered offering the whole of British industry to the United States in return for their continual supply of arms and raw materials. Privately the Prime Minister did not hide his disappointment with the Americans, telling some guests at Chequers that they were 'very good in applauding the valiant deeds done by others'.[17]

On December 8th Churchill composed a telegram to Roosevelt (which he later decided not to send) in uncompromising terms, explaining Britain's precarious financial position. In it he wrote: 'The moment approaches when we shall no longer be able to pay cash for shipping and other supplies.' At that moment Britain faced a bill for over $1 billion and had just over half that amount in gold and US dollar balances. The telegram ended: 'I believe you will agree that it would be wrong in principle and mutually disadvantageous in effect if at the height of this struggle Great Britain were to be divested of all saleable assets, so that after the victory was won with our blood, civilisation saved, and the time gained for the United States to be fully armed against all eventualities, we should stand stripped to the bone.'[18]

The reason the telegram was not sent was the announcement of what came to be known as the 'Lend-Lease Program'. The Lend-Lease Act permitted the President of the United States to 'sell, transfer title to, exchange, lease, lend, or otherwise dispose of, to any such government whose defense the President deems vital to the defense of the United States'. Using Lend-Lease, the United States was about to aid all its Second World War allies with war materials, including tanks, airplanes, trucks and food. Without this vital assistance, Britain could not long have continued in the war. But altruism it was not. The Americans insisted on some form of repayment after the war, leading Churchill to say in exasperation that 'we are not only to be skinned, but flayed to the bone'.[19] Lend-Lease incorporated an element of self-interest in another important way too. As long as Britain was holding off the Nazi enemy, it would provide more time for the Americans to complete their own rearmament programme.

In February 1941 Churchill called on President Roosevelt to provide material assistance so that Germany could be defeated. In a moving oration he declared: 'We shall not fail or falter; we shall not weaken or tire. Neither the sudden shock of battle, nor the long drawn trials or vigilance and exertion will wear us down. Give us the tools, and we will finish the job.'[20] The President had set out his stall by describing America as the 'arsenal of democracy', and he was as good as his word. In February one million rifles and fifty million rounds of ammunition made their way to Britain, and in the following month Congress passed the Lend-Lease Act.

The Americans also promised a merchant shipbuilding programme from 1942 which would help to replace Britain's crippling losses in the Battle of the Atlantic. To help further, Roosevelt told Churchill that America's security zone and patrol areas would be extended eastwards so that the Americans could inform Britain of enemy planes and ships. Later in 1941, Roosevelt announced a significant increase in tank production, which would allow the Americans to arm Britain more effectively for the months ahead.

While Churchill was grateful for this vital assistance, he was aware that it fell short of the one thing he really craved – America's entry into the war. At different times in 1941, Churchill appealed directly to Roosevelt to issue a firm declaration of war. One such appeal followed the German invasion of Greece in April 1941. He predicted grave consequences were Egypt to fall under Axis control, warning that it would 'seriously increase the hazards of the Atlantic and the Pacific'. Furthermore, if the Axis were to control great swathes of Europe, Asia and Africa, then any war against such a mighty agglomeration would be 'a hard, long, and bleak proposition'.[21] Roosevelt chose not to respond to this plea.

However, the prospects of American military co-operation brightened somewhat in 1941. In June Roosevelt sent over engineers and mechanics to Egypt to service American military equipment in the Middle East. In the same month he froze all German and Italian assets in the United States and sent American troops to Iceland to help the British garrison there. On September 11th Roosevelt announced that any German or Italian war vessels that entered the American protected Atlantic zone would 'do so at their own peril'. In addition, after June 1941, when Germany invaded the Soviet Union, the United States supplied a vast array of munitions and materials to Stalin.

But the most significant moment in the US-UK relationship prior to Pearl Harbor was the signing of the Atlantic Charter in August 1941. Churchill and Roosevelt met on August 9th in Placentia Bay in Newfoundland. During their first talk, Churchill handed Roosevelt a draft declaration which had been discussed by the British Cabinet. The document contemplated 'a world at peace after the final destruction of the Nazi tyranny' and pledged 'an effective international organisation' giving nations security 'within their own boundaries ... without fear of lawless assault'. The key point was that Britain and the United States would seek 'no aggrandisement' from the war and that there would be no territorial changes that did not accord 'with the freely expressed wishes of the peoples concerned'. They would also 'respect the right of all peoples to choose the form of government under which they will live.'

For Churchill, the staunch imperialist, this last commitment did not include the indigenous population in India, or other parts of the British Empire. Another clause, calling for free trade and unhindered access to the markets of the world, was effectively nullified by the phrase 'with due respect for existing obligations', which took account of British-imposed imperial tariff barriers.

To posterity, this event has signalled a dramatic escalation of American intervention in the war. Churchill told the crew of the *Prince of Wales* that a 'surer hope of final and speedy victory' had been obtained following the conference. However, in a press conference after the meeting, Roosevelt described his meeting with Churchill as an opportunity for 'an exchange of views' and emphatically denied that the United States was a step closer to war. The Chiefs of Staff assessment was that their American counterparts were 'thinking in terms of the defence of the western hemisphere', with no formulation of a 'joint strategy for the defeat of Germany'.[22]

In truth, despite the growing American contribution, both in terms of military supplies to the Allies and the Atlantic convoys, there was no sign of an imminent declaration of war on Germany. As Churchill candidly revealed to his son in a letter, 'one is deeply perplexed to know how the deadlock is to be broken and the United States brought boldly and honourably into the war'.[23] That deadlock would be broken, not by Churchillian sentiment or appeals to a common moral cause, but by Germany's declaration of war on the United States in the days following Pearl Harbor.

The story of the Anglo-American relationship in the first two years of war is hidden beneath a cloak of romantic mythology. The sentimentalists hide the fact that, until July 1940, there was a spirit of defeatism in Washington. Roosevelt seemed more interested in safeguarding American interests at Britain's expense than providing material assistance. Even when much-needed support was given, as with Lend-Lease, it reflected not altruism but American self-interest. Roosevelt was buying valuable time for the United States before its probable clash with Germany. However, 1941 saw a powerful increase in American military and economic assistance. Here, Churchill's obduracy in winning concessions from the President merits praise. When he became Prime Minister in May 1940, in highly unpropitious circumstances, isolationism was prevalent in the United States, matched by a belief that Britain would likely fall under Nazi domination. As a result of the action at Oran, and through his invigorating speeches, Churchill persuaded the Americans that Britain would fight on and he forged a close, if at times troubled, relationship with the President. The 'special relationship' was undoubtedly stronger for having Churchill at the helm.

Was there a cover-up over Pearl Harbor?

ON DECEMBER 7th 1941 the Japanese navy carried out a devastating raid on America's Pacific fleet at Pearl Harbor. Ever since, a vigorous debate has raged about how much American officials knew about the attack beforehand. Some critics allege that Roosevelt had fore-knowledge of the operation but allowed it to proceed in order to force a stubbornly isolationist Congress to enter the war. This is the central charge made by John Toland in his book *Day of Infamy*. Others allege that Roosevelt, far from being the chief culprit, was in fact Churchill's dupe. Russbridger and Nave, in *Betrayal at Pearl Harbor*, claim that Churchill had advance warning of the Japanese attack but chose not to inform Roosevelt in order to trick him into declaring war on Germany. The authors claim that, on hearing the news of the Pearl Harbor attack, Churchill 'was jubilant at having won his battle to let Japan drag America into the war'.[24] If true, the claim is sensational, making the British Prime Minister complicit in the deaths of thousands of American servicemen.

According to Rusbridger and Nave, Churchill took a gamble by withholding vital intelligence information from the unsuspecting Roosevelt. Churchill believed, they claimed, that if he shared the advance knowledge of Japanese intentions Roosevelt would warn his commanders at Pearl Harbor, who would, in turn, thwart the Japanese attack. The chance to bring the United States into the conflict would then be lost. Churchill appeared to have the motive, means and opportunity to carry out an elaborate deception of the President and the American people.

Churchill was certainly capable of ruthlessly manipulating intelligence to serve his country's national interests. During the visit of Harry Hopkins to London in January 1941, Churchill received an Ultra report which suggested that a German invasion was unlikely. He chose not to share this fact with Hopkins, talking instead of the anti-invasion measures Britain was adopting in the event of a German landing. Churchill could not afford to share Ultra until the

Americans were partners in war.[25] Neither did Churchill shirk from callous action if it was in the greater interest of the war effort, as the attack on the French fleet clearly demonstrated. But a close analysis of the facts reveals that neither Churchill nor Roosevelt had the advance knowledge their critics contend.

Central to this conspiracy theory is the allegation that both Churchill and Roosevelt's codebreakers had intercepted Japanese ciphers, thereby discovering the country's military plans. By late 1941, several Japanese ciphers (such as the diplomatic code 'Purple') had indeed been broken by the Allies. Given that Purple was a high-security Japanese foreign office cipher, this undoubtedly represented a considerable cryptographic success. Crucially, however, Purple carried little information about the planning for Pearl Harbor. This was partly because the military, who dominated Japan's wartime policy, did not trust their country's foreign office and thus left it 'out of the loop'.

The Allies had also succeeded in cracking the Japanese naval cipher JN-25. This, too, proved redudant, for the code had been superceded by another, improved code, JN-25B, which proved to be practically unreadable. The first JN-25B decrypt was made on January 8th 1942, and the first twenty-five decrypts were short messages of little intelligence. As Duane Whitlock stated, 'The reason that not one single JN-25B decrypt made prior to Pearl Harbor has ever been found or declassified is not due to any insidious cover-up ... it is due quite simply to the fact that no such decrypt ever existed ... It simply was not within the realm of our combined cryptologic capability to produce a usable decrypt at that particular juncture.'[26] Detailed month-by-month progress reports have shown no reason to believe that a single message was fully decrypted before the start of the war.

More important still is the fact that America's intelligence agencies suffered from a crippling failure of co-ordination. The US army's Signal Intelligence Service (SIS) worked separately from the navy's intelligence service, OP-20-G. The former concentrated on Japan's diplomatic codes and the latter on Japan's naval messages. More confusingly, by 1940 SIS and OP-20-G were jointly processing Japanese diplomatic material, though entirely separately from each other, while the US navy withheld all details of its success with Japanese naval crypto-systems from the army. As Russbridger and Nave comment, 'it is hard to think of an arrangement likely to cause more mistakes and misunderstandings'.[27]

The conspiracy theorists allege that there was foreknowledge of the attack via the so called 'Bomb Plot message'. On September 24th 1941 a message was sent from Tokyo to the Japanese consul in Honolulu. The message divided Pearl Harbor into five key areas and also requested information on the disposition of warships and air-craft carriers there. For Russbringer and Nave, 'the purpose of the message could not have been clearer' for it 'divided Pearl Harbor into a number of target areas for an aerial attack'.[28]

For many this is the crucial smoking gun that proves that top echelons of the US government, including Roosevelt himself, were privy to Japanese plans but chose to keep naval commanders Kimmel and Short in the dark. Crucially, as Stinnett maintains, neither Admiral Kimmel nor Lieutenant General Walter Short received the Bomb Plot message. Stinnett has claimed that this was a deliberate ploy by FDR to ensure the destruction of Pearl Harbor and Amer-ica's entry into the Second World War. Yet the message contained nothing about a deliberate plot to destroy Pearl Harbor, or any date for an impending attack. As historian Warren Kimball has argued, Washington was receiving a huge amount of information about Japanese behaviour and the issue was how to separate mere 'noise' from specific and detailed information.

In addition, only a small number of people in Tokyo had been told of the plan and its operational details were distributed to the task force by hand. The Japanese were also careful not to refer to the raid on the air waves; as the Japanese fleet sailed, it maintained strict radio silence. All surviving officers from Nagumo's ships maintained that no radio traffic could have been overheard and that their radio operators in Japan had faked traffic for the benefit of listeners (i.e. military intelligence traffic analysts in other countries). It was claimed that all radio transmitters aboard Nagumo's ships had been physically disabled to prevent inadvertent broadcast and subsequent tracking of the attack force. After the war, the Strategic Bombing Survey found the Japanese military's after-action report, which cred-ited the success of the attack to the fact that secrecy was maintained.

Historian Robert Stinnett has claimed that, despite the order for radio silence, Japanese commanders made radio communication as the fleet travelled south-eastwards towards Pearl Harbor. These mes-sages, he says, were picked up by naval intelligence around the Pacific Rim. But the messages were coming not from the attack fleet but from Japanese shore stations. The stations were trying to deceive the

United States into thinking that the noise was coming from the ships themselves and that the ships were still in Japanese waters.[29] The Pearl Harbor attack has to be seen, therefore, as a major triumph for Japanese intelligence.

The absence of two American aircraft carriers, *Enterprise* and *Lexington*, from Pearl Harbor is often cited as evidence supporting the conspiracy theory. The two carriers were in fact on missions to deliver additional fighters to Wake and Midway. The carriers travelled west, towards Japan and the Japanese navy, and were lightly escorted. At the time of the attack, the *Enterprise* was about two hundred miles west of Pearl Harbor; it was scheduled to be back on December 6th, but was delayed by a storm. It was then scheduled to return at 7am on December 7th, almost an hour before the attack started, but was again delayed. One aircraft carrier was therefore scheduled to return to Pearl Harbor prior to the Japanese attack and only fortuitous and unexpected circumstances prevented this from happening. This makes no sense in the light of the conspiracy theory.

Churchill's behaviour prior to Pearl Harbor does not suggest that he wanted a showdown with Japan. Indeed, he did a great deal to *deter* Japanese aggression in the weeks prior to Pearl Harbor. By the end of July 1941 the Japanese had occupied French Indo-China (now Vietnam) *en route* to creating a South East Asian empire. The US and Britain had imposed an embargo on oil exports, a move welcomed by Churchill as a 'very great advance towards the gripping of Japanese aggression by united forces'.[30] In order to discourage further Japanese aggression, Churchill sent two battleships, the *Prince of Wales* and the *Repulse,* to the Far East, and described sending the former as 'the best possible deterrent'.[31] At the same time he told the President that the firmer the Allied attitude, 'the less chance of [Japan's] taking the plunge'.[32] This hardly sounds like the language of a warmonger.

Even more important was Churchill's reaction to the Japanese suggestion of a *modus vivendi*. Roosevelt had not dismissed the suggestion out of hand, suggesting to Churchill that the Allies could relax some of the economic sanctions and permit some items to be exported to Japan. On November 23rd 1941 Churchill had minuted to Eden: 'My own feeling is that we might give Hull the latitude he asks. Our major interest: no further encroachments and no war, as we have already enough of the latter...' He told Eden that, subject to certain conditions, 'it would be worth while to ease up upon Japan economically sufficiently for them to live from hand to mouth'. He added: 'I must say I should feel pleased if I read that an American-Japanese agreement had been made'.33

In general, Britain's policy was to avoid becoming directly involved in a war with Japan unless there was guaranteed United States involvement. Above all, Britain could not take 'forward action in advance of the United States'.34 Far from secretly goading Japan to war, Churchill wanted to avoid opening another front in the Far East which would tie down large numbers of British troops indefinitely. The reason was simple and summed up in a War Office memorandum on November 30th: 'The effect of war with Japan on our main war effort might be so severe as to prejudice our chances of beating Germany.'35 Revisionist historians more often accuse Churchill of downplaying the Japanese threat, rather than covering up knowledge from the Americans.36

But, while the conspiracy theory is unsound, it would be incorrect to suggest that the Allies were unaware of *any* threat in the Pacific. Throughout 1941 the US, Britain and the Netherlands were aware that Japan imperilled their interests in the Far East. There were warnings of attacks against Thailand (the Kra Peninsula), Malaya, French Indochina, the Dutch East Indies and even Russia. In late November both the US navy and army sent war warnings to all Pacific commands. Although these clearly stated the high probability of war with Japan, they did not mention the likelihood of an attack on Pearl Harbor itself, concentrating instead on the probability of an attack in the Far East. This was inherently plausible as the Japanese attack on the US in December was essentially a side operation to the main Japanese thrust south against Malaya and the Philippines. Far more resources, especially imperial army resources, were devoted to these attacks as compared to Pearl Harbor. In general, intelligence was aware of an imminent attack in late October but this suggested that the principal target would be Russia or Thailand.

The allegation that Churchill had foreknowledge of the Pearl Harbor attack continues to reverberate on both sides of the Atlantic. The combined evidence points in a very different direction.

Could Churchill have been toppled from power during the Second World War?

IT IS OFTEN assumed that Churchill's position was unassailable throughout the war. Such is his stature that it seems almost heretical to suggest that he was not the right man to be Prime Minister. But we know that he was intensely vulnerable during the first few months of his premiership, and that his rise to power was not due to the inexorable workings of destiny. What is less well known is that Churchill's domestic standing was even less secure in 1942, and that he faced a challenge to his leadership from a highly ambitious rival. Only military victory in the Egyptian desert guaranteed Churchill's position for the rest of the war but this victory was far from certain at the time. Even though he may well have survived defeat at the hands of Rommel's Africa Korps, he would have come under pressure to resign, something that seems almost unthinkable today. To understand Churchill's vulnerability, one must consider Britain's parlous military standing after the Battle of Britain.

Having survived the onslaught of the *Luftwaffe* in 1940, Britain found herself engaged on a number of fronts with Axis forces. But 1941 was to be a bleak year in the history of the British army. Initially there were successes in the North African theatre of war with Wavell overrunning Italian forces in Libya, occupying the port in Tobruk in January 1941 and taking Cyrenaica the following month. However, a disastrous decision was taken to send troops to Greece to defend against an imminent German invasion from Romania. The result was the evacuation of fifty thousand troops to Crete and Egypt. When the Germans invaded Crete in May 1941, with parachute and airborne troops, the British and New Zealand forces, after bitter resistance, were forced to withdraw, and some twelve thousand troops became prisoners of war.[37]

Much worse was to follow in the shape of the Japanese threat to Britain's Far East Asian Empire, in particular the fortress of Singapore and Hong Kong. Both these imperial possessions were vulnerable to a Japanese attack, yet Churchill chose not to heed Sir John Dill's advice to provide them with urgent reinforcements. In part this stemmed from Churchill's fatal underestimation of the Japanese navy and air force and, in part, his mistaken overestimation of British resistance in Singapore. To make matters worse, mistakes in defence planning were made by the commander on the spot, General Percival. This was to prove a fatal cocktail of strategic misjudgements.

After conquering Hong Kong on Christmas Day 1941, the Japanese captured the whole of Malaya by January 1942, and a month later Percival surrendered in Singapore. Churchill was to describe this defeat as 'the worst disaster and largest capitulation in British history'.[38] The surrender of over a hundred thousand men haunted him; his words to Violet Bonham-Carter were particularly significant: 'We have so many men in Singapore, so many men – they should have done better.'[39] In his wartime diary, Harold Nicolson feared 'a slump in public opinion which will deprive Winston of his legend'.[40]

The humiliation did not end there. On February 12th 1942 the government was stunned when three German warships, the *Scharnhorst*, the *Gneisenau* and the *Prinz Eugen*, slipped through the English Channel from Brest *en route* to Germany. This seemed to many a striking demonstration of Britain's failure to defend her home waters, even though the two main warships had been damaged in their Channel dash. According to Henry Channon, the political reaction was dynamite: 'Everyone is in a rage against the Prime Minister. Rage; frustration.'[41]

Under pressure, Churchill was forced to carry out a Cabinet reshuffle; on February 19th the new War Cabinet was announced. The key figure now included was the austere Sir Stafford Cripps, who had arrived in Britain in January 1942 after eighteen months as Ambassador to the Soviet Union. While stationed there, Cripps had sent telegrams home demanding full-scale British support for the USSR and a wholesale alliance. When he arrived in Britain, after effectively resigning his post, he was hailed as the symbol of a new progressive mood in British politics.

Cripps' pro-Russian sentiments were timed to perfection for they coincided with a remarkable resurgence of sympathy in Britain for the Soviet Union. Given that the Russians were bearing the brunt of Nazi attacks, this was understandable, but Churchill was so worried that this would translate into support for communism that he temporarily banned the BBC from playing the Soviet Russian anthem, the *Internazionale*. He was later forced to revoke this ban.

Aware that Cripps was a potential rival, Churchill offered him the position of Leader of the House of Commons and Lord Privy Seal. Shortly afterwards Cripps undertook a mission to negotiate the

terms of a new settlement with the Indian Congress. He offered
India dominion status after the war, with the right to withdraw from
the Commonwealth, and independence for the princely states. The
mission was a failure, Cripps making enemies of both the Viceroy
and a highly distrustful Congress, but when he returned he found
that his personal popularity, at least with the public, had scarcely
been dented. Opinion polls throughout 1942 regularly showed that,
behind Anthony Eden, Cripps, rather than Bevin or Attlee, was the
popular choice of minister to succeed Churchill.[42]

Churchill's domestic crisis came to a head in the summer of 1942,
following the disastrous fall of Tobruk. Thirty-three thousand
British soldiers surrendered to Rommel's forces in what Churchill
would later describe as 'one of the heaviest blows' of the war.[43] A few
days later the *Daily Express* columnist Tom Driberg won the Tory seat
of Maldon in a by-election, standing on a left-wing platform. How
much the fall of Tobruk contributed to this defeat is hard to gauge;
it could hardly have helped. The by-election saw the Conservative
share of the vote plummet by 22 per cent. The Prime Minister's personal popularity had fallen to 78 per cent – high by modern standards, but the lowest figure of the war.[44]

Churchill now faced a vote of no confidence in the House of
Commons. Led by Conservative MP John Wardlaw-Milne, the
motion stated: 'That this House, while paying tribute to the heroism
and endurance of the Armed Forces of the Crown, has no confidence
in the central direction of the war'. Churchill survived the debate
with relative ease, winning by 475 votes to 25, though 27 MPs also
abstained. Wardlaw-Milne had given Churchill an inadvertent boost
when he proposed that the Duke of Gloucester, the King's brother,
be made Commander in Chief of the forces, an absurd suggestion
that was met with ironic cheers in the House. Nonetheless the forces
of opposition knew that, without some military victory, Churchill's
position was assailable. With Japan building up its Far East Asian
Empire and the Germans laying siege to Stalingrad, the situation for
the Allies looked far from secure.

Roosevelt had given the go-ahead for Operation Torch, the Allied
landings in North Africa which were designed to drive out Axis
forces and divert German divisions from the Russian front. Before
any Allied troops landed, it was necessary for the British Eighth
Army to defeat Rommel's forces at El Alamein, sixty miles from
Alexandria. Defeat here was unthinkable. A victory for the Germans

would have presaged a push to the Suez Canal, threatening British oil supplies and inflicting a greater psychological wound than the loss of Singapore.

During the summer of 1942 Cripps believed he could exploit this uncertainty to bring down Churchill. He sounded out both Conservative and Labour MPs about his chances of succession, telling his family that he might resign in order to campaign for changing the direction of the war. In September he demanded wholesale changes, proposing a new War Planning Directorate to help direct military strategy and operations, as well as innovative measures of social reform. Cripps informed Churchill that, if these measures were not implemented, he would resign. Churchill persuaded him to delay this decision until they knew the outcome of the battle at El Alamein. Cripps agreed, and secured his fate.

On October 23rd Montgomery's forces launched a blistering attack on Rommel, aided by three hundred Sherman tanks supplied by the United States. After twelve days of heavy fighting, Montgomery's forces had broken through German lines and were overwhelming the enemy. With a majority of German tanks destroyed, Rommel was forced to retreat, handing Britain its first victory on land against the *Wehrmacht*. Churchill ordered church bells to ring out in celebration of a famous victory. He now turned on Cripps and demanded that he follow through with his resignation. The former Leader of the House was given a minor role in the Ministry of Aircraft Production, crucially outside the War Cabinet.

The victory at El Alamein guaranteed Churchill's position until the election of 1945. Later he would say that the two summer months in 1942 were the most anxious of the war, and that without victory in Egypt he would have been finished. In this, there was a degree of exaggeration. While some Tory discontents, notably ex-Chamberlainites, might have accepted a diminution of Churchill's powers, transferring his role as Minister of Defence to another figure, it is unlikely they would have wanted another disfiguring leadership contest. Despite this, Cripps certainly gave the Prime Minister the most jittery moments of his premiership.

Did Churchill refuse to open a
second front in Europe?

THE DECISION to delay an Allied invasion of Western Europe is frequently cited as one of the great strategic blunders of the war. It is also one of the most common criticisms of Churchill's war leadership. Critics have long claimed that he hesitated to commit troops to the liberation of Europe, fearing a bloodbath and the protracted saga of another Western Front. He is often accused of overruling the Americans, who were enthusiastic for a second front, and delaying an operation that could have considerably shortened the war.

For one historian, Churchill's procrastination ensured that the Soviets 'had to do most of the fighting, suffer most of the casualties and take most responsibility for victory', all of which ensured that, by 1945, 'the Soviets had advanced further west than they otherwise would have'.[45] For the Anglophobic American General Albert Wedemayer, Churchill's alternative strategies for 1942-3, namely his 'diversionary' campaigns in North Africa and the Mediterranean, were 'a trap which prolonged the war in Europe by a year' and which 'cost many unnecessary lives'.[46]

As with much mythology, there are grains of truth in this account. Churchill was reluctant to oversee a premature cross-Channel operation, the failure of which would have seriously impaired the chances of an Allied victory. He became highly skeptical about the fighting qualities of the British army and feared an Allied bloodbath if British (and American) troops were pitted against the better prepared German forces.

But, as Britain was a democracy, not a dictatorship, Churchill had to defer to his military Chiefs of Staff on matters of grand strategy. It was they, particularly the indomitable Alan Brooke, Chief of the Imperial General Staff, who vetoed any such operation in 1942-3. Their reservations came to be accepted by Roosevelt himself and (reluctantly) his Chief of Staff, George Marshall, though they caused understandable irritation in Moscow.

Throughout the 1930s the British army remained the 'Cinderella service', receiving far less from the government's defence budget than its sisters, the Royal Navy and the RAF. Unlike the Continental powers, there was no British tradition of conscription: the 'volunteer principle' of army recruitment held sway. In practice, this meant that

Britain had a relatively small army, much of which was dispersed abroad in the defence of imperial interests.

Successive British governments practised a doctrine of limited liability, knowing that in any continental war they could mobilise the Indian army while relying on fortress France to stem the tide of German attacks. Even in May 1940, the British Expeditionary Force was a mere ten divisions, compared to 134 French, Belgian and Dutch ones. Strategy in 1940 was largely based on the naval blockade of Germany, and aerial bombing in order to weaken Germany from without while it collapsed from within. Even though the Chiefs of Staff contemplated 're-establishing a striking force on the Continent' with which to 'enter Germany', they did not seek to 'raise, and land on the Continent, an army comparable in size to that of Germany'.47 Prior to Pearl Harbor, the American army was also relatively small, numbering some two hundred thousand men, though this would increase to over eight million by the end of the war. These facts must be borne in mind by those who question the lateness of D-Day in the Second World War. The liberation of the Continent would require the greatest amphibious assault in history, over one million men and vast quantities of fuel, ammunition and landing craft. It could never have succeeded through half measures.

The question of a second front was raised by Stalin in July 1941, a month after the German invasion. He urged Churchill to establish two fronts against Hitler, one in France and another in the Baltic, the object being to divert German forces from the Russian front. In deference to his military advisers, Churchill had to turn this request down. He cited Britain's lack of sufficient military forces as well as the formidable German coastal defences in France. As he told Stalin:

> The Germans have 40 divisions in France alone, and the whole coast has been fortified with German diligence for more than a year, and bristles with cannon, wire, pill boxes and beachmines ... This is one mass of fortifications with scores of heavy guns, commanding the sea approaches, many of which can fire right across the Straits ... To attempt a landing in force would be to encounter a bloody repulse, and petty raids would only lead to fiascos doing far more harm than good to both of us.48

In a letter to Sir Stafford Cripps, Churchill spelt out the extent of the difficulties that Britain would face:

The French coast is fortified to the limit, and the Germans still have more divisions in the West than we have in Great Britain, and formidable air support. The shipping available to transport a large army to the Continent does not exist, unless the process were spread over many months. The diversion of our flotillas to such an operation would entail paralysis of the support of the Middle Eastern armies and a breakdown of the whole Atlantic traffic. It might mean the loss of the Battle of the Atlantic and the starvation and ruin of the British Isles.

What counted for Churchill was that the Chiefs of Staff were 'united in the views expressed here'.[49]

In March 1942 Roosevelt, spurred on by General Marshall, expressed an interest in opening a second front in Western Europe. Again the logistics strongly militated against this. Roosevelt cited figures for America's shipbuilding programme, which was, he said, 'about the maximum that could be obtained'. The total number of troops that could be transported in mid-1942 was 130,000, rising to 270,000 by the end of 1943 and 400,000 by June 1944. These shipping figures meant that it would not be feasible for the US to join in any imminent campaign on European soil. In effect, they were signaling that any cross-Channel attack would have to comprise predominantly British and imperial, not American troops.

General Brooke was adamant that, with Britain's lightweight army, there was little prospect of a successful second front. Brooke wrote in his diary for March 1942 that he had spent a number of hours 'discussing possibilities of some form of offensive in northern France to assist Russia in the event of a German attack being successful...' He went on to say that it was hard to contend with the 'universal cry' for action, yet 'what can we do with some ten Divisions against the German masses'.[50] With military advice such as this, Churchill had little option but to argue against a cross-Channel attack that year.

In April 1942 US Chiefs Hopkins and Marshall arrived in London with suggestions for opening a second front the following year. The plan, which would involve forty-eight divisions, thirty American and eighteen British, and nearly six thousand combat aircraft, entailed an amphibious assault on various French beaches with nearly a hundred thousand men a week augmenting the invasion forces. Due to the paucity of current American troops, the plan was for an invasion in 1943, though a much smaller number of American troops would be available for more immediate action.

The British Chiefs of Staff derided any plan for invading Europe in 1942, though it was thought that some form of military action the following year would be more viable. According to Brooke's own account, Churchill appeared to be favourably disposed to the American proposals, while Brooke himself had numerous misgivings. However, in order to paper over their strategic disagreements, both sides agreed that they shared the common aim of jointly destroying Nazi Germany and restoring European democracy. As Churchill told the Commons in a secret session, the liberation of Europe was 'the main war plan of our two nations'.[51]

Churchill constantly pressed his Chiefs of Staff about the possibility of opening a second front. In May 1942, at a meeting of the Chiefs of Staff committee to determine what operations could be launched in Western Europe that year, Churchill was informed that, with the landing craft that were available, only 4,300 men and 160 tanks could be put ashore 'in the first flight'. This small force 'would have the greatest difficulty in establishing a bridgehead wide enough to permit the disembarkation of supporting forces without serious interference from the coast defence guns'. Mountbatten added that it would take about three more weeks to get a further six divisions ashore. Later in the year the Joint Intelligence Committee reinforced these doubts after making calculations of German military strength.

Churchill was disappointed with this analysis, but nonetheless conceded that a fruitless attempt to open a second front would have terrible consequences for the French while it 'would be no consolation to the Russians'.[52] He was aware that the Germans could hold the Russians at bay with fifty or sixty divisions while bringing back huge numbers of troops to reinforce Western Europe. However, Churchill remained open to a large-scale invasion of Europe in 1943, involving more than one million men. This was named 'Operation Round-Up'.

If a second front could not be opened on the Continent in 1942, an alternative had to be found if Stalin was to be appeased. Roosevelt wanted American soldiers in action against German forces that year. He was aware that congressional elections were due in November 1942 and that political pressure would demand some form of military involvement.[53] That alternative was Operation Torch, the plan agreed unanimously by the British Cabinet (and accepted by Roosevelt) to launch an invasion of North Africa to drive out the Axis forces. The aim was to establish Allied control on impregnable rocks from the Atlantic coast of Africa up to the Suez Canal.

It is worth dealing here with a related historical controversy that concerns the reasons for the North African operations. The campaigns in North Africa have been described as a 'sideshow to the war to liberate German occupied Europe'.[54] Churchill is sometimes accused of betraying Stalin and ruling out a second front for the sake of preserving Britain's imperial interests. It is argued that, by concentrating the military campaign from late 1940 until late 1942 in the North African theatre, Churchill was struggling to preserve key colonial interests in the Mediterranean, principally Egypt and the Suez Canal, and the Indian Empire which lay beyond. According to historian William Deakin, many American strategists believed that the Mediterranean operations were 'designed to further exclusively British interests'.[55] The war is thus seen as a means of preserving imperial interests at the expense of a key ally who subsequently bore the brunt of Hitler's war machine.

It is certainly true that Churchill had a fondness for the Mediterranean. As Michael Howard has put it, 'This was, for him, after India, the very heartland of the British Empire, worth retaining for its own sake irrespective of its significance in the conduct of the war.'[56] Churchill was aware that the preservation of the Indian Empire was central to the retention of British power, and that the key trade route to India was the Suez Canal. British interest in the Middle East was augmented with the discovery of oil and the concern to preserve cheap supplies for the Royal Navy.

But in the 1930s the interest in the Middle East was given a new focus with the threat of both Italian and German fascism. For both countries, the countries of south-eastern Europe had a particular appeal, leading Britain to take an interest in creating a 'Balkan' barrier that included Greece and Turkey. On the outbreak of war, the need to preserve supplies of oil for the Royal Navy (and deny them to the Germans) gave the British one powerful impetus for staying in the Middle East. Preserving this vital flow of Middle East oil, necessary for the British war machine, gave the Allies a powerful argument for preventing any German advance across North Africa and into the Middle East itself.

But there were other reasons for staging a fight in this part of the world. Churchill was desperate for neutral countries, including the USA, to join the Allied cause, while equally concerned that they did not lean towards the Axis powers. Among the wavering countries were Britain's Arab allies, including Egypt itself. He believed that this would be achieved by bold, direct offensives against the enemy rather than a strategy of passive defence. Italy had a number of African possessions, all of which could only be reinforced by sea, but its army and navy were weaker than their German counterparts, and there were additional question marks about Italian morale.

At the same time, Britain also possessed a large imperial force in the region, including the famous 7th Armoured Division (the Desert Rats), the 4th Indian Division and units from Australia and South Africa. If the British were to fight the Italians, it would at least be on highly favourable terms. In the absence of fighting the German army, Churchill had the opportunity for a successful military offensive. In this sense, A.J.P. Taylor was wrong when he wrote: 'If you ask what the Mediterranean campaign was about, why the British were ever in the Mediterranean, one can give the simple answer of the Second World War ... they were there because they were there – because they were there.'57 In December 1940 Britain launched a counter-attack against the Italian forces and achieved a spectacular success, routing ten divisions and capturing 130,000 prisoners.

Moving forwards to 1942, the decision to launch Operation Torch now seems eminently sensible. In the absence of a cross-Channel invasion, but with the need for a second front to appease Stalin, North Africa was a logical area for operations. Less resistance could be expected landing in North Africa rather than attacking the heavily defended French coast. It also helped that British and American forces would largely meet Italian rather than German opposition, while controlling the North African seaboard would provide the much needed springboard for an invasion of southern Europe, the soft underbelly of the Axis powers. Churchill also argued, and Stalin later accepted, that this operation would draw off some German divisions from the Soviet Union.58 In addition, if Britain were to save her shipping, which was being hemorrhaged in the Battle of the Atlantic, she needed control of the Mediterranean, and this necessitated clearing North Africa of Axis troops. In the final analysis, as Andrew Roberts shows in his masterful *Masters and Commanders*, it was pressure from Roosevelt, not Churchill, that won over the American Chiefs of Staff to Operation Torch.

Despite Roosevelt's expressing enthusiasm for Torch, another strategic disagreement was to follow. The Americans made it clear that Operation Torch in 1942 would preclude any large-scale cross-Channel landing in 1943. That this was not Churchill's view was made clear at his meeting with Stalin in 1942, when Churchill explained that Torch 'should be considered in conjunction with the 1943 operation'.[59] He made it clear to the Chiefs of Staff in September 1942 that Torch was 'no substitute' for a European cross-channel invasion.[60] Indeed, he even set a date, July 12th 1943, showing he was clearly not reneging on his promise to Stalin earlier that year.

In the end it was the failure to bring about a speedy defeat of German forces in Tunisia that scuppered any chance of Operation Round-Up, the proposed 1943 cross-Channel invasion. This resulted from Hitler's determination to keep control of Tunisia, which he did by sending men and supplies from Sicily to Tunis in late 1942 and early 1943. But this could not have been known to Churchill at any time in 1942. He maintained the case for a cross-Channel landing in 1943, provided only that sufficient troops could be assembled.[61]

Here again he was met with a torrent of skepticism from Brooke, who presented the Prime Minister with a paper from the Chiefs of Staff rejecting the case for a Western Front in 1943. In particular, they cited the strength of the German railway network that had been established in Western Europe, which would allow the Germans to meet advancing Allied troops very easily. The Chiefs argued in favour of an alternative strategy, whereby forty German divisions would be tied down in Western Europe in the expectation of an attack while the Allies attempted to remove Italy from the war. Churchill gave way, stating that he saw 'no alternative to the strategy recommended by the Chiefs of Staff'.[62]

One key factor in his decision was the weakness of the American military contribution. It was the inadequate number of American troops, and particularly landing craft, that made a 1943 cross-Channel operation, in concert with Torch, an unlikely proposition. Another factor was Britain's inadequacy in being able to provide assault shipping and landing craft. Again the Chiefs of Staff pointed out that, even without Torch, only a small assault force could be landed by the limited number of British manned craft. Furthermore, the decision to launch an invasion of Sicily following Torch meant that the landing craft previously earmarked for a 1943 cross-Channel landing were going to be needed for the Sicily landings.

At the Casablanca Conference held in early 1943, the Chiefs of Staff discovered that Roosevelt did not share Marshall's enthusiasm for a cross-Channel invasion that year, and in this fully concurred with the British Chiefs of Staff. Instead, Roosevelt favoured a Mediterranean strategy that would involve attacking Sardinia, Sicily, Italy, Greece and other areas in the Balkans. It was this project that inspired Churchill to talk of attacking 'the soft underbelly' of Europe. Churchill and Roosevelt agreed that there should be a maximum build-up of American troops in Britain ready to invade the Continent in Autumn 1943 if there were signs of a German collapse.[63] The American Chiefs of Staff were skeptical that German morale would crack without any direct military offensive.

While Churchill was open to a cross-Channel operation, he voiced simultaneous doubts about a premature operation carried out with too few troops. His main concern was that any Allied invasion force would be too weak for the German forces in France and that an Allied bloodbath would result. As Lord Moran recalls in his diary, 'Why did Winston so much dread this particular operation? He feared the casualties.'[64] 'In my view,' Churchill wrote, 'and that of all my expert military advisers, we should, even if we got ashore, be driven into the sea, as the Germans have forces already in France superior to any we could put there this year...'[65] He also felt that American troops were not 'sufficiently hardened to be war worthy on the battlefields of Europe'.[66]

All along Churchill had advocated a second front in Europe predicated on the assumption that Allied forces were sufficient and that German forces had been weakened. In 1943, as he contemplated an invasion the following year, his fears of a premature assault became more pronounced. While he was fairly sure that an initial lodgement could be secured, he was worried that, in the later stages of the operation, the Germans could 'inflict ... a military disaster greater than that of Dunkirk', which could resuscitate the Nazi regime.[67] But at the Teheran Conference late in 1943, unlike earlier in the war, Churchill was a marginalised figure in the making of Grand Strategy and he accepted a cross-Channel invasion for May 1944.

One year later, in June 1944, the world witnessed the largest amphibious assault in the history of war – Operation Overlord. Hours before D-Day on June 6th 1944, as he was going to bed, Churchill told his wife: 'Do you realise that by the time you wake up in the morning twenty thousand men may have been killed?'[68] The dreaded fear of mass casualties haunted Churchill until the moment the second front was opened. This was due, in no small part, to his belief in the superior fighting qualities of the *Wehrmacht*, a belief that had been reinforced throughout the dark days of 1940. The incontrovertible truth was that, in engagements between the British and the German armies, the Germans inflicted much higher casualties. In order to defeat them, the Allies needed considerable numerical superiority.

Churchill, like Brooke, was not an obstinate opponent of a second front *in principle*. During 1942 and 1943 he continually pressed his Chiefs of Staff for a cross-Channel invasion, arguing that it was compatible with a Mediterranean strategy. As the historian Michael Howard has written: 'Paper after paper was put up by the Chiefs of Staff arguing the impossibility of Round-Up in 1943, which the Prime Minister analysed line by line, challenged in minutest detail and reluctantly accepted; only to question their conclusions a few days later when some fresh victory spurred his unquenchable optimism.'[69] But the Chiefs told Churchill that such operations were impracticable given British and American military weaknesses. When he therefore denied in his memoirs that he 'was inveterately hostile to the plan of a large scale Channel crossing in 1943' he was largely telling the truth.[70]

Was Churchill indifferent to the Holocaust?

'THERE IS NO DOUBT that this is probably the greatest and most horrible single crime ever committed in the whole history of the world, and it has been done by scientific machinery by nominally civilised men in the name of a Great State and one of the leading races of Europe.'[71] These were Churchill's words to Anthony Eden in 1944 when he learnt of the horrors of Auschwitz. Six decades on, they remain a resonant commentary on history's greatest crime. The Holocaust remains the paradigm example of man's inhumanity to man and one of the greatest justifications for the Allied stand against the Nazis.

Since the 1970s, however, the increasing trend among the liberal intelligentsia has been to condemn the wartime British and American governments for their perceived inaction and passivity, their failure to 'intervene' while the Holocaust was taking place. The wartime governments have frequently been denounced for their 'bystander apathy' in the face of appalling evil.

Typical of the critical school is Bernard Wasserstein in his *Britain and the Jews of Europe* (1979). He criticised the British authorities for failing to allow more German Jewish refugees to settle in British territory, including Palestine. He concluded that this obstructionist policy showed an insensitivity to Jewish suffering and was even marked by official anti-Semitism. He assumed that Jewish lives could have been saved if a more generous policy had prevailed within the Palestine administration.

Other scholars correctly point out that Churchill never repudiated the Palestine White Paper, which restricted Jewish immigration to the country, although he had the power to do this. The result, it is argued, was that Palestine was permanently shut off as an escape route for thousands of Jews fleeing Nazi persecution. Perhaps the most frequently cited criticism of both Churchill and Roosevelt is that they did not order the bombing of either Auschwitz itself (and other camps) or the railway tracks leading up to it, but stood by while millions perished. Richard Davis in *The Bombing of Auschwitz* says that both Roosevelt and Churchill erred in not ordering the bombing of the camp or, in Churchill's case, not following up this order.

William Rubinstein and Lucy Dawidowicz stand out among modern historians for exempting the Allies from indirect responsibility for the Holocaust. In *The Myth of Rescue*, Rubinstein deals impressively with the charges against the Allied nations and shows how, in each case, it would have been extremely difficult to rescue Europe's Jews from the Nazis. He concludes: 'In searching for a rational explanation of modern history's greatest crime, it is important that we not assign guilt to those who were innocent.'[72]

The arguments of the critical school are flawed in quite obvious ways. Of course, there *was* vacillation and indifference among officials in Whitehall, and many civil servants were hostile to Jews generally, but it does not necessarily follow that a greater level of philo-Semitism among officialdom would have made a significant difference. The issue to be addressed is whether it was feasible, given the full demands of total war, to rescue Europe's Jews from the clutches of an implacable, paranoid dictator who was intent on their destruction. With Hitler in control of mainland Europe, the escape routes for the Jews of Central and Eastern Europe were largely shut off from the middle of 1941.

Certainly the decision to suspend Jewish immigration to Palestine in 1939 was an egregious form of appeasement designed to win Arab support during the war. A more generous policy after 1939 would have seen limited numbers of Jews (those who could escape from Nazi-occupied Europe) travel to Palestine and claim asylum there. Undoubtedly Churchill should have lifted the White Paper while he had the power to do so.

But to indict the British government on a charge of indirect responsibility for genocide would be misguided. It would be to attribute a fantastic level of post-historical foresight to the British government, for in 1939 no reasonable official or minister could have discerned that the Holocaust was coming. Despite Hitler's violently anti-Semitic speeches, and Germany's pre-war persecution of the Jews, it did not follow that a programme of systematic genocide was about to be exacted upon European Jewry. Indeed, it was not until the middle of 1942 that news of the Final Solution filtered out to the Western Allies.[73] As Michael Cohen points out, 'It is a somewhat misplaced judgement to indict the British for complicity in a crime which they could not be expected to have imagined was about to be committed.'[74]

In regard to the bombing of Auschwitz, some points ought to be borne in mind. Until the capture of Foggia air base in December 1943, Auschwitz was beyond the range of Allied bombers from both east and west. In addition, it was not until May 1944 that anyone suggested bombing the camp. This was two years after the camp had begun exterminating European Jews and less than six months before the killings stopped. Indeed, the initial demand was to bomb one of the railway lines to Auschwitz, not the camp itself. But Auschwitz was a major railhead junction for eastern and south-central Europe, and there were seven railway lines running from Hungary to Auschwitz. Thus even the successful bombing of one line would not have impeded the deportation process elsewhere.

Logistically it would have been possible to mount a raid on the camp itself, but even with Auschwitz out of action the Nazis would have found other means for murdering their hapless victims. It should not be forgotten that vast numbers of Europe's Jews perished outside the death camps, victims of mass shootings, death marches and ghettoisation. The destruction of the gas chambers, even if feasible, would only have delayed the extermination process, not ended it.[75]

Despite the constraints on his government and the overriding need to win the war, Churchill's record on the Holocaust is far from negative. Prior to 1939, he had vigorously denounced the harsh anti-Semitism in Nazi Germany. In 1934, he condemned the way that Jews were being baited 'for being born Jews' and had to be 'insulated by regulation and routine on particular days of the week or month and made to feel the ignominy of the state of life to which the Creator [had] called them'.[76] In 1935 he attacked the 'ferocious' doctrine that had seen the German Jewish population 'stripped of all power, driven from every position in public and social life, expelled from the professions, silenced in the press, and declared a foul and odious race'.[77] He endorsed the proposed Jewish boycott of German goods, arguing in 1937 that the Jews had a right to use their influence round the world to pressurise any governments that persecuted them.

Following the invasion of the USSR, news filtered out of the hideous massacres of Jews that were being perpetrated by the Nazis and their collaborationist allies. 'We are in the presence of a crime without a name,' Churchill declared in a world broadcast. He wrote to the *Jewish Chronicle* 'a special message of good cheer to Jewish people in this and other lands':

> None has suffered more cruelly than the Jews the unspeakable evils wrought upon the bodies and spirits of men by Hitler and his vile regime. [The Jew] bore the brunt of the Nazis' first onslaught upon the citadels of freedom and human dignity. He has borne and continued to bear a burden that might have seen beyond endurance. He has not allowed it to break his spirit; he has never lost the will to resist. Assuredly in the day of victory the Jew's suffering and his part in the struggle will not be forgotten. Once again, at the appointed time, he will see vindicated those principles of righteousness which it was the glory of his fathers to proclaim to the world.[78]

After *The Times* reported in September 1942 that four thousand Jewish children had been deported from France, Churchill condemned the Nazi regime in the House, and in particular 'the most bestial, the most squalid and the most senseless of all their offences, namely the mass deportation of Jews from France, with the pitiful horrors attendant upon the calculated and final scattering of families.'[79]

On October 29th 1942 Anglo-Jewry organised a huge demonstration at the London Albert Hall, chaired by the Archbishop of Canterbury, to condemn the mass extermination of Europe's Jewry. Churchill sent a message to the Archbishop, protesting 'against Nazi atrocities inflicted on the Jews'. He went on: 'The systematic cruelty to which the Jewish people – men, women and children – have been exposed under the Nazi regime are among the most terrible events in history, and place an indelible stain upon all who perpetrate and instigate them.'[80]

On December 17th 1942, at a protest rally organised by the Women's International Zionist organisation in London, Clementine Churchill read out a message from her husband in which he vehemently denounced Hitler's 'satanic design to exterminate the Jewish people in Europe'.[81] That same day the Allies issued a declaration, read out simultaneously in London, Washington and Moscow, that condemned 'this bestial policy of cold blooded extermination'. The Allies had been receiving reports which, taken together, indicated that Jews from across Europe were being deported *en masse* to the East where they faced a horrendous fate.

Churchill also endorsed a policy of retribution with the following statement: 'They [the Allied governments] re-affirm their solemn resolution to ensure that those responsible for these crimes shall not escape retribution, and to press on with the necessary practical measures to this end.' This policy was welcomed by the *Jewish Chronicle* as coming 'not a moment too soon'.[82]

The policy of retribution was reflected in the Three Power Declaration of October 1943, personally drafted by Churchill, in which he affirmed that the perpetrators of 'atrocities, massacres and cold blooded mass executions' would be 'brought back, regardless of expense, to the scene of their crimes and judged on the spot by the peoples whom they have outraged'. On November 1st 1943 the Allies issued the famous Moscow Declaration which followed the spirit of the policy Churchill had previously outlined. The Allies declared that they would pursue 'the ranks of the guilty to the uttermost ends of the earth' and would deliver them to their accusers 'in order that justice may be done'. After the war leading Nazis were put on trial at Nuremberg. Churchill supported the principle of war crimes trials, commenting: 'Terrible evidence has been presented against the accused, and there is no doubt that the trials are just.'[83]

But mere words of condemnation were never enough for a man of action like Churchill. There were times when he was called upon to act and, despite the pressures he was under, he made some important and decisive interventions.

During the early years of the Second World War, Jews living in central and southern Europe made repeated attempts to escape to the safety of Palestine, usually via the Balkans. In 1940 1,771 Jewish immigrants reached Palestine from Europe on two ships, the *Milos* and the *Pacific*. On arrival, they were treated as illegal immigrants and transferred to a French liner, the *Patria*, which was travelling to the French island of Mauritius. In an attempt to immobilise the ship, the Haganah[84] used explosives to blow it up. The force was greater than intended and the ship sank, killing over 250 passengers.

In view of the tragedy, the government decided to allow the remaining refugees to enter Palestine, but General Wavell protested, arguing that the action would alienate opinion in the Arab world. Churchill personally wrote back to Wavell, pointing out the necessity 'on compassionate grounds' not to 'subject them again immediately to the hazards of the sea'. He added: 'It would be act of inhumanity unworthy of British name to force them to re-embark.'[85] Churchill's persuasiveness won the day.

In 1942 the Royal Navy intercepted a ship, the *Darien II*, carrying 793 Jewish refugees who were bound for Palestine. Churchill wanted the refugees to settle in Palestine but Moyne, Minister Resident in Cairo, insisted that they be sent to Mauritius. This was important, he argued, because it would confirm Britain's 'reputation in the Middle East for trustworthiness and firmness'. Churchill got his way and the refugees were allowed into Palestine. At the same time, the War Cabinet suggested that 'all practicable steps should be taken to discourage illegal immigration into Palestine'. But Churchill never approved of a hard-hearted application of restrictive laws on immigration to Palestine. As he told his Cabinet colleagues in 1943, 'I cannot in any circumstances, contemplate an absolute cessation of immigration into Palestine at the discretion of the Arab majority.'[86]

In 1942 Churchill heartily approved a request from the Jewish Agency to allow 4,500 Bulgarian Jews (mainly children) to enter Palestine. 'Bravo!' he wrote to the Colonial Secretary, Oliver Stanley, who had put the request to Churchill. But the plan, which included allowing the transit of 29,000 Jews from south-eastern Europe to Palestine, came to the attention of the Germans and the Palestinian Grand Mufti, Haj Amin al-Husseini. As a result, the Bulgarian government, under German pressure, closed their border to Turkey to prevent the exodus of Jews.

When there was opposition to allowing Jews to enter Palestine, Churchill considered other destinations. At the Bermuda Conference in April 1943, Britain agreed to allow all Jewish refugees who had reached neutral Spain to flee to Allied-controlled North Africa, where they could seek sanctuary. Overcoming objections from President Roosevelt, Churchill said that 'the need for assistance to refugees, in particular Jewish refugees, has not grown less since we discussed the question'. Many hundreds of Jews were subsequently able to leave neutral Spain for safer destinations.[87]

Churchill was aware that other European leaders would be tempted to collaborate with Nazi persecution, or simply ignore the suffering of Jews. When he learned in 1941 that the Iron Guard in Romania had hunted down and massacred hundreds of Jews, he warned Romania's leader, Ion Antonescu, that if he allowed further atrocities to be committed he would be held to account after the war. Sadly his words had little effect; throughout 1941 tens of thousands of Jews were deported and killed by Antonescu's pro-Nazi regime.

In April 1943 Churchill lunched with the Spanish Ambassador to Britain, the Duke of Alba. During their conversation, he raised the issue of the Spanish government's decision to close the Franco-Spanish border to Jewish refugees and prisoners of war. He told the Ambassador 'that if his Government went to the length of preventing these unfortunate people seeking safety from the horrors of Nazi domination, and if they went farther and committed the offence of actually handing them back to the German authorities, that was a thing which would never be forgotten and would poison the relations between the Spanish and British peoples.'[88] Within a few days the Spanish authorities had re-opened the border to allow Jewish refugees to leave. In 1943 Churchill successfully insisted on the immediate repeal of the anti-Semitic Vichy laws that were still in force in Algeria.

In March 1944 Germany occupied Hungary. Churchill was aware that three quarters of a million Jews were at risk from the Nazis and he asked Marshall Tito to protect any Jews who escaped from Hungary to partisan-held Yugoslavia. Tito consented to this request. Within two months the deportation of Hungarian Jewry was under way and, after receiving information that confirmed this, Churchill wrote to Eden the words quoted at the beginning of this section. The point was reiterated in a letter to the Archbishop of Canterbury: 'I fear we are the witnesses of one of the greatest and most horrible crimes ever committed in the whole history of the world.'[89]

In July 1944 representatives of the Jewish Agency asked the British government to consider bombing Auschwitz and the railway lines leading up to it. This followed the release of a report showing that the destination in the east to which vast numbers of Hungarian Jews were being sent was the camp of Auschwitz-Birkenau in Poland. At this site thousands of Jews were being gassed every day. The report was based on the eyewitness testimony of two Jewish inmates who had escaped and fled to Slovakia, from where they compiled their account.[90] The news was subsequently relayed across the globe and found its way to Chaim Weizmann and the Jewish Agency.

Churchill received the request directly from Anthony Eden and responded favourably. He told Eden: 'Get anything out of the Air Force you can, and invoke me if necessary.'[91] Eden passed on Churchill's request to the Air Ministry at once, but it was flatly rejected in September 1944 on 'logistical' grounds. Sinclair wrote that the distance from British bases to Silesia was so great as to rule out an effective operation.

On the assumption that the operation would have saved lives, one might ask why Churchill did not ensure that Auschwitz was bombed. As wartime Prime Minister, he had the power to overrule his officials. But at the time Churchill was dealing with numerous issues of Grand Strategy: the vexed question of Polish independence, the fate of Greece, the Normandy landings, the V1 rocket campaign, the battle raging in Italy and, above all, the imminent threat of Soviet control in Eastern Europe. He could not deal with every issue or operation at length and was forced to reply on subordinates who did not always share his philo-Semitism. Furthermore, Admiral Horthy's government announced an end to the deportation of Hungarian Jews on July 8th, which for Churchill may have ruled out the need to bomb Auschwitz in any case.[92]

At the same time, Churchill was forced to consider the infamous 'trucks for humans' offer that was being made by the Nazis. On May 19th 1944 Joel Brand, a leading Hungarian Zionist, brought to British officials a proposal from Adolf Eichmann, the man in charge of implementing the Final Solution. Eichmann proposed to release all surviving Hungarian Jews in return for ten thousand trucks, which were only to be used on the Eastern Front. Churchill flatly rejected any notion of bargaining with the Nazis, stating that there 'should be no negotiations of any kind on this subject'. He was also aware that accepting the offer would have contradicted the aim of unconditional surrender; it would have divided the Allies and further alienated the Russians.

Following 'trucks for humans' came the less sinister 'Horthy offer'. Regent Admiral Miklos Horthy, spurred on perhaps by pressure from the Allies, offered to put a halt to all deportations of Hungary's Jews. Those people in possession of entry visas for other countries would be allowed to leave. There was some suspicion that Horthy's offer would see Palestine 'swamped' with refugees but, under American pressure, on August 16th the British government announced it would accept Horthy's proposal. Churchill was personally in favour, writing to Eden that he 'should not like England to seem to be wanting to hunt [the Hungarian Jews] down'.[93]

Moved by the plight of European Jewry, Churchill also heartily approved a request for the creation of a Jewish brigade to fight alongside Allied forces in Italy. Despite the objections of other members of the War Cabinet, he felt that, 'in view of the sufferings which the Jewish people were at present enduring there was a strong case for sympathetic consideration of projects in relation to them'. He continued: 'I like the idea of the Jews trying to get at the murderers of their fellow countrymen in Central Europe', and added that they should be allowed to fight with a Jewish Star of David flag.[94] Churchill won the argument and the Jewish Brigade Group was duly formed on September 19th 1944.

Undoubtedly, the British government did not prioritise the rescue of Europe's Jewry during the Second World War. Many officials and ministers remained indifferent to Nazi persecution, harbouring the belief that to single out Jewish suffering would encourage a Zionist movement that they viewed with suspicion or hostility. But even a doggedly philo-Semitic administration that was intent on rescuing European Jewry would have been thwarted by an implacable and determined enemy. Within these constraints, however, Churchill made a number of interventions to try to alleviate the suffering of persecuted Jews. In the face of overwhelming evil, he was far from indifferent.

Did Churchill support the policy of area bombing?

THE DELIBERATE and indiscriminate bombing of the German civilian population by the RAF (and USAAF), also known as area bombing, remains one of the most controversial issues of the Second World War. The policy, which was put into effect from 1942 onwards, was designed to demoralise the enemy and destroy civilian morale. It is estimated that over 600,000 German citizens died following the destruction of major cities such as Berlin, Cologne and Hamburg, and it has led one German historian, Jorg Friedrich, to denounce Churchill as a 'war criminal'. There is no doubt that Churchill authorised and took ultimate responsibility for the policy of area bombing, but for much of his life he had rejected the bombing of civilian populations in war as a crime which would not achieve any military objective. Unknown to many, he expressed the same reservations right up until the end of the Second World War.

During the First World War, Churchill considered the effects of bombing on several occasions. In August 1918 he urged Louis Loucheur, the Under-Secretary of State for Munitions, to 'attack the enemy' and 'carry the war into his own country'. He urged a bombing campaign to 'harry his hungry and dis-spirited cities' so as to 'affect [the enemy's] morale'.[95] But he did not intend the slaughter of civilians. In a memorandum produced for the War Cabinet some months before, Churchill had discussed the tactic of targeting civilians and his views proved to be remarkably prescient. 'It is improbable,' he wrote, 'that any terrorisation of the civil population which could be achieved by air attack would compel the Government of a great nation to surrender ... In our own case we have seen the combative spirit of the people roused, and not quelled, by the German air raids.' The German people, with their capacity for suffering, would not be 'cowed into submission by such methods' and might be 'rendered more desperately resolved by them'.

The raids he was referring to were those launched from German aeroplanes, such as the Gotha, and the Zeppelins. Churchill recommended that air power be directed, not at civilian targets, but at the 'bases and communications upon whose structure the fighting power of the enemy's armies and his fleets of the sea and of the air depends'.[96]

Twenty years later his views had not changed. In an article for *The News of the World* he wrote: 'I do not believe in reprisals upon the enemy civilian population. On the contrary, the more they try to kill our women and children, the more we should devote ourselves to killing their fighting men and smashing up the technical apparatus upon which the life of the armies depends.' It was acceptable to destroy purely military targets upon which the enemy army relied, such as 'railway junctions' and 'military depots'.97

Throughout the 1930s British politicians panicked about the likely effects of aerial bombardment. Baldwin famously declared that the bomber would 'always get through' and that the only way to protect a civil population was to promise retribution against any enemy willing to attack first. Churchill rejected the case for 'the murdering of women and children as an orthodox and legitimate means of civilised war'. It was a 'horrible, senseless, brutal method of warfare'.98

Churchill's skepticism about the value of bombing civilian targets was reinforced by the Spanish Civil War. In an article published in 1938, he considered that, when the cities of 'Madrid, Barcelona and Valencia' had been attacked from the air, 'the psychological effects upon the civil population' were 'the opposite of what the German and Italian air bombers had expected'. Instead of inducing panic and submission to the enemy will, the bombers 'aroused a spirit of furious and unyielding resistance among all classes'. The destruction of the civilian population through bombing was described as a 'base and barbarous' method of warfare.99

Later he prophesied that a period of immense suffering resulting from the aerial slaughter of non-combatants, if 'borne with fortitude', would only 'seal the comradeship of many nations to save themselves'.100 He re-emphasised the futility of bombing civilians a year later. Reflecting once more on the experience of the Spanish Civil War, he wrote that 'the whole effect of the German and Italian bombing of the Spanish towns has been to animate and exhilarate the whole people'. He went on: 'Murdering women and children from the air has not sapped the spirit either of the fighting men or of the surviving women and children themselves. On the contrary, the hostile airplanes ... have been the best recruiters.'101 Prior to the Second World War, Churchill did not consider it strategically wise or morally acceptable to target civilians using air power.

At the height of the Blitz in October 1940, there were numerous calls for reprisals to be carried out against German cities. Churchill had already staked his faith in the power of bombers to provide 'the means of victory'. He had declared: 'There is one thing that will bring [Germany] ... down, and that is an absolutely devastating, exterminating attack by very heavy bombers from this country upon the Nazi homeland.'[102]

But he continued to insist on attacking only military targets. Nicolson recorded in his diary an exchange between Churchill and the MP Robert Cary, who made the point that public opinion demanded the unrestricted bombardment of Germany as retaliation for the Blitz. Churchill replied that this was 'a military and not a civilian war' and that, whereas others had a 'desire to kill women and children', his government wished only 'to destroy German military objectives'.[103] In March 1941, according to John Colville, Churchill remained 'unmoved by bloodthirsty demands for the destruction of Germany' and would 'never condone atrocities against the German civil population'.[104]

In a minute from September 1941, he wrote that it was 'very disputable whether bombing by itself [would] be a decisive factor in the present war'. Repeating some of the arguments he had produced in the previous world war, he wrote that the Blitz had merely 'stimulated and strengthened' the British people, while the effects of British bombing on the enemy's morale were 'greatly exaggerated'.[105] Daylight bombing of German factories, if it were possible, would provide 'a different picture'.[106]

Clearly something changed between 1941 and 1942 when area bombing became a central tactic in Britain's air duel with Germany. In 1940 the British authorities feared that their heavy bombers were at risk from defending German fighters and they were aware that the Germans had a larger air force. Bombing attacks that were mounted without the protection of escorting fighters therefore took place at night. This provided additional protection for the British bombers with the disadvantage that the targets, such as oil installations and aircraft factories, could not be accurately seen or hit. If a bombing offensive was to continue, and in 1940-1 it was the only means of taking the war to Germany, the bombers needed larger targets, and it became rapidly clear that the smallest ones to be hit were towns.

From this operational 'problem' the doctrine of area bombing was born. But the Chiefs of Staff were also arguing that, unlike in Britain, German morale would be affected by targeting German cities. The reason they cited was that the Germans had been 'undernourished

and subjected to a permanent strain equivalent to that of war conditions during almost the whole period of Hitler's regime'.[107] That
the Chiefs' assessment was open to doubt mattered less than their
overall conclusions. Churchill was also influenced by his chief scientific adviser, Professor Lindemann. In 1942 Lindemann presented a
'dehousing' paper to the Cabinet in which he advocated the area
bombardment of German cities.

The policy of area bombing is usually associated with Air Chief
Marshal Sir Arthur 'Bomber' Harris, who became Commander in
Chief of the British Bomber Command. In 1942 he launched the
thousand-bomber raids on Cologne, Essen and Bremen which caused
extensive damage to all three cities. Thereafter he embarked on
'a systematic attempt to tear the heart out of the major German
industrial and transport towns from the Ruhr to Berlin'.[108] In July
1943 a massive raid on Hamburg (Operation Gomorrah) caused forty
thousand German fatalities, and an enormous and sustained air
offensive was launched against Berlin between November 1943 and
March 1944, greatly damaging the city but also costing thousands of
bombers.[109]

It may seem that Churchill was prepared to bury his earlier
qualms about targeting civilians. After all, he was aware that the
bombing of cities would involve a huge loss of civilian life as well as
the destruction of non-military infrastructure. Towards the end of
1942 he argued that the 'severe, ruthless bombing of Germany on an
ever increasing scale will not only cripple her war effort ... but will
also create conditions intolerable to the mass of German population.'
The bomber offensive, he went on, could break 'her war-will'.[110]

Private documents reveal, however, that he maintained his
scepticism about the effectiveness and morality of area bombing. In
1942, while watching a film showing the bombing of German towns,
he suddenly and dramatically turned round to his assembled guests
and blurted out: 'Are we beasts? Are we taking this too far?'[111]

In truth, Churchill was ambivalent about the policy of area
bombing. One reason why he sanctioned it was that it would make
up for the delay in opening the second front. Since 1941 Stalin had
been urging the Western Allies to launch an invasion of continental
Europe and take the heat off his beleaguered Soviet forces. A sympathetic Churchill repeatedly disappointed Stalin by revealing how ill-
prepared British troops were for the task. A bombing campaign was
therefore offered as 'compensation'.

At no point was area bombing more controversial than with the destruction of Dresden. On February 13th and 14th 1945, more than eight hundred planes of the RAF and six hundred planes of the USAAF bombed the town, causing such a devastating firestorm that temperatures rose to over 1,800 degrees Fahrenheit.[112] It was estimated that between 40,000 and 135,000 people died, though the figures are hotly disputed. There is no doubt that the ancient, historic city noted for its splendid architecture was reduced to ruins very quickly.

Dresden's status as a cultural icon has allowed it to be portrayed as lacking any military value whatever. This is quite false. The city included the Zeiss-Ikon optical works which made lenses for submarine periscopes, the Siemens electrical plant and a number of factories that produced engines for fighter planes. It also had a number of important bridges and railways. Dresden was thus as much of a 'legitimate' target as any other German city that Bomber Command had attacked and only its cultural significance turned it into a pawn of Nazi propaganda. This can be appreciated by examining the background to the operation.

In January 1945 the air ministry drew up plan Thunderclap, which would involve bombing raids on Berlin and other eastern German cities. This was designed to tie in with the Soviet advance into Germany, which appeared to be the main means of bringing the war to an end. Decoded Enigma messages, which were passed to the Russians, indicated that the Germans were withdrawing many of their best divisions from Germany, Italy and Norway to launch a counter-attack against the Soviet army in Silesia. One of the deciphered messages was a German order to transfer troops through Dresden to attack the Soviets in the Breslau area. It was the Soviets who requested the bombing of Dresden so as to impede this transport of troops.

In any event, Churchill never ordered the bombing of Dresden. At the time the Soviet request was made, he was on his way to the Yalta conference, leaving responsibility in the hands of his deputy, Clement Attlee. Furthermore, Churchill's minute of March 28th 1945 suggests that he was uneasy about the attack on Dresden: 'It seems to me that the moment has come when the question of bombing of German cities simply for the sake of increasing the terror ... should be reviewed. Otherwise we shall come into control of an utterly ruined land ... The destruction of Dresden remains a serious query against the conduct of Allied bombing.'[113] True, Churchill wrote that minute in the midst of concerted criticism of the attack and he may have simply been trying to distance himself from blame, but it tallies with the qualms he expressed on earlier occasions.

Churchill's critics contend that he never overruled Harris, though he undoubtedly lacked his crusading zeal. Indeed in 1944, in a major speech to the House of Commons on war strategy, Churchill talked of how the 'marauding states' had used air power as a chief 'tool of conquest' by which to subjugate others. There was now, he said, a 'strange, stern justice in the long swing of events'.[114] Perhaps it was for this reason that Churchill fought for Sir Arthur Harris to receive a post-war honour when the former Air Marshal was shunned by some of his former colleagues. Clement Attlee refused, but Churchill bestowed on him a baronetcy when he became Prime Minister again in 1951.

For much of his career, Churchill adamantly opposed deliberate warfare against civilians, preferring to concentrate on purely military targets, yet, during the Second World War he oversaw the ruthless destruction of cities with their large civilian populations. He consistently expressed ambivalence about the operations and, to some, these reservations are to his credit. Others remain sharply critical of a policy that, they believe, put Britain on a moral par with their Nazi foe.

It is as well for the critics to remember that Britain was fighting a total war against a military hegemonic power. From the outset, Churchill realised that Britain could not match Germany in military terms but a bombing campaign could soften up the enemy in readiness for a future Allied invasion. He also knew that, because his enemy had ruthlessly targeted British cities, public morale demanded a suitable and equivalent response. But crucially, from June 1941, Britain's Soviet ally was bearing the brunt of German agression. Churchill could not provide Stalin with a second front in Europe but he could appease him with the knowledge that bombers were destroying German infrastructure and lowering civilian morale. One should consider the words of Albert Speer in this regard:

> The real importance of the air war consisted in the fact that it opened a second front long before the invasion of Europe. That front was the skies over Germany ... The unpredictability of the attacks made the front gigantic.[115]

This is surely the legitimate context for viewing the horrors of area bombing, a policy in which Churchill reluctantly acquiesced after years of public opposition.

Did Churchill betray Eastern Europe during the Second World War?

THE COLLAPSE of the Berlin Wall in 1989 brought an end to an era of communist domination in Eastern Europe. One by one communist governments were toppled in the 'velvet revolution', leading to an upsurge in nationalist sentiment across the Continent. Having broken the shackles of foreign domination, the long-suffering peoples of Poland, Hungary, Romania, Bulgaria and Czechoslovakia were finally able to embrace the rights and freedoms that had been denied them for so long. For those who had prophesied the collapse of the Soviet Empire, this was a moment to savour. As a lifelong foe of Communism, Winston Churchill would have been among them. Churchill condemned the post-war Soviet takeover of Europe and spoke of how an 'iron curtain' had descended upon the Continent. But he never lost faith in democracy and once told his private secretary that, while he would not live to see the collapse of the Iron Curtain, his secretary would.

It seems deeply ironic, then, that in the post-communist era Churchill has been accused of engineering the Soviet domination of Eastern Europe. By a curious twist of fate, Churchill has even been blamed for appeasing a tyrant, masterminding a second Munich and selling out the interests of his allies. Can there be any substance to these allegations? Churchill's role in the post-war settlement merits careful scrutiny but the picture that emerges is more nuanced than his critics imagine.

Poland
In 1939 Britain went to war, ostensibly, to defend Poland. On March 31st 1939 Chamberlain broke with decades of foreign policy tradition by giving Poland a guarantee that, if her independence as a sovereign state was violated, Britain would help to restore it. Militarily, this made little sense, for Poland could not realistically be defended from a German attack. The guarantee was largely designed as a form of psychological reassurance and a way of deterring further aggression

from Germany. In the event Poland was easily overcome in September 1939 by a combination of German and Russian firepower;[116] Britain and France could only watch from the sidelines. However, after Operation Barbarossa Stalin re-established diplomatic relations with the Poles at the end of July 1941.

In 1941 the Russians made it clear that one of their post-war aims was to secure their borders from attack. This would inevitably involve redrawing their border with a post-war Poland, incorporating some of the land they had seized in September 1939. The establishment of the new border, which became known as the 'Curzon Line', would mean that Russia would incorporate one fifth of Polish territory and several million Polish people. Unsurprisingly, the Polish government in exile strongly rejected the proposal.

Churchill had been adamant in July 1941 that 'His Majesty's government did not recognise territorial changes affecting Poland made since August 1939.'[117] He therefore emphatically rejected Stalin's demand, made to Eden in December 1941, that the Baltic States as well as eastern Poland be transferred to Russia after the war. Churchill recognised that any forcible transfer of people to an alien country would violate the spirit of the Atlantic Charter and shatter the principles of freedom for which the war was being fought. When the Anglo-Soviet treaty[118] was signed in May 1942, Churchill told Stalin that there would be no compromise on the undertakings made to Poland.

There was little discussion on the Polish question until the startling revelations of the Katyn massacre in April 1943. German troops in the Katyn forest[119] discovered the corpses of nearly 4,500 Polish officers, all of whom had been shot from behind. These officers had previously been interned by the Soviet authorities and the conclusion was drawn that they had been brutally murdered on the orders of the Kremlin. When the commander-in-chief of Polish forces in the west, General Sikorski, publicly denounced the Soviet regime for the murders, against Churchill's advice, Stalin promptly cut off relations with the London Poles. At the same time, Stalin continued to insist that the post-war Russo-Polish border be reconstructed on the basis of the Curzon Line.

Churchill's reaction to the Katyn massacre demonstrated that he was susceptible, like Chamberlain, to the charge of appeasement. While Churchill admitted to the Poles that the officers had probably been shot by the Soviets ('the Bolsheviks can be very cruel'), he denied their request for an International Red Cross inquiry. He also warned Sikorski not to raise the Katyn issue publicly and used censorship on Polish language newspapers in Britain to ensure that they did not 'endorse the German claims'.[120]

Churchill now had to balance the competing needs of two important allies: the interests of the Poles in not seeing their country dismembered and the Soviet requirement for post-war security. Given that the Soviets were bearing the brunt of attacks by Hitler's forces, he could hardly ignore them; but Churchill was to spend the next eighteen months in a fruitless search for compromise.[121]

The future of Poland was discussed at the 1943 Teheran Conference. While Churchill stressed the need to have a strong and independent Poland, he drew suggested frontier lines for a post-war Soviet-Polish border. Poland would lose land in the east, which Russia would gain, but gain land in the west, at the expense of Germany. This was demonstrated with the help of three matches. Stalin claimed the city of Lvov, which Churchill and Roosevelt appeared to accept, and Poland would receive some compensation in the north, together with the German city of Konigsberg. Churchill made it clear to Stalin that he agreed with these arrangements, but he stressed that 'he had no power from Parliament ... to define any frontier lines'.[122] At best he could seek to recommend the frontiers agreed at Teheran to the Poles in London. He accepted that a 'decision to resist' was the 'privilege of every nation'.[123]

When Churchill met the London Poles in January and February 1944, he tried in vain to persuade them to accept Stalin's border proposals. He tried to impress on them the sheer scale of Russian losses (twenty million deaths), and that without their contribution Poland would have ceased to exist. Initially there were signs of a *rapprochement* as the London Poles ordered the Polish Underground to co-operate with the Soviets in fighting the Germans.

But the London Poles were suspicious of Soviet promises, shaken as they were by revelations of the Katyn massacre and Stalin's decision to break off all diplomatic relations. As a result, they were very wary of compromise. Despite the fact that the new leader of the London Poles, Stanisław Mikolajczyk, was willing to discuss the question of frontiers in a post-war settlement, Stalin insisted that they accept the new frontiers straight away and reconstruct their government on lines favourable to Moscow. These were conditions that Mikolajczyk simply could not accept.

On first inspection, Churchill's behaviour appears to suggest a classic volte-face. Was this not the cynical betrayal of a weaker ally in the face of pressure and intimidation? Such a facile view misses the essential context of the discussions. In recommending that the Poles accept his suggested territorial revisions, Churchill was aware that in due course the Red Army would be on Polish soil. From that position they would, by *force majeure,* settle the border issue themselves. When the Poles made the reasonable point that the frontier changes would mean an unwarranted population transfer, Churchill asked whether this was worse than waiting 'while the Russian army rolled on' and left the 'ultimate fate' of the Poles 'to the decision of the Soviet government'.[124] He was thinking along these lines when, in January 1944, he minuted Eden that 'the questions of Bukovina and Bessarabia have very largely settled themselves through the victories of the Russian armies'.[125]

By July 1944 Soviet forces had crossed the temporarily designated western frontier of Poland, which was known as the Curzon Line. Churchill tried to browbeat Mikolajczyk into accepting changed borders but his language revealed all too clearly the new realities of power: 'brutal facts could not be overlooked. He could no more stop the Russian advance than stop the tide coming in.'[126] On more than one occasion he told the London Poles that it would be 'unthinkable' for Britain to go to war with the Soviet Union to defend disputed borders. More importantly for Churchill, 'the United States would certainly never do so'.[127] Again in February 1944 he told the Poles that 'Britain would always do her best against tyranny in whatever form it showed itself. But Britain, though better situated, was not much bigger than Poland. We would do our best, but this would not save Poland.'[128] It was a stark admission of British weakness and of the dangerous shift of power in international relations.

Churchill's concern was to salvage something for Poland before the Red Army occupied the country and set up a puppet state under the communists. He had repeatedly warned the London Poles that, if there was no agreement with the Russians, the Red Army, on reaching Warsaw, 'would probably set up a Polish government, based on a plebiscite, having every aspect of democratic and popular foundation, and in full accord with the Russian view'.[129] This explains his warning to the Poles later that, if they continued to hold out for their pre-1939 borders and also Vilna and Lvov, the Soviets would set up a puppet government and a plebiscite 'under which the opponents of Soviet plans would be unable to vote'.[130]

A future puppet government was revealed in July 1944 when Stalin set up the Lublin Committee of National Liberation (an organisation which was stuffed with communists) to administer the liberated areas of Poland. Stalin had not trusted the London Poles, declaring that he was 'more convinced than ever that men of their type are incapable of establishing normal relations with the USSR'. However, the closest that they came in agreement to Stalin's request was that a new government should discuss. 'as part of a general settlement, a new frontier between Poland and the Soviet Union', though this would be in a future peace settlement.[131]

When the Red Army occupied Lublin on July 23rd 1944, the Committee declared that it was the only legal executive power in the country. Churchill was adamant that the Soviets should recognise the London Poles as the provisional government and not set up their own puppet government in Warsaw. 'It would be a great pity and even a disaster,' he telegraphed to Stalin on July 27th, 'if the Western Democracies found themselves recognising one body of Poles and you recognising another'.[132]

It was at this moment that the Warsaw uprising took place. On July 29th 1944 Moscow Radio broadcast to the people of Warsaw, encouraging them to rise up against their German oppressors and aid the coming Russian onslaught. In response, forty thousand Poles, together with the remnants of the country's Jewish population, rose up against the Germans in order to liberate themselves rather than wait to be liberated by the Russians. Churchill immediately responded to their call for arms, announcing a delivery of sixty tons of equipment and ammunition and calling on Stalin for a reciprocal gesture. But Stalin doubted that the Polish Home Army was in any position to capture Warsaw, given the strength of the German opposition. He spoke of the uprising as a 'reckless and terrible adventure which is costing the population large sacrifices'.[133]

Meanwhile the Red Army, which had entered the city, met heavy German resistance and halted any further advance. Stalin, who knew that the underground supported the London rather than the Lublin Poles, saw a chance for the Germans to kill off troublesome opposition to Soviet domination. This is certainly how Churchill saw it later: 'It certainly is very curious that the Russian armies should have ceased their attack on Warsaw and withdrawn some distance at the

moment when the underground army had revolted. It would only be
a flight of 100 miles for them to send in all the necessary quantities
of ammunition and machine guns the Poles need for their heroic
flight.'[134]

In the end Britain could not deliver aid safely as deliveries
required Russian help that was unforthcoming. As W. Averell Harriman put it: 'Churchill's repeated appeals for help in behalf of the
Warsaw insurgents had no effect except to sharpen Stalin's rage
against the Poles for their effrontery.'[135] Churchill, by contrast, paid
statesmanlike tribute to the Polish resistance which the Germans
brutally crushed. 'I wish', he told the Commons, 'to express our
respect to all those Poles who fell, fought or suffered at Warsaw and
our sympathy with the Polish nation in this further grievous loss.'[136]
The idea that Churchill, rather than Stalin, betrayed the Poles
during the uprising is another egregious myth.

Churchill hoped, in vain, that the London Poles would work with
the Lublin committee. A meeting in Moscow in October 1944
between Stalin and Mikolajczyk ended acrimoniously with the latter
unable to accept either Stalin's conditions or the British guarantees
of security. By December 8th 1944 Stalin had told Churchill that
Mikolajczyk was incapable of helping a Polish settlement. Despite
the protests of his Allies, Stalin formally recognised the Lublin committee as the provisional government of Poland on January 5th 1945.

By the time of the Yalta conference in February 1945, Russian
forces were in control of Poland, strengthening Stalin's diplomatic
hand. Churchill and Roosevelt both stressed the need for a representative 'provisional' government in Poland which would consist, in
part, of the London Poles. Churchill then hoped for 'free and unfettered elections on the basis of universal suffrage and a secret ballot',
in which democratic parties would have the 'right to participate and
run candidates'. By contrast, Stalin argued that the Lublin Poles
should form the provisional Polish government and that they, unlike
the London Poles, were popular throughout the country.

Roosevelt now changed tack, agreeing with Stalin's request to
allow the Lublin Poles to have at least majority control of the
provisional government. This change of heart somewhat distressed
Churchill, as did Stalin's refusal to allow monitors to oversee a Polish
election. Churchill's commitment to a democratic Poland was unwavering, but without Roosevelt's political support he was reduced
to a position of sheer diplomatic impotence.[137]

By the end of the Yalta conference there was an Allied commit-ment to a 'strong, free, independent, and democratic Poland'. While acknowledging the role of the Lublin Poles, there was a call for the 'inclusion of democratic leaders from Poland itself and from Poles abroad'. Over the next few months, however, Stalin would exclude all Poles whom he deemed unfriendly to the Soviet Union, while banning outside electoral observers. In practice, this meant the exclusion of almost all the London Poles.[138] With the Red Army's iron grip on the country complete, legislative elections were delayed, and when they took place in 1947 they were inevitably controlled by the Communist government.

One has to conclude that Churchill did what he could for the Poles from the disadvantageous position of military and diplomatic weakness.

Greece and Balkans

Churchill is also accused of engineering Soviet domination in the Balkans through his infamous 'percentages agreement' with Stalin in October 1944. In May 1944 the Soviet ambassador in London heard a suggestion from Eden that Britain would regard Romania as a Russian concern provided that the Russians left Greece to Britain. When Churchill consulted his US ally about this proposal, the reaction was one of scepticism. Cordell Hull, the Secretary of State, rejected the notion of a spheres-of-influence arrangement patched together in war.

On October 9th 1944, during his visit to Moscow, Churchill handed a document to Stalin proposing to divide Eastern Europe into 'spheres of influence'. This is Churchill's account of the meeting:

> The moment was apt for business, so I said [to Stalin], 'Let us settle about our affairs in the Balkans. Your armies are in Roumania and Bulgaria. We have interests, missions, and agents there. Don't let us get at cross-purposes in small ways. So far as Britain and Russia are concerned, how would it do for you to have ninety per cent predom-inance in Roumania, for us to have ninety per cent of the say in Greece, and go fifty-fifty about Yugoslavia?' While this was being translated I wrote out on a half-sheet of paper:

> *Roumania*
> Russia   90
> The others   10

Greece	
GB	90
Russia	10

Yugoslavia	50-50

Hungary	50-50

Bulgaria	
Russia	75
The others	25

I pushed this across to Stalin, who had by then heard the translation. There was a slight pause. Then he took his blue pencil and made a large tick upon it, and passed it back to us. It was all settled in no more time than it takes to set down ... After this there was a long silence. The pencilled paper lay in the centre of the table. At length I said, 'Might it not be thought rather cynical if it seemed we had disposed of these issues so fateful to millions of people, in such an offhand manner? Let us burn the paper'. 'No, you keep it,' said Stalin.'[139]

This one-off piece of personal diplomacy has gone down in folklore as a classic Anglo-Russian carve-up of the Balkans, a cynical piece of *Realpolitik* which preserved Britain's imperial interests at the expense of smaller nations. For many, it has come to symbolise how Churchill sacrificed the right to self-determination of millions of Eastern Europeans on the altar of British imperial power. According to Clive Ponting, this was an agreement 'steeped in *Realpolitik* and self interest' which resembled the Munich Agreement of 1938 to which Churchill was so bitterly opposed.[140] The historian Warren Kimball said that this was 'not Churchill's finest hour'.[141]

It is possible to see this 'cynical deal' in a very different light, however. In October 1944 Churchill could do very little to prevent a full Soviet takeover of Hungary, Bulgaria and Rumania. The Red Army was in the process of overrunning Rumania and Bulgaria and was slowly making its way through Hungary. As Carlton puts it, the Soviet armies in Rumania and Bulgaria 'stood in no real need of British blessing'.[142] In the armistice agreements of 1945, the occupation of former Axis countries was decided by the military power in occupation and, in the three cases mentioned, this was the Soviet Union.

Aware of Britain's lack of diplomatic leverage and the unwillingness of President Roosevelt to open a breach with Stalin, Churchill, at his cunning best, salvaged the best deal he could get for British (and Greek) interests. Far from cynically disposing of the interests of millions, Churchill tried to put a limit on Stalin's takeover of Europe by securing a free, non-communist Greece. He explained to Eden his hopes for the future of the Balkans: 'If we manage these affairs well we shall perhaps prevent several civil wars and much bloodshed and strife in the small countries concerned.' He went on: 'Our broad principle should be to let every country have the form of government which its people desire.'[143]

Armed with Stalin's signature, Churchill sent British paratroopers to intervene in the Greek Civil War between liberal monarchists and a partisan communist army that had spearheaded resistance to Hitler since 1941. This was a vital action at the time for it was likely that, by the end of 1944, a 'communist insurrection would overwhelm Athens'.[144] Without his intervention, the communists might easily have seized power in Greece. As David Carlton, a critic of Churchill's policy towards Russia, puts it: 'the truth seems to be that at a time of great national weakness Churchill, without a single decent card in his hand, effectively bluffed Stalin into giving him a free hand in Greece.'[145] Though damned at the time for appeasing Stalin, Churchill's far-sighted policy in saving Greece from communism was eventually lauded in Washington.

Did Churchill appease Stalin?

THROUGHOUT THE 1930s Churchill staked his reputation on opposing the craven appeasement of Hitler by British politicians. 'It seems a mad business', he wrote once, 'to confront dictators without weapons or military force.'[146] Another time he expressed it differently: 'Short of being actually conquered, there is no evil worse than submitting to wrong and violence for fear of war.'[147] He condemned the injudicious and short-sighted concessions made to avoid direct confrontation with the Nazis and described the signing of the Munich Agreement as a 'black day' for Britain. But was the arch anti-appeaser guilty of the very same crime during the Second World War? Some historians would now argue that Churchill appeased Joseph Stalin as naively as Chamberlain appeased Hitler. They charge that he misguidedly trusted Stalin's good intentions while remaining blind to his plans for a post-war domination of Eastern Europe.

Some evidence undoubtedly supports this interpretation. According to Lord Moran, Churchill expressed the view that Stalin was not 'unfriendly' to British interests.[148] He sought to 'win Stalin's friendship' for he was sure Stalin 'would be sensible' and that 'once he says something, he sticks to it'.[149] In an echo of Chamberlain's declaration of peace in our time, Churchill told the Commons after his return from Yalta that Stalin wanted 'to live in honourable friendship and equality with the Western democracies', and said of the Russians: 'Their word is their bond.'[150]

The accusation of appeasement is closely connected to the issue of Polish independence in 1943-4. Churchill is usually accused of writing off the Poles in the way that Chamberlain wrote off the Czechs in 1938. Churchill accepted Stalin's request to change the Polish borders, knowing that this would displace millions of people. He repeatedly tried to get the Polish government in exile to agree to the changes, arguing that their failure to acquiesce could lead to a major diplomatic rupture. He also silenced the London Poles after they were justifiably outraged following revelations of the Katyn massacre. Worse, his percentages agreement appeared to offer far-reaching concessions to Stalin in his control of Romania, Bulgaria and Hungary while Britain was in a position of military and diplomatic weakness.

Harold Nicolson recalled Churchill's view that the Polish settlement was the best Britain could get, given the enormous power of the Russian army, but it also 'seemed to him a mistake to assume that the Russians [were] going to behave badly'.[151] It took *The Economist* to call for an end to the 'policy of appeasement' towards Stalin (and Roosevelt) which had been carried out for years 'at Mr. Churchill's personal bidding'.[152]

When he returned from Yalta, Churchill sought to persuade the War Cabinet of Stalin's honourable intentions. According to one eye witness at the meeting, he declared: 'Stalin I'm sure means well to the world and Poland. Stalin has offered the Polish people a free and more broadly based government to bring about an election.' He added, 'Stalin had a very good feeling with the two Western democracies and wants to work quite easily with us. My hopes lie in a single man, he will not embark on bad adventures.'[153] In retrospect, these sentiments seem embarrassingly myopic.

Churchill is also open to other charges of appeasement. During the summer of 1944, he was forced to agree to the repatriation of

thousands of Soviet prisoners of war. These soldiers had been captured by the Germans and had subsequently decided to fight on the
German side against the Allies, but now sought asylum in the West.
It was generally acknowledged that the men would face a terrible fate
if they returned to the Soviet Union, but offering them sanctuary in
the West would be equally damaging for Anglo-Soviet relations.[154]

Churchill agreed to Eden's request for repatriating the men but it
is worth pointing out, as does his official biographer, that Churchill
expressed severe doubts about the morality of such an action. What
weighed on Churchill's mind at the time of Yalta was the fate of
thousands of British prisoners of war in the East. In imploring Stalin
to turn the men over, a reciprocal arrangement had to be made
involving the Soviet POWs.

Finally, the 1944 percentages agreement was based on a 'naughty
document' signed by Churchill and Stalin which relied implicitly on
the trust of the Russian dictator. Nigel Knight comments on the
irony that Churchill 'believed that a piece of paper assented to by a
dictator constituted a binding agreement between nations'.[155]

The appeasement comparison works up to a point. Both
Churchill and Chamberlain could be conceited and egocentric in
their dealings with dictators. To one colleague Churchill remarked:
'If only I could dine with Stalin once a week, there would be no
trouble at all. We get on like a house on fire.'[156] Referring to the 'Big
Three', Churchill is said to have commented, 'If we three come
together everything is possible.'[157] These sentiments sound dangerously like Chamberlain's comment, in a letter to his sister, that all he
had to do was 'sit down at a table with the Germans and run through
all their complaints with a pencil'.[158] Churchill's roseate perception
derived, in part, from his Whig belief that great men were the motor
force of history, and that Stalin was 'already one of the great figures
of history'.[159] Churchill's occasional myopia was shared by Roosevelt,
who told a former ambassador to France that Stalin only wanted to
'work for a world of democracy and peace'.[160]

Churchill certainly had his blind spots about Stalin, but blind
spots are less fatal than full-blown myopia. From early on, Churchill
was more than alert to the political machinations emanating from
the Kremlin, while Chamberlain, as late as March 1939, did not fully
believe in the Nazi threat to Europe. In 1942 Churchill spoke of the
'measureless disaster' that would follow 'if Russian barbarism over-
laid the culture and independence of the ancient states of Europe'.[161]

Harold Macmillan once recalled a wartime conversation with Churchill in which the premier reflected on Oliver Cromwell: 'Cromwell was a great man ... but he made one terrible mistake. Obsessed in his youth by fear of the power of Spain, he failed to observe the rise of France. Will that be said of me?'[162] For France, one has to read Russia. During the Quebec Conference in 1943, Churchill reflected on his dealings with the Soviet Union and foresaw 'bloody consequences in the future'. Stalin was, he thought, 'an unnatural man'.[163]

While Churchill was prepared to negotiate the borders of Poland with Stalin, having previously said that the Soviet Union would never be allowed to benefit from the territorial gains of 1939-40, this was not peace at any price. Britain would not agree to Poland becoming a mere 'puppet state of Russia' where 'the people who don't agree with Stalin are bumped off'.[164] Churchill's firm handling of the London Poles was based on his knowledge that, without a settlement over Poland, Stalin would impose his own solution on the country which would be to its profound detriment. He also saw quite clearly that the Lublin Poles were servants of the Russian regime with little interest in a post-war democratic Poland.

Churchill was certainly aware that appeasing Stalin carried disagreeable connotations. On one occasion he told Eden: 'Although I have tried in every way to put myself in sympathy with these communist leaders, I cannot feel the slightest trust or confidence in them. Force and facts are their only realities.' Later he would write with foreboding that 'the Russians are drunk with victory and there are no lengths they may not go'.[165] To Tommy Lascelles Churchill admitted: 'If my shirt were taken off now it would be seen that my belly is sore from crawling to that man.' He added, 'I do it for the good of the country, and for no other reason.'[166] And, in a more humourous vein, he would compare the Soviets to a crocodile: 'When it opens its mouth you cannot tell whether it is trying to smile or preparing to eat you up.'

Throughout 1944 and 1945, Churchill was haunted by the fear that Stalinist rule would spread across Eastern Europe. The 'Red Army', he declared, 'was spreading like a cancer from one country to another'.[167] It was this obsessive fear of a post-war Soviet domination of Eastern Europe that galvanised him into trying to alter Allied strategy in 1945. As the Russians advanced westwards into Europe, Churchill was determined to see the Allied armies meet the Russians as far east as possible.

He therefore called for a British force to arrive in Vienna before the Red Army, but this idea was rejected by the Americans. When, in March 1945, the Allied armies were racing faster across Germany than the Russians, Churchill saw the real possibility of an Allied march towards Prague or Berlin ahead of the Russians. But Eisenhower scuppered any such move, informing Stalin that the Allied armies would not advance in that direction.[168] In one sense, Eisenhower was right. Berlin was deep inside the Russian zone allocated at Yalta and any occupation would have had to be reversed swiftly. It is also doubtful whether the western armies could have reached Prague or Vienna, via southern Europe, before the Red Army.[169]

At one point Churchill even went so far as to instruct Montgomery to collect German arms and hold them in reserve in case they needed to be used against the Russians. When this was revealed later, it caused a sensation.

As one of his private secretaries recalled of Churchill, 'He pleaded, in vain, that the Western forces should not fall back from the positions they had won in battle to the lines of the occupation zones until there had been a further parley with the Russian leaders to test their long-term intentions.'[170] Among these conditions were assurances about the future of Poland, as well as the 'character of the Russian occupation of Germany' and the 'conditions to be established in the Russianised or Russian-controlled countries in the Danube valley, particularly Austria and Czechoslovakia, and the Balkans.'[171] The failure of Roosevelt and his commanders to accept his dire warnings was not due to 'any slackening in the force and vehemence with which [Churchill] sought to exercise his influence over the development of Western policy'.[172] In the end, the Red Army would reach Prague, Vienna and Berlin with deleterious consequences for all three.

It was for this reason that Churchill called the final volume of his war memoirs *Triumph and Tragedy*. The fact that he was prepared to change Allied strategy and take a more forceful position with Stalin removes much of the criticism that he was a mere dupe of the Russian dictator. Churchill understood that force and the logic of possession would help convince Stalin of Allied intentions. For this reason he quipped at Yalta that, while Stalin professed a desire for peace, this really meant that he wanted 'a piece of Poland, a piece of Czechoslovakia, a piece of Romania'.[173] So why did Churchill's view not prevail?

The answer lies in the changed realities of British power. With the Red Army crossing Poland's eastern frontier, and in near complete occupation of Romania and Bulgaria, Britain's diplomatic leverage was very limited. Churchill was reliant on Stalin to sweep away Hitler's armies and needed to retain his goodwill for as long as possible. But without the back-up of the United States, Britain alone could not take a forceful stand on Poland or the impending Soviet occupation of Eastern Europe. For this reason one can argue that Churchill did the best that he could for the Poles, given the slender diplomatic and military resources at his disposal. Britain was the weakest of the Allied triumvirate in 1945 and Churchill recognised this better than anyone.

What role did Churchill play in the bombing of Hiroshima?

TWICE IN 1945, the United States unleashed the atomic bomb on Japan, ending the Second World War in Asia. When 'Little Boy' and 'Fat Man'[174] exploded above Hiroshima and Nagasaki on August 6th and 9th respectively, the world entered a new era of warfare with immense repercussions for global security. Though it was an American operation carried out by the USAAF, it required British approval, and the story of Churchill's involvement is fascinating.

Churchill arguably anticipated the atomic age by at least two decades. In his 1924 essay, 'Shall We All Commit Suicide?', he had shown uncanny prescience when he penned the following reflection: 'May there not be methods of using explosive energy incomparably more intense than anything heretofore discovered? Might not a bomb no bigger than an orange be found to possess a secret power ... to concentrate the force of a thousand tons of cordite and blast a township at a stroke?'[175]

But, as with all his reflections on war, there was a curious ambivalence in his thinking. In 1931 he wrote that nuclear energy was 'incomparably greater' than molecular energy and that, properly harnessed, it could bring mankind immeasurable benefits as well as catastrophic disaster. If the latter, it would involve 'explosive forces, energy, materials, machinery' which would 'be available upon a scale which [could] annihilate whole nations'.[176] On both occasions he was aware of the potential as well as the pitfalls of new super-weapons.

With the rise of the Nazis in the 1930s, a number of German Jewish scientists sought refuge abroad to avoid persecution. Two of these, Otto Frisch and Rudolph Peierls, came to Britain, where they worked at the University of Birmingham. Frisch and Peierls produced a memorandum which suggested that a bomb with no more than five kilogrammes of Uranium U235 could be produced with an explosive power equivalent to 'several thousand tons of dynamite'.[177] This memorandum led to the formation of the MAUD committee, under the physicist George Thompson, to investigate the possibilities of producing an atomic weapon.

Throughout 1940 British scientists worked in earnest on producing a nuclear weapon. They were ahead of their American counterparts in researching nuclear fission, and received an immense boost when they received the world stock of heavy water. By the middle of 1941 the 'British nuclear bomb project' was officially launched and Churchill was informed that a uranium bomb was 'practicable'.[178] He told the Chiefs of Staff that, although 'content with the existing explosives', he did not wish to 'stand in the path of improvement'.[179]

For most of the war Churchill wrote little about the atomic project and there are very few minutes expressing his views. This was understandable, given that it was by no means certain that atomic weapons would become a reality, or that they would be developed before the end of the war. Given the immense strain he faced, it was only natural that Churchill would concentrate on the weapons that were available rather than novel ones that were not. Churchill maintained a remarkable secrecy over the nuclear programme throughout the war. The Chiefs of Staff heard nothing of the project from their initial approval in 1940 until 1944, and their scientific advisor, Sir Henry Tizard, was not told at all. Attlee, the Deputy Prime Minister, claimed not to have been told until the Potsdam Conference. Churchill believed that this project, like Ultra, required as few eyes and ears as possible.

In 1941 American scientists expressed an interest in joint research with their British counterparts, leading Roosevelt to propose to Churchill 'a co-ordination of efforts'. Roosevelt's approach was initially rebuffed, but in December 1941, with both countries at war, the response became favourable. American scientists were given access to all Britain's secrets and this eventually led to the instigation of the 'Manhattan Project', the codename for America's wartime project to build the bomb. American research now moved ahead rapidly but, much to Churchill's chagrin, they began to exclude their former 'junior partner'. Security precautions played a part: General Groves, the director of the project, was wary of sharing information with 'aliens'. Nonetheless, Churchill refused to see Britain shut out of this important area of research and raised his concerns with Harry Hopkins in 1943.

As a result of his personal intervention, Churchill's signature appeared on the Quebec Agreement of August 19th 1943. Under the terms of this (largely) Anglo-American agreement, both countries undertook not to use atomic weapons against each other and, more crucially, not to use them against a third party without each other's consent. Britain and the USA were now partners in atomic bomb research, but the focus was the USA, not Britain.

Then in 1944 came the Hyde Park Agreement, a hastily drafted memorandum between Churchill and Roosevelt in which both leaders agreed to maintain the secrecy of the nuclear project and collaborate in developing it after the defeat of Japan. But, if Churchill believed he had secured Britain's long-term partnership in the field of atomic warfare, he was sadly mistaken. After the war Churchill believed that the wartime agreements which stipulated the sharing of atomic secrets would remain valid in peacetime; that Britain would be supplied with atomic secrets or weapons by her transatlantic ally if the need arose. But the Americans were determined to exploit the new-found atomic technology for both commercial and military purposes, and this required its exclusive use. In 1946 Congress passed the McMahon Act,[180] which forbade the exchange of atomic information between the United States and other nations.

On July 1st 1945 Churchill, on his own initiative and without the approval of the War Cabinet, gave Roosevelt's successor, Harry S. Truman, his approval to use nuclear weapons if the test at Alamagordo, New Mexico proved successful. Thus, when the bomb was dropped on Hiroshima on August 6th 1945, Churchill became the first and, to date, the only British Prime Minister to authorise the use of nuclear weapons against another country. Churchill certainly did not contemplate a conventional assault on the Japanese mainland using American and British troops with equanimity. He recollected a meeting with Henry Stimson, the US War Secretary, who conveyed news of the successful atomic test in New Mexico. He later wrote:

To quell the Japanese resistance man by man and conquer the country yard by yard might well require the loss of a million American lives and half that number of British – or more if we could get them there: for we were resolved to share the agony. Now all this nightmare picture had vanished. In its place was the vision of the end of the whole war in one or two violent shocks ... Moreover we should not need the Russians...[181]

It would be wrong to think that Churchill tamely acquiesced in this decision. At Potsdam he told Truman that the insistence on a Japanese 'unconditional surrender' would lead to tremendous American losses. He suggested that the very term 'unconditional surrender' ought to be expressed in a different way which 'guaranteed the essentials for future peace and security' but which also allowed the Japanese a way of saving face and honour.[182] One way of saving face and honour was the retention of Emperor Hirohito, a figure of cardinal importance to the Japanese nation.

Truman was unmoved, believing that, after Pearl Harbor, the Japanese had lost any sense of honour. More importantly, there were many in Washington who believed that a nuclear explosion would send the most powerful deterrent signal to the Russians, who were contemplating their own imminent occupation of the Japanese mainland. The famous Potsdam Declaration of July 26th gave the Japanese the impression that the Emperor might have to abdicate.[183] When the Japanese rejected the declaration, Japan was warned that it would face further aerial bombardment. This strategy culminated in the devastating atomic attacks of August 6th and 9th on Hiroshima and Nagasaki.

Churchill's post-war comments show that he clearly saw the deterrent power of the new weapons. Indeed, he may have been one of the first public figures to appreciate the logic of nuclear deterrence. Addressing Congress in 1952, he urged the members 'never to let go of the atomic weapon until ... other means of preserving peace' were available. The bomb was one way, but not necessarily the only way, of 'accumulating deterrents ... against aggression', which would 'ward off the fearful catastrophe'.[184]

In 1953, talking of the proliferation of the new and deadlier hydrogen bomb, Churchill commented that there had been a 'diminution of tension' and less likelihood of another world war. He considered that the 'annihilating character of these agencies may bring an utterly unforeseeable security to mankind'. He spelt out the reason why:

'it seems pretty safe to say that a war which begins by both sides suffering what they dread most ... is less likely to occur than one which dangles the lurid prizes of former ages before ambiguous eyes.'[185] Churchill clearly understood how the new atomic age represented a startling revolution in warfare. Instead of long-protracted campaigns involving the movement of whole armies, and decisions spread over many months or even years, a nuclear war would begin 'with horrors of a kind and on a scale never dreamed of before by human beings'.[186]

In a speech which he was due to broadcast following the atomic attacks, but which was delivered instead by Clement Attlee, Churchill ended with these reflections on the new age of atomic power: 'This revelation of the secrets of nature, long mercifully withheld from man, should arouse the most solemn reflections in the mind and conscience of every human being capable of comprehension.' They could wreak 'measureless havoc upon the entire globe' or 'become a perennial fountain of world prosperity'.[187] Blessing or cursing, Churchill's ambivalence to war remained as strong as ever.

NOTES

1 E. Nel, *Mr. Churchill's Secretary*, p.82.
2 WSC Bio 7, p.1301.
3 Speeches V, p.5129.
4 M. Gilbert, *Churchill and America*, p.149.
5 *Ibid.*, p.150.
6 In 1921 Roosevelt was struck down by an illness, possibly polio, which left him paralysed from the waist down.
7 M. Gilbert, *Churchill and America*, pp.164-5.
8 *Ibid.*, p.159.
9 S. Berthon, *Allies at War*, p.26.
10 *War Papers 2*, p.45.
11 In London, US Ambassador John Kennedy's defeatist view of Britain's chances had great influence.
12 *War Papers 2*, p.93.
13 T. Clayton and P. Craig, *Finest Hour*, p.98.
14 *War Papers 2*, p.255.
15 M. Gilbert, *Churchill and America*, p.195.
16 Roosevelt had received a more upbeat assessment of Britain's chances of

survival from American military and naval institutions, as well as from his envoy in London, Colonel Donovan.

17 John Colville, *The Fringes of Power*, p.234.
18 M. Gilbert, *Churchill and America*, p.208.
19 *Ibid.*, p.219.
20 Speeches VI, p.6350.
21 *Churchill War Papers III*, p.600.
22 R. Lamb, *Churchill as War Leader – Right or Wrong*, p.80.
23 *Churchill War Papers III*, p.1132.
24 E. Nave and J. Russbridger, *Betrayal at Pearl Harbor*, p.28.
25 D. Stafford, *Churchill and Secret Service*, pp.232-3.
26 'The Truth About Pearl Harbor: A Debate', Stephen Budiansky, The Independent Institute, January 30 2003.
27 E. Nave and J. Russbridger, *Betrayal at Pearl Harbor*, p.63.
28 *Ibid.*, p.131.
29 The ruse worked because, on December 1st 1941, naval intelligence in Washington asserted that Japanese aircraft carriers were still in home waters even as they were heading to Hawaii.
30 *War Papers III*, p.1057.
31 *Ibid.*, p.1373.
32 *Ibid.*, p.1399.
33 *Ibid.*, p.1499.
34 *Ibid.*, p.1551.
35 *Ibid.*, p.1530.
36 J. Ramsden, *Man of the Century*, p.206.
37 H. Pelling, *Britain and the Second World War*, p.122.
38 *Ibid.*, p.140.
39 P. Addison, *Churchill on the Home Front*, p.350.
40 WSC Bio 7, p.59.
41 R.R. James (ed), *Chips*, p.393.
42 P. Addison, *Road to 1945*, p.200.
43 WSC Bio 7, p.128.
44 P. Addison, *Road to 1945*, p.159.
45 N. Knight, *Churchill: The Greatest Briton Unmasked*, p.256.
46 A. Roberts, *Masters and Commanders*, p.580.
47 M. Dockrill and B. McKercher, *Diplomacy and World Power*, p.213.
48 *War Papers III*, p.964.
49 *Ibid.*, p.1171.
50 WSC Bio 7, p.80.
51 *Ibid.*, p.94.
52 *Ibid.*, p.113.
53 A. Roberts, *Masters and Commanders*, p.199.
54 N. Knight, *The Greatest Briton Unmasked*, p.173.
55 A. Roberts, *Masters and Commanders*, p.295.
56 M. Howard, *Continental Commitment*, p.141.
57 A.J.P. Taylor, *The Warlords*, pp.82-3.
58 M. Donnelly, *Britain in the Second World War*, p.100.
59 WSC Bio 7, p.180.

60 *Ibid.*, p.232.
61 Churchill stressed this point with the Americans, partly out of a fear that they would sift priorities away from the defeat of Germany to the defeat of Japan.
62 R. Lamb, *Churchill as War Leader – Right or Wrong*, p.218.
63 *Ibid.*, p.221.
64 Moran, *Churchill: The Struggle for Survival*, p.36.
65 WSC Bio 7, p.431.
66 Moran, *Churchill: The Struggle for Survival*, p.43.
67 M. Dockrill and B. McKercher, *Diplomacy and World Power*, p.218.
68 WSC Bio 7, p.794.
69 Michael Howard, *Grand Strategy IV*, p.208.
70 T. Ben Moshe, *Churchill: Strategy and History*, p.204.
71 M. Gilbert, *Auschwitz and the Allies*, p.341.
72 W. Rubinstein, *The Myth of Rescue*, p.216.
73 For a detailed account of Allied knowledge of the Holocaust during the war, see W. Lacquer's *The Terrible Secret*.
74 M. Cohen, *Churchill and the Jews*, p.262.
75 Yet it is also true that the reasons given at the time for not bombing Auschwitz (the distance to the camp was too great; a bombing raid was not logistically feasible; more Jewish inmates than Nazis would be killed) were essentially bogus.
76 M. Gilbert, *Wilderness Years*, p.111.
77 WSC Bio 5, p.681.
78 *Jewish Chronicle*, November 14th 1941.
79 M. Gilbert, *Auschwitz and the Allies*, p.68.
80 *Jewish Chronicle*, November 6th, 1942.
81 M. Gilbert, *Auschwitz and the Allies*, p.104.
82 *Jewish Chronicle*, January 16th 1942.
83 WSC Bio 8, p.190.
84 A military organisation set up in Palestine in the 1920s to protect Jewish settlements from attack by neighbouring Arabs. It later formed the core of the Israel Defence Force.
85 WSC Bio 6, pp.910-11.
86 M. Gilbert, *Churchill and the Jews*, p.189.
87 *Ibid.*, p.198.
88 WSC Bio 7, p.377.
89 M. Gilbert, *Churchill and the Jews*, p.216.
90 W. Laqueur (ed), *The Holocaust Encyclopedia*, p.43.
91 WSC Bio 7, p.846.
92 M. Cohen, *Churchill and the Jews*, pp.296-7.
93 O. Rabinowicz, *Winston Churchill on Jewish Problems*, p.135.
94 M. Gilbert, *Churchill and the Jews*, pp.216-17.
95 Companion IV (i), p.377.
96 W. Churchill, *World Crisis*, p.1448.
97 *News of the World*, May 1st 1938.
98 Speeches V, p.5232.
99 W. Churchill, *Step by Step*, p.266.

100 M. Weidhorn, *Sword and Pen*, p.135.
101 'Let the tyrant criminals bomb', *The Collected Essays of Sir Winston Churchill* I, pp.426-7.
102 N. Knight, *Churchill: The Greatest Briton Unmasked*, p.279.
103 WSC Bio 6, p.852.
104 J. Wheeler-Bennett, *Action This Day*, p.85.
105 *War Papers III*, p.1270.
106 WSC Bio 6, p.1206.
107 R. Callahan, *Retreat from Empire*, p.126.
108 Dear, I. (ed), *Oxford Companion to World War II*, p.832.
109 Increasingly from 1944, the USAAF carried out systematic bombing operations.
110 N. Knight, *Churchill: The Greatest Briton Unmasked*, p.283.
111 WSC Bio 7, p.437.
112 Contrary to popular belief, the attack on Dresden was an Anglo-American operation.
113 WSC Bio 7, pp.1257-8.
114 Speeches VII, p.6884.
115 N. Knight, *Churchill: The Greatest Briton Unmasked*, p.297.
116 In August 1939 the Soviet Union and Germany signed the 'Molotov-Ribbentrop Pact', or Nazi-Soviet Pact, in which both countries agreed not to attack each other and to remain neutral if either country was attacked by a third party. A secret protocol in the treaty divided Poland up into German and Russian spheres of influence.
117 C. Ponting, *Churchill*, p.652.
118 A twenty-year Anglo-Soviet treaty of mutual political and military assistance signed on May 26th 1942.
119 The village of Katyn is near the town of Smolensk in western Russia. In total some 22,000 Poles were murdered on Stalin's orders in separate locations in Russia.
120 D. Carlton, *Churchill and the Soviet Union*, p.105.
121 See Chapter XIV of W. Averell Harriman and Elie Abel, *Special Envoy* for a detailed account of the negotiations.
122 WSC Bio 7, p.577.
123 *Ibid.*, p.750.
124 *Ibid.*, p.659.
125 D. Carlton, *Churchill and the Soviet Union*, p.109.
126 WSC Bio 7, p.684.
127 *Ibid.*, p.658.
128 *Ibid.*, p.682.
129 *Ibid.*, p.664.
130 *Ibid.*, p.682. Note: The Polish government did understand Stalin's desire for security and incorporated in a message to Stalin the view that, in any Polish government, there would be 'none but persons fully determined to co-operate with the Soviet Union' (*ibid.*, p.687). Stalin rejected this formula.
131 *Ibid.*, p.686.
132 *Ibid.*, p.863.

133   *Ibid.*, p.901.
134   *Ibid.*, p.895.
135   W. Harriman, *Special Envoy*, p.337.
136   WSC Bio 7, p.982.
137   The President's rapidly declining health did not help matters.
138   Pressure from Churchill allowed Mikolajczyk to attend talks on the Polish government in June.
139   W. Churchill, *The Second World War: Triumph and Tragedy*, p.198.
140   C. Ponting, *Churchill*, pp.660-1.
141   D. Carlton, *Churchill and the Soviet Union*, p.115.
142   *Ibid.*, p.116.
143   WSC Bio 7, p.999.
144   J. Lukacs, *Churchill: Strategy and History*, p.41.
145   D. Carlton, *Churchill and the Soviet Union*, p.115.
146   Companion V (iii), p.94.
147   Companion V (i), p.917.
148   Moran, Lord, *Churchill: The Struggle for Survival*, p.241.
149   *Ibid.*, pp.204, 250.
150   W. Harriman, *Special Envoy*, p.419.
151   N. Nicolson (ed), *Harold Nicolson: Diaries and Letters, 1939-45 II*, p.440.
152   M. Dockrill and B. McKercher, *Diplomacy and World Power*, p.198.
153   A. Roberts, 'Winston Churchill: Secret conversations reveal views on Stalin and Gandhi', *Daily Telegraph*, September 26th 2008.
154   D. Carlton, *Churchill and the Soviet Union*, p.113.
155   N. Knight, *Churchill: The Greatest Briton Unmasked*, p.320.
156   WSC Bio 7, p.664.
157   Moran, Lord, *Churchill: The Struggle for Survival*, p.204.
158   F. McDonough, *Neville Chamberlain: Appeasement and the British Road to War*, p.48.
159   Moran, Lord, *Churchill: The Struggle for Survival*, p.322.
160   A. Roberts, *Masters and Commanders*, p.557.
161   R. Callahan, *Retreat from Empire*, p.204.
162   WSC Bio 2, p.283.
163   W. Harriman, *Special Envoy*, p.226.
164   Moran, Lord, *Churchill: The Struggle for Survival*, p.235.
165   D. Carlton, *Churchill and the Soviet Union*, p.112.
166   D. Hart Davis (ed), *King's Counsellor*, p.198.
167   Moran, Lord, *Churchill: The Struggle for Survival*, p.185.
168   WSC Bio 7, p.1322.
169   A. Roberts, *Masters and Commanders*, p.517.
170   J. Wheeler-Bennett, *Action This Day*, p.34.
171   WSC Bio 7, p.1330.
172   J. Wheeler-Bennett, *Action This Day*, p.34.
173   N. Knight, *Churchill: The Greatest Briton Unmasked*, p.324.
174   The names of the first two atomic bombs.
175   W. Churchill, 'Shall we all commit suicide?', *Thoughts and Adventures*, pp.188-9.
176   W. Churchill, 'Fifty Years Hence', *Thoughts and Adventures*, pp.208, 211-12.

177 Dear, I. (ed), *The Oxford Companion to World War II*, p.55.

178 R. Lamb, *Churchill: War Leader – Right or Wrong*, p.321.

179 G. Best, *Churchill and War*, p.205.

180 Also known as the Atomic Energy Act.

181 WSC Bio 8, p.86.

182 *Ibid.*, p.68.

183 With the Japanese cabinet so divided on the question of surrender, it is debatable whether a change of wording in the Potsdam Declaration would have brought an end to the war.

184 WSC Bio 8, pp.689-90.

185 *Ibid.*, p.908.

186 *Ibid.*, pp.510, 769 for more.

187 War Speeches 3, p.511.

CHAPTER EIGHT

Churchill as War Leader

What were Churchill's greatest qualities as a war leader?

CHURCHILL'S IMMENSE reputation rests on the leadership he displayed throughout the Second World War. In particular, he is remembered for heroic feats of statesmanship from May 1940 until June 1941, when Britain and the Empire stood alone against the seemingly unstoppable might of Nazi Germany. During this time, and in the absence of military victories, he galvanised the nation with stirring oratory that seemed to breathe new life into the war effort. He showed a vital energy, a sense of unflinching resolve and a ruthless desire to win the war at all costs. But these qualities were not manufactured by the exigencies of conflict: they came from unrivalled political experience and an inner conviction in the rightness of Britain's cause.

What follows is a short analysis of those Churchillian qualities that were vital in the successful leadership of the war.

Ceaseless energy

In the 1920s Churchill had written that war leadership required 'a frenzied energy at the summit' and an 'effort to compel events'.[1] From the moment he became Prime Minister, Churchill lived up to this standard, providing a dramatic increase in the tempo of government. His private secretary, John Colville, noted early in the war how impressed he was with 'Winston's ceaseless industry'. He wrote: 'He is always having ideas which he puts down on paper in the form of questions and dispatches to Ismay or the C.I.G.S. for examination.'[2]

Churchill's constant prodding of his officials and generals was reflected in his famous minutes, known as 'Prayers' because they invariably started 'Pray enquire', and his 'Action This Day' tags. Some of these minutes concerned minor issues: one sought to determine the number of apes left on the Rock of Gibraltar; another expressed concern about the protection of animals at London Zoo during the Blitz. Churchill took a meticulous interest in every conceivable aspect of the war. According to Colville, he would scrutinise 'every document that has anything to do with the war and does not disdain to enquire into the most trivial point'.[3] Every day he would pour out a ceaseless stream of instructions to cut red tape, reduce bureaucracy, overcome obstacles, clarify information, question objections and demand positive action.

There were several advantages to this strategy of continuous prodding. Firstly, Churchill helped to ensure that no aspect of the war was overlooked by others. Secondly, he kept a close eye on whether instructions had actually been carried out and how the business of war could be done more efficiently. He did not take the conduct of the war for granted, preferring to search out better alternative strategies and tactics. He constantly spurred on his ministers, generals and officials to greater effort in the conduct of the war.

The vast number of minutes he dictated was testament to the fertility of his brain, if not necessarily to the brilliance of every idea. Roosevelt was famous for declaring: 'Winston produces 100 ideas a day, of which only 6 are any good.' Australia's Prime Minister, Sir Robert Menzies, made the same point slightly differently: 'The truth is that he had ten times as many ideas as other people. He lived with the problems of the nation. He made them *his* problems, and let his powerful imagination loose around them. *All* his ideas could not be right. But he was so fertile in ideas that he could afford a high rate of wastage and still be in credit.'[4] Macmillan, writing in the middle of the war, said that the 'the vigour and originality of his mind' was 'extraordinary'.[5]

Churchill energised those around him and prevented them from falling into the habits of complacency and laziness. He was, in the words of Peter Stansky, the war's 'great animator'. Colville was later to write: 'I doubt if there has ever been such a rapid transformation of ... the tempo at which business was conducted'.[6] According to Lord Normanbrook, the effect of Churchill's interventions was 'immediate and dramatic'. His probing 'quickened the pace and improved the tone of his administration', adding 'a new sense of purpose and of urgency' as people 'realised that a firm hand, guided by a strong will, was on the wheel'.[7]

This prodigious energy was maintained throughout the war years. In 1944 Churchill chaired a committee to oversee preparations for

Operation Overlord. As Ismay later recalled, 'The Chairman's fiery energy and undisputed authority dominated the proceedings'. In order to move things forward, Churchill 'tongue-lashed' those who were 'seemingly slothful or obstructive' so that 'decisions were translated into immediate action'.[8]

As a war leader, Churchill made enormous demands of his staff, something that is often cited as evidence that he was a domineering bully. As Colville pointed out, this did cause 'great inconvenience'; working for Churchill meant working 'very long hours ... with very little let-up'.[9] His late-night conversations taxed his most hardened colleagues. Sometimes he would change his plans without telling anyone; meetings would be 'arranged, cancelled and re-arranged to suit nobody's convenience but his own'.[10] But, as Colville remarks, it did not occur to those working for the Prime Minister to regard their chores as a hardship; nor did they feel any overriding resentment.

Working for Churchill was, by all accounts, highly invigorating and a source of constant fascination. Take this account by Elizabeth Nel, one of Churchill's secretaries: 'We of his personal staff were called upon to put forth the maximum effort of which our frames, nerves and minds were capable ... He [had], to make use of one of his adjectives, a prodigious capacity for work and, in those days at any rate, he expected those around him to devote themselves heart and soul to the cause to which he had dedicated himself.' Far from complaining about the strain of working for Churchill, Nel offers a paean of praise: 'From first to last we were utterly devoted to him.'[11]

One can also take this statement from an Admiralty bureaucrat, Sir Clifford Jarrett: 'He practically killed people by overwork and at the same time inspired people to extreme devotion.'[12] Another official, Sir George Mallaby, commented that Churchill 'was not kind or considerate'; he was 'free with abuse and complaint' and 'exacting beyond reason'. But Mallaby went on to offer this list of superlative qualities: 'He was unusual, unpredictable, exciting, original, stimulating, provocative ... a great man.'[13]

Energy only really mattered if it was harnessed to the right ends. In Churchill's case, this meant a relentless, single-minded focus on the problems of the war. As Sir Ian Jacob recalled: 'In the circumstances of 1940, when the fight for survival was all absorbing, the whole of his energies were concentrated on this fight ... there were no distractions.' Even meal times and journeys were 'never wasted' as 'useful conversations could be held or Minutes dictated'.[14]

Churchill's ability to concentrate forcefully on the pressing issues of the moment was picked up by Lord Normanbrook, deputy secretary to the War Cabinet: 'His general method of work was to concentrate his personal attention on the two or three things that mattered most at any given moment, and to give to each of these all the time and attention that it merited.'[15]

Led by example

Churchill was able to exhort others to greater effort because he pushed himself to the limit too. He thus exemplified one of the most important values of leadership: the ability to lead by example. When he told his staff in December 1940 to spend 'a busy Christmas', he meant this edict to apply to himself too. He spent much of Christmas Day 1940 dictating minutes on a variety of important matters.

One of his private secretaries noted the following: 'The Prime Minister has made a great point of working as usual over the holiday and yesterday morning was like almost any other here, with the usual letters and telephone calls and of course many Christmas greeting messages thrown in.'[16] When Churchill stated that 'We must keep working, like the gun horses, till we drop', he meant what he said.[17] Acutely aware of the pressures of war to which he was subject, Churchill once told Colville: 'Each night I try myself by Court Martial to see if I have done anything effective during the day. I don't mean just pawing the ground, anyone can go through the motions, but something really effective.'[18]

Doing something effective often meant being seen on the front line near to the troops and war workers. It was not enough for Churchill to receive and fire off reports and memos; he wanted direct, unmediated access to the war so that he could judge it for himself. Thus in 1940 he personally inspected Britain's coastal defences with General Montgomery, listening to the General's concerns about his soldiers' lack of mobility. He toured Britain's bombed-out streets during the Blitz and saw for himself the effects of German aerial bombardment. His visits raised cheers from the crowds and lifted national morale at a time of crisis. The essence of these visits was *visibility* – Churchill wanted to be seen among his people so that they could appreciate the government was on their side. Harriman writes, 'At Swansea, I recall, he got out of his car and walked into the dock area. The dockers crowded round him and I am sure the security men accompanying him must have been concerned for his safety. But Churchill called out, 'Stand back, my man. Let the others see.'[19]

Indomitability

In the challenging days of 1940 the British government faced an enemy of colossal military power. It would have been understandable for any British government, unsure of winning allies and in a precarious financial position, to have buckled under the strain and negotiated a compromise peace. But at no point did Churchill consider such an option as morally or politically feasible.

From the moment he became Prime Minister, Churchill had only one thought in mind: the total defeat of Nazi Germany and its allies. In an early speech to Parliament (and the British people) as Prime Minister, Churchill tried to rally the nation for the impending trial against Nazi Germany. He told them it was 'the appointed time for all to make the utmost exertions in their power'. The coming battle for Britain would call forth the full reserves of effort from the British people and the aim of both the British and French nations would be 'to wage war until victory is won'.[20]

Churchill famously told his daughter-in-law and wife that, in the event of a German invasion, he expected them to 'take at least one German'. When his daughter-in-law protested that she did not carry a gun or know how to fire one, Churchill retorted, 'But my dear you can always use a carving knife!'[21] No anecdote could better sum up his single-minded focus, his utter devotion, to winning the war.

When, at the beginning of June 1940, the Director of the National Gallery suggested that its paintings be shipped to Canada, Churchill gave the emphatic retort: 'No, bury them in caves and cellars. None must go. We are going to beat them.'[22] In a similar vein, he criticised the 'stampede from this country', of British children being sent to Canada, which encouraged 'a defeatist spirit'.[23] There was nothing like courage in adversity.

Churchill knew he had to exude confidence if he was to carry the public with him. It is much to his credit that he understood this aspect of war leadership so well. As Field Marshal Montgomery put it, the leader 'must ... radiate confidence, even when he himself is not too certain of the outcome'.[24] There is no doubt that Churchill had an infectious confidence and buoyancy which was conveyed to all those who met him during the war. John Martin, one of his private secretaries, wrote that the words used to describe Pitt – 'Nobody left his presence without feeling a braver man' – were no less true of Churchill.[25] The scientist R.V. Jones, describing the effect of war-time meetings with Churchill, said that he had 'the feeling of being recharged by contact with a source of living power'.[26] In even more poetic terms, Harriman wrote that Churchill had the 'glow of Mount Sinai on him'.[27]

But it was no good radiating resolve and confidence if this was not shared by other responsible people. In a famous memorandum from 1940, Churchill made this very point: 'In these dark days the Prime Minister would be grateful if all his colleagues in the government, as well as high officials, would maintain a high morale in their circles; not minimising the gravity of events but showing confidence in our ability and inflexible resolve to continue the war till we have broken the will of the enemy to bring all Europe under his domination.'[28]

Again on July 1st, with intelligence reports suggesting an imminent German invasion, Churchill wanted to dampen down alarmist or defeatist sentiments. He therefore penned the following message for the three fighting services and civil departments:

> On what may be the eve of an attempted invasion or battle for our native land, the Prime Minister desires to impress upon all persons holding responsible positions in the Government, in the Fighting Services, or in the Civil Departments, their duty to maintain a spirit of alert and confident energy ... The Prime Minister expects all His Majesty's servants in high places to set an example of steadiness and resolution ... They should not hesitate to report, or if necessary remove, any officers or officials who are found to be consciously exercising a disturbing or depressing influence, and whose talk is calculated to spread alarm and despondency.[29]

Churchill made morale-building a central goal of his leadership, realising that, however the fates played, it would always be an immense asset in wartime. Once his course was set there was, as Menzies put it, 'no defeat in his heart'.[30]

Despite rejecting defeatism outwardly, Churchill privately expressed doubts about Britain's prospects. On the day he became Prime Minister, he told an aide, 'I hope that it is not too late. I am very much afraid that it is. We can only do our best.'[31] Shortly after becoming Prime Minister, Churchill was greeted by well-wishers outside Downing Street who shouted out, 'Good luck, Winnie!' As Ismay recalled, Churchill was moved and said, 'Poor people. They trust me, and I can give them nothing but disaster for quite a long time.'[32]

Brendan Bracken noted Churchill's feelings of 'profound anxiety' early in his premiership. Churchill once told Eden that there were days when he would awaken with dread in his heart.33 Almost always, the radiant optimism expressed Churchill's own feelings – as his bodyguard remembered, his sentiments were mostly, 'We shall win, Thompson, we shall win.'34 But there were times when the optimism was just an act, a clever confidence trick – and certainly one played to perfection. He fully realised that displays of high morale would prove infectious and discourage defeatistism. It was as if he had taken to heart the famous verse from Corinthians: 'For if the trumpet gives an uncertain sound, who shall prepare himself to the battle' (1 Corinthians 14:8).

Churchill conveyed this indomitable resolve to his French allies in May and June 1940. He told Reynauld and Weygand that he was convinced that England and France needed to 'remain in the closest accord', that by so doing 'they could best ensure that their spirits remained high'. Britain and France needed 'only to carry on the fight to conquer'.35 His words moved many that were present, in both the British and the French camps. Amid signs that the French were about to ask for an armistice, Churchill later declared that 'Britain would continue the struggle in all circumstances'. When Reynaud asked Churchill what he would do if the Germans invaded Britain, Churchill's reply showed his usual courage and quick-fire humour: 'If they swim, we will drown them. If they land, we will hit them on the head, *frappez* them *sur la tete*.'36 De Gaulle was hugely impressed. Recalling in his memoirs his first visit to Churchill, he wrote: 'The impression he gave me confirmed me in my conviction that Great Britain, led by such a fighter, would certainly not flinch.'37

In 1942, while meeting Roosevelt at the White House, Churchill received his heaviest blow of the war, hearing of the fall of Tobruk. Twenty-five thousand British troops had surrendered. Churchill felt humiliated in the presence of his friend and political colleague but, after reflection, his spirits revived. Eleanor Roosevelt noted: 'To neither of these two men was there such a thing as not being able to meet a new situation.'38

During the war Churchill had a little motto for when times were bad. He would tell his staff, 'Just KBO' – 'keep buggering on'. KBO was one of Churchill's secret weapons.

Wartime oratory

Throughout the war, Churchill's inspiring oratory provided a ray of hope to subjugated people across Europe. Some of his phrases are now part of the national vocabulary; to listen to his parliamentary performances is to appreciate a true master of the English language. His tribute to the fighter pilots who were engaged in a daily battle of wills against their German counterparts will live long in the memory: 'Never in the field of human conflict has so much been owed by so many to so few.' As one writer has observed, this was 'the most resonant sentence to have emerged from the Second World War.'[39]

There is no better expression of defiance and resolution than the conclusion of his Dunkirk speech of June 1940: 'We shall fight them on the beaches, we shall fight them on the landing grounds, we shall fight them on the fields and on the streets, we shall fight them on the hills, we shall never surrender.' The clever use of repetition amplifies the qualities of indomitability and courage demanded from his listeners. His promise of 'blood, toil, tears and sweat' is a classic example of the use of pithy monosyllables.

His speeches were enthused with hope for a better future. On May 13th 1940 he told Parliament that he was sure 'our cause will not be suffered to fail among men'.[40] Though France had fallen, he talked of his faith that 'a liberated France [would] once again rejoice in her greatness and her glory, and once again stand forward as the champion of freedom and the rights of man.' Though the peoples of Czechoslovakia, Poland, France and the Low Countries had lost their freedom, he was certain that they would 'not be ruled for long by the Nazi Gestapo'. Those enslaved Europeans would feel each British victory as 'a step towards the liberation of the Continent from the foulest thralldom into which it has ever been cast.' Though Britain stared into a dark valley, he could see 'the sunlight on the uplands beyond'.[41]

Following an air raid in October 1940, Churchill talked of how cities 'would rise from their ruins' and be rebuilt 'more to our credit than some of them were before'.[42] Even after the fall of Singapore in 1942, one of the lowest points of the war, he talked of a supreme moment in which Britons could 'display that calm and poise combined with grim determination, which not so long ago brought us out of the very jaws of death'.[43]

In the House of Commons in 1941, in the last speech he gave before the Old Chamber was bombed, Churchill gave another ringing declaration of confidence in victory: 'When I look back on the perils which have been overcome, upon the great mountain waves through which the gallant ship has driven, when I remember all that has gone wrong ... I feel sure we have no need to fear the tempest. Let it roar, and let it rage. We shall come through.'44 This was his message to those nations, free or subjugated, that cared for the cause of freedom: 'Lift up your hearts. All will come right. Out of the depths of sorrow and sacrifice will be born again the glory of mankind.'45

From the outset Churchill clearly grasped the monumental significance of this global conflict. As First Lord of the Admiralty, he spelt out his belief that this conflict was not about rescuing Danzig, Poland or any other small state, though they were intermediate aims; it was 'to save the whole world from the pestilence of Nazi tyranny and in defence of all that is most sacred to man.' The war would establish 'on impregnable rocks the rights of the individual' and would 'revive the stature of man'.46

In his first speech to the Commons as Prime Minister, Churchill described the Nazi regime as 'a monstrous tyranny, never surpassed in the dark, lamentable catalogue of human crime'.47 When the Battle of Britain was about to begin, he realised its true dimension immediately. In one of his most celebrated speeches, delivered on June 18th 1940, he declared that upon the outcome of the battle rested 'the future of Christian civilisation'. He went on:

> Hitler knows that he will have to break us in this island or lose the war. If we can stand up to him, all Europe may be free and the life of the world may move forward into broad, sunlit uplands. But if we fail, then the whole world, including the United States, including all that we have known and cared for, will sink into the abyss of a new Dark Age made more sinister, and perhaps more protracted, by the lights of perverted science.48

The issue at stake, as he spelt it out in January 1941, was simple: 'Are we to move steadily forward and have freedom, or are we to be put back into the Middle Ages by a totalitarian system that crushes all forms of individual life and has for its aim little less than the subjugation of Europe and little more than the gratification of gangster appetites.'49 Failure to meet the challenge posed by Hitler would mean a dehumanising enslavement to the forces of barbarism. For five years, Churchill enthused the war effort, not just in Britain or

Europe but around the world, with an unmistakable clarity of purpose.

Above all, Churchill never downplayed the dangers faced by his countrymen. Unlike his predecessors, Baldwin and Chamberlain, Churchill believed it was right to tell the truth to the British people, whenever this was possible. In his first speech as Prime Minister, he reminded the country that they had to face 'an ordeal of the most grievous kind' which would involve 'many, many long months of struggle and of suffering'.[50] After the ignominy of Dunkirk he did not shirk from describing the evacuation of troops and the considerable loss of military hardware as a 'colossal military disaster'.[51]

Broadcasting to the British people in September 1940 on the dangers of invasion, he warned that 'no one should blind himself to the fact that a heavy, full scale invasion of this Island is being prepared with all the usual German thoroughness and method, and that it may be launched now...'[52] In a secret session of Parliament in September 1940, he gave a stark analysis of what a German invasion would look like, prompting Harold Nicolson to write: 'I must say that he does not try to cheer us up with vain promises.'[53] In the 1930s Churchill had argued that the British people were 'robust' and would appreciate being told the 'truth' about the crises in international relations. This was a prescription for honesty and frankness in discussing the dangers Britain faced in a hostile world. As Prime Minister he followed this prescription, giving startlingly frank assessments of the dangers ahead.

'Words', Churchill once said, 'are the only things which last forever', and this was an apt description of his own words.[54] But, as Harold Nicolson observed in his diaries, these were 'never words for words' sake'. They had a 'massive backing of power and resolve behind them, like a great fortress'.[55] Without the strength of his convictions and the backing of his resolve, Churchill's words could never have resonated so with the public.

Sense of history

Churchill was able to inspire hope through oratory because he was able to tap into his nation's historical imagination. His sense of history allowed him to criticise what he saw as the folly of appeasement in the 1930s. He wrote to Lord Rothemere, resisting Hitler's suggestion of an Anglo-German pact: 'If [Hitler's] proposal means that we should come to an understanding with Germany to dominate

Europe I think this would be contrary to the whole of our history. We have on all occasions been the friend of the second strongest power in Europe and have never yielded ourselves to the strongest power. Thus Elizabeth resisted Philip II of Spain. Thus William III and Marlborough resisted Louis XIV. Thus Pitt resisted Napoleon, and thus we all resisted William II of Germany.'[56] Adolf Hitler was but the latest incarnation of Continental despotism. This theme, of the need to preserve the European balance of power, was taken very seriously by Churchill.

For some years he had called for a Grand Alliance of anti-fascist powers to resist Germany, arming himself with historical precedents in support of this strategy. In a letter to Lord Londonderry in 1936, he spelt out the case: 'British policy for four hundred years has been to oppose the strongest power in Europe by weaving together a combination of other countries strong enough to face the bully. Sometimes it is Spain, sometimes the French monarchy, sometimes the French Empire, sometimes Germany. I have no doubt who it is now.'[57]

To Lord Linlithgow he added: 'I have come to think ... one should always look back upon the history of the past, study it and meditate upon it. Thus one learns the main line of advance.'[58] In 1939 Churchill warned Hitler to study British history so as not to under-estimate British resolve against aggressors. 'He had only to read the last two years of the reign of King William III and the opening years of Queen Anne to learn that an improvident unwillingness to enter a quarrel may be succeeded by unwearying and triumphant leadership in that same quarrel at a later date and more difficult stage.'[59]

Thus, in 1940, Churchill could regale the British people with a sense of the past, reminding them that their national story demanded yet another struggle against evil and oppression. He declared that the Battle of Britain ranked 'with the days when the Spanish Armada was approaching the Channel, and Drake was finishing his game of bowls, or when Nelson stood between us and Napoleon's Grand Army at Boulogne.' He went on: 'We have read all about this in the history books; but what is happening now is on a far greater scale and of far more consequence to the life and future of the world and its civilisation...'[60] Hitler was just the latest, though deadliest, despot to threaten the liberties of Englishmen. He shared his own unconquerable faith in the British people and inspired them to think that they were living at a glorious time when they could match the deeds of past heroes. This would only have been possible in a country with a profound sense of its own history.

In a passage from his book *Sword and Pen*, Manfred Weidhorn sums up the usefulness of history to Churchill during both world wars:

> As one of the few among politicians and military men to appreciate the relevance of history, he pointed out in 1917, when everyone thought that the Russian revolution and the American entry would spur Germany into peacemaking, that nothing in the Napoleonic wars, the American Civil War, or the Boer War could give one such a hope, for men will often fight on without good prospects. In World War II, remembering the ultimate triumph of encircling alliances, he was not unnerved by the fall of France, or the German penetration of Russia.[61]

Looking for initiatives

One outstanding feature of Churchill's wartime leadership was his belief that attack was the best form of defence. Whereas Chamberlain believed that an economic blockade would weaken Germany and buy time for the Allies, Churchill had no time for such defensive tactics.

While at the Admiralty in December 1939, he floated the idea of dropping aerial mines into the River Rhine to disrupt military traffic. Later, in January 1940, he battled hard for his plan to mine Norwegian waters, which was designed in part to wrest the initiative from Germany. The Cabinet minutes are revealing: they record Churchill lamenting the fact that, since the beginning of the war, Britain had let the initiative rest with Germany. 'If we opened up a new theatre of operations in Scandinavia,' he declared, 'we had a fine chance of forcing Germany into situations which she had not foreseen, and of seizing the initiative for ourselves.'[62] 'The offensive', he declared, 'is three or four times as hard as passively enduring from day to day.'[63]

Churchill's belief in taking the initiative lay behind his support for the British bomber offensive. Realising in 1940 that Britain lacked a continental army to match Germany's, and that a German march eastwards was unstoppable, Churchill proposed that 'an absolutely devastating, exterminating attack by very heavy bombers from this country' would bring Nazi Germany to its knees. He told Beaverbrook: 'We cannot accept any lower aim than air mastery.'[64]

Whereas others might have despaired at the lack of options available in 1940, Churchill proposed a vigorous policy that would dent the enemy's resources.

Speaking again in early June 1940, he deprecated the notion of a 'passive resistance war' and called for bold initiatives and enterprises. He wanted a 'vigorous, enterprising and ceaseless offensive against the whole German-occupied coastline'; sitting back and waiting for events to take their natural course was not an option.[65] He told General Wavell in the same year that defensive inactivity imposed 'intolerable shackles' which it was necessary to cast off. For this reason he was delighted at the announcement of a plan to attack Axis forces in North Africa. 'Wars', he said, 'are won by superior will power'; it was necessary to 'wrest the initiative from the enemy and impose our will on him.' A year later, hearing that no major offensive was being planned against Axis forces in North Africa, Churchill wrote to General Smuts, dreading 'this long delay'. 'In war', he said, 'one cannot wait to have everything perfect, but one must fight in relation to the enemy's strength and plight.'[66]

Churchill did not want the subjugated European populations to remain enslaved to the enemy will. For this reason he set up the Special Operations Executive or SOE in July 1940 with Hugh Dalton. The SOE provided a means of conducting warfare without direct military engagement. Its mission was to encourage and facilitate espionage and sabotage behind enemy lines and to serve as the basis of a resistance movement in Britain should Germany invade. In Churchill's words, the task of its agents was to '*set Europe ablaze*'.

It is arguable that these enterprises (particularly the SOE) did not have the effect Churchill intended, but they do reflect his belief that the enemy would not be defeated by passivity; that victory would 'never be found by taking the line of least resistance'.[67]

Ruthlessness

Churchill knew that, in order to defeat a deadly and amoral foe, he would need a degree of ruthlessness. As early as 1915, his wife Clementine noted this facet of her husband's character. In an effort to save her husband's career, she wrote to Prime Minister Asquith: 'Winston may in your eyes and in those with whom he has to work have faults, but he has the supreme quality which I venture to say very few of your present or future Cabinet possess, the power, the imagination, the deadliness to fight Germany.'[68] Throughout the war, Churchill was certainly ruthless when the situation demanded it, and sometimes this involved bending the normal rules of conflict.

Shortly before he became Prime Minister, Churchill was the driving force behind the ill-fated Narvik expedition. He wanted to prevent the passage of Swedish iron ore to Germany via Norway – an important lifeline for the enemy. However, the operation would involve the violation of Norwegian territorial waters while that country was still officially neutral. Others in the Cabinet made the fair point that Britain should not be seen to violate international law when that was exactly what Nazi Germany was doing. For Churchill the issue was clearer cut. 'Our defeat', he said, 'would mean an age of barbaric violence, and would be fatal not only to ourselves, but to the independent life of every small country.' What mattered was that British breaches of law would not be accompanied by 'inhumanity'.[69] At the same time Churchill put himself out of joint with public opinion by refusing to condemn the Soviet attack on Finland. The Soviets, he declared, should 'increase their strength in the Baltic' and limit 'German domination in that area'.[70]

After the Franco-German armistice was signed, Churchill feared that the French fleet would fall into German hands, empowering an already deadly foe. British admirals negotiated with French Admiral Gensoul on July 3rd, offering him the chance to either scuttle his ships or sail them to a British port. When it became clear that Gensoul would accept neither option, Churchill had little hesitation in ordering their destruction. The action claimed over twelve hundred French lives, something that was particularly galling for the Francophile Prime Minister, but it was dictated by the even more terrible circumstances of war. The action helped persuade the wavering Roosevelt administration that Churchill's government was determined to persevere in the war against Germany. His decision in June 1940 to withhold further aircraft for the French also revealed a tough streak that was necessary for British national survival.

When Britain faced invasion, Churchill was prepared to adopt a similarly ruthless attitude to the enemy. Confronting the possibility of a German landing on the English coast, he told the War Cabinet not to 'hesitate to contaminate our beaches with gas if this course would be to our advantage'. He added that, 'We had the right to do what we liked with our own territory.'[71] Later he asked General Ismay for a report on current stocks of mustard gas which could be used to drench the beaches if the enemy landed. An alternative plan was to send fire ships into German-held French ports to 'scatter burning all over the harbour, possibly with most pleasing results'.[72] Operation Razzle involved dropping incendiary pellets into German forests.

Later in the war, with the terrifying V1 and V2 rockets raining down on British cities, Churchill was prepared to consider the use of poison gas again. 'We could drench the cities of the Ruhr and many other cities in Germany in such a way that most of the population would be requiring constant medical attention.' He added, 'I do not see why we should always have all the disadvantages of being the gentlemen while they have all the advantages of being the cad.'[73] Though Churchill was overruled by colleagues on this occasion, it is not difficult to see the lengths to which he was prepared to go in defeating a far more ruthless enemy.

Humanity

Despite his capacity for ruthlessness, Churchill often showed concern at the scale of wartime suffering. He was deeply touched by the plight of families during the Blitz and moved by the devastation caused by air raids. He sent a memo to John Reith, then Minister of Works and Buildings, to provide some material assistance to people whose houses had been damaged in this way: 'Sometimes I see a whole row of houses whose windows are blown out, but are not otherwise damaged, standing for weeks deserted and neglected. Active measures should be taken to replace the tiles and to close up the windows with fabric, with one small pane for light ... You ought to have a regular corps of workmen who would get this job done so that the people may get back into their homes...'[74] He also arranged a scheme of compensation for shopkeepers whose livelihoods had been destroyed by the Blitz.[75]

Churchill consistently championed a cross-Channel invasion of Europe and welcomed Operation Overlord. However, on the eve of battle, he expressed concern at the expected number of Allied casualties. He was haunted by the mass carnage on the Western Front and feared that a repeat would wipe out another generation. Prior to the landings, Churchill shared these concerns with John J. McCloy, US Under-Secretary for War: 'If you think I'm dragging my feet, it is not because I can't take casualties; it is because I am afraid of what those casualties will be.'[76]

He also expressed concern at the planned bombing of French railway bridges and railways in 1944, fearing the heavy toll in French and

Belgian civilian casualties. According to Brooke, Churchill was 'scared of casualties to the French entailed by this policy'; he believed that 'this slaughter was likely to put the French against us'.[77] Whereas Churchill sought to place a limit on the civilian death toll in any raid, Roosevelt had no such qualms.[78]

It was not just an excess of Allied causalities that concerned Churchill. He came to harbour doubts about the wisdom and morality of area bombing, too. In June 1943 he was shown footage of British bombing raids on German cities in the Ruhr. After witnessing the devastation wrought on the cities, those assembled around Churchill waited for his expected approval. Instead, he looked at them and said: 'Are we beasts? Are we taking this too far?'[79] Reviewing the policy of area bombing in 1945, he said, 'It seems to me that the moment has come when the question of bombing of German cities simply for the sake of increasing the terror, although under other pretexts, should be reviewed.' Dresden, he added, 'remains a serious query against the conduct of Allied bombing'.[80]

No matter how much Churchill revelled in the intricacies of wartime strategy, he never forgot what war really meant to those caught up in it. Sarah Churchill recollects her father's words during the Teheran Conference: 'War is a game played with a smiling face, but do you think there is laughter in my heart? We travel in style and round us there is great luxury and seeming security, but I never forget the man at the front, the bitter struggles, and the fact that men are dying in the air, on the land, and at sea.'[81] Perhaps for this reason Attlee said that one of Churchill's greatest gifts was 'his compassion'.[82]

Magnanimity

In order to lead the country successfully, Churchill had to ensure that pre-war feuds were laid to rest during the conflict. His ability to do this without hesitation reflects an abiding belief in magnanimity. During the war he led a coalition government consisting of Conservative, Labour and Liberal MPs, former foes and allies from various previous political campaigns. He also achieved the rare feat of leading a largely united nation during the period of his prime ministership. A lesser man would have felt entitled to lecture Parliament on the evils of appeasement and remind them of his regular and unheeded warnings. What mattered to Churchill was winning the war, not engaging in partisan political squabbles.

As he was the leader of the dominant Conservative Party, Churchill felt obliged to include its two foremost figures, Chamberlain and Halifax, in his-five man War Cabinet. For much of 1940, in a climate of bitter hostility towards the appeasers, calls were frequently made to sack them and their associated supporters.

Typical of these calls was one in the Labour *Daily Herald* on May 21st 1940. The article called for the removal of 'deadweight' in the government, adding: 'If a man has been incapable of estimating the probabilities of the war up to now, of what use will he be when – as must happen soon – its problems become infinitely more complex, its surprises more frequent, its dangers more dire.'[83] Churchill would have none of it. It would be 'a foolish and pernicious process' to hold a Commons inquest on the conduct of former governments, he said. He gave this advice to those who looked back at the past rather than forward to the future: 'Let each man search his conscience and his speeches. I frequently search mine ... Every minister who tries each day to do his duty shall be respected, and their subordinates must know that their chiefs are not threatened men, men who are here today and gone tomorrow, but that their directions must be punctually and faithfully obeyed.' He went on: 'Of this I am quite sure, that if we open a quarrel between the past and the present, we shall find that we have lost the future.'[84] In the titanic struggle with Nazi Germany, national unity was the overriding goal.

His magnanimity towards the former Tory leaders, Baldwin and Chamberlain, was particularly striking. Churchill had had bitter exchanges with Baldwin over Indian reform, and had not forgiven him for being excluded from office, but when he heard that crowds had thrown stones at Baldwin's car he invited the former Prime Minister to Downing Street for lunch. Neville Chamberlain had been the supreme appeaser and leading advocate of the Munich settlement, but when he was struck down with terminal cancer Churchill ensured that he was sent a daily round of political dispatches.[85]

This generousity was extended to the French government after it signed the armistice with Germany. The French, Churchill said, were like a 'friend and comrade' who had been 'smitten down by a stunning blow'. Under such circumstances, it was 'necessary to make sure that the weapon that [had] fallen from his hand' could not 'be added to the resources of [the] common enemy'. Crucially, however, Churchill added that there could be 'no room in war for pique, spite or rancour'.

Though scornful of the Vichyites, he was prepared to work with former Vichy collaborators like the Anglophobe Admiral Darlan, in an attempt to shorten the war in North Africa. While this may have seemed pernicious to some, for Churchill it was necessary in order to save more lives in the long term.[86] The same holds true of his alliance with Stalin in June 1941. Churchill declared that, while he would not 'unsay one word' of criticism of the communist ideology, he would enthusiastically embrace the Soviet dictator in their common fight against Nazism. This involved setting aside ideological differences and the bitterness of past exchanges. When Churchill famously declared that he had 'only one purpose, the destruction of Hitler', he truly meant it.

Welcomed criticism

As wartime Prime Minister, Churchill possessed more power over military strategy than any previous premier in history. He created a new role for himself, that of Minister of Defence, and established a level of civilian control over the military that Lloyd George could not have dreamed of. But, despite the vast powers at his disposal, Churchill was always prepared to tolerate dissent from his political and military colleagues, a fact that is often overlooked.

Churchill certainly *appeared* dictatorial in manner, and clearly disliked censure and criticism. 'I feel very biteful and spiteful when people attack me,' he told Violet Bonham-Carter. 'I don't want to be surrounded in the War Cabinet by a lot of people who want to beat me up.'[87] Certainly, his immense political experience and his commanding personality daunted many of his colleagues in government. When he felt certain about a strategic point, he would press others to accept it and 'was reluctant to abandon' it.

From first-hand accounts of Cabinet meetings, it certainly sounds as if Churchill was a dictator. Sir Ian Jacob recalls the way he chaired his meetings: 'Churchill talked a great deal, and though he could listen when he wanted to, he could also debate, browbeat, badger and cajole those who were opposed to him, or whose work was under discussion.'[88]

Eisenhower recalled that he had 'a very hard time withstanding his arguments'. And, according to Harold Nicolson's diaries, none of the great political figures of the past 'would have been so frightened of Winston as the whole Cabinet are today'.[89] Many, like General Dill, were unable to accept this adversarial style of leadership and did not fare well under Churchill. Dill wrote: 'He has such drive and personality that no one seems able to stand up to him'.[90] In a jovial passage in his memoirs, he reminded people that he only 'expected compliance with his wishes after reasonable discussion'.

There were clear advantages to this adversarial style of leadership. As Eisenhower recalled, 'More than once he forced me to re-examine my own premises, to convince myself again that I was right – or accept his solution.' Furthermore, he was far from being *impervious* to argument: as the Cabinet Secretary, Lord Normanbrook, pointed out, 'on many issues he kept an open mind and was ready to follow advice from men whose judgement he trusted.'[91]

Genuine dictators cannot tolerate those who criticise their ideas. Sir Ian Jacob remembered that the only way to stand up to Churchill was to offer 'a vigorous reply, even a counter-attack, and a clear and accurate statement of the case.' Those who could do this 'earned his respect'.[92] Air Marshal Portal was one of those who rejected one of Churchill's proposals quite forcefully. Portal recalled: 'During my tirade he fixed me with a glassy stare and at the end, when I said I was sorry if I had seemed rude, a broad smile appeared across his face and he said: 'You know in war you don't have to be nice, you only have to be right.'[93] Lord Bridges remarked: 'I cannot recollect a single minister, serving officer or civil servant who was removed from office because he stood up to Churchill.'[94] According to Macmillan, Churchill could be 'dogmatic', but he added: 'Actually, if one stands up to him in argument I do not think he resents it.'[95]

At the same time Churchill never once overruled the Chiefs of Staff on a military issue. As Attlee put it, 'He'd get some idea he wanted to press, and after we had considered it the rest of us would have to tell him there was no value in it ... Winston was sometimes an awful nuisance ... but he always accepted the verdict of the Chiefs of Staff when it came to it ...'[96] Strategic decisions were made collectively, sometimes with disastrous consequences, as in the decision to send troops to Greece in 1941. The War Cabinet in a democratic country could never have survived with a dictatorial leader at the helm.

Far from packing his Cabinet with congenial 'yes men' who would comply with his every wish, the Prime Minister sought colleagues who would challenge his views. As Colville put it, he 'retained unswerving independence of thought' and was not 'liable to be swayed by the views of even his most intimate counsellors'.[97] As early as September 4th 1939, as First Lord of the Admiralty Churchill submitted minutes to his naval colleagues 'for criticism and correction'.[98] He had no intention of gaining unthinking and uncritical approval for his ideas. Indeed, Churchill's relations with his Generals were more liable to become strained if they *failed* to stand up to him.[99]

Perhaps for this reason he kept on Sir Alan Brooke as army chief from 1941 until the end of the war. The two men frequently had ferocious exchanges of views, Churchill describing them in the following terms: 'When I thump the table and push my face towards him, what does he do? Thumps the table harder and glares back at me.'[100] Churchill and Alan Brooke remained a formidable team until the end of the war. As Lord Portal recollected of Churchill: 'He knew his own weaknesses, and knew that he needed to have around him men who from their experience and their expert training could keep his imagination in check.'[101]

Neville is wrong to say that, 'Ultimately Churchill's power was only circumscribed by the fact that Britain acquired allies who were far more militarily powerful than she was.'[102] It is certainly true that by late 1943 Britain's influence over wartime strategy had diminished now that both the United States and Soviet Union were flexing their military muscles. But, irrespective of allies, the Chiefs of Staff and Cabinet exercised their own control mechanisms to prevent Churchill's every strategic whim from being turned into reality.

Personal diplomacy

Finally, Churchill's war leadership epitomised the importance of personal diplomacy. He did not believe in the informal conduct of foreign policy through intermediaries or impersonal dispatches, preferring instead direct one-to-one meetings with other leaders. To this end, he undertook several lengthy and arduous journeys, often in perilous conditions, to meet his wartime allies. During the first month of his premiership he made five visits to France in order to boost the sagging morale of the French leaders. De Gaulle was impressed with the courage Churchill displayed, recalling in his memoirs his impression that 'Great Britain, led by such a fighter, would certainly not flinch.'[103] But, with France out of the war, Churchill needed to court the Americans.

Churchill crossed the Atlantic a number of times to visit President Roosevelt, a journey which was never reciprocated by the

American President. In June 1941 they met in Newfoundland, where the historic Atlantic Charter was signed, and following Pearl Harbor Churchill crossed the Atlantic again for a wartime summit with his new ally. In 1942 he made hazardous visits to Washington and Moscow, in the latter case to persuade Stalin of the Allies' goodwill and continuing military support. In 1943 he attended the Big Three conference in Teheran, but not before he had met Roosevelt at Casablanca, visited Canada and the United States in the *Queen Mary*, and travelled to Algiers, Malta and Egypt for important meetings. In 1944 he made visits to Gibraltar, France and Italy, followed by another visit to Canada and the United States for the Second Quebec Conference. In total he clocked up in excess of 110,000 air miles during the war.

The dangers of some of these wartime travels should not be underestimated. Travelling in the *Duke of York* in 1941 meant traversing the same route taken by German U-boats and coming perilously close to German airfields in Brittany. For one day of the week-long voyage, the battleship sailed without any accompanying vessel. Churchill's first trip to Moscow in 1942 was undertaken, not in a luxurious ocean-bound vessel, but in a cold, unpressurised Liberator bomber. For most people this would pose a considerable risk, and it was especially dangerous for the 67-year-old Prime Minister who was prone to bouts of pneumonia. In January 1943 Lord Moran, Churchill's personal physician, recounted another episode of Churchillian bravery in the face of physical adversity. He described how he awoke one night on a leaky aircraft to find the Prime Minister trying to keep out the draught by putting his blanket against the side of the plane: 'He was shivering: we were flying at 7,000 feet in an unheated bomber in mid winter. I got up, and we struggled, not with much success, to cut off the blast ... The P.M. is at a disadvantage in this kind of travel, since he never wears anything at night but a silk vest. On his hands and knees, he cut a quaint figure...'[104]

One can therefore understand the thoughts of General Douglas McArthur: 'If disposal of all the Allied decorations were today placed by Providence in my hands, my first act would be to award the Victoria Cross to Winston Churchill. Not one of those who wear it deserves it more than he. A flight of ten thousand miles through hostile and foreign skies may be the duty of young pilots, but for a Statesman burdened with the world's cares it is an act of inspiring gallantry and valour.'[105]

Despite their wartime disagreements, Stalin appreciated this side of Churchill's leadership. In 1944, during Churchill's second visit to Moscow, Stalin heard that the Big Three had been described as 'the Holy Trinity'. He quipped: 'If that is so, Churchill must be the Holy Ghost. He flies around so much.'[106]

These brave and vital wartime journeys exemplify Churchill's raw courage and his desire to lead by example. But above all they reflect his belief that foreign policy should be conducted by one-to-one personal diplomacy rather than being left to experts, committees or informal meetings.

NOTES

1 W. Churchill, *Great Contemporaries*, p.115.
2 John Colville, *The Fringes of Power*, p.143.
3 *Ibid.*, p.159.
4 Sir Robert Menzies, *Afternoon Light*, p.70.
5 H. Macmillan, *War Diaries: The Mediterranean 1943-5*, p.250.
6 J. Wheeler-Bennett (ed), *Action This Day*, p.49.
7 *Ibid.*, p.22.
8 *Memoirs of General The Lord Ismay*, London 1960, p.345.
9 J. Wheeler-Bennett (ed), *Action This Day*, p.238.
10 *Ibid.*, p.57.
11 E. Nel, *Mr. Churchill's Secretary*, pp.11-12.
12 WSC Bio 6, p.156.
13 A. Roberts, *Masters and Commanders*, p.111.
14 J. Wheeler-Bennett (ed), *Action This Day*, p.175.
15 *Ibid.*, p.21.
16 WSC Bio 6, p.962.
17 M. Gilbert, *Winston Churchill's War Leadership*, p.71.
18 WSC Bio 6, pp.758-9.
19 W. Harriman, *Special Envoy*, p.28.
20 Speeches VI, p.6222.
21 W. Churchill Jr, *Memories and Adventures*, p.10.
22 J. Colville, *The Fringes of Power*, p.145.
23 J. Lukacs, *The Duel*, p.164.
24 D. Littman and C. Sandys, *We Shall Not Fail*, p.174.
25 WSC Bio 6, p.436.
26 D. Jablonsky, *Churchill: The Great Game and Total War*, p.90.
27 *Ibid.*, p.91.
28 *War Papers 2*, p.187.
29 *Ibid.*, p.464.

30 R. Menzies, *Afternoon Light*, p.66.
31 W. Thompson, *Sixty Minutes with Winston Churchill*, pp.44-5.
32 WSC Bio 6, p.333.
33 J. Lukacs, *The Duel*, p.127.
34 T. Hickman, *Churchill's Bodyguard*, p.91.
35 WSC Bio 6, p.444.
36 D. Littman and C. Sandys, *We Shall Not Fail*, p.152.
37 C. de Gaulle, *The Call to Honour*, p.63.
38 D. Stafford, *Churchill and Roosevelt*, p.141.
39 J. Paxman, *The English*, p.84.
40 Speeches VI, p.6220.
41 *Ibid.*, pp.6247-50.
42 *Ibid.*, p.6286.
43 *Ibid.*, p.6587.
44 *Ibid.*, p.6399.
45 *Ibid.*, p.6425.
46 *Ibid.*, p.6153.
47 *Ibid.*, p.6220.
48 *Ibid.*, p.6238.
49 *Ibid.*, pp.6330-1.
50 *Ibid.*, p.6220.
51 *Ibid.*, p.6232.
52 *Ibid.*, p.6276.
53 N. Nicolson (ed), *Harold Nicolson: Diaries and Letters, 1939-45 II*, p.112.
54 R. Langworth (ed), *Churchill by Himself*, p.581.
55 N. Nicolson (ed), *Harold Nicolson: Diaries and Letters, 1939-45 II*, p.90.
56 Companion V (ii), p.1170.
57 Companion V (iii), p.143.
58 *Ibid.*, p.828.
59 W. Churchill, *Step by Step*, pp.329-30. In the same period, Churchill was working on a multi-volumed biography of his ancestor John Churchill, the first Duke of Marlborough. One of the themes of his biography was a celebration of the Grand Alliance created by Marlborough which was designed to secure Europe's liberty, and of which England was the undoubted lynchpin.
60 Speeches VI, p.6276.
61 M. Weidhorn, *Sword and Pen*, p.221.
62 *War Papers I*, p.629.
63 *Ibid.*, p.493.
64 WSC Bio 6, pp.656.
65 *Ibid.*, p.472.
66 M. Gilbert, *Winston Churchill's War Leadership*, p.55.
67 *War Papers I*, p.642.
68 Companion III (ii), p.921.
69 M. Gilbert, *Winston Churchill's War Leadership*, pp.41-2.
70 WSC Bio 6, p.100.
71 *Ibid.*, p.434.
72 D. Jablonsky, *Churchill: The Great Game and Total War*, p.178.

73 *Ibid.*, p.179.
74 WSC Bio 6, p.939.
75 T. Hickman, *Churchill's Bodyguard*, p.112.
76 M. Gilbert, *Winston Churchill's War Leadership*, p.87.
77 WSC Bio 7, p.738.
78 *Ibid.*, p.739.
79 *Ibid*, p.437.
80 *Ibid.*, p.1257.
81 S. Churchill, *A Thread in the Tapestry*, p.63.
82 D. Stansky, *Churchill: A Profile*, p.192.
83 WSC Bio 6, pp.474-5.
84 Speeches VI, p.6232.
85 J. Wheeler-Bennett (ed), *Action This Day*, p.55.
86 M. Weidhorn, *Sword and Pen*, p.167.
87 V. Bonham-Carter, *Champion Redoubtable*, p.236.
88 J. Wheeler-Bennett (ed), *Action This Day*, p.185.
89 N. Nicolson (ed), *Harold Nicolson: Diaries and Letters, 1939-45 II*, p.171.
90 D. Jablonsky, *Churchill: The Great Game and Total War*, p.129.
91 J. Wheeler-Bennett (ed), *Action This Day*, p.28.
92 *Ibid.*, p.185.
93 D. Jablonsky, *Churchill: The Great Game and Total War*, p.125.
94 *Ibid.*, p.105.
95 H. Macmillan, *War Diaries*, p.304.
96 G. Best, *Churchill and War*, p.169.
97 J. Colville, *Fringes of Power*, p.125.
98 WSC Bio 6, p.7.
99 D. Jablonsky, *Churchill: The Great Game and Total War*, p.124.
100 G. Best, *Churchill and War*, p.181.
101 A. Roberts, *Masters and Commanders*, p.106.
102 P. Neville, *Churchill: Statesman or Opportunist*, p.109.
103 C. de Gaulle, *The Call to Honour*, p.63.
104 D. Jablonsky, *Churchill: The Great Game and Total War*, p.90.
105 C. Sandys, *Chasing Churchill*, p.131.
106 D. Jablonsky, *Churchill: The Great Game and Total War*, p.90

CHAPTER NINE

Elder Statesman

THE BIG THREE (Truman, Churchill and Stalin) now met at Potsdam in July 1945 to decide on the shape of post-war Europe. Tensions were already evident, not least because Stalin had reneged on promises made at Yalta to allow free elections in Poland. Churchill returned home halfway through Potsdam to face a general election. His defeat at the hands of Clement Attlee's Labour Party was an electoral shock, though opinion polls and by-election results had long suggested a leftward tide in public opinion.

As leader of the opposition and the 'man who had won the war', Churchill was now a commanding figure on the world stage. In 1946 he travelled to Fulton, Missouri to deliver a landmark speech. He warned of an 'iron curtain' drawn down upon the Continent, and called for transatlantic unity in reaching a settlement with the Russians. He was widely criticised as a warmonger but events in the following years would vindicate his warnings. At the same time he declared that peace in Europe could come only from Franco-German harmony, and he became the champion of European unity, albeit without direct British involvement.

In the Middle East, the new state of Israel was formed in 1948, following Britain's withdrawal at the end of her mandate. In contrast to the Labour government, Churchill warmly recognised the country, which was in keeping with his long-standing Zionist sentiments. He would continue to support the Jewish state for the rest of his life.

Churchill lost the general election of 1950, though Labour was returned with only a five-seat majority. When Labour went to the polls again in 1951, the Conservatives won, and Churchill became Prime Minister for the second time. Leaving domestic policy in the hands of trusted ministers, he now concentrated on his final campaign in international affairs, an attempt to bring the Cold War to an end. He knew that a nuclear conflict would be devastating and that Britain would not be immune to any superpower conflagration. Thus he called for a high-level summit between the leaders of the Big Three, harking back to the personal diplomacy of the war years. His suggestion was met with a torrent of scepticism in Washington and London.

Churchill's campaign had a renewed urgency with the American testing of the hydrogen bomb in the Pacific Ocean in 1952. When Stalin died in 1953, Churchill tried to persuade new American President Eisenhower to meet the Russians. But with the McCarthyite scare raging in Washington, there was little chance of an agreement and Churchill was derided as an appeaser.

During his second premiership Churchill was showered with honours. He accepted the Order of the Garter from Elizabeth II, the sixth monarch he had served in his public career. He was also awarded the Nobel Prize for Literature, in part for his mammoth six-volume semi-autobiographical *History of the Second World War*, but lamented not receiving the Nobel Prize for peace.

In 1955 Churchill retired as Prime Minister and Conservative leader. He was still a back-bencher, though he would increasingly distance himself from public life. He was returned at Epping in 1963 but a year later, at the age of 89, he retired from Parliament after more than six decades of public service. Only William Gladstone, a century earlier, had served Parliament for a longer period. On January 24th 1965, Sir Winston Churchill died of a stroke, seventy years to the day that his father had passed away. He was awarded the ultimate accolade of a state funeral and, in a break with convention, even the monarch attended.

In 2002 the British public was asked to vote for their greatest national hero. Beating off rivals Isambard Kingdom Brunel and Princess Diana, Winston Churchill emerged by popular acclaim as 'The Greatest Briton' of all time. It was an accolade he would have heartily welcomed.

Why did Churchill lose the 1945 election?

In July 1945 Churchill's Conservatives lost the general election to the Labour Party in one of the greatest election upsets in British history. Labour swept to power securing half the popular vote and 393 Commons seats to the Tories 213. It was a landslide victory by any standard and few political commentators had anticipated it. Most expected that Churchill would win the 'khaki election', triumphing on the back of his victory against Nazi Germany. Churchill took the result badly and went on an extended holiday abroad to recover from the shock of defeat.

In retrospect, the defeat still seems surprising. Churchill was a much esteemed and popular war leader, as judged by the consistency of wartime opinion polls. During the war, his personal ratings rarely fell below 80 per cent and, even during the darker periods of war in 1942, his popular appeal scarcely waned. Yet here lies the historical irony. While Churchill was seen as a great and indispensable war leader, he was not trusted with Britain's immediate post-war future. As the war unleashed pent-up demands for reconstruction and welfare, the public turned to Labour, not the Conservatives, to fulfil their aspirations.

Labour's outright victory clearly owed something to the Tories' disastrous election campaign, and for this Churchill must bear some responsibility. After co-operating well with the Labour leadership in the wartime coalition, he adopted an unmistakably vituperative and aggressive tone as the war drew to a close. With coalition politics now obsolete, Churchill went to battle in the trench warfare of party politics. In a speech to the Conservative Party conference in March 1945, he claimed that a Labour government's control over the economy would destroy 'the whole of our existing system of society, and of life, and of labour...'[1]

In his first election broadcast he declared that socialism was essentially 'an attack not only upon British enterprise, but upon the right of an ordinary man or woman to breathe freely without having a harsh, clumsy, tyrannical hand clapped across their mouth and nostrils.' He went on to make the disturbing claim that any socialist government would 'have to fall back on some form of Gestapo, no doubt very humanely directed in the first instance.' This was because no socialist government 'could afford to allow free, sharp, or violently worded expressions of public discontent.'[2]

The conflation of socialist economic policy with totalitarianism was unfair to a Labour leadership that had loyally supported Churchill throughout the war. It is now well known that he had taken advice from Lord Beaverbrook, but no doubt he was also influenced by F.A. Hayek's anti-totalitarian tract, *The Road to Serfdom*, which referred to the socialist origins of Nazism. But Churchill's venomous attack on a wartime colleague was also an astonishing political miscalculation. The speech went down badly with much of the electorate, who felt 'real distress and concern that a figure so admired, even by his opponents, should lose his prestige.'[3]

But it would be a mistake to blame the Tory defeat entirely on the poor campaign. The seeds of defeat had long been implanted during, and even before the war. If sections of the electorate were becoming disenchanted with Churchill, it was largely because of, rather than in spite of, his links with the Tory Party. Churchill had become Tory leader in November 1940, following the death of Neville Chamberlain. A move that was born of political necessity during the war became a hindrance to Churchill after it. The Tories were dominant in Parliament throughout the 1930s and they were inextricably associated with a host of unpopular memories. They were the party that presided over much of the Depression and unemployment; they were the party that had advocated appeasement; they were in charge during the Phoney War, marked by Chamberlain's complacent retort that 'Hitler had missed the bus'. Churchill was revered as the leader of humanity but not as the leader of the Tory Party.

To some extent this represented an ironic and spectacular act of collective amnesia. In 1935 a majority of the British electorate had voted for a Tory government committed to only limited rearmament, while appeasement was popular in many quarters. The Labour Party took advantage of the Conservatives' declining stock because they had been out of government throughout the 1930s. The public were therefore unable to blame Attlee and his party for appeasement, Dunkirk or the failures of pre-war planning. People knew little of Labour disunity in the 1930s, and how they voted against rearmament on several occasions. Collective amnesia happens in elections and the Tories paid the price for it in 1945.

Perhaps the most important reason why Labour trounced their opponents was that it was they, rather than the Conservatives, who championed social reform. In the aftermath of war, the mood of the working-class electorate seemed to be quite simple: they wanted to end mass unemployment, slum housing and the enormous wealth inequalities associated with the pre-war years. Harold Laski summed up the feelings of many when he said that post-war Britain had to see 'no more distressed areas, no more vast armies of unemployed, no more slums, no vast denial of equality of opportunity.'[4]

This feeling did not suddenly spring from nowhere in 1945. The Beveridge Report, published in November 1942, the brainchild of civil servant William Beveridge, was hugely popular, selling over 600,000 copies when it was released. It proposed a comprehensive 'social service state', instead of the safety net system for lower income groups, with a free national health service, family allowances, housing reforms and an extended system of national insurance. The report outlined a plan according to which the state would, in Churchill's words, take care of the citizen 'from the cradle to the grave'. Beveridge's proposals received enthusiastic endorsement from the media, so much so that the coalition 'came under sustained pressure to give serious, rather than token, attention to the problems of reconstruction'.[5]

Most Tories rejected the wide-ranging levels of state intervention implied by the report. In a report submitted to the Prime Minister, Tory back-benchers comprehensively dismissed the notion of social security, arguing that the main post-war economic priority was to reduce taxation. This was music to Churchill's ears for he considered Beveridge to be 'an awful windbag and a dreamer' and he did not attend the subsequent Commons debate on the report. In a private letter, Beveridge was led to write: 'It seems to me that any Government under Winston will not do more for social progress than they are driven to by opposition and peace-making.'[6]

Later on March 21st 1943, Churchill broadcast on the subject of welfare reform. He talked of a four-year plan based on extending national insurance and welcomed the broadening of opportunities in education. He also embraced the National Health Service, commenting famously that there was 'no finer investment for any community than putting milk into babies'.[7]

Churchill's commitment to post-war reconstruction was limited, however. He did not mention the Beveridge Report by name and, while prepared to endorse new schemes of social security, was reluctant to ponder the question too deeply. One reason was that he believed the war had to take priority above all other issues. In 1941 he told the editor of the *Manchester Guardian*: 'The necessary thing was to win the war, and any statement on peace aims would either be a collection of platitudes or would be dangerous to the present unity.'[8] To focus too much on divisive matters of domestic policy would risk the fragmentation of the wartime national consensus.

This attitude was likened by Sir Alan ('Tommy') Lascelles to 'a man with a gun looking for a mad dog, solely concerned with the shooting of the dog, and not with the fate of those whom it may have bitten.'9 As Colville put it, 'His interests were predominantly defence, foreign affairs and party politics.'10 Churchill would later claim that it would be unrealistic to bind the government or its successor, to new expenditure in future conditions which could not be foreseen. This was one of the reasons he gave to Butler for rejecting suggestions for post-war educational reform: 'I certainly cannot contemplate a new Educational Bill. I think it would be a mistake to stir up the public schools question at the present time. No one can possibly tell what the financial and economic state of the country will be when the war is over.'11

Perhaps for this reason Churchill was soon out of touch with the electorate on this most vital issue of domestic reform. Throughout the war he had taken a backseat on questions of domestic policy. The management of the war economy had been delegated to the Lord President's Committee, chaired by Chamberlain, Anderson and Attlee, while a prominent Labour figure, Ernest Bevin, became Minister of Labour.

From 1943 the tide was turning in a leftward direction, and towards a leftward party. According to the British Institute of Public Opinion pollsters, from June 1943 onwards the numbers of people planning to vote Conservative markedly decreased until the figure stood at 24 per cent in May 1945. Labour's share in the meantime increased to 40 per cent, which seemed to accurately reflect wartime electoral trends. Between 1942 and 1945 eight Conservative candidates whose seats were not contested by Labour were defeated by left-wing independent candidates.

After 1943 the Conservative Party was defeated four times, either by independent socialists or by the new radical Common Wealth Party, in what were essentially safe seats. Meanwhile, in the armed forces there was ample evidence of antipathy towards the Conservatives and an acceptance of the Beveridge Report.12 Churchill sensed that 'a strong tide was flowing left', though 'not in the direction of any particular left Party.'13 In a meeting with Alan Lascelles in June 1945 Churchill said he was convinced that 'all the young men and women in the Services' would 'vote against him'.14

The Conservatives in 1945 relied on their revered wartime leader, little realising that, in the aftermath of war, the electorate would have a new set of political priorities. As Woolton wrote, 'People wonder whether the great war leader will be a good peace leader. "Is he really interested in reconstruction and social reform" is the question that I find people asking.'[15] While the Conservatives tried to frighten the electorate away from the Labour Party, the Labour Party campaigned on a programme of comprehensive reform, nationalisation and economic planning. Their programme, rather than the Conservative Party's anti-socialist scaremongering, fitted the mood of the new electorate.

Speaking of the election defeat in 1945, Clementine remarked, 'It may well be a blessing in disguise.' As ever, Winston had a witty riposte: 'At the moment it seems quite effectively disguised.'[16]

What was the true message of the 'iron curtain' speech?

IN MARCH 1946 Churchill delivered a speech at Westminster College in Fulton, Missouri that helped to change the course of history. It would not be an overstatement to describe Churchill's Fulton speech as the most influential of his illustrious career, and certainly one of the most influential of the twentieth century. It introduced new phrases into the political lexicon, such as 'Iron Curtain' and 'the special relationship', while projecting Churchill to the world as a prophet in the emerging Cold War. As Pamela C. Harriman put it so aptly, the speech 'cut like a thunderbolt through the public dialogue'.[17]

But, far from being credited for prescient statesmanship, Churchill has often been denounced as a warmonger. Ponting argues that he rejected 'any policy of accommodation with the Soviet Union' in his Fulton speech. At the time, the *Chicago Sun* interpreted it as a call for 'world domination through arms',[18] while *The Wall Street Journal* was at pains to deny that the United States needed another alliance, even though Churchill had not explicitly called for one. Many came to view the speech as a clarion call to arms, even though it was actually titled 'The Sinews of Peace'. A close examination of the speech reveals that Churchill, far from seeking a showdown with the Soviet Union, wanted a renewal of Western unity in the face of Soviet pressure, and an urgent settlement with the Russians.

Throughout late 1944 and 1945 Churchill became obsessed with the threat of Soviet domination in Europe. The 'Red Army', he said, 'was spreading like a cancer from one country to another'.[19] Churchill's fear of Soviet intentions made him determined to alter

Allied strategy, firstly through his 'percentages agreement' and
secondly by calling for the Allied armies to meet Russian forces as far
eastwards as possible. As the war in Europe was ending, Churchill
was perturbed at the gradual disappearance of the American army
from Europe, and its transfer to the Pacific theatre of war. He sent
a message to new US President, Harry S. Truman, warning that an
'iron curtain' was drawn down upon the Russian front and that only
a firm Allied stand against Stalin could save Europe from 'another
bloodbath'.[20]

That Churchill had pre-war appeasement in mind was clear from
a telegram he sent to Field Marshal Smuts. 'I am sure', he wrote, 'that
any sign that we can be bluffed and pushed about would have a
deadly effect upon the future of Europe, which I regard with as much
anxiety as I did before the outbreak of the war.'[21] At the July 1945
Potsdam Conference Churchill made it clear to Truman that the
Eastern European countries under Red Army occupation needed to
have fair and free elections as promised at Yalta. Later Stalin
appeared to endorse this demand.[22]

The growing East-West confrontation, which so preoccupied
Churchill in 1945, emerged as the dominant theme of his address at
Fulton. At the beginning of his speech, Churchill noted one important but unpalatable fact, namely that the Grand Alliance he had
striven to create in wartime was being dissolved in peacetime.
Churchill stressed the urgent need to re-establish the alliance
between those he called 'the English speaking peoples'. While
acknowledging that the United States stood at 'the pinnacle of world
power', he added that she had an 'awe-inspiring accountability to the
future'[23] and that the United Nations could only become an effective
instrument of international diplomacy if it was buttressed by an
Anglo-American 'special relationship'. Without realising it, he had
just coined a key term of the post-war political lexicon.

He waxed lyrical on the ideological affinity between Britain and
America, stressing their mutual regard for democratic freedoms
within their respective constitutions. But a key emphasis within this
relationship had to be the projection of strength. Thus he spoke of
the 'continuance of the intimate relationship between [our] military
advisers ... the similarity of weapons and manuals of instructions
and ... the interchange of officers and cadets at technical colleges'.[24]
He wanted to see a permanent defence agreement between the
United States and the entire British Commonwealth and eventually

common citizenship. Only this relationship, he argued, could ensure the stature and strength of the United Nations.

But Churchill's words were not words for their own sake. There was a need for an urgent alliance for, as he put it, a 'shadow' had 'fallen upon the scenes so lately lighted by the Allied victory'. He went on:

> From Stettin in the Baltic to Trieste in the Adriatic, an iron curtain has descended across the Continent. Behind that line lie all the capitals of the ancient states of Central and Eastern Europe. Warsaw, Berlin, Prague, Vienna, Budapest, Belgrade, Bucharest and Sofia ... lie in what I must call the Soviet sphere, and all are subject in one form or another, not only to Soviet influence but to a very high, and in many cases, increasing measure of control from Moscow ... The Communist parties ... have been raised to pre-eminence and power far beyond their numbers and are seeking everywhere to obtain total-itarian control.

He talked of communist fifth columns in some European countries which worked 'in complete unity and absolute obedience to the directions they receive from the Communist centre'. He concluded: 'This is certainly not the Liberated Europe we fought to build up.'[25]

Much of this was fair comment. Since February 1945, when Stalin had promised free and fair elections in Eastern Europe, the communist parties and the Red Army had extended their grip on the countries of Poland, Hungary, Czechoslovakia, Bulgaria, Romania and Albania, and democratic freedoms were being slowly extinguished. The solid bloc of pro-communist states owed their allegiance to Moscow and, in the Middle East, Persia [now Iran] stood at the mercy of the Red Army. This Soviet threat had to be faced by a new unity in Europe which would see the abolition of struggles between its individual nations. To this unified Europe (by which he did not mean a federated Europe), Churchill hoped that American power could be added.

This was not a ringing declaration of war against the Soviet Union; he did not believe that a new conflict was inevitable or even imminent. Indeed, he denied that Soviet leaders wanted war so much as 'the fruits of war and the indefinite expansion of their power and doctrines'. The call for transatlantic unity, in whatever form, was essential for, as he put it, 'there is nothing [the Russians] admire so much as strength, and there is nothing for which they have less

respect than weakness, especially military weakness.'[26] In his inim-
itable style, he sounded a grave warning to the Americans not to
avert their eyes from the potential danger or engage in a fruitless
policy of appeasement.

While the 'iron curtain' speech was a call for the unity of the
Western democracies, it was not intended to endorse a confrontation with the Soviet Union. Churchill talked of the need to reach a
settlement with the Russians, or, in his own words, 'a good understanding on all points with Russia under the general authority of the
United Nations Organisation'.[27] This included an understanding of
the difficulties endured by the 'valiant' Russian people, to whom
Churchill paid generous tribute. He talked of Russia requiring
security on her western borders and the 'removal of all possibility of
German aggression'. Far from casting Russia aside as a pariah state,
he welcomed her 'to her rightful place among the leading nations of
the world' while lauding the 'constant, frequent and growing contacts
between the Russian people and our own people'.[28]

But this settlement had to be backed up with the strength of all
the major powers on the other side of the Iron Curtain. As Churchill
observed, the combined populations of the English speaking
commonwealths, in military, diplomatic, scientific and industrial
contexts, would ensure an 'overwhelming assurance of security' and
not a 'precarious balance of power'.[29]

Clive Ponting's assessment of the speech as 'recycling anti-Soviet
rhetoric of the 1920s and early 1930s' and 'rejecting outright any policy of accommodation with the Soviet Union' is somewhat facile.[30]

Far from being an enemy of the new United Nations, Churchill
welcomed its creation, urging that it become 'a force for action, and
not merely a frothing of words'. But, in order to function effectively,
it had to be properly equipped with international armaments. As he
put it, courts and magistrates 'cannot function without sheriffs and
constables'.[31] Churchill even suggested that each of the world's major
countries should contribute a number of air squadrons to the service
of the United Nations should they be required. He believed in the
efficacy of international organisations provided that they would not
repeat the mistakes of the impotent League of Nations.[32] In a sense,
Churchill's call for unity was a means to an end: reaching a settlement with the Soviet Union, backed up by force, that would permanently remove the causes of future conflicts and lead to a period of
peace.

Thus, far from being the speech of a warmonger, Churchill's guiding strategic interest at Fulton was 'the permanent prevention of war', as well as 'the establishment of conditions of freedom and democracy'.33 He talked of preserving the 'the safety and welfare, the freedom and progress, of all the homes and families of all the men and women in all the lands'. These people had to be 'shielded' from the 'giant marauders' of 'war and tyranny'.34 It was the supreme responsibility of all the powers not to engage in another destructive conflict but rather to 'guard the homes of the common people from the horrors and miseries of another war'.35

In a much ignored passage later in the speech, Churchill talked of how, in the absence of tyranny and war, the fruits of science could be used to bring about 'an expansion of material well-being beyond anything that has yet occurred in human experience'. He approvingly quoted his mentor, the great American orator Bourke Cochran, who wrote: 'The earth is a generous mother; she will provide in plentiful abundance food for all her children if they will but cultivate her soil in justice and in peace.'36

Churchill's speech was enormously influential as the contours of the Cold War were emerging. But initially there was such a hostile reaction in many American newspapers that Truman and Acheson intentionally distanced themselves from Churchill, though the speech had not taken Truman or the American administration by surprise. There is evidence that Truman, Leahy and other senior figures very much appreciated the most controversial parts of the speech, suggesting amendments where necessary, and only backed away because of the unexpected public reaction.37

The speech soon became a defining moment in the early rhetoric of the Cold War. This was partly a result of fortuitous timing. The date of the speech, March 5th 1946, coincided with a period of heightened tension with the Soviets. On March 1st, Russia had halted its withdrawal from Iran, a withdrawal that had been required by the treaty of 1942. Shortly afterwards, there was a Soviet announcement from Ankara that the Russians desired to see a more pro-Soviet Turkish government. On the day of the Fulton speech, the Americans issued not one but two stiff notes of protest, one that concerned Russian behaviour in Manchuria. As Churchill himself acknowledged seven months later, 'if I were to make that speech at the present time and in the same place, it would attract no particular attention'.38

Churchill enjoyed a unique position as the Western world's foremost statesman, not just because of his record as a war leader but more particularly from his record as an anti-appeaser in the 1930s. He was rightly seen as the most vigorous critic of pre war appeasement, as the man who could have prevented 'the unnecessary war'. In his call for unity and resolve against Hitler, he had been proved right. Now he was calling for the same unity and resolve against the emerging Russian threat. For once Ponting got it right when he said, 'Churchill had convinced himself that by virtue of his prophecies in the 1930s he was a reliable forecaster of world events in the 1940s.'[39]

Churchill believed that lessons had to be learnt from turning a blind eye to Hitler in the 1930s. As he put it in his speech, 'Last time I saw it all coming and cried aloud to my own fellow countrymen and to the world, but no one paid any attention.'[40] Of course, Churchill was not alone in criticising the approach to Hitler, nor was he the sole champion of strength against the Soviets. There were a myriad of voices, mostly notably that of George Keenan,[41] arguing for a tougher line with the USSR and the view of Churchill as a unique prophet is myth-making at best. But he understood the contours of the new East-West conflict and proposed a genuinely statesmanlike solution. In years to come, the Truman Doctrine, Marshall Aid and the establishment of NATO would all reflect the very Western unity that Churchill had called for.

Did Churchill believe in a federal Europe?

TODAY CHURCHILL is claimed as an ally by both sides in the debate on a united Europe. The federalists point to his enthusiasm for the cause of a 'United States of Europe' after the Second World War. They point out that he was an influential presence at various postwar European congresses and that, in 1958, he received the Charlemagne Prize for services to the cause of European unity. The Eurosceptics interpret matters rather differently, pointing out that, during his second prime ministership from 1951 to 1955, he distanced Britain from binding federal commitments. They also claim that his references to a common Europe were designed to exclude British involvement.

Was he a fellow traveller of the skeptics or the federalists? The evidence taken as a whole shows that, while Churchill did embrace a vague aspiration for European unity, largely to ward off the Soviet threat during the Cold War, he did not believe in a binding British commitment to the Continent.

Churchill mused about the benefits of a united Europe as early as 1930. In an article aptly titled 'The United States of Europe' he compared the Continent, with its high tariff barriers and national rivalries, to the United States. In the United States there was 'no obstacle or barrier of any kind except those which nature has raised, and which science was overcoming'. By contrast, the organisation of Europe was 'onerous and less economically efficient than it was before the war' owing to different frontiers, stamps and currencies. He argued that a merging of frontiers in Europe could provide great economic benefits to the people of the Continent.

But he also saw Europe as a seething cauldron of hate and national rivalries which the post-war treaties had done little to assuage. It was but a short step to arguing that a united Europe could quell national rivalries and appease the 'obsolete hatred and vanished oppressions' between nations. He wrote: 'In so far as the movement towards European unity expresses itself by the vast increase of wealth which would follow from it, by the ceaseless diminution of armies which would attend it, by ever increasing guarantees against the renewal of war, it bodes no ill toward the rest of the world.'

Churchill appeared to stamp his federalist credentials more strongly when he wrote: 'from every man will some day be required not the merging or discarding of various loyalties, but their simultaneous reconciliation in a complete or larger synthesis.'

Today's Euro-enthusiasts see this as the first British call for a supranational European body, one that would be able to reconcile British national interests with those of the Continent. But they would be mistaken. At the same time as he lauded European unity, Churchill simultaneously disclaimed any role for Britain, declaring: 'We are with Europe but not of it. We are linked but not compromised. We are interested and associated, but not absorbed.' His sentiments would reverberate within Conservative Party ranks for decades.

Churchill welcomed plans for European unity because his country's economic wellbeing required a harmonious and stable Continent. As he put it, 'The prosperity of others makes for our own prosperity; their peace is our tranquillity; their progress smooths our path.' His advocacy of a United Europe was based on a perception that it served British imperial interests, for the Empire's safety depended on 'reconciling and identifying British interests with the larger interests of the world'.[42]

At different times during the Second World War, Churchill discussed various proposals for post-war European unity. The most shocking proposal (to posterity) was the plan for an 'indissoluble union of the French and British peoples', hastily proposed and accepted in June 1940. Rene Pleven, Jean Monnet and Charles de Gaulle had all conceived of a political union between Britain and France, with their two governments acting as one, their two armies fighting as one and their two peoples possessing automatic citizenship in both countries. Churchill, though initially wary of such a monumental constitutional alteration, accepted the plan, convinced that it was the only way to keep the French in the war. Ultimately he was unable to avert the French armistice of June 22nd 1940, and with that fateful decision the Pleven plan was consigned to history. In any case, it is hard to imagine that this sudden enlargement of the national realm would have survived long after the war ended.

Later in 1940 Churchill contemplated the future of a post-war Europe. According to Colville's recollection:

> When we had won the war he visualised five great European nations: Great Britain, France, Italy, Spain and Prussia. In addition, there would be four confederations: the Northern, with its capital at the Hague; the Middle European with its capital at Warsaw or Prague; the Danubian including Bavaria, Wurttemberg, Baden, Austria and Hungary, with its capital at Vienna; and the Balkan with Turkey at its head ... These nine powers would meet in a Council of Europe, which would have a supreme judiciary and Economic Council, and each would contribute men to a Supranational Air Cohort.

Churchill was already contemplating Britain as a bridge between Europe (of which she would be part) and the English-speaking world, including the USA. But Britain would not itself be tied into any such confederation.[43]

In 1942 he told Anthony Eden that he hoped for a 'United States of Europe' in which the barriers between nations would be 'greatly minimised' in order to facilitate 'unrestricted travel'.[44] He talked of the same confederation the following year but already made clear that one of his motivations was fear of Russia. As he told Barrington-Ward, editor of *The Times*, 'I do not want to be left alone in Europe with the Bear.'[45] He was also thinking of how Europe's ancient hatreds might be quietened by the opening of commercial links and the breaking down of economic barriers. But there was little hint about what role, if any, Britain would play.

Again during a trip to Washington in 1943, Churchill discussed the idea of a World Council. In it there would be three regional bodies, the European one consisting of twelve states or confederations of lesser powers. There was little sign that he envisaged Britain as one of these twelve states, though he did talk of a fraternal association between the United States and the British Commonwealth. Much of this was akin to table talk, the spontaneous eruption of thoughts on issues which could only receive sustained attention at war's end.

Having lost the general election in 1945, the following year Churchill made two seminal speeches which set out his vision of the post-war world. At Fulton, he talked of a 'new unity in Europe' and 'a grand pacification of Europe' but this grand vision was couched in language that was deliberately vague and ambiguous. Then in 1946 Churchill travelled to Zurich, where he made an appeal for 'a United States of Europe'. What astonished his audience was the suggestion that the first step in achieving the 're-creation of the European family' would be 'a partnership between France and Germany', and that a revived Europe required at its core 'a spiritually great Germany'. The two countries, he argued, had to take a moral lead in European rejuvenation while the shadow of the atomic bomb was hanging over the Continent. In the immediate aftermath of war, these were highly prescient sentiments.[46]

The Zurich speech may have lit the spark for European unity but, once again, there was no suggestion of British involvement. Britain and its Commonwealth would be 'friends and sponsors of the new Europe' rather than an integral part of the new structure. In short, Britain's involvement would be one of benevolent association only.[47] The reason for Britain's proposed looser ties was a perception that the national interest lay elsewhere. Churchill spoke of three great interlocking circles, the Empire/Commonwealth, the United States and a Europe in which Britain would exercise its interest and maintain its influence.

Shortly after the Zurich speech, Churchill accepted the leadership of the movement for a United Europe, and he justified it in these terms:

In the mechanised world of today, the small nation States of the past
can scarcely hope for political or economic survival as isolated units.
The peoples of Europe, or as many of them are as willing to make a
start, should come together in order to create an effective European
union ... designed to maintain their common peace, to restore their
common prosperity and above all to preserve their common heritage
of freedom.[48]

There was plenty of fine sounding rhetoric but little suggestion of
the concrete steps that might be required to make this work. However he did make a point of ruling out 'currency reform' and urged
his followers: 'We must stick to our sentimental line – the spiritual,
cultural side. Let hatreds die.'[49] Nothing would induce him to be a
federalist.[50]

Again at the Hague Conference in 1948, Churchill appeared to
take a step towards federalism when he called for 'closer political
unity' which might involve 'some sacrifice or merger of national
sovereignty' by the countries involved. Churchill appeared willing to
accept this consequence of European unity. In his view, this sacrifice
would be counterbalanced by the 'gradual assumption, by all nations
concerned, of that larger sovereignty which can alone protect their
diverse and distinctive customs and characteristics, and their
national traditions.'[51]

But he said precious little about British involvement and, beyond
the call for a European assembly, was more prone to offer fine sounding phrases about European 'glory' than practical suggestions for
creating a federal superstate. When he later addressed the European
Assembly, an organisation he had helped to create, he declared his
trust in 'the growth and gathering of the united sentiment of Euro-
peanism' rather than in more concrete machinery. In truth, he was as
sceptical as the Labour Party about the surrender of national sovereignty to a federalist parliament.

What is significant about his vague embrace of European unity is
the timing. In 1946 he was terrified about the growing menace of
Soviet power and fearful of the progressive withdrawal of American
forces from Europe. He had already failed to convince Roosevelt to
make a permanent American commitment to defend Western
Europe and the position of his successor, Harry S. Truman, was
unlikely to differ. It was these sobering considerations that gave
added impetus to the idea of European unity. A solid Continental
power bloc would act as a counterweight to growing Soviet power,

deterring Russian aggression against Western Europe. The theory went that this would ease Cold War tensions, and reduce Britain's perilous financial and military liabilities, which would in turn ensure her survival as a post-war power. But such a solid power bloc was always a second best option compared to American participation in Europe. Until the formation of NATO in 1949, British policymakers could not be sure of American commitments, and thus a united Europe was a compromise solution.

After his Zurich speech, Churchill was concerned about the possible exclusion of Germany from any European bloc as there would be 'no force of nationhood in the West which could hold the balance with the Soviet power'.[52] In 1950 he called for a Franco-German alliance at the heart of Europe, a solid bloc that would serve as a 'nucleus upon which all the other civilised democracies of Europe, bound or free' could 'one day rally and combine'. By 'bound' he meant those countries currently under Soviet domination, which, in combination with Western Europe, could be a counterweight to Russian power.[53] This largely explains his post-war enthusiasm for a European army of sixty or seventy divisions to which each free nation would contribute. This armed force would help close 'the hideous gap in the protection of Western Europe from a Russian-Communist onrush to the sea'.[54]

In 1949, in Strasbourg, Churchill made another dramatic intervention. Supported by the Americans and, later, the British Chiefs of Staff, he urged the creation of a unified European army to include a German military contingent. A year later Rene Pleven and Jean Monnet put forward the notion of a European Defence Community, designed to allow the Germans to rearm, but under cover of a regional force. Churchill publicly endorsed the EDC and German rearmament within the body. Without a German force, he argued, it would not make sense to talk of 'the defence of Europe against Russia'. An armed Germany would be a 'deterrent to the Soviets'.[55]

Churchill later admitted the crucial Soviet dimension to his post-war dreams for European unity in 1954 when he told the Commons: 'Nothing but the dread of Stalinised Russia could have brought the conception of united Europe from dreamland into the forefront of modern thought.'[56] In 1955 he stated that, if the Western powers abandoned the EDC and had nothing to put in its place, Europe itself would appear 'divided and in vacuity before the mighty Communist oligarchy and dictatorship and its satellites'.[57] He even told Moran, 'If we'd got EDC, then we could have spoken to Russia from strength, because German rearmament is the only thing they are afraid of. I want to use Germany and EDC to keep Russia in the mood to be reasonable – to make her play ... It sounds cynical.'[58] But he was little interested in Britain joining a European bloc or in advancing a federal agenda.

Indeed Churchill consistently disclaimed any major role for his own country. While he stressed the need for a military alliance on the Continent, he made it clear that Britain would be 'with EDC but not in it'.[59] This somewhat half-hearted approach understandably led Eisenhower to complain that Britain had not provided any leadership on the Continent. 'Britain', he added, 'had been rather flat and colorless in the [whole] European business'.[60]

This 'flat and colorless' approach was to continue when Churchill became Prime Minister again in 1951. Much to the disappointment of Euro-enthusiasts like Jean Monnet, Churchill took little interest in the various supranational initiatives that were being proposed. Like his Labour predecessors, he refused to commit Britain to the European coal and steel community (ECSC) which was the forerunner of the EEC and made no effort to link Britain more closely with the EDC. He summed up his noncommittal approach in November 1951 by saying that he had 'never thought that ... Britain should become an integral part of a European federation'.[61]

In general there were few discussions in Cabinet about European integration and his choice of the Eurosceptic Anthony Eden as Foreign Secretary was revealing. In January 1952 he described the European army as a 'sludgy amalgam' and again refused to commit British troops to the EDC. For the remainder of his peacetime premiership, Churchill's energies were concentrated on a fruitless attempt at recreating a Big Three summit in order to ease tensions in the Cold War. European countries would have been excluded from any such summit.

By the time that Britain sought membership of the EEC in the early 1960s, Churchill's scepticism about a surrender of British sovereignty had scarcely waned. He published an open letter (written in fact by his secretary Anthony Montague-Brown) supporting Britain's application to join the EEC, but he stressed that the country could not afford to sacrifice her Commonwealth interests during negotiations. He added that at no time in his life had he 'contemplated the diminution of the Commonwealth'.[62]

Conclusion

Churchill has been accused of inconsistency, of espousing pro-European sentiments when out of power and abandoning the 'cause' when he was Prime Minister. In a sense, Churchill sowed the seeds of confusion. His talk of creating a 'United States of Europe' was couched in grand utterances and vague commitments, with little thought given to the substantive issues involved. After the war he sought to encourage a spirit of reconciliation which would forever remove the possibility of war. He wanted to exchange the pre-war bitterness and mutual hostility between continental nations for 'moral, cultural, sentimental and social affinities throughout Europe'.[63] His abiding fear of Soviet territorial ambitions led him to assert that only a strong and united European power bloc could unsettle and deter the USSR.

But Britain would only help Europe from the sidelines. One reason was the supreme importance attached to the British Commonwealth. As Churchill put it in November 1949, 'For Britain to enter a European Union from which the Empire and Commonwealth would be excluded would not only be impossible but would, in the eyes of Europe, enormously reduce the value of our participation.'[64] Colville summed matters up even better when he said that Churchill 'never for one moment during or after the war contemplated Britain submerging her sovereignty in that of a United States of Europe or losing her national identity. He wanted to see Europe one family ... but in his vision of the future, Britain was only linked to Europe. Her true destiny was the moral leadership of the English speaking peoples...'[65]

When it came to the three circles of British influence, the Commonwealth came first and Europe came third. Sandwiched in between was the United States, on whose role British security came to rest.

How did Churchill try to end the Cold War?

CHURCHILL IS REMEMBERED as the implacable opponent of world communism and one of the chief ideologists of the Cold War. He is well known for his tirade against Bolshevism and his attempt to strangle the Soviet regime at birth. His term the 'Iron Curtain' came to symbolise the seemingly irreconcilable gulf between East and

West. Americans often champion Churchill as much for his Cold War anti-communism as for his inspiring war leadership.

What is less well known is that Churchill spent his remaining years in office trying to end the Cold War. In the late 1940s and 1950s he was gripped by the spectre of nuclear conflict and spent a number of years seeking to lessen tensions between the superpowers. He called for a 'summit conference' between Britain, the USA and the Soviet Union in the style of the Big Three conferences of the Second World War. It was the final remarkable battle of his political career.

Churchill had long believed that his powers of persuasion could solve the most intractable crises. Throughout the war he had engaged in a form of shuttle diplomacy, traversing the skies and the seas to meet with his superpower allies. His inclination was to 'personalise international politics', reflecting a deeply held Whiggish conviction that great men could alone influence world history.[66] 'The progress of the world', he once said, was 'dependent on eminent individuals'.[67]

In 1946, at Fulton, Churchill called for the strengthening of the Anglo-American alliance. One of his central (though understandably unstated) aims was to ensure that Britain remained a powerful and influential player on the world stage. Far from speaking like a warmonger, however, Churchill called for a negotiated settlement with the Russians from a position of Allied unity and strength. He criticised the policy of drift and irresolution and argued that war was not inevitable, but it could be prevented only by timely diplomatic intervention.

What added to the urgency of these negotiations was the West's military advantage. Despite the USSR's quantitative edge in conventional weapons, they lacked atomic weapons. The American monopoly was a trump card. 'When this Parliament[68] first assembled,' Churchill argued, 'I said that the possession of the atomic bomb would give three or four years' breathing space ... But more than two of those years have already gone. I cannot think that any serious discussion which it may be necessary to have with the Soviet government would be more likely to reach a favourable conclusion if we wait till they have got it too.'[69]

He remained convinced that the atomic bomb would exercise a deterrent effect on the Soviet government, arguing that, were it not for this weapon in American hands, 'Europe would have been communised and London under bombardment some time ago'.[70] Indeed, he maintained this position throughout 1949, when the USSR first tested an atomic bomb, arguing that it would take them time to catch up with the United States. He privately mused on how the atomic arsenal could be used to the advantage of Britain and America in their dealings with the Soviets. He must have believed that the Russians would be forced into a settlement, backing down when threatened with a nuclear strike on their soil. But this notion of nuclear brinkmanship, if taken seriously, was not shared by Truman.

By 1950 Churchill appeared to have shifted his position somewhat, talking more in terms of 'peaceful co-existence' than a showdown between the powers. He was telling Parliament that there was a need to 'create a friendly atmosphere and feeling of mutual confidence and respect'.[71] Given that mutual paranoia and mistrust lay at the heart of the Cold War, this could hardly have been interpreted as a facile suggestion. In the same year, he spelt out his strategy for healing wounds between East and West: 'The idea appeals to me of a supreme effort to bridge the gulf between the two worlds, so that each can live their life, if not in friendship at least without the hatreds of the cold war.' He then called for 'a parley at the summit'.[72] In order to alleviate the suspicion that this represented weakness in the face of Soviet strength, Churchill conceived of a dual-track approach: Britain and America would continue to rearm, not to avoid dialogue but in order to pursue it more effectively. Discussions, he declared, would only be viable if they were pursued from a position of military power. Henceforth he would call for a form of appeasement through strength, the opposite of the policy he had condemned so forcefully at Munich.

Churchill's appeal for political summitry reflected a major change in strategic realities. During the Berlin blockade in 1948-9 the Americans had established a number of bomber bases in East Anglia. It was widely feared that American bomber crews could carry nuclear cargoes at the behest of the US President in any military showdown with the Soviet Union. The disturbing implication was that these American bases would in turn become prime targets for Soviet attack in a Third World War. When the Soviet Union tested its first atomic weapon in August 1949, Churchill became exercised, like his contemporaries, by the prospect of nuclear war being brought home to British cities.[73]

When he returned to power in 1951, Churchill was intent on ending the Cold War stalemate. He got his first chance when he visited President Truman on an extended tour of the USA in 1952. The

mood in Washington was not favourable to proposals for a summit
and such was the level of skepticism that Truman delayed Churchill's
visit by two months. At the time, America was in the grip of
McCarthyism, while a war raged against communists on the Korean
peninsula. Dean Acheson in particular did not believe that any
solution to the Cold War was feasible in the foreseeable future.
Churchill was aware of the depths of American scepticism and for
this reason barely touched on the issue when he addressed Congress.
He did, however, hold out the hope of 'a new mood' behind the Iron
Curtain.[74]

The case for a summit conference was undermined by 'the battle
of the notes'. In 1952 Stalin proposed the creation of a united Germany, formed on condition that it remained neutral between East
and West and did not join any international organisation that would
compromise its neutrality. The Anglo-American response was to
insist on free and fair elections (something that Stalin would not do
until after reunification) under the supervision of the four powers
and to insist that the new united Germany should be able to join a
peaceful organisation recognised by the UN.

Stalin's rejection of these terms reinforced the perception, widely
held among Western policymakers, that the Soviet leader was trying
to drive a wedge between West Germany and its allies. Churchill did
little to influence the Battle of the Notes and seemed pessimistic
about the chances of a summit conference. By this stage he realised
that, with Stalin in the Kremlin, there was little chance of making
significant political progress. Neither did he hope for a breakthrough
with an American administration beset by McCarthyism.

When Truman was succeeded by Eisenhower, his old wartime
colleague, Churchill's hopes for a three-way high-level summit were
raised. They may have been bolstered by a speech the President
made in which he said that he would, in principle, 'meet anybody
anywhere' if 'there was the slightest chance of doing any good'.[75]
However, in private Eisenhower had little time for Churchill's
schemes, believing that the ageing Prime Minister, beyond his prime,
was trying to re-create his glorious leadership of the war years.

What appeared to transform the situation was the death of Stalin
in March 1953. Replacing the paranoid dictator was a Kremlin
triumvirate of Molotov, Beria and Malenkov, headed by Malenkov,
who talked of 'prolonged co-existence' between the two systems of
capitalism and socialism. There were rumours that traffic restrictions

between East Berlin and the West could be eased, that the Soviet Union could obtain a truce in the Korean War and that long-standing Russian demands in Turkey could be waived. Churchill seized on these rumours as evidence of a new mood in the Kremlin but his optimism was shared in neither London nor Washington.[76] The Foreign Office and State Department believed (rightly) that there was a power struggle going on in Moscow and that this apparent liberalism was no more than an elaborate smokescreen.

That Eisenhower was not serious about peace overtures to the Soviet Union was confirmed in a famous speech he delivered in 1953. In the speech, broadcast across the world, Eisenhower called on the Russians to 'turn the tide of history'. He demanded the end of the Korean War, a solution to the German and Austrian questions, a general disarmament treaty overseen by the UN and a move towards democratic governance across Eastern Europe. Some commentators have called this speech the most effective of Eisenhower's presidency, even of his entire career. But Eisenhower was speaking in hope, not expectation. Even in his wildest dreams, he could not have expected such profound largesse from the new rulers of the Soviet Union.

Nonetheless, Churchill was not deterred. On April 20th 1953 he told the Commons of his hope that there would soon be 'conversations, on the highest level, even if informal and private, between some of the principal powers concerned'. Writing to Eisenhower, he suggested that the Big Three meet in neutral Stockholm to reconvene the Potsdam Conference, but he now added an ominous caveat: 'If nothing can be arranged I shall have to consider seriously a personal contact'.[77] He went further and sent Eisenhower the draft of a telegram that he proposed to send to Malenkov, with the suggestion that he travel to Moscow at Malenkov's express invitation. As he wrote, Churchill had the advantage of being acting Foreign Secretary while Anthony Eden was convalescing from a serious illness.

Eisenhower was not convinced but, while trying to dissuade Churchill from meeting the Soviets personally, he realised he could hardly stop him. He suggested that a unilateral diplomatic mission to Moscow could have adverse consequences for the Western powers, though he stopped short of a veto. While outwardly sympathetic, Eisenhower remained as implacably anti-Russian as his hard-line Secretary of State, John Foster Dulles.

In a ground-breaking speech of May 11th 1953, Churchill made a number of points of far-reaching significance. The Soviet Union, he declared, was justifiably concerned at renewed aggression from Western Europe; she needed a long-term guarantee of security. 'I do not believe that the immense problem of reconciling the security of Russia with the freedom and safety of Western Europe is insoluble ... Russia has a right to feel assured that, as far as human arrangements can run, the terrible events of the Hitler invasion will never be repeated'.[78] He also called for a Locarno-style agreement[79] to ensure the balance of power in Europe, extending the 1925 system of security to Central and Eastern Europe.

He finally made a link between German reunification and European security by saying that Germany ought to be neutral in the Cold War. But he insisted that the West continue its rearmament programme so as to negotiate from a position of strength. However, Churchill's concept of negotiation through strength was greeted badly in the United States. For Senator Knowland, the Republican majority leader, Churchill was pursuing a policy of appeasement and he compared this speech to Neville Chamberlain's visit to Hitler at Munich.

The remainder of the year went badly for Churchill, on a personal as well as a political level. Firstly, the crushing of the East German uprising by Soviet armed forces in June 1953 turned the Russians decisively away from a Big Three summit. Secondly, Churchill was incapacitated for over two months by a stroke that might have finished his prime ministership. By the time he had recovered, he was repeating his support for a summit conference at the 1953 October Conservative Party conference. He continued to press on Washington that, if it did not agree with his plans, he might make a solitary visit to see Malenkov in Moscow. Finally, in December 1953 came the unsuccessful Bermuda Conference, where the heads of government and foreign ministers of Britain, France and the USA met. Churchill tried to revive interest in a summit conference but found Eisenhower hostile.

Churchill came to believe that a summit conference could be successful even if it did not produce consensus among its participants. It was the mere presence of the Big Three at a summit that would be of paramount significance. What was required first was the building of confidence between the parties, prior to agreements being forged for, as he put it, 'Even if we had to go through a decade of cold war bickerings punctuated by vain parleys, that would be preferable to the catalogue of unspeakable and also unimaginable horrors which is the alternative.'[80]

His perception of 'unimaginable horrors' grew intensely in March 1954 with the American announcement of the hydrogen bomb test at Bikini Atoll in the South Pacific. The explosion was over one thousand times more powerful than the atomic blast at Hiroshima and caused widespread radioactive fallout. Churchill would come to talk of the hydrogen bomb as a 'ghastly invention' that would bring an 'equality of ruin to east and west'.[81] He also knew that, in any atomic showdown between the United States and the Soviet Union, Britain could be attacked, given the presence of American air bases in East Anglia.

For a decade Churchill had been pursuing the notion of 'peace through strength'. In 1954 he continued to talk on this theme, arguing that détente could be achieved by 'building up the defensive strength of the free world against Communist pressure'.[82] It was for this reason that in 1954 he authorised the production of Britain's own hydrogen bombs. This followed a claim by the Chiefs of Staff that Britain needed such a weapon 'in order to wield enough influence in the world to prevent a nuclear war happening'.[83] It would be a full year before this programme was revealed to the public and Churchill successfully pressured the BBC into not showing documentaries on the effects of a nuclear attack.

It may seem paradoxical that Churchill was simultaneously calling the hydrogen bomb a 'ghastly' weapon and pursuing talks that could lead to nuclear disarmament, while at the same time authorising the creation of a British nuclear arsenal. Surely it was better to follow the lead of the unilateral disarmers and ensure that there were less of the weapons in existence? Was not the very notion of rearmament itself a barrier to mutual understanding, given that countries on friendly terms did not generally arm 'against' each other? Geoffrey Best has summarised how Churchill's dual-track approach, rearming while pursuing a high level conference, reflected a consistent political philosophy:

> ...the advent of atomic weaponry had introduced an unfamiliar factor into the military equation. Here were weapons which, he was coming to think, were better not used at all. But, paradoxically, they could not be dispensed with, as the early nuclear disarmers were beginning to assert, because of the very nature of international relations. Power, of whatever sort, would assert itself as surely as water finds its own level ... A great preponderance of power in any one state, unless it was to impose itself on all other states, had to be met

by an equivalent presence of power among those others. Churchill still held the time honoured doctrine of the balance of power...

Best goes on to answer the second conundrum:

Co-existence suggested amity; deterrence implied menace. How could a statesman speak of his desire for improved relations with a foreign country at the same time as he was improving his own country's means of doing damage to that country? For Churchill the matter was simple. His policy was analogous to that of the homely maxim, 'Strong fences make good neighbours.' It was in the nature of international relations that a powerful state won more respect than an impotent one. It was in the nature of a Communist great power to take advantage of its neighbours' weaknesses, but it would be natural for any realistic Great Power to respect its neighbours' strengths. The Soviet Union was a Great Power as well as a Communist one.[84]

Churchill wanted to appease the Russians from a position of military strength, which was the only sure way of guaranteeing their respect. To do this he needed a nuclear capability with deterrent power.

Churchill's fear of mutual nuclear annihilation galvanised him into trying one last time to win over Eisenhower. In his final Washington visit, in June 1954, he again tried to persuade the President to agree to a summit with the Russians. It was here that he is believed to have said over dinner that 'to jaw-jaw is always better than to war-war', but the words were in fact those of Harold Macmillan. Despite hesitation and scepticism from Eisenhower and Dulles, expressed ambiguously in Eisenhower's case, Churchill was buoyed up by what he interpreted (falsely) as tacit approval for a Moscow visit.

Now came the last initiative in Churchill's final political battle. He composed a telegram which he was to send to Molotov, the Soviet foreign secretary, rather than Malenkov. The telegram proposed that Churchill should visit Moscow for initial bilateral talks. Instead of sending this to the Russians, he submitted it first (with Eden's prior approval) to his Chancellor, Rab Butler, as a 'private and personal' communication. The message duly went out on July 4th 1954 and the reply from Molotov was favourable.

Churchill now faced a triumvirate of righteous objectors. Firstly, foreign office officials believed that even sending the telegram initially would impact negatively on Britain's international standing, and Eden was condemned for allowing it to be sent. Secondly, when

Eisenhower was asked for his approval, he replied somewhat indignantly. 'When you left here,' he told Churchill, 'I had thought, obviously erroneously, that you were in an undecided mood about this matter, and that when you had cleared your own mind I would receive some notice if you were to put your program into action.' He added that he could not see how a Big Three meeting 'could serve a useful purpose at this time'.[85]

Throughout July, Churchill faced even worse problems in his Cabinet. Some ministers, notably Lord Salisbury, were threatening to resign if a summit went ahead without American approval. In the end the Russians scuppered any hope of talks when they suggested that multilateral discussions on European security would have to include Communist China. A final opportunity for high-level talks in March 1955 also foundered, this time on Eisenhower's unwillingness to meet the Russians, and the fall of Malenkov in the Soviet Union.

In his farewell speech to the Commons, and to the nation, Churchill reflected on the implications of nuclear war. In an ideal world there would be a 'trustworthy and universal agreement upon disarmament' overseen by 'an effective system of inspection', but in the real world an alternative policy, that he termed 'defence through deterrence', was necessary. Far from making the world more dangerous or war more likely, he believed that nuclear deterrents could become 'the parents of disarmament'. This was because, in any nuclear war, both sides at the outset would suffer what they most dreaded, namely 'the loss of everything that it has ever known of', while an aggressor, tempted to launch a first strike against another nuclear power, would know that the other side possessed 'the certain power to inflict swift, inescapable and crushing retaliation'. He concluded from this: 'Then it may well be that we shall by a process of sublime irony have reached a stage in this story where safety will be the sturdy child of terror, and survival the twin brother of annihilation.'[86]

In one resonant sentence, he had perfectly grasped the logic of mutually assured destruction. Following Churchill's retirement in June 1955, a summit conference between the major powers did indeed take place at Geneva. This time the Americans agreed to attend, encouraged by the Soviet withdrawal from Austria as part of the Austria state treaty and their proposals for arms reduction in Europe.[87] Churchill was understandably disappointed that the event which had eluded his grasp for so long had now taken place in his absence.

Remembering the strength of Eden's opposition to such summitry, he quipped rather cynically, 'how much more attractive a top level summit seems when one has reached the top'.[88]

For half a decade Churchill had sought to end a state of hostility between East and West that threatened the most devastating consequences. He was haunted by the prospect of nuclear war, in particular how it would lead to an irreversible loss of British power. From 1951 to 1955 he 'wished to go down in history as the politician who had enabled his nation to survive during the Second World War and had then managed to preserve Britain as a great power by creating a less a dangerous world.'[89]

David Carlton is wrong to dismiss suggestions that Churchill was serious about a high-level summit. According to Carlton's analysis, Churchill was simply a feeble and idealistic old man, intoxicated by power, who used endless excuses to remain in office.[90] He interprets Churchill's obsession with high-level summitry as a classic British case of *innenpolitik*, the primacy of domestic over foreign policy.

This is to misread the situation. Churchill *did* want to cling on to power but only because he had deep and genuine anxieties about Britain's future in the nuclear age. He also deeply wished to be remembered as a peacemaker, and not just as a war leader.[91] That Churchill was unsuccessful was due to the uncompromising stance of both superpowers, as well as an exaggerated belief in his own powers of persuasion. He entirely failed to appreciate that the Soviets viewed him with deep misgivings. He had, after all, a long record of anti-Bolshevism, while his 'iron curtain' speech of 1946 was widely blamed for aggravating East-West tensions.

Churchill put too positive a gloss on his communications with the White House, and failed to appreciate the depth and potency of Eisenhower's anti-communism. At the 1953 Bermuda Conference, according to Colville, Eisenhower's view of the Soviets was uncompromising: 'Russia was a woman of the streets and whether her dress was new, or just the old one patched, it was certainly the same whore underneath. America intended to drive her off the present beat into the back streets.'[92]

Nonetheless, Churchill pioneered the notions of *détente* and summit diplomacy which characterised relations between East and West in the 1970s. Even if his efforts were doomed to failure, his concept of nuclear diplomacy offered a respectable alternative to the martial rhetoric of the Cold War.

NOTES

1 Speeches VII, p.7131.
2 *Ibid.*, p.7172.
3 P. Addison, *Churchill*, p.215. Note: Lascelles commented on the speech that it sounded like 'a tired man unwillingly reading something that had been written for him and that he didn't much like' (Lascelles, p.331).
4 P. Addison, *Churchill on the Home Front*, p.357.
5 S. Hylton, *Finest and Darkest Hours*, p.51.
6 *Ibid.*, p.55.
7 Speeches VII, p.6761.
8 P. Addison, *Churchill on the Home Front*, p.360.
9 D. Hart-Davis (ed), *King's Counsellor*, p.65.
10 J. Colville, *The Fringes of Power*, p.127.
11 P. Addison, *Churchill on the Home Front*, p.364.
12 Nicolson II, p.348.
13 V. Bonham-Carter, *Champion Redoubtable*, p.313.
14 D. Hart-Davis (ed), *King's Counsellor*, pp.335-6.
15 P. Addison, *Churchill on the Home Front*, p.383.
16 M. Soames (ed), *Speaking for Themselves*, p.536, note 3.
17 P. Harriman, 'The True Meaning of the Iron Curtain Speech', *Finest Hour* 58, Winter 1987-8.
18 *Chicago Sun*, March 6th 1946.
19 Moran, *Diaries*, p.185.
20 WSC Bio 8, p.8.
21 *Ibid.*, p.27-8.
22 This rather blunts the force of Carlton's criticism that Churchill could be little surprised at the emergence of the Iron Curtain following the percentages agreement.
23 Speeches VII, p.7286.
24 *Ibid.*, p.7289.
25 *Ibid.*, pp.7290-1.
26 *Ibid.*, p.7292.
27 *Ibid.*, p.7293.
28 *Ibid.*, p.7290.
29 *Ibid.*, p.7293.
30 C. Ponting, *Churchill*, pp.732-3.
31 Speeches VII, p.7287.
32 In the 1930s the reputation of the League of Nations was stained by its failure to deal with Japan's invasion of Manchuria (in China) and Italy's invasion of Abyssinia.
33 Speeches VII, p.7292.
34 *Ibid.*, p.7286.
35 *Ibid.*, p.7287.
36 *Ibid.*, p.7288.
37 J. Ramsden, *Man of the Century*, p.178.
38 *Ibid.*, p.182.
39 C. Ponting, *Churchill*, p.735.

40 Speeches VII, p.7292.
41 An American diplomat, historian and strategist who served as deputy head of the US mission in Moscow from 1944 to 1946. For many he was the most influential voice in American strategy in the Cold War.
42 'The United States of Europe', *The Collected Essays of Sir Winston Churchill II*.
43 Blake/Louis, *Churchill*, p.446.
44 WSC Bio 7, p.239.
45 *Ibid.*, p.373.
46 Speeches VII, pp.7380-1.
47 K. Larres, *Churchill's Cold War*, p.143.
48 WSC Bio 8, p.278.
49 V. Bonham-Carter, *Daring to Hope*, p.36.
50 *Ibid.*, p.50.
51 Speeches VII, p.7636.
52 WSC Bio 8, p.279.
53 Speeches VIII, p.7981.
54 *Ibid.*, p.8082.
55 WSC Bio 8, p.926.
56 Speeches VIII, p.8532.
57 *Ibid.*, p.8638.
58 Moran, *Diaries*, p.459.
59 WSC Bio 8, p.927.
60 K. Larres, *Churchill's Cold War*, p.147.
61 *Ibid.*, p.153.
62 J. Ramsden, *Man of the Century*, p.321.
63 Blake/Louis, *Churchill*, p.454.
64 Speeches VII, p.7900.
65 J. Wheeler-Bennett, *Action This Day*, p.97.
66 K. Larres, *Churchill's Cold War*, pp.xii, xvi.
67 Speeches V, p.5129.
68 The 1945 Parliament that was dominated by Labour.
69 Speeches VII, p.7589.
70 *Ibid.*, p.7809.
71 Speeches VIII, p.7983.
72 *Ibid.*, p.7944.
73 Before the advent of inter-continental ballistic missiles this was not a threat that the United States had any cause to fear.
74 K. Larres, *Churchill's Cold War*, p.161. But Washington could not afford to ignore Churchill either. They needed continuing British support in Korea while they were also aware that their important strategic bases in East Anglia were a launching pad for an attack on the Soviet Union.
75 K. Larres, *Churchill's Cold War*, p.186.
76 Moran, *Diaries*, p.429.
77 K. Larres, *Churchill's Cold War*, pp.215-16.
78 Speeches VIII, pp.8483-4.
79 Under the Locarno agreement of 1925, Germany, France and Belgium undertook not to invade each other's territory except in self-defence, and to guarantee each other's borders.

80 K. Larres, *Churchill's Cold War*, p.322.
81 D. Cannadine and R. Quinault, *Winston Churchill in the Twenty First Century*, p.209.
82 Speeches VIII, p.8538.
83 *History Today*, October 2005, p.41.
84 G. Best, *Churchill and War*, p.227.
85 K. Larres, *Churchill's Cold War*, p.346-7.
86 Speeches VIII, p.8625-9.
87 The Austria treaty gave Austria sovereignty but required the country to be neutral in the Cold War. In practice, Austria's political allegiances were with the West.
88 K. Larres, *Churchill's Cold War*, p.373.
89 *Ibid.*, p.156.
90 D. Carlton, *Churchill and the Soviet Union*, p.187.
91 A. Montague-Brown, *Long Sunset*, p.133.
92 D. Carlton, *Churchill and the Soviet Union*, p.184. Churchill came to realise this. According to Lady Violet Bonham-Carter's diary, he told her after his resignation that he 'would have stayed on if there had been any chance of four power meetings – but Ike won't have it' (*Daring to Hope*, p.147).

CHAPTER TEN

Churchill's Political Philosophy

Was Churchill a Liberal or a Conservative?

MOST POLITICIANS are, first and foremost, *party* politicians. They look to their party for political bearings and a sense of tribal allegiance while in return they are expected to provide loyal support on key issues. It is usually possible to categorise politicians according to their party loyalties or the philosophical outlook they articulate.

As a politician, Winston Churchill defies simplistic categorisation, which is owed in part to his shifting party allegiances. He entered the House of Commons as a Conservative in 1900, then switched to the Liberals in 1904, and finally returned to the Conservative fold as a 'Constitutionalist' in 1924. 'Any one can rat,' he once famously declared, but 'it takes a lot of ingenuity to re-rat'. Churchill was certainly not captive to any political party and, early in his career, he advocated the creation of a 'Government of the Middle'. As he explained to the Liberal Prime Minister, Lord Rosebery, this party would be 'free at once from the sordid selfishness and callousness of Toryism ... and the blind appetites of the Radical masses.'[1]

During the 1930s he was regularly at odds with the Conservative government on issues as diverse as Indian independence, the Abdication and the pace of rearmament; and in his Finest Hour he was the leader of a coalition government and the 'leader of the nation' rather than the Tory leader. When one takes into account Churchill's monumental egotism and his unashamed pursuit of power, it is easy to accuse him, as his sternest critics do, of blatant political opportunism. Indeed it has become increasingly fashionable to deny that he had any political philosophy at all.

Yet, despite these apparent contradictions, Churchill was a highly capable party politician who possessed a fairly consistent political viewpoint. Throughout his life he espoused, if not the orthodox

conservatism of his forbears, a kind of hybrid liberal-conservatism –
Burkean social conservatism and the emerging 'new liberalism' which
sought to raise the working man.

At the turn of the twentieth century, as today, Conservatives
believed that their nation had a set of customs, values and institutions which formed the bedrock of its identity and which needed to
be preserved for the future. These factors were seen as a solemn
inheritance that required vigorous defence and constant vigilance
from the forces of radicalism. Conservatives felt a profound attachment to monarchy, the enduring symbol of national continuity, and
to Parliament as the sovereign political force in the land. They
shared an abiding attachment to the nation's land and its deeply
rooted heritage and traditions. Conservatism was thus patriotic to
the core and saw love of nation as a unifying social force.

That did not make the Conservatives averse to political change,
but they believed that change, when it came, had to be managed
through the existing institutions of society rather than through a
process of revolutionary change.[2] In part, this was because they were
deeply suspicious of utopian fantasists promising to remake the
world. For centuries they had seen dictators and tyrants lay waste to
entire nations on the basis of grand ideas and first principles. Burke's
reflections on Revolutionary France offered a salutary reminder of
how the most idealistic revolutions could end in terror and bloodshed. Conservatives therefore tended to prefer earthy, pragmatic
thinking to the abstract calculations of idealists.

Liberals, like Conservatives, believed profoundly in the freedom
and dignity of the individual. They sought to limit the remit of
government wherever possible and to safeguard individual liberty.
For this reason, both were traditionally ardent champions of free
trade, low taxation and private property; yet they also recognised
that, unless the community as a whole prospered, there could never
be the communal harmony that was requisite for a stable society.
As a result, both Liberals and Conservatives argued that the plight
of the poor had to be ameliorated through progressive measures of
social reform. But for Conservatives, far more than liberals, legitimate authority was a necessary check on individual behaviour. At the
level of the state, this required the maintenance of law and order and
a robust stand on defence and security issues.

Churchill was to imbibe this liberal conservatism from an early
age. He wrote in 1899 that the coming twentieth century would

witness 'the great war for the existence of the Individual'.3 Quite what was meant by freedom soon became clear in the first decade of the twentieth century. In response to Joseph Chamberlain's call for a scheme of imperial tariffs, Churchill eagerly embraced the principle of free trade, becoming a staunch advocate of what he called 'cheap food'. The population, he argued, had to be 'free to purchase its supplies of food ... in the open markets of the world' rather than being restricted in their choice through protected markets.4

In economics, he was a believer in low taxes and sound enterprise – the fiscal prudence championed by both Liberals and Conservatives. 'Taxes', he declared early in his career, 'are an evil, a necessary evil but still an evil, and the fewer we have of them the better.'5 He never hesitated to defend the capitalist system, which he described as 'the only system that has ever been devised for regulating the economic relations between man and man and for appraising the value of services which men render to each other'.6 As Chancellor he championed capitalism as 'the only system that had been invented as a substitute for slavery'.7 When, in the aftermath of the 1929 Crash, he was told that capitalism was finished, he responded: 'More mush! Capitalism will right itself.'8

But in the first decade of the twentieth century Churchill defined himself as a classic liberal. 'Free trade', he told a friend, 'is so essentially Liberal in its sympathies and its tendencies that those who fight for it must become Liberals.' At the same time he felt able to say: 'I am an English liberal. I hate the Tory party, their men, their words and their methods.'9 His friend Violent Bonham-Carter recalled that Churchill, 'though born and cradled in the purple of the Tory fold was not of it.'10 Indeed free trade would cause Churchill's departure from the Conservatives and switch to the Liberal Party.

As a result of these leanings, Churchill also staunchly supported freedom of speech. When Lloyd George, a notable opponent of the Boer War, had been prevented from speaking at Birmingham Town Hall in 1901, Churchill leapt to his defence. Writing to the President of the Birmingham Conservative Association, Churchill observed: 'If people say things which are treasonable ... they should be prosecuted and dealt with accordingly, but within the law every man has a perfect right to express his own opinions, and that they should be shouted down because they are odious to the majority in the district is a very dangerous, fatal doctrine for the Conservative Party.'11

But from the outset, Churchill believed that a liberal economy required a minimum standard of life. As he put it, 'political freedom, however precious, is utterly incomplete without a measure at least of social and economic independence.'[12] Freedom and grinding poverty simply could not co-exist. Indeed, he saw social deprivation as a threat to the community, as when he told an audience in 1909: 'The greatest danger to the British Empire and to the British people is not to be found among the enormous fleets and armies of the European Continent ... it is here in our midst ... in the dwindling and cramped villages of our denuded countryside.'[13] From early on, therefore, he sought to make the improvement of the British breed a key goal of his political life.

When the Liberals swept to power in 1906, he talked of 'the universal establishment of minimum standards of life and labour...' and of helping 'the left-out millions'. In a speech in 1906 he talked of how the state could embark on 'various novel and adventurous experiments' without impairing 'the vigour of competition'. The idea was not to dampen the competitive spirit of capitalism but to protect the most unfortunate in society: 'We want to draw a line below which we will not allow persons to live and labour, yet above which they may compete with all the strength of their manhood.'[14] Thus freedom in liberal terms necessitated a route out of extreme poverty that the state could help to provide. Among his 'novel and adventurous experiments' were labour exchanges, designed to alleviate unemployment, and a generous scheme of social insurance. He was a driving force behind the old-age pension system and introduced legislation restricting coal miners' working days to eight hours. His Trade Boards Act established a minimum wage in a small number of the 'sweated trades'.

His liberal belief in alleviating poverty continued into the 1920s. As Chancellor of the Exchequer in that decade he saw an opportunity to continue the social legislation of the pre-war Liberal era. He introduced an old-age and widows' pension scheme in his first budget of 1925. Every male worker and his employer would contribute fourpence a week, and female employees tuppence. This would provide ten shillings a week for widows, various payments for their children under the age of 14, and ten shillings a week for pensioners between the ages of 65 and 70 from January 1st 1926.[15] He also extended health insurance to cover millions of wage-earners and their dependents.

Churchill's belief in lowering taxes also came to the fore: he reduced income tax in his first budget, in particular for lower income groups. He wanted to 'stimulate enterprise and accelerate industrial revival' by 'liberating the production of new wealth from some of the shackles of taxation'.[16] Here he carefully distinguished between earned and unearned wealth, arguing that it was essential to encourage the energetic creation of new wealth at the cost of a 'penalty on inertia'. This echoes his earlier belief that the tax burden had to be shifted from income to (unearned) land value, in order to create a fairer society.

His liberal credentials were also on impeccable display during the strikes of 1909-11. As President of the Board of Trade, Churchill was asked to intervene in the shipbuilding and engineering strikes of 1908 and, in each case, a settlement was reached between employers and unions. Despite his willingness to send troops to the port strikes of 1911, Churchill first allowed negotiations to proceed. Accordingly, G.R. Askwith, the chief Industrial Conciliator at the Board of Trade, was given time for mediation and a settlement was reached on August 18th. The trade unionist Ben Tillett paid tribute to Churchill's refusal to bow to pressure: 'He refused to listen to the clamour of class hatred, he saved the country from a national transport stoppage becoming a riot and incipient revolution.'[17] Churchill consistently defended the right of men to join trade unions and to suspend their labour by non-violent means.

But he was willing to defend individual rights, including the right to strike, only if, in the exercise of those rights, citizens were not threatening the social order. When an exercise of individual freedom threatened anarchy and social breakdown Churchill had few qualms about a resort to force.

During the dockers' strikes of 1911, he sent troops to Hull at the request of the local authorities. During the 1911 railway strike he adopted an even more belligerent posture: in preparation for the strike he 'employed the army in a display of force calculated to make the strikers back down'.[18] This insistence on asserting authority through the use of force, even if it overrode the right to strike, shocked many of Churchill's liberal contemporaries and reflected his strong Conservative instincts.

The rest of his career witnessed a playing out of this hybrid philosophy. He took a much criticised belligerent stand during the General Strike, believing that it reflected Bolshevik ideas and that the unions had effectively declared war within Britain. He also supported actions that were likely to inflame the situation. On May 7th he called for the Territorial Army to combat the strike but was overruled by colleagues. When the government organised a food convoy from the London docks to bring supplies into the country, Churchill suggested that it should be accompanied by an escort of tanks and armoured cars to deter the strikers. He also favoured outright control of the nominally independent BBC in order to demonstrate the government's authority, but he was overruled in Cabinet. However, once the strikers had stood down, Churchill worked in earnest to reach a negotiated settlement of the coal dispute.

Churchill's belligerence during the strike made many people doubt his liberal leanings. His close friend Violet Bonham-Carter believed he was 'by temperament an intellectual autocrat' who 'never shared the reluctance which inhibits Liberals from invoking force to solve a problem'.[19] But there was little contradiction between his positions. So long as the social order was not threatened, Churchill sought to placate the forces of labour through progressive, reformist legislation; when he detected the whiff of revolution, he was prepared to use force to *conserve* the existing order.

Translated into foreign affairs, Churchill's Conservative leanings implied a robust defence of national and imperial interests. Though hardly a warmonger, he was quite prepared to use force to settle international disputes. He oversaw a period of naval expansion prior to the First World War and urged a speedy increase in aerial power before the Second World War. He poured scorn on those who advocated pacifism and utopian internationalism, believing instead in the tried and tested principle of the 'balance of power'. This was in keeping with orthodox Conservatism – the rejection of policy built around rational first principles.

During the two major global conflicts of his era, Churchill believed in the vigorous prosecution of the war, ruling out premature compromises with the enemy. Thus he rejected the arguments of Lord Halifax in May 1940, arguing that they would fatally undermine the war effort and Britain's resolve to defeat Germany. He was also an ardent champion of the British Empire throughout his life, which he defended in typically Victorian paternalistic terms. While prepared to criticise abuses of power, such as the massacre at Amritsar in 1921, he remained committed to the imperial project as a means of projecting British power across the world.

His conservatism shone through in other respects. His romantic sense of the past and his belief in the 'great man theory of history' combined to produce a genuine reverence for the monarchy. He saw the British constitutional monarchy as the embodiment of centuries of history and tradition and as a unifying force for the nation. While he questioned the qualities of individual sovereigns, especially Edward VII and George V, he never doubted that the institution they served was a cherished part of Britain's national life. In the words of Isaiah Berlin, Churchill possessed a belief in a 'natural, social, almost a metaphysical order, a sacred hierarchy which it was neither possible nor desirable to upset'.[20] This explains, in part, his misplaced support for Edward VIII during the Abdication Crisis. He felt that the abdication of the King could cause irreparable harm to the institution of monarchy and that, in any case, the British people had 'sworn allegiance to him'.[21]

Hand in hand with support for the monarchy came a profound attachment to the British constitutional tradition. He celebrated the organic character and 'venerable structure' of the Constitution which had grown from 'the wisdom of our ancestors' and 'the practice of former times'.[22] 'No one generation', he wrote, 'has the right to overturn the whole constitution and traditions of our island.' In Burkean language, he referred to the current generation as only the 'trustees and life tenants' of Britain; we have 'to do our duty by the future'.[23] Amery put it succinctly: 'The key to Winston is to realise that he is mid-Victorian, steeped in the politics of his father's period.'[24] Nonetheless, his attachment to the Constitution never blinded him to the need for change, particularly during the crisis of 1909, when he challenged the Tory peers over the budget.

Churchill's profound belief in ceremony, custom and tradition imbued his historical writings with a strong conservative and aristocratic outlook. His histories show little interest in the life of the common man and little regard for what might be termed 'social history'. He did not speculate on the causes of events using abstract philosophical theories or metapsychological concepts. He was fascinated by the machinations of 'the great men' of the past, the kings and politicians whose daring exploits were alone deemed to be responsible for historical progress. These individuals were the colourful motor of events, their deeds shaping the societies around them.

Like all Conservatives, Churchill believed that Britain's past held vital lessons for its future. He would cite historical episodes as guidance for contemporary struggles. He rejected Lord Rothemere's proposal of an Anglo-German pact by arguing that this contravened centuries of successful British foreign policy. He told Rothemere: 'We have on all occasions been the friend of the second strongest power in Europe and have never yielded ourselves to the strongest power.'[25]

In 1940 he viewed the battle with Nazi Germany as just another example of rousing British defiance of Continental despotism. He declared that the Battle of Britain ranked 'with the days when the Spanish Armada was approaching the Channel, and Drake was finishing his game of bowls, or when Nelson stood between us and Napoleon's Grand Army at Boulogne.'[26] Only a man who believed in preserving the lessons of history would eulogise the past in this way.

In many ways, then, Churchill retained the stamp of his mid-Victorian origins. He believed in conserving the institutions and values which the past had bequeathed and in learning the vital lessons of history. But he was not averse to innovation and social change, so long as progressive legislation did not threaten the social order.

Was Churchill a reactionary imperialist?

> I have always served two great public causes which I think stand supreme – the maintenance of the enduring greatness of Britain and her Empire and the historical continuity of our Island life.[27]

PERHAPS NO OTHER twentieth-century British statesman, except Joseph Chamberlain, has shown as much zeal for the Empire as Winston Churchill. At the outset of his public career, Churchill saw active service in India and South Africa, revelling in the chance to defend Britain's imperial status. He fought in a number of conflicts and wrote celebrated accounts that were well received at home. As Colonial Under-Secretary, he was largely responsible for the political settlement in the Transvaal, while as Colonial Secretary in the 1920s he played a prominent role in peacemaking, both in Ireland and in the Middle East. He is often remembered as a thundering and implacable opponent of Indian independence during the 1930s, while inevitably, as war leader, he maintained a watchful eye on imperial matters. At the end of his career, the Empire he had lauded for so long progressively crumbled in the era of decolonisation. During these times, he never resiled from the view that the Empire was an 'indispensable prop of British power and greatness'.[28]

For many this implies he had a dogmatic, wholly unquestioning belief in British imperial power. Ponting writes that Churchill believed 'in the supremacy of white nations' and that 'he accepted without question the greatness of the British Empire'.[29] Andrew Roberts in *Eminent Churchillians* argues that Churchill was a 'zealous child' and 'true believer' in the imperial mission, and also an 'Anglo-Saxon supremacist'.[30] For these and other authors, Winston Churchill was simply a British embodiment of unrepentant imperialism. Certainly, Churchill's occasional intransigent outbursts, such as his contemptuous dismissal of Gandhi as a 'seditious Middle Temple lawyer'[31] did not help his cause, but his views were actually more enlightened than many imagine, making him more a liberal progressive than a diehard reactionary.

As early as 1898, when he saw action in the River War in the Sudan, he eschewed the unbridled imperialism and jingoistic sentiments of more conventional reporters. He paid tribute to the courage and fighting spirit of the 'valiant' Dervishes, who were 'as brave men as ever walked the earth'.[32] He also criticised the decision not to spare the lives of wounded Dervish soldiers and condemned 'atrocious' acts of cruelty by British soldiers, telling his mother that the victory was tainted by 'inhuman slaughter'.[33] The worst of these acts was the desecration of the Mahdi's tomb and the disinterring of his corpse, a 'wicked act, of which the true Christian ... must express his abhorrence'.[34] In condemning these outrages, Churchill suggested that there was a code of honour to which any imperial nation had to aspire if it was to rule successfully.

This code applied to any imperial power, not just the British. In 1895 he had visited Cuba to observe at first hand the native rebellion against Spanish rule. In one of his dispatches, he described some of the natives' economic grievances, particularly over-taxation and corrupt administration, before he concluded: 'A national and justifiable revolt is the only possible result of such a system.'[35] Early in *The River War* he condemned the Egyptian rule of the Sudan as 'a hateful sham', perpetrated by a 'tyrannical government' whose 'aim was to exploit, not to improve the local population'. There was, he said, 'no better case for rebellion than presented itself to the Soudanese', adding: 'Their country was being ruined; their property was plundered; their women were ravished; their liberties were curtailed.'[36]

Churchill believed that imperial rule was indefensible if it was exploitative; it had to be based on nobler principles of governance. If the only basis for controlling a territory and population was the controlling nation's power to expand, it was tantamount to tyranny. Furthermore, as in the examples above, tyrannical rule would only encourage native rebellions which would have to be ruthlessly suppressed at considerable moral and economic cost. Empire building required enlightened rule, with duties to those who were governed, rather than the imposition of arbitrary force.

This benevolent paternalism expressed a thoroughly Victorian view of the colonial mission. True to his nineteenth-century origins, Churchill championed the notion of an imperial 'civilising mission' that could improve the lives of native populations while fulfilling the nobler aspirations of imperial overlords.[37] Churchill was to take these twin themes – imperialism as a civilising mission, and the avoidance of tyranny – with him into the twentieth century. Indeed, in one of his first statements on Empire as a radical MP, he railed against the 'unbridled imperialists' who sought to 'pile up armaments, taxation and territory' while neglecting domestic issues.[38]

Examples of his opposition to cruelty are legion. In 1903 a British mission was sent by the Viceroy of India to the Tibetan border to negotiate outstanding boundary disputes. A misunderstanding developed when the mission reached the town of Guru and in the ensuing clash six hundred Tibetan soldiers were mown down. Churchill condemned this action in the strongest terms: 'Surely it is vy wicked to do such things. Absolute contempt for the rights of others must be wrong.'[39] The following year he was unsparing in his condemnation of British behaviour in Tibet following a local dispute:

> We were told that the Tibetans had sent an embassy to Russia, that they had pulled down some boundary posts, that they failed to answer the Viceroy's letters, and had wished to put a 10 per cent duty on imported manufacturers. What did we do? We broke into the country, we tore the veil from a mysterious shrine, we butchered more than 1,000 Tibetans who endeavoured, as they were bound by every human right to do, to defend their country against us. What parity is there between the delinquencies of Tibet and the revenge of Great Britain?[40]

The attack on Tibet he described as a 'criminal and unrighteous invasion'.[41]

During a conversation with the Kaiser in 1906, Churchill heard of the fighting qualities of the Herero tribe, then under ruthless attack by the Germans in South West Africa. Far from agreeing with German tactics, Churchill declared: 'Our chief difficulty had not been to kill the rebellious natives, but to prevent our Colonists (who so thoroughly understood native war) from killing too many of them.'[42] In general he sought to condemn all forms of cruelty to native populations, the most odious of which was 'the exploitation of natives for the purposes of gain'.[43]

While he was at the Colonial Office in 1906-8, Churchill sought to inject a liberal tone into the administration of Colonial justice. When he read that the Governor General of Nigeria proposed reprisals against northern Nigerian tribes following an act of arson, Churchill wrote: 'Of course if the peace and order of the Colony depend on a vigorous offensive we must support him with all our hearts. But the chronic bloodshed which stains the West African seasons is odious and disquieting.'[44]

In the same year there was a Zulu revolt in Natal in which some three thousand Zulus were killed and over four thousand taken prisoner. Churchill described this as 'the disgusting butchery of natives' which represented 'the kind of tyranny against which these unfortunate Zulus have been struggling'.[45] On a visit to Malta in 1907, Churchill took up the grievances of the local population and, in an echo of his dispatches from Cuba, wrote to Eddie Marsh: 'they were never conquered by England but ... now we spend their money without allowing the Maltese any sort of control'. The Maltese complaint was 'a vy real' and 'vy painful one'.[46]

From an early age Churchill had a strong aversion to slavery and recognised how it had been used to mistreat black Africans. In *The River War* he had called the slave trade 'the most odious traffic in the world'. When the trade was officially abolished in Zanzibar, a British protectorate, in 1907, Churchill welcomed the change. He believed that no empire could be sustained by an arbitrary use of force; it required 'the assent of free peoples, united with each other by noble and progressive principles'.[47]

Hand in hand with his rejection of cruelty came a Victorian belief in Britain's civilising mission towards the natives. In *The River War*, written towards the end of the nineteenth century, Churchill wrote that no enterprise of an enlightened community (such as Britain) was nobler than 'the reclamation from barbarism of fertile regions and large populations'. It was a great virtue to 'give peace to warring tribes, to administer justice where all was violence, to strike the chains off the slave ... to plant the earliest seeds of commerce and learning.'[48]

When, in 1907-8, Churchill toured East Africa, he pondered the role of imperial governors in dealing with the less 'advanced' indigenous population. His view of the 'East African negro' was certainly not favourable. He talked of a 'native race still plunged in its primary squalor, without religion, without clothes, without morals', a race separated by 'a veritable abyss of knowledge and science'. Under these circumstances, the ruling government could provide 'suitable robes for ceremonial occasions to the chiefs' and 'gradually encourage, and more gradually still enforce, their adoption throughout the population'.[49] Here were the elements of a more cautious approach to change than mere arbitrary compulsion. Later he described the Kikuyu tribes, whose children were 'tractable' yet 'brutish' and needed to be 'raised from their present degradation'. The British government had a 'grave' and 'inalienable' responsibility to care for the tribe and this required 'impartial and august administration'.[50]

Churchill was incredibly optimistic about improving the natives through Western enlightened rule. Take the following passage about the natives of Uganda: 'Just and honourable discipline, careful education, sympathetic comprehension, are all that is needed to bring a very large proportion of the native tribes of East Africa to a far higher social level than that at which they now stand.'[51] Baganda people in Uganda were said to be 'an amiable, clothed, polite and intelligent race' living in a society with 'discipline', 'industry', 'culture' and 'peace'.[52] They were fortunate to be subject to a trio of beneficial influences – a 'secular, scientific, disinterested' imperial administration, a native government and feudal aristocracy 'corrected of their abuses', and the missionary movement. Churchill's paternalism was summed up when he called for Uganda to be a 'planter's land' rather than one exploited by a 'petty white community' with 'harsh and selfish ideas'.[53] The British administration in Uganda had no end, he said, other than 'the improvement of the country'; in no other way could they win 'approbation or fame'.[54]

Churchill's paternalistic concern for just colonial administration led to some interesting interventions when he served at the Colonial Office. Unlike some politicians, he did not assume that the officials on the spot were automatically right and he insisted on investigating apparent breaches of justice.[55]

Another notable feature of Churchill's time as Colonial Under-Secretary was his magnanimous settlement with the Boers in 1906. When the Boer War ended in victory for Britain in 1902, questions were raised as to what place, if any, the Boers should have within the Empire. Despite the jingoistic clamour in some quarters, Churchill argued that the Boers of the Transvaal and Orange Free State should be brought into the emerging Union of South Africa on equal terms with the British settler populations of the Cape and Natal. He also wanted a new constitution that would 'advance the principle of equal rights of civilised men irrespective of colour'. This was a little misleading for in his scheme there was discrimination between 'the different classes of coloured men' – immigrant Indians had privileges over native Africans. However, if Churchill had afforded more rights to native Africans he would have faced a revolt by the Boers as well as the British settlers, both of whom rejected equality for the Africans.

Nonetheless, as Colonial Under-Secretary he played an important role in drafting the new constitution that eventually gave self-government to the Boer republics in 1907. One reason for his magnanimity was his belief that reconciling the Boers would ensure South Africa's future loyalty to Britain. Just as he had hoped, South Africa rallied to the motherland when war was declared in 1914.

Churchill's magnanimity and his rejection of imperial abuses were never better on display than in the debate that followed the Amritsar massacre. In 1919 General Reginald Dyer, a senior British officer in India, ordered his troops to fire on an unarmed Indian mob at Amritsar. Three hundred Indians were killed and nearly two thousand injured. Dyer was later relieved of his military command at Churchill's insistence. A year later in the House of Commons, during a stormy debate, Churchill defended his decision. Describing what had happened as 'a monstrous event' which stood 'in singular and sinister isolation', he outlined a number of simple tests that any officer had to follow in deciding whether to open fire on a crowd: 'First of all, I think he may ask himself, is the crowd attacking anything or anybody? Surely that is the first question ... The second question is this: Is the crowd armed? ... By armed, I mean armed with lethal weapons.' At Amritsar, he continued, the crowd 'was neither armed nor attacking'. Thirdly, the officer had to follow the doctrine 'that no more force should be used than is necessary to ensure compliance with the law.'

Though he admitted that it was easy to debate such matters in 'safe and comfortable England', he believed these to be 'sound, simple tests' which could be used in a time of crisis. Dyer had claimed that it was necessary to 'teach the Punjab a moral lesson'. Churchill characterised this as 'frightfulness', the 'inflicting of great slaughter or massacre upon a particular crowd of people, with the intention of terrorising not merely the rest of the crowd, but the whole district or the whole country.' Such 'terrorism' was 'foreign to the British way of doing things'. He quoted Macaulay: 'And then was seen what we believe to be the most frightful of all spectacles, the strength of civilisation without its mercy.'[56]

In the 1920s, as Colonial Secretary, Churchill played a key role in securing the Irish Treaty of 1922, the cornerstone of modern Ireland. This brought into being the Irish Free State as a dominion within the British Empire. The British monarch remained head of state and one of the oaths taken by members of the Free State parliament was to 'be faithful to His Majesty King George V, his heirs and successors by law, in virtue of the common citizenship'. As with the Boers in South Africa, Churchill was prepared to make concessions as long as he secured the loyalty of the previous 'colony'. In this he was to be disappointed by events. When De Valera, the leader of the anti-treaty faction that was later defeated in Ireland's civil war, became Taoiseach, he gradually undid the treaty clause by clause. He helped to turn the Free State into a Catholic Republic and ensured that it remained neutral during the Second World War.

Churchill is most often remembered as a diehard opponent of Indian constitutional reform and it is certainly true that he fought a long battle against the India Bill in the 1930s. His opposition to granting democratic rights to African or Asian natives had a distinctly Victorian taint. As early as 1897 he had told his mother that 'East of Suez Democratic reins are impossible' and that India had to be governed 'on old principles'.[57] In 1922 he argued that it was wrong to grant 'democratic institutions to backward races which had no capacity for self-government'.[58]

He added in 1931 that only a 'fraction' of the Indians were 'interested in politics and Western ideas', and in typical Victorian fashion declared that Indians were 'dependent for their livelihood and for the happiness and peace of their humble homes upon the rule of a very small number of white officials' who had no personal interests of their own to serve. He added: 'I do not admit, for instance, that a great wrong has been done to the Red Indians of America, or the black people of Australia. I do not admit that a wrong has been done to these people by the fact that a stronger race, a higher grade race, or at any rate, a more worldly wise race ... has come in and taken their place.'[59]

Nonetheless, he showed an enlightened concern for India's untouchables and feared that they would be persecuted if they lived under direct Hindu rule. In 1935 Churchill told one of Gandhi's friends that the Indian leader had gone up in his estimation because he was championing the rights of the untouchables.

As a staunch believer in the British Empire, Churchill unsurprisingly took decolonisation hard. He had already declared in 1942: 'I have not become the King's First Minister in order to preside over the liquidation of the British Empire.'[60] He also took pains to exclude British colonies from the promises of the Atlantic Charter, leaving Roosevelt to describe Churchill as a 'great man for the status quo.'[61]

After 1945 he opposed what he called 'the handing over of India to caste rule' and berated the Attlee government for a policy of 'scuttle'. 'It is with deep grief', he said in 1947, 'I watch the clattering down of the British Empire with all its glories, and all the services it has rendered to mankind.'[62] But he could be magnanimous in defeat and, after partition in 1948, he welcomed India into the Commonwealth. When Churchill first met Nehru, he told him that he was 'like the prodigal who has returned to the fold of the family'.[63] Though Churchill could not reconcile his belief that the Indians were not ready for self-rule, his bitterness had started to recede.

During the 1950s he was often reluctant to grant self-government to former colonies. But at the same time he reluctantly accepted that Britain's imperial fortunes were on the wane and he did not stand in the way of making concessions when necessary. Both of his colonial ministers, Lyttelton and Lennox-Boyd, were 'given a wide degree of freedom in determining colonial policy' and it does not seem that Churchill impeded their work or 'actively discouraged the political advance towards independence in the colonies'.[64] During the Malayan insurrection, Churchill called for the restoration of law and order and even expressed the hope that the country would soon gain independence.[65] During the Mau Mau insurrection in Kenya, he questioned 'the wisdom of harsh measures' and believed 'that mass executions would be opposed by the British public'. Though he failed to prevent the internment of thousands of rebels in camps, he regarded the Kikuyu tribe as people of 'considerable fibre, ability and steel' and sympathised with their economic grievances.

Out of office he criticised Macmillan's 'wind of change' speech, believing that it had led to an irresponsible pace of decolonisation and the replacement of benign colonialism with tribal dictator-ships.[66] One of the dictators he condemned was Nkrumah, the leader of Ghana. He opposed the Queen's visit to Ghana in 1960 as he felt it was tantamount to endorsing a regime which had 'impris-oned hundreds of Opposition members without trial' and which was 'thoroughly authoritarian in tendency'.[67] Even at this late stage, he was concerned lest the Commonwealth be tainted by association with a corrupt regime.

Towards the end of his life, Churchill reflected on the decline of the Empire. He told his private secretary, Anthony Montague-Brown: 'I have worked very hard all my life, and I have achieved a great deal – in the end to achieve nothing.'[68] The Empire he had believed in had gone. But Churchill had never been prepared to accept Empire at any cost. His imperialism was of a liberal hue in which the duty of beneficent and enlightened rule was paramount.

Was Churchill a racist?

ONE OF THE COMMONEST charges levelled at Churchill, by friend and foe alike, is that he was a racist. Clive Ponting, ever eager to blacken Churchill's reputation, argued that he 'accepted without question the idea of the inherent superiority of white people'.[69] Andrew Roberts, though not in the revisionist anti-Churchill camp, wrote in *Eminent Churchillians* that he was a 'white – not to say Anglo-Saxon supremacist' who 'thought in terms of race to a degree that was remarkable even by the standards of his own time'.[70] In 2005, on the fortieth anniversary of Churchill's death, South African President Thabo Mbeke echoed these views and suggested that Churchill's attitude towards black peoples was both racist and patro-nising.[71]

Churchill certainly held controversial views on some racial issues. As one trawls through the reminiscences of his Cabinet colleagues and friends, one reads some of Churchill's less guarded utterances, which could be highly derogatory and distasteful. The Indians he found 'the beastliest people in the world next to the Germans', and when he was told that the Cabinet was considering 'constitutional reform in Ceylon' he 'mumbled for a quarter of an hour or more in order to ventilate his emotions of disgust at anything that could extend self-government to brown people'.[72]

In her wartime diaries Violet Bonham-Carter recalled Churchill talking of India: 'The only quality of the Hindus is that there's a lot of them and that's a vice.'[73] According to Colville, the Prime Minister regarded the Hindus as 'a foul race protected by their mere pullulation from the doom that is their due.'[74] He told the Indian representative on the War Cabinet that Indians had to practise birth control, describing the increase in population as a 'vast and improvident efflorescence of humanity'.[75]

Such attitudes had been imbibed from an early age and already in *The Malakand Field Force* (1897) Churchill had described the Pathan tribesmen with contempt: they 'reveal a state of mental development at which civilisation hardly knows whether to laugh or weep'.[76] This confirms what he told Moran many years later: 'When you learn to think of a race as inferior beings it is difficult to get rid of that way of thinking; when I was a subaltern the Indian did not seem to me to be equal to the white man.'[77]

His views on Oriental peoples were no less unfavourable. Violet Bonham-Carter recalls a conversation with Churchill on the subject of the Labour Party's visit to China in 1954: 'I hate people with slit eyes and pig tails. I don't like the look of them or the smell of them – but I suppose it does no great harm to have a look at them.'[78] He contemptuously dismissed the Chinese Army with 'four million pigtails don't make an army' and he referred to the Japanese as 'the Wops of the Pacific'.[79] In general, Oriental people were 'the yellow peoples'.[80] When Churchill dined with Chiang Kai-shek, Moran commented that the PM was 'sceptical of China as a great power' and added in explanation, 'Winston thinks only of the colour of their skin'.[81]

Black people were referred to scornfully as 'blackamoors' and South African blacks as 'Hottentots'.[82] 'He is alas very anti-black', wrote Bonham-Carter in one of her diary entries.[83] Perhaps not surprisingly, Churchill expressed concern at 'the continuing increase in the number of coloured people coming to this country' and believed their presence would be resented by huge numbers of the British people. Churchill's favoured slogan was 'Keep England White'.[84]

In this he undoubtedly reflected growing concerns about what the *Sunday Times* termed 'a serious colour problem'.[85]

Racial assumptions also played a part in his imperial world view. When he gave evidence to the Peel Commission, he said that he felt no wrong had been done to the Arabs in Palestine, just as no wrong had been done to the Red Indians of America or black people of Australia 'by the fact that a stronger race, a higher grade race, or at any rate, a more worldly wise race ... has come in and taken their place'.[86] Churchill requested that his evidence to the Commission should not be published. As he explained to Lord Peel, 'There are a few references to nationalities which would not be suited to appear in a permanent record.'[87] His views on Arabs could be particularly severe. In 1952 he dismissed Egyptians as 'lower than the most degraded savages now known'.[88]

In assessing these views we must never forget that Churchill unmistakably bore the stamp of his Victorian origins. He shared the widely held assumption that Anglo-Saxon civilisation was superior to 'primitive' cultures, a notion which justified imperial control around the world. His early writings on empire reveal his Victorian ancestry – the smugness of the aristocratic, imperial British elite rationalising its control over 'backward' races. Of all his character flaws, this one seems to jar most with modern sensibilities, in an age when equality and anti-discrimination are the defining values of liberal society.

We must be wary, however, of applying twenty-first-century values to an era in which those standards did not apply. Many of Churchill's intellectual contemporaries, such as H.G. Wells and the Webbs, held racial views that were equally distasteful, yet they were regarded as progressive thinkers for their time. The moral *Zeitgeist* on race has clearly shifted over a century and this must be acknowledged in any assessment of Churchill's views. In any case, there is much more to say about Churchill and race than the previous brief summary.

While some of his language towards black people and 'natives' was intemperate, his views were more enlightened than those of his contemporaries. As a young man, he claimed to despise slavery and he regarded its abolition as a fine achievement of the British Empire. In his observations on the Cuban revolt against Spanish rule, he noted that 'by far the bravest and best disciplined part of the rebel forces are pure negroes'. In *The River War* he also stressed the important role played by African troops in the Anglo-Egyptian conquest of the Sudan.[89]

Though he wrote in *The River War* about killing the 'odious Dervishes', Churchill paid generous tribute to their fighting spirit. They were 'as brave men as ever walked the earth', 'valiant' and 'confident in their strength, in the justice of their cause, in the support of their religion'.[90] His description of Muslim warriors was a mixture of contempt and generosity: 'All the warlike operations of Mohammedan peoples are characterised by fanaticism'; some, 'fought in the glory of religious zeal', others, 'fought in defence of the soil' and yet others 'in the pride of an army'. He concluded: 'Fanatics charged at Shekan; patriots at Abu Klea; warriors at Omdurman.'[91] While he said that the indigenous Sudanese were 'simple minded savages' with 'cruel and thriftless' natures, people who 'displayed the virtues of barbarism', he qualified that negative assessment by admitting that they were 'brave and honest'.[92]

When it came to imperial administration, Churchill showed an enlightened attitude that would please today's progressives. In devising a constitution in South Africa, he sought to 'advance the principle of equal rights of civilised men irrespective of colour'. He pledged that he would not 'hesitate to speak out when necessary if any plain case of cruelty or exploitation of the native for the sordid profit of the white man can be proved'.[93] He also condemned 'harsh laws' such as those which excluded 'the natives from walking on the footpath in a town', for these were liable to 'offend against our sense of democratic equality'.[94] However, in order not to alienate the Boers, some discrimination had to be accepted.

In discussing the racial tensions in East Africa, he was similarly adamant in applying the principle 'of equal rights for all civilised men', which would include 'natives and Indians alike' who conformed 'to well marked European standards'.[95] In discerning who could fully exercise civic rights, what mattered for Churchill was their education and breeding rather than their racial background. In 1921 he wrote: 'We must make a continuous effort to live up to the principle that racial distinctions do not determine the status or position of any man in the British Empire who is otherwise qualified to occupy a position or exercise a function of responsibility.'[96]

In 1935 Churchill denounced Mussolini's conquest of Ethiopia in uncompromising terms. This was repeated in *The Second World War* (1948-54), where he described the invasion as 'unsuited to the ethics of the twentieth century' as it belonged to an age when 'white men felt themselves entitled to conquer yellow, brown, black or red men, and subjugate them by their superior strength and weapons'.97 Despite the vitriol he directed at Indians, he insisted, in a minute about Indian sailors serving in the Royal Navy, that there should be no discrimination 'on grounds of race and colour' and failed to see any objection to qualified Indians serving on HM ships – though he added, 'not too many of them, please'.98

There was one group about which Churchill rarely expressed any form of prejudice and that was the Jews. 'No thoughtful man can doubt that they are the most formidable and the most remarkable race which has ever appeared in the world', he wrote in 1920. Churchill's basis for this judgement was partly the Jewish system of ethics, which he regarded as 'the most precious possession of mankind, worth, in fact, the fruits of all other wisdom and learning together'.99 From this ethical system had come 'the whole of our existing civilisation', including Christianity.

He liked to expound his belief in the supremacy of Jewish (and Judaeo-Christian) ideals. In his essay 'Moses' he wrote that the Jews 'grasped and proclaimed an idea of which all the genius of Greece and all the power of Rome were incapable. There was to be only one God.'100 He admired the way that the Jewish spirit acted as a 'bond of union', an 'inspiration' and 'a source of great strength'.101

Throughout his career he consistently opposed anti-Semitic prejudice. In 1904 he denounced the Aliens Act as an unfair and discriminatory piece of legislation which would be harmful to immigrant Jewry. He believed that it would be a mistake to grant the police or customs officers the power to refuse entry to immigrants as it could lead to 'bullying and blackmail', and, in the hands of an anti-Semitic Home Secretary, it could become 'an instrument of oppression'.102

A year later, following a wave of Russian pogroms that claimed thousands of lives, Churchill expressed his unqualified horror and indignation at the massacres of Jews and denounced those responsible. Then, during the Russian Civil War of 1919-21, Churchill warned the anti-Bolshevik leader Denikin that there could be a pogrom of Russian Jews, saying 'this danger must be combated strongly.'103

On several occasions in the 1930s, he denounced the racial bigotry of the Nazi system. In a newspaper article in 1934, he condemned the situation in Nazi Germany where Jews were being baited 'for being born Jews' and 'insulated by regulation and routine on particular days of the week or month and made to feel the ignominy of the state of life to which the Creator has called them'.104

In an article in 1935 he lamented how the Jews of Germany had been 'stripped of all power, driven from every position in public and social life, expelled from the professions, silenced in the Press, and declared a foul and odious race'.[105] He went on: 'No past services, no proved patriotism, even wounds sustained in war, could procure immunity for persons whose only crime was that their parents had brought them into the world.'[106] Two years later he declared that it was a 'horrible thing' that 'a race of people should be attempted to be blotted out of the society in which they have been born'.[107] His stance against this form of bigotry was clear and unequivocal.

On one issue, however, Churchill has been accused of pandering to anti-Semitic prejudice. During his attack on Bolshevism after the First World War, he appeared to subscribe to a conspiracy theory that directly linked Bolshevism and Jewry. He referred to the Soviet government as a 'tyrannic government of these Jew commissars' and in 1922 described the Bolsheviks as 'these Semitic conspirators'. He even spoke of the Russian government as 'a world-wide communistic state under Jewish domination'.[108] In an article written in 1920, he described the Jewish revolutionary agitators (such as Trotsky) as 'terrorist Jews' who had 'fearfully excited' the mob passions of anti-Semites.[109]

Churchill was dabbling here in paranoid conspiracy theories that linked Jewry with international subversion. *The Jewish Chronicle* rounded on him for engaging in a 'reckless and scandalous campaign' based on 'flashy generalisations and shallow theories',[110] but it is worth noting that in the same article Churchill contrasted these 'revolutionary' Jews with the rest of the Jewish community. He praised the patriotic contributions of 'national Jews', whose role in the Great War had been particularly distinguished, and applauded the efforts of the Zionist pioneers in Palestine, whose 'inspiring movement' was seen as an antidote to the rootless nature of Bolshevism. But his sympathy with Zionism was also a logical extension of the philo-Semitism he so commonly expressed throughout his life.

Churchill was at pains to demand an end to the anti-Semitic excesses of the anti-Bolsheviks. He urged White leader General Denikin to prevent 'the ill treatment of the innocent Jewish population', while also condemning the 'fearful massacres of Jews' in other Russian districts.[111]

Churchill's belief in Anglo-Saxon superiority is often cited as evidence of his unapologetic racism. He talked on many occasions of the sentimental and historical bonds uniting Britain and the United States, and as early as 1911 called for closer attachments between the two countries. Throughout his life he sought to forge, in Colville's words, 'an indissoluble family connection between the English speaking peoples', and he never shied away from asserting the superiority of Western, specifically Anglo-Saxon, values and institutions.[112] As L.L. Harper has admitted, if there were such a creed as 'Anglo-Saxon brotherhood' then Churchill was its 'Pontiff'.[113]

Tempting as it may be to regard Churchill's Anglo-Saxonism as racist, that would be to misunderstand the creed. His references to the Anglo-Saxon race were linked more closely to culture, history and values than pure ethnicity. In a speech to the American people in 1938, he expounded on the achievements of Western Christian English-speaking peoples:

> Since the dawn of the Christian era a certain way of life has slowly been shaping itself among the Western peoples, and certain standards of conduct and government have come to be esteemed. After many miseries and prolonged confusion, there arose into broad light of day the conception of the right of the individual; his right to be consulted in the government of his country; his right to invoke the law even against the State itself.[114]

A year later he spoke of the English-speaking peoples as the authors and trustees of a set of sacred principles, among them 'freedom and law' and 'the rights of the individual'.[115] Then in 1954 he talked of the bonds that united Britain and America: 'We have history, law, philosophy, and literature; we have sentiment and common interest.'[116] These references suggest that, for Churchill, the term 'race' had a very different connotation from that it has today. He was little interested in the racial purity of the Anglo-Saxons, or in discovering among them some common physical stock. What mattered was a unifying political culture and value system, a spiritual, historical and linguistic thread that united people of diverse appearance and origin. Throughout his life, he unapologetically celebrated this common thread among the Anglo-Saxon people.

Some of Churchill's views on race seem unpalatable by modern standards. But to paint him as an implacable foe of racial minorities is to deny the complex strands in his thought and action.

Was Churchill a democrat?

The only sure foundation for a State is a government freely elected by millions of people, and as many millions as possible. It is fatal to swerve from that conception.[117]

OVERLOOKING THE Houses of Parliament on Westminster Green is a rather imposing bronze statue of Churchill on a plinth. The brooding figure stares solemnly towards Big Ben, with a resolute pose and indomitable glare. It serves as a vivid reminder of Churchill's days as war leader and is a fitting tribute to a staunch defender of parliamentary democracy. He was, in his own words, a child of the House of Commons, a body that he served for almost his entire public life.[118]

The House of Commons, which provided 'the enduring guarantee of British liberties and democratic practices', was in many ways Churchill's true 'spiritual home' and the scene of his greatest triumphs.[119] He was proud of Britain's democratic traditions and its (largely) unwritten and vaguely defined Constitution, which he traced back to Magna Carta. He never believed that democracy was perfect; he was said to have regarded it as the worst form of government apart from all the others that had been tried from time to time, but he never swerved from his commitment to a form of democratic politics that was centred on Britain's parliamentary system.

In his first decade as a young and ambitious MP, he was concerned lest the legislature lose its influence over the executive. In 1905 he introduced a motion calling for parliaments to have a reduced duration (from seven years down to five) and an extended time for general election campaigns. Contrary to popular belief, he voted in favour of extending the franchise to women on an equal basis in 1904. However, his confidence in the suffragist campaign was undermined by the more militant tactics of the suffragettes and he was forced to modify his position on this issue. He would later condemn suffragette activity as 'undemocratic'.

His stance on House of Lords reform also showed he was in tune with prevailing democratic sentiments. He condemned the Lords' veto of the 1909 budget as 'the whole foundation of democratic life depended on the control of the finances being wielded by the House of Commons'. He denounced the Lords as a 'small, limited and unrepresentative class' whose considerable power and influence had to be reduced.[120] He envisaged the struggle over the budget as a battle between 'a representative assembly and a miserable minority of titled persons who represent nobody, who are responsible to nobody and who only scurry up to London to vote in their party interests, their class interests and in their own interests.'[121]

During the First World War, parliamentary debates were often stifled by the need to avoid giving useful information to the enemy. Alert to this potential danger, Churchill called for Parliament to be allowed secret sessions, without the press being present, where urgent issues could be discussed by its members. In these secret sessions an 'intelligent, instructive, real, vivid discussion' was possible 'on nearly all the great questions now pending before the country'.[122] The Commons, he argued, was being sidelined if it did not 'exercise a real, vital, earnest, active, vigilant influence upon the conduct of public affairs'.[123]

He was quick to remind fellow parliamentarians that a powerful and effective Commons was a crucial difference between the British and Prussian constitutions, and that if the Commons were muzzled it would violate one of the crucial issues of the war, the preservation of Britain as a free and democratic state. 'It would indeed be the irony of fate', he declared to Parliament, 'if we liberated Germany and enslaved ourselves, and if at the same time that we were Anglicising Prussia we found that we had Prussianised England.'[124]

The European political landscape was transformed in the aftermath of war. Within a few years, authoritarian and undemocratic regimes had appeared in Russia and Italy, while a violent political undercurrent could be felt nearer to home. The rise in militant, populist politics tested Churchill's faith in the political process. In particular, he was alarmed by the rise of Bolshevism which he believed could rapidly undermine the fabric of Western civilisation. Many historians believe that, in the inter-war years, Churchill ceased to be a democrat and looked to any regime that would check the growth of Bolshevism in the West. Thus, during a visit in 1927, he praised Mussolini's revolution for 'being a bulwark to the agitation of revolutionary socialism'. Sebastian Haffner goes further and argues, in an otherwise brilliant biography, that, 'It is no exaggeration or unjust imputation to say that the Churchill of the 1920s was really a fascist.'[125]

This is an unjust imputation. Those who make this argument overlook the fact that Churchill's opposition to revolutionaries of either left or right rested on the same foundations: that they abused the democratic process, tyrannised their populations and clamped down on fundamental freedoms. Bolshevism was condemned because it introduced 'awful forms of anti-democratic tyranny', as well as 'bloody and devastating terrorism'.[126] Despite appearing to prefer fascism to communism, Churchill rejected Mussolini's political system as alien to the British heritage, and went on to denounce all forms of authoritarianism as 'equally odious'.[127]

In the 1930s it became ever clearer to Churchill that a vigorous stand against Nazism required an equally vigorous defence of democracy. In a speech in 1936, he surveyed the political heritage of Britain, France, Belgium, Holland and the United States. In those countries, he declared, 'thought is free; speech is free; religion is free; no one can say that the press is not free.' These were advantages that had to be protected and liberties that had to be cherished.

The alternative across great swathes of central and Eastern Europe (and of course Russia) were the Scylla and Charbydis of fascism and communism, which he called 'two violent extremes'. In those totalitarian 'utopias' one could be 'gagged and muzzled', facing 'eavesdroppers and delators at every corner'; one could be 'arrested and interned without trial' or 'tried by political or party court for crimes hithero unknown to civil law'. Rather than submit meekly to 'oppression', Churchill declared that 'there is no length we would not go to' to resist totalitarian government.[128] Faced with such oppressive choices, he always advocated the middle path of civilised and tolerant democracy.

During his 'wilderness years' Churchill was relentless in his ideological critique of fascism, communism and tyranny. As he surveyed the Spanish Civil War in an article in 1936, he condemned the 'cruelties and ruthless executions' of both the fascists and the communists, arguing that a victory for either would be followed by 'a prolonged period of iron rule'.[129]

The following year, speaking in the House of Commons about the same conflict, he declared: 'I refuse to become the partisan of either side.' He went on: 'I will not pretend that, if I had to choose between Communism and Nazi-ism, I would choose Communism', but then added, 'I hope not to be called upon to survive in the world under a Government of either of these dispensations ... I cannot feel any enthusiasm for these rival creeds. I feel unbounded sorrow and sympathy for the victims.'[130] His recommendation to the British government was that it should pursue a policy of neutrality.

Elsewhere he penned the hope that 'in the passage of years, these Dictators will disappear like other ugly creatures of the aftermath'.[131] In a speech at Oxford in 1937, Churchill emphasised again the affinity between Communist and Nazi societies. 'It is sometimes said that Communism and Fascism are poles apart ... But what difference is there between life at the North Pole and life at the South Pole? Perhaps as one crawls out of life's igloo there may be a few more penguins at the one or polar bears at the other. At both, life is miserable. For my part I propose to remain in the Temperate Zone.'[132] The Houses of Parliament were a key part of this temperate zone and provided an 'effective buffer against every form of revolutionary and reactionary violence'.[133]

Churchill's support for parliamentary democracy was not just a luxury of peace time: it was maintained during the war. As early as October 1939 Churchill was forecasting a prominent role for Parliament in the war. Parliament, he declared, was 'the shield and expression of democracy' in which one could debate 'all grievances or muddles or scandals'. As before it would prove itself to be 'an instrument of national will-power capable of waging stern wars'.[134]

On many occasions Churchill was assailed by the House on a military or political issue but he always relished the chance to put his case before the nation. Debates, he declared, were 'of the very greatest value to the life thrust of the nation', and they were 'of great assistance to His Majesty's Government'.[135] Sir John Martin wrote that, 'At no time was Parliament's right of criticism restricted and, if anything, he seemed over sensitive to parliamentary opinion, insisting on debates and votes of confidence even when it was clear that he enjoyed the support of the overwhelming majority.'[136] In a more humorous vein, Churchill likened parliamentary criticism to 'pain in the human body'. 'It is not pleasant,' he said, 'but where would the body be without it?'[137] He rightly described himself as 'the servant of the House'.[138]

Churchill never shirked from revealing the gravity of events during the war. If the news was bad, he would inform Parliament at once. As Colville has written, 'his sense of caution disposed him to overstate, rather than understate bad news'.[139]

Even though Churchill relished holding the reins of power during the Second World War, he realised that a mandate from the people was required if he was to make the transition from war to peace. 'The foundation of democracy', he said in 1944, 'is that the people have the right to vote'; if that right were taken away, it would 'make a mockery of all the high sounding phrases which are so often used'. He went on: 'I cannot think of anything more odious than for a Prime Minister to attempt to carry on with a Parliament so aged, and to try to grapple with the perplexing and tremendous problems of war and peace ... without being refreshed by contact with the people.'[140] Even in war, democracy could never rest on foundations of violence, coercion and terror. It was built on 'reason, on fair play, on freedom, on respecting the rights of other people'.[141]

During the Second World War he set out a number of key tests for an aspiring democracy. The people, he wrote, had to possess 'the right to turn out a Government of which they disapprove'. They had to be subject to 'courts of justice free from violence by the executive and from threats of mob violence' which would 'administer open and well established laws' based on 'decency and justice'. Above all, any democracy had to exalt 'the rights of the individual, subject to his duties to the State'.[142]

There is another side to 'Churchill the democrat' which must be considered. The great defender of democracy was no fan of what we might term 'populist politics'. Democracy, for Churchill, was not about MPs blindly following the will of the people. It was about electing representatives who could lead the nation in a responsible and intelligent manner, and according to their reasoned judgement rather than the whims of the press. This was a vision of politics centred on the Houses of Parliament rather than the people. In his words, democracy was 'the association of us all through the leadership of the best'. He therefore rejected any notion of populist politics in which elected representatives would become mere slaves to the prevailing public mood. MPs were the guides as well as the servants of the nation.

From this Churchill took on a dislike of referendums on political issues. In 1934 he told Baldwin not to resist a firm rearmament policy because of public opinion. 'You need not go and ask the public what they think about this,' he declared. 'Parliament and the Cabinet have to decide, and the nation has to judge whether they have acted rightly as trustees.'[143] Though he flirted with holding referendums on certain issues, such as votes for women, he believed in general that they would not 'conduce to the good government of our country'.[144] In Churchill's mind, elections existed for the sake of the House of Commons rather than the other way round.

Indeed, he was sceptical that public opinion could ever reliably inform political action. 'Nothing is more dangerous in wartime', he once wrote, 'than to live in the temperamental atmosphere of a Gallup Poll, always feeling one's pulse and taking one's temperature'.[145] The true statesman had to 'have his eyes on the stars rather than his ears on the ground'.[146]

The same rules applied to the winning of elections. Shortly before an election defeat, Churchill remarked that it would be better for the Conservatives 'to go down telling the truth and acting in accordance with the verities of our position than gain a span of shabbily bought office by easy and fickle froth and chatter'.[147] In the words of Tony Benn, Churchill was a 'signpost' rather than a 'weathercock'.[148]

Churchill's rejection of populism also stemmed from a belief that the public were politically ill-educated and thus reliant on a superficial and sensationalistic press. Political opinions, he believed, were not being formed by intellectual reflection, but from an uncritical acceptance of the views of the press. The newspapers, he commented scathingly, 'do an immense amount of thinking for the average man and woman', supplying them with a 'continuous stream of standardised opinion' which is 'borne along upon an equally inexhaustible flood of news and sensation'.

This was not an educative process because it was 'superficial' and produced 'standardised citizens'.[149] The press was therefore 'a spectacle of immense democratic irresponsibility'. He added: 'No one can pretend that reasoned discussion or careful study of the facts play any appreciable part of the decision of [the] modern mass electorate.' In somewhat elitist fashion, Churchill disparaged a press that catered 'for the millions with headlines, snappy paragraphs and inexhaustible sensationalism'.[150] For a modern generation, inundated with media soundbites and sensationalist headlines, Churchill's concerns seem highly pertinent.

In short, Churchill favoured a 'somewhat deferential and hierarchical form of democracy' in which the public could be trusted to make sound judgements as long as 'they were properly informed and led'.[151] But to be effective MPs had to resist not just the lure of opinion polls and 'froth and chatter' but also their own parties' ideological dogmas. In 1904 he was infuriated that, on the great question of free trade, the House of Commons was being 'gagged and smothered by a cynical and ingenious abuse of its own procedure.'[152]

In 1934 he made an impassioned plea to the government not to regard dissenting members of Parliament as a 'public nuisance' or to resent their 'awkward way of thinking things out for themselves'.[153] This came at a time when he was foremost among the Indian diehards and regarded as a political nuisance. When he seconded the nomination of Neville Chamberlain as Prime Minister in 1937, he made an appeal for a non-dictatorial form of leadership. He hoped that Chamberlain would not resent honest differences of opinion that might arise between them when their aims were largely similar, and that party opinion would not be stifled.'[154] One of those honest differences of opinion, to use his polite euphemism, was over Czechoslovakia. As German troops marched into Prague on March 14th 1939, vindicating Churchill's warnings that war had not so much been avoided as postponed at Munich, he made an impassioned defence of his dissenting stand:

> What is the use of sending Members to the House of Commons who say just the popular things of the moment, and merely endeavor to give satisfaction to the Government Whips by cheering loudly every Ministerial platitude ... People talk about our Parliamentary institutions and Parliamentary democracy; but if these are to survive, it will not be because the Constituencies return tame, docile, sub-servient Members, and try to stamp out every form of independent judgement.[155]

Churchill was haunted by the fear that, if Parliament failed to stand up to the executive, it would enter a state of inexorable decline. During the First World War he lamented the growing power of the executive at Parliament's expense, a development that saw the House of Commons become, in Churchill's view, 'a useless addition to the Constitution.[156]

Worse, he believed that parliamentary debate itself was in decline. Its high point was in the mid-nineteenth century, when the Commons witnessed the stirring debates of Peel, Gladstone and Disraeli; Parliament now lacked figures of 'the same commanding eloquence' and 'mental force'.[157] The public, he argued later, were being switched off politics, while the House of Commons 'steadily declined in public repute', showing itself 'increasingly inadequate to deal with the real topics of public interest.'[158] The key to re-engaging them, he argued was resuscitating fierce public debate and re-engaging the public. In recent years, much attention has been paid to voter apathy and the narrowing of ideological debate between the parties, concerns that Churchill would have readily understood.

He was also concerned to ensure that Parliament exert its proper constitutional check on the growth of executive power. In 1911 he was at pains to stress the checks and balances on Cabinet power. The Cabinet, he declared, 'springs from the House of Commons and dwells in the House of Commons. It is checked and corrected by the House of Commons, and by the shrug of the shoulder of the Private Members of the House the Cabinet can be scattered.'[159] He would later speak of a particularly British 'genius' for 'the division of power', with its 'balanced rights and divided authority'.[160]

Why are so many of Churchill's concerns pertinent today? The last quarter century in British politics has witnessed the rise of 'spin doctors' with a relentless focus on media manipulation and personality politics. This seismic shift has been accompanied by the advent of a presidential style of politics, notably under Margaret Thatcher and Tony Blair, who oversaw a shift of power away from Parliament and towards the Cabinet and 10 Downing Street. Each Prime Minister has reduced the amount of time spent in Parliament while using his or her large parliamentary majority to stifle dissenting backbench opinion.

Churchill would have ridiculed such developments while lamenting the decline of parliamentary power. He argued consistently that docile and subservient MPs were simply not discharging their duty, and that their sterile approach to political debate was feeding voter apathy. But he would never have accepted a mood of indifference towards elections and voting. His valet recalled a conversation with Churchill in London on the morning of the 1951 general election:

> 'What are you doing about your vote? Have you arranged to vote by post, or are you registered up here?"
>
> I replied that as a resident of Chartwell I would have to vote down there, but being in London I would not trouble about it.
>
> 'But you must vote,' he said firmly. 'It doesn't matter for which party you vote so long as you do so. I will arrange for you to be sent down there so you can go to the polls.'[161]

Two years later Churchill declined the offer of a dukedom but reluctantly accepted the Order of the Garter. He was proud of being the Great Commoner and wanted to retain the title 'Mr.' even after being awarded the Garter. He told Norman Brook: 'Why should I not continue to be called Mr. Churchill as a discourtesy title?'[162] Nothing better illustrates his reverence for democracy and parliamentary sovereignty.

Was Churchill a monarchist?

THROUGHOUT HIS LIFE Churchill was a zealous supporter of Britain's constitutional monarchy. His long public career spanned the reigns of six monarchs, a feat in itself, and he found himself on personal and usually cordial terms with nearly all of them. 'You are monarchical no. 1 and value tradition, form and ceremony,' Clementine Churchill told her husband, a description that was at once succinct and apposite.[163]

For a man of Churchill's age and background, his respect for the monarchy was hardly surprising. He described himself as a 'child of the Victorian age' and within this framework came a number of important assumptions about class and society. He possessed a belief in a 'natural, social, almost a metaphysical order, a sacred hierarchy which it was neither possible nor desirable to upset'. His reading of history was influenced by classic Victorian historians such as Macaulay, Carlyle and Gibbon, whose narratives were dominated by a 'cavalcade of the great public figures ... headed and dominated by kings and queens'.[164]

Churchill cherished the monarchy for a number of reasons. He firstly saw it as the romantic embodiment of centuries of British history, an institution that connected the past, the present and the future in one mysterious and intangible sweep. It also stood above the ebb and flow of party political strife, allowing individual monarchs to absent themselves from political wrangles. As a result, the monarchy was never bound to one faction or political party but was truly representative of all Britons, regardless of their background or class. This meant that the monarchy was a great unifier, both at home and abroad within the Empire.

While the monarchy could stand above politics, it was also an effective bulwark against tyranny. After the Abdication Churchill wrote that 'the ancient constitutional monarchy of this country' was the 'most effectual barrier against one-man power or dictatorship, arising whether from the Right or from the Left'.[165] In 1942, in a letter to George VI, he wrote of how the 'ancient and cherished monarchy' was 'the true bulwark of British freedom against tyrannies of every kind'.[166] Finally, he valued the pomp, glitter and ceremony that were inextricably linked to royal occasions. 'How proud we may be', he wrote, 'to have preserved the symbols and traditions of our glorious past, enshrined and perpetuated in an hereditary monarchy'.[167]

However, Churchill did not admire every style of monarchy. In *Great Contemporaries* he wrote that 'An hereditary monarchy without responsibility for government is for many countries the most sagacious policy'.[168] What Churchill valued was the peculiarly *British* style of monarchy with its limited powers and purely ceremonial functions. He was always at pains to stress that the monarch's government was answerable to Parliament rather than the Crown, and that the Royal prerogative was exercised on the advice of elected ministers. 'Criticism of all debatable acts of policy', he told his wife, 'should be directed to ministers – not to the Crown'.[169] He carefully reminded Edward VIII that 'when our kings are in conflict with our constitution, we change our kings',[170] and drew strength from the Glorious Revolution which had strengthened Parliament at the monarch's expense.

But the portrait thus far reveals only a part of the truth. For, while Churchill undoubtedly valued the institution of monarchy, his relations with individual monarchs were not always marked by automatic respect and deference.

Edward VII

Edward VII, as Prince of Wales, played an important part in Churchill's life. It was he who introduced Jennie Jerome to Randolph Churchill at the races at Cowes in 1873. Thereafter Edward maintained close relations with the Churchills and it was even rumoured that Jennie had been one of the Prince's many mistresses.

Initially Churchill had a good relationship with the Prince of Wales, sending him a copy of *The Story of the Malakand Field Force* and receiving a favourable response. The Prince later gave Churchill good advice, suggesting that he would prefer a parliamentary career to one in the army. As Churchill's political career blossomed, King Edward took an interest, expressing his pleasure that Churchill was a 'reliable minister and ... serious politician', which was possible only because he was 'putting country before party'.[171]

But the goodwill did not last. As a young liberal firebrand, some of Churchill's interventions met with distinct royal displeasure.

While at the Board of Trade, Churchill's call for reductions in military expenditure angered the King and led him to suggest that his minister was 'well named' because his initials were WC. In 1909, during the fierce debates over the future of the Lords, Churchill outraged the King with his frank description of the peers as 'a miserable minority of titled persons'.

Indeed so incensed was Edward that his Private Secretary, Lord Knollys, protested to *The Times*, leading Churchill to fulminate privately at what he perceived to be an abuse of the royal prerogative. 'He and the King must really have gone mad', was his somewhat impolite response.[172] However, the King did not accept Knollys's view that Churchill could never act from settled conviction or principle, and despite their disagreements Churchill told Edwina Ashley on the King's death that he had 'lost a good friend whose like I shall never see again'.[173]

During the year of Edward's death, Churchill intervened in a Commons debate on the Regency Bill. Here he spoke against allowing regents to be Catholic, arguing that, if the monarch was to be 'in communication with the Church of England', it was essential for the regent, who was 'to guide the mind and convictions of the young Sovereign', to be dissociated from 'the Church of Rome'.[174]

George V
Relations with Edward's son, George V, did not get off to an auspicious start. As Home Secretary, it fell to Churchill to write a daily report of Commons proceedings for the King, a communication which the King found 'very interesting'. However, in one letter Churchill commented that there should be labour colonies for tramps and wastrels, but added that 'there are idlers and wastrels at both ends of the social scale'. The King took offence at these 'very socialistic' ideas and Churchill was politely rebuked via Knollys, leading to a temporary falling out in which Churchill threatened to discontinue his daily letters to the King. The inevitable patching up occurred, but not without hurt feelings on both sides.

When Churchill went to the Admiralty in 1911, full of reformist zeal, he further antagonised a naval monarch who was a stickler for tradition. Churchill suggested to the King that a new battleship be called *HMS Oliver Cromwell*. Remembering the fate of the monarchy under Cromwell, the King understandably declined and was much irritated when Churchill persisted with his request. Eventually

Churchill gave way, persuaded by his own First Sea Lord. Nonetheless it was unusually insensitive behaviour from the monarchist politician. Churchill had little affection for the views of his monarch, believing that, on naval matters at least, he was full of 'cheap and silly drivel'.[175] By the outbreak of war in 1914, the damage had been done and the King privately welcomed Churchill's downfall from the Admiralty, commenting that he had become 'impossible' and a 'real danger'.[176]

By the start of the 1920s the King had gone up slightly in Churchill's estimation and the reason is not hard to discern. The First World War had transformed Europe's social and political landscape. A settled and harmonious order dominated by the great ruling houses of Central Europe had been brutally swept away, and in its wake had come the aftershocks of revolution, dictatorship and extremism. The passing of monarchies marked the symbolic end of a fixed and peaceful social order, something lamented by Churchill. Duff Cooper wrote in his diary how after the war Churchill 'swore we would have all the kings back on their thrones, even the Hohenzollerns' and how 'he attributed the calamitous state of Central Europe to the incompetence and corruption of the new republics'.[177]

At least in Britain the constitutional monarchy survived intact, and remained a potent symbol of tradition and continuity. During the negotiations in Ireland in 1921, the Colonial Secretary and his monarch paid each other compliments, reflecting a mutual esteem that had been absent in previous years. Late in the King's reign Churchill even accepted a request from Alexander Korda to produce a script for a film on the life of George V in time for the Silver Jubilee. The plan was later cast aside.

When George V passed away in 1935, Churchill offered fulsome praise. As the crisis of war loomed, he wrote that the King 'adhered unswervingly to the Constitution' and 'strove to mitigate the fury of parties'. 'The King,' he added, devoted himself to 'every form of war work' and 'tirelessly ... inspected and reviewed the growing armies', while he also 'encouraged and assisted his Ministers'. For Churchill, the King 'was the holding ground in which all the anchors of British strength were cast'.[178] Churchill reflected on the King's political impartiality which 'revived the idea of Constitutional Monarchy throughout the world'.[179]

Edward VIII

Prior to the events of 1936, Churchill had known Edward for more than a quarter of a century. In 1913, when Edward was Prince of Wales, the two men went through the Admiralty boxes together and Winston told his wife that they had become good friends.[180] During the 1920s they exchanged letters and played polo together, and Edward contributed to the cost of the Daimler that was bought for Churchill following his accident in the United States in 1931.[181] According to Colville, Churchill found Edward to be 'a shining example of all that youth should be'.[182] In 1936 Churchill warmly welcomed Edward's ascent to the throne and sent him heartfelt wishes for what he hoped would be a long and glorious reign. He hoped that 'in the long swing of events Your Majesty's name will shine in history as the bravest and best beloved of all the sovereigns who have worn the island crown'.[183]

During the Abdication Crisis, Churchill was under no illusions that the King had to be talked out of his plans to marry the divorcee Wallis Simpson. At no time did he seriously support the King's proposed marriage, and indeed secretly hoped that the King would change his mind. As he told Mrs Belloc Lowndes, 'He falls constantly in and out of love. His present attachment will follow the course of all the others.'[184] He also told Colville years later that he saw Edward's love for Wallis as a 'passing infatuation'. But his sense of loyalty to the King was 'axiomatic' and he felt that the King should be given adequate time to see the folly of his ways.

When he visited Edward in December 1936 at Fort Belvedere, he told him that 'the hereditary principle must not be left to the mercy of politicians trimming their doctrines to the varying hour'. He felt aggrieved only that the King was being rushed into making a decision of grave importance. For Churchill the principal issue at stake in 1936 was the future of the monarchy itself, which he thought would be irreparably damaged by a forced abdication. Churchill's position was unrealistic, not only in underestimating Baldwin's own resolve and the mood of the Commons (which supported Baldwin) but in failing to see that the King was intent on marrying Wallis. Far from being an opportunist, Churchill was prepared to risk grave political fallout in order to support a King, and a monarchical principle, that were both deeply important to him.

During the war relations were strained to say the least. After a brief spell as a Major General in France at the outset of war, the

Duke had gone to Madrid with the Duchess, at a time when Spain was a neutral country. In June 1940 he asked Churchill for permission to come to England and requested, as a condition, that he receive an official post while in the country. Churchill rejected the notion, reminding the King that he had taken military rank so that 'refusal to obey direct orders of competent military authority would create a serious situation'.[185] Aware of the Duke and Duchess's pro-Nazi sympathies, and the antipathy with which the couple were held by the Royal Family, Churchill offered the Duke the Governorship of the Bahamas. After some hesitation and further wrangling, the Duke accepted.

George VI

The Abdication left its mark on Edward VIII's brother, King George VI. Without doubt, George and Elizabeth, and George's mother Mary, collectively hated Wallis and viewed with extreme suspicion any of her husband's previous supporters. Churchill fell into this category and was thus viewed as *persona non grata* following the Abdication. It scarcely helped Churchill's cause that he was the most strident critic of Neville Chamberlain's appeasement policy, a policy that received ringing approval from members of the House of Windsor. When Chamberlain returned from Munich bringing 'peace with honour', he appeared on the balcony of Buckingham Palace with the King and Queen, a deeply unconstitutional act in a constitutional monarchy.

One of the royal household's favourites, the upright, decent, churchgoing Lord Halifax, was expected to succeed Chamberlain in 1940. This was certainly the outcome the King hoped for. One of his diary entries reads: 'I thought H. was the obvious man, and that his peerage could be placed in abeyance for the time being'.

However, the King put aside his reservations and became a staunch supporter of Churchill during the five years of war. There were occasional disagreements: Churchill was sometimes late for royal meetings; the King objected to appointing Brendan Bracken as a Privy Councillor, and to the inclusion of Lord Beaverbook in the government; and he occasionally felt sidelined by Churchill. But in general the relationship between PM and sovereign was a healthy and mutually beneficial one. In 1942, after the victory at El Alamein, Churchill wrote to the King to thank him for his support: 'No minister in modern times, and I dare say in long past days, has received more help and comfort from the King.'[186] His wartime letters to the King display abundant flattery and 'exaggerated displays of deference'; they were warmly appreciated by the Royal Household.

A powerful example of the King's affection was observed in 1944. Churchill was keen to witness the Allied landings in Normandy on June 6th from a nearby cruiser squadron but the King would not hear of this, promptly informing the Prime Minister that, if he was going to risk his life in this way, the King would do likewise. Understandably, Churchill backed down; he did not visit the beaches of Normandy until several days later.

A year later, when Churchill was turfed from office, the King wrote: 'I thought it was most ungrateful to you personally after all your hard work for the people'. He added, 'I shall miss your counsel to me more than I can say.'[187]

The King died in 1952 and Colville recalls Churchill's reaction: 'He sat in bed, with tears streaming down his face, recalling his comradeship with the King during the war and the love he had felt for him.'[188] He later paid fulsome tribute to the King's personal courage during his battle with lung cancer: 'He walked with death, as if death were a companion, an acquaintance, whom he recognised but did not fear'. As in his eulogy to George V in 1936, Churchill respected also the late King's propriety, noting that he was 'uplifted above the clash of party politics'.[189]

Elizabeth II

With the last monarch he served, Churchill enjoyed perhaps the fondest relations. Elizabeth II was said to have 'dazzled' him, with Churchill describing her as a 'truly remarkable person'.[190] There was a curious blend of the old and the new, of a wise, experienced and sagacious politician and a refreshingly new and forward-looking monarch. Again, his praise was exaggerated and eloquent. Churchill had first met the Princess Elizabeth in 1928, when she was aged just two; he had remarked on her 'air of authority and reflectiveness', which he judged 'astonishing' in one so young.[191]

At her coronation, he spoke of the new monarch as a 'gracious' and 'noble' figure at the 'summit of our world wide community', and expressed the hope that 'her reign shall be as glorious as her devoted subjects can help her to make it'.[192] He described the royal tour of the Commonwealth in 1954 in glowing terms: it had 'reasserted human values, and given a new pre-eminence to the grace and dignity of life ... I assign no limits to the reinforcement which this Royal journey may have brought to the health, the wisdom, the sanity and hopefulness of mankind.'[193]

Churchill enjoyed his weekly audiences with the Queen where they could discuss not just affairs of state but also mutual interests such as horse-racing and polo. For her part, the Queen became fond of her first Prime Minister, bestowing on him the Order of the Garter, which he had declined from her father. She even offered him a dukedom as a reward for his services to the nation, having previously been assured that he would not accept it. There was no doubting the cordial relations between the youthful Queen and her avuncular Prime Minister.

After his resignation in April 1955, Churchill was at pains not to mention a choice of successor, even though Anthony Eden was his obvious heir apparent. As Colville remarks, 'He wished it to be on record that Eden was chosen without any prompting or advice from the outgoing Prime Minister.'[194] Churchill took constitutional issues seriously and firmly believed that the royal prerogative of choosing a prime minister should remain.

On Churchill's death in 1965, the Queen bestowed upon him the highest possible posthumous honour, not only agreeing to a State funeral but also attending in person. This went against centuries of tradition and precedent and was something that Queen Victoria had never done during her reign.

Churchill's romantic instincts and his love of history had combined to produce a genuine reverence for the monarchy. As a minister and war leader, he showered his sovereigns with the kind of praise that might have embarrassed even Disraeli, but as a pragmatic politician he viewed some of his monarchs as flawed creatures prone to lapses of judgement. While outwardly deferential, Churchill never forgot that, in a constitutional monarchy, the will of the people expressed in Parliament was always paramount, not the whims of a hereditary monarch. Nonetheless, if individual sovereigns did not always meet with Churchill's approval, he remained 'monarchical no. 1' to the very end.

Was Churchill a warmonger?

IF ONE CHARGE sticks to Churchill more than any other, it is that he was a warmonger. One of his earliest biographers wrote: 'The whole spirit of his politics is military. It is impossible to think of him except in the terms of actual warfare. The smell of powder is about his path, and wherever he appears one seems to hear the crack of musketry and the hot breath of battle.'[195] Writing in *The Observer* in 1922, J.L. Garvin accused Churchill of a 'tendency to rush into war-like enterprises' which was 'the very bane of his life'.[196] John Maynard Keynes observed that Churchill adored 'the intense experiences of conducting warfare on the grand scale which [only] those can enjoy who make the decisions'.[197]

There is no doubt that he enjoyed war talk, both discussing high strategy and recounting his own battle experiences. Duff Cooper wrote in his diaries in 1920: 'Winston prefers military conversation to all other. It has become an obsession with him.'[198] There were also unguarded moments when Churchill's comments revealed a deep fascination with war. On the eve of the Great War he wrote to his wife that he was 'interested, geared up and happy', and tellingly added: 'Is it not horrible to be built like that?'[199]

These are often taken to be the sentiments of a warmonger, yet in 1909 Churchill also described war as 'vile and wicked folly and barbarism'.[200] His attitude to war was in fact marked by a deep ambivalence. His fascination for conflict and strategy co-existed with a belief that war had to be avoided whenever possible.

Churchill was brought up in the magnificent Blenheim Palace, a towering monument to his illustrious ancestor John Churchill, the first Duke of Marlborough. Without doubt Marlborough was one of Britain's greatest combat heroes, a man whose military genius in the seventeenth and early eighteenth centuries laid the foundations of English world power and imperial greatness for centuries to come. From an early age Churchill dreamt of emulating the exploits of his illustrious forbear and making a name for himself on the battlefield.

Churchill's early life revolved around military affairs. As a young boy he would delight in playing with his collection of over a thousand toy soldiers, arranging them in colourful military formations. He recalled one time when his father inspected him with his toy soldiers: 'He spent twenty minutes studying the scene – which was really impressive – with a keen and captivating smile. At the end he asked me if I would like to go into the army. I thought it would be splendid to command an army, so I said "Yes" at once...'[201] Training followed at the Sandhurst Military Academy and his first experience of war came in 1897 in Afghanistan, where he was both soldier and war correspondent. His dispatches, designed for public consumption, were usually full of praise for the British army. He described one particular infantry battalion as being 'as fine a picture in the pages of history as the legions of Caesar, the Janissaries of the Sultans or the Old Guard of Napoleon'.[202] He took little issue with the army's tactics in subduing the Pathan tribes and was happy to comment on the bravery of individual soldiers.

But in his letters home a slightly different picture emerges. To his grandmother he described the 'shattering effects' of the new and controversial dum-dum bullet: 'I believe no such bullet has ever been used on human beings before but only on game – stags, tigers etc. The picture is a terrible one, and naturally it has a side to which one does not allude in print.'[203] In another letter, this time to a friend, he commented on the cruel aspects of war: 'There is no doubt that we are a very cruel people ... At Malakand the Sikhs put a wounded man into the incinerator and burnt him alive.'[204] Already we can sense that he would recoil if there was any departure from his own lofty conceptions of how war should be fought.

The same mixture of fascination and horror can be found in *The River War*, his account of the conflict in Sudan in 1898. He wrote to his mother that 'the victory at Omdurman was disgraced by the inhuman slaughter of the wounded ... Kitchener was responsible for this'.[205] The killings of the wounded Dervishes were 'acts of barbarity' which could not be justified by 'the fierce and treacherous nature of the Dervish'.[206] The desecration of the Mahdi's tomb and the removal of his head for 'future disposal' raised his indignation more than anything else: 'If ... the people of the Sudan still venerated the memory of the Mahdi then I shall not hesitate to declare that to destroy what was sacred and holy to them was a wicked act, of which the true Christian, no less than the philosopher, must express his abhorrence.'[207]

In one of the most stirring and eloquent passages in the book, he dealt with the sight of enemy corpses left to rot on the battlefield of Omdurman. His account of the Dervish dead revealed that he had been disabused of any romantic notion of war:

> Occasionally there were double layers [of bodies] ... It is difficult to
> imagine the postures into which man, once created in the image of
> his Maker, had been twisted. It is not wise to try, for he who succeeds
> will ask himself with me, 'Can I ever forget?' I have tried to gild war,
> and to solace myself for the loss of dear and gallant friends, with the
> thought that a soldier's death for a cause that he believes in will
> count for much, whatever may be beyond this world ... But there
> was nothing *dulce et decorum* about the Dervish dead; nothing of the
> dignity of unconquerable manhood; all was filthy corruption ... Yet
> these were as brave men as ever walked the earth.[208]

Though the Dervish were 'destroyed, not conquered' by machinery, that same technological prowess would catch up with the victors. He wrote: 'Time, which laughs at science, as science laughs at valour, will in due course contemptuously brush both combatants away.'[209]

In a war of machine guns and technology, Churchill saw few displays of chivalry and valour. This was a theme he would return to when he recounted his experiences in the Boer War. As both officer and war correspondent, Churchill revelled in the chance to make history on the battlefield; there is an exhilarated tone to some of his writing. Typical was his dispatch to *The Morning Post* describing the armoured train episode: 'Nothing was so thrilling as this: to wait and struggle among those clanging, rending iron boxes, with the repeated explosions of the shells and artillery'.[210] He paid tribute at Spion Kop to the 'magnificent' defence, the 'devoted heroism' of the Irish soldiers, but also to the 'stout endurance' of the Boers.

But, in his description of the battle of Spion Kop, Churchill also showed how attuned he was to the horror of mechanised warfare. Take this passage from one of his dispatches to *The Morning Post*:

> The terrible power of the Mauser rifle was displayed. As the
> charging companies met the storm of bullets they were swept away.
> Officers and men fell by scores on the narrow ridge. Though assailed
> in front and flank by the hideous whispering death, the survivors
> hurried obstinately forwards, until their own artillery were forced to
> cease firing...[211]

In both of these conflicts Churchill showed himself to be no outright jingoist. Indeed, he was even on record as saying that in war 'neither side has a monopoly of right or reason'.[212] Certainly, war aroused within him an elemental passion, and he revelled in the chance to be centre stage in battle, but his excitement was tempered by experiencing at first hand the immense cruelty and suffering it brought.

With the Boer War in mind, one of his first interventions as a newly elected MP was to oppose Brodrick's scheme for army expansion in 1901. Brodrick, the Secretary of State for War, planned to create six army corps, three of which would be held ready to be dispatched abroad. Churchill rejected the idea that this would give Britain more security in a future war against a Continental power: 'They are enough to irritate; they are not enough to overawe,' he declared.

He was at pains to point out what such a Continental war would look like: 'A European war cannot be anything but a cruel, heartrending struggle, which, if we are ever to enjoy the bitter fruits of victory, must demand, perhaps for several years, the whole manhood of the nation, the entire suspension of peaceful industries, and the concentrating to one end of every vital energy in the community.'

The reasoning behind this analysis was simple enough. In previous wars that were fought by small armies of professional soldiers, it was possible to 'limit the liabilities of the combatants'. However, in modern Continental warfare, 'mighty populations' would be 'impelled on each other', using the resource of science to 'sweep away everything that might mitigate their fury'. He went on: 'A European war can only end in the ruin of the vanquished ... and exhaustion of the conquerors.'[213]

These were remarkably prescient sentiments, anticipating as they did the immense national sacrifice of the twentieth century's total wars. But his foreboding only reinforced the ambivalent views he had held since 1898. While he would undoubtedly relish the experience of military engagement, he would also strive, from a ministerial position, to deter opponents from being belligerent. At no time was this better displayed than in the run-up to 1914.

Years before the First World War, Churchill was deprecating the colossal arms race between the Great Powers. He talked of the 'boon and advantage' of de-escalating the arms race which would 'lighten the burden of armaments'. Future ages, he said, would see the arms race as 'the blackest reproach upon the civilisation, the science and the Christianity of the twentieth century'.[214] A good liberal, he said at the time, had 'to keep cool in the presence of Jingo clamour'.[215]

Amid worsening Anglo-German relations, on March 18th 1912 Churchill put forward his idea for a 'naval holiday'. This involved freezing the arms race for one year in Britain and Germany, meaning that neither country would build Dreadnoughts during this period and 'any retardation or reduction in German construction' would be promptly followed in Britain. The German government feared that any cancellation of shipping orders would lead to domestic turmoil and promptly turned down Churchill's suggestion. Churchill renewed his proposal for a naval holiday in a speech in 1913 in Manchester, and a year later called for direct talks between himself and his German counterpart, Admiral von Tirpitz. Both suggestions were declined.

When war broke out Churchill sought to meet the challenge with conviction and resolution. He had great confidence in tactical combinations and felt so sure that he was at his true war station that he offered to resign in 1914 to take command in Antwerp. He eschewed any notion of a compromise peace and urged instead a vigorous offensive against Germany. In August 1918, in response to a call for a compromise peace from Lord Lansdowne, Churchill declared that there was no 'substitute for victory'. 'We have but to persevere to conquer,' he wrote. A compromise peace would 'defraud and defile the destiny of man'. The 'indispensable preliminary to a cessation of hostilities' was not a negotiated peace but the German people being 'decisively beaten in the field by the armies of the Allies'.[216]

To try and achieve this victory Churchill thought in an innovative fashion. He expended much energy on supporting the use of the tank and the aeroplane, while being ever alert to alternative theatres of war, such as the Balkans.

Certainly, there were moments when Churchill appeared to show an unhealthy zest for conflict. On the eve of war in 1914 he had revealed how military preparations had 'a hideous fascination' and prayed to be forgiven for such 'fearful moods of levity'.[217] He also reprimanded Edward Grey, the Foreign Secretary, for not showing 'a sufficiently elate spirit' at the outset of the conflict.[218]

In 1914, when it looked as if Antwerp was about to fall, Churchill was sent there to restore the morale of the Belgian government. Asquith noted Churchill's relish for 'adventure' and that he 'was quite ready to take over in Belgium'.[219] In Violent Bonham-Carter's diary for 1915 she recounts a conversation with Churchill in the build-up to the Dardanelles operation in which he told her: 'I think a curse should rest on me – because I love this war.'[220] All observers noted Churchill's courage, iron will and valour throughout the war, in contrast to the lethargy and defeatism of other colleagues. The downside of his undoubted bravery was that he appeared eager for military confrontation and oblivious to the suffering of others.

In his war memoirs, however, Churchill's tone was more sober. He reflected on the mass carnage of the previous four years: war had been 'stripped of glitter and glamour' and the Western Front had become a byword for the futility of mass industrialised warfare. What stunned him more than anything was how war itself had changed. It was no longer a heroic and chivalrous enterprise decided by acts of individual glory. Instead, war had become an impersonal exercise in mass slaughter, directed by the misguided calculations of aloof generals:

> No longer will Hannibal and Caesar, Turenne and Marlborough, Frederick and Napoleon, sit their horses on the battlefield and by their words and gestures direct and dominate between dawn and dusk the course of a supreme event ... No longer will they share their perils, rekindle their spirits and restore the day ... They have been banished from the fighting scene ... Instead our generals are to be found on the day of the battle at their desks in their offices fifty or sixty miles from the front, anxiously listening to the trickle of the telephone for all the world as if they were speculators with large holdings when the market is disturbed.[221]

This language is reminiscent of his outrage following the massacre of the Dervish at Omdurman and his horror over Spion Kop. It is hardly surprising that Keynes described Churchill's memoirs, *The World Crisis*, as a tractate against war.

In March 1919, as Secretary of State for War, Churchill introduced a bill to prolong conscription for certain classes of men who were already in the army. At the same time he passionately supported the intervention against the Bolsheviks during the Russian civil war but promised that no conscripts would be sent there. This persuaded many on the left that he was a vainglorious and unbalanced adventurer with Napoleonic ambitions. The editor of *The Nation* went so far as to accuse Churchill of recommencing 'this crazy game of war'.[222]

But Churchill had no interest in the recommencement of war. The start of the inter-war period was marked by a concerted effort on Churchill's part to avoid another terrible European conflict. Understanding the French fear of a resurgent Germany, while sensing the festering German hatred of the Treaty of Versailles, he called for a binding alliance between Britain, France and Germany. He felt this would strengthen France's security but allow for 'a profound revision of the Treaty of Versailles' so that Germany could be 'an equal partner in the future guidance of Europe'.[223] A warmonger might have relished the growing Franco-German antagonism, but not Churchill.

Perhaps at no stage was Churchill's position on war more misunderstood than in the 1930s. Throughout this decade, he warned of Hitler's growing power and of the futility of appeasing dictators. He also called for an urgent speeding up in Britain's own rearmament programme, as well as advocating a Grand European Alliance of anti-fascist states. Many parliamentarians, including supporters of appeasement, believed that Churchill's dire forebodings about Nazism were the alarmist rantings of a military adventurer.

But he was not relishing a conflict, nor did he think one was imminent. He wrote to his wife in 1935 that, if war broke out again, it would be 'the end of the world'. He added: 'How I hope and pray we may be spared such senseless horrors.'[224] In 1937 he wrote an article entitled 'War is not imminent' in which he declared: 'there is a good chance of no major war taking place again in our time'.[225] Far from offering a shrill voice of alarm, Churchill advocated 'vigilance and preparation without panic, and cool heads without cold hearts or cold feet'.[226] Nor was his opposition to Hitler's aggression a form of anti-German prejudice. As late as August 1939 Churchill could write in *Picture Post*: 'I have said repeatedly that it is a major interest of Great Britain that there should be in Europe a prosperous and happy Germany, taking an honoured and leading part in the forward guidance of the world.'[227]

Of course Churchill could hardly be accused of being a warmonger once the Second World War had started. He wrote in his memoirs that, as he went to bed on May 10th, he felt as if he was 'walking with destiny' and that his 'entire life had been but a preparation for this hour and this trial'. His prosecution of the war was marked by vigour, persistence, resolve, ceaseless energy and an unalterable conviction about the aims of the conflict. These qualities would have been impossible in a man who felt ill at ease as a war leader. After the war he told his physician, Lord Moran, that he felt 'very lonely without a war'.[228]

But as war leader he was ever sensitive to the casualties entailed during conflict. Thus on the eve of D-Day he told the US under-secretary for war: 'If you think I'm dragging my feet, it is not because I can't take casualties; it is because I am afraid of what those casualties will be.'[229] He was alarmed at American plans to bomb French railway bridges and railways, fearing a heavy toll in Allied civilian deaths. He was 'scared of casualties to the French entailed by this policy', arguing that 'this slaughter was likely to put the French against us'.[230]

Nor was it just Allied casualties that haunted him. He came to doubt the wisdom and moral viability of area bombing and, after watching a raid on German cities in 1943, asked those assembled with him: 'Are we beasts? Are we taking this too far?'[231] As the war ended, he wrote to his wife: 'I am free to confess to you that my heart is saddened by the tales of the masses of German women and children flying along the roads everywhere in 40 mile long columns to the West ... I am clearly convinced that they deserve it; but that does not remove it from one's gaze. The misery of the whole world appals me ...'[232] These reservations would not have interfered with his judgement that some actions were necessary for the greater good of winning the war. But that he *had* reservations is telling in itself.

Again in 1946 Churchill was accused of being a warmonger after his 'iron curtain' speech at Fulton. He warned of the Russian encroachment in Eastern Europe, the Soviet desire for 'the fruits of war' and the need for transatlantic unity in the face of this danger. But this was not a call to arms or, as Ponting claims, anti-Soviet rhetoric recycled for the post-war era. Churchill talked of the need to reach a settlement with the Russians under the general authority of the UN, which took into account the difficulties endured by the Russian people, to whom Churchill paid tribute. He talked of Russia requiring security on her western borders and the removal of any possibility of future German aggression.

Towards the end of his life Churchill sought in vain to end the Cold War by bringing together the Big Three for a summit conference. He was fully aware of the horrific consequences of all-out nuclear war and how it would shatter the foundations of civilised life in every country affected. He came to talk of the hydrogen bomb as a 'ghastly invention'[233] that would bring an 'equality of ruin to east and west'. This new type of war, he sensed, could bring no appreciable gain to the victor save the taste of ashes in his mouth. But Churchill was also an early believer in the 'nuclear deterrent' and ordered the construction of Britain's own nuclear arsenal. 'Peace through strength' was the real Churchillian motto.

Conclusion

Churchill's reputation was sealed by war. He fought in several conflicts himself and commanded a battalion in the trenches of the Western Front. He never shirked from battle once it had commenced and was exhilarated by the demands and challenge of wartime leadership. Battles, he thought, 'were the principal milestones in secular history'.[234] At no point did he subscribe to the pacifist view that war was always an evil and that violence never solved problems. For Churchill, the choice was not between war and peace but between a limited war now and a much worse one later. He would have argued that, to safeguard peace in the future, war was sometimes a necessary evil; but the charge that he was a reckless warmonger is unfounded. All truly great statesmen are aware of the agony of conflict and seek whenever possible to prevent it. Geoffrey Best sums up this ambivalence when he writes of Churchill: 'When he was in it he fought to win, but he was statesman and moralist enough to wish that wars could be avoided.'[235]

Was Churchill an appeaser?

CHURCHILL'S STRONG STAND against appeasement, especially at Munich, is frequently used to justify a vigorous foreign policy in the face of growing international threats. In 1956 Anthony Eden was confronted by the belligerent posturing of Egypt's Gamal Nasser. Eden launched his ill-fated expedition to Suez, convinced that Nasser was an Arab Hitler who should not be appeased at any cost. In 1965 President Johnson, weeks after committing troops to Vietnam, justified his policy with echoes reverberating from Munich: 'From Munich until today, we have learnt that to yield to aggression brings only greater threats and brings even more destructive wars.'[236]

Three decades later, Margaret Thatcher faced up to the Argentine invasion of the Falkland Islands in 1982. The leader of the opposition, Michael Foot, co-author of a devastating indictment of the 1930s 'appeasers', talked of the need to 'ensure that foul and brutal aggression does not succeed in the world', while others accused the Foreign Office of appeasement for not foreseeing Argentina's aggression.[237] And in 1998, while contemplating the use of force against Slobodan Milosevic, Tony Blair insisted that 'we have learnt by bitter experience not to appease dictators'.[238]

In each case these world leaders were invoking Churchillian rhetoric to justify their tough stands against foreign aggression. They saw Churchill's defiant pre-war critique of British appeasement, and the consequent failure of the appeasers, as a justification for their postures. But what few now realise is that Churchill often talked about the need for 'appeasement' and conciliation in foreign affairs during a lifetime of international statesmanship. Why the apparent contradiction?

Appeasement can be defined as the attempt to resolve the grievances of other powers though the use of concessions and diplomacy, without recourse to war or the threat or force. Judged in this light, it does not have the usual negative connotations of 'giving in' to aggressors. For Churchill, appeasement could be either good or bad, depending on the circumstances and the power relationship between appeaser and appeased. When one nation appeased another from a position of strength, it could be honourable and magnanimous. But when appeasement was offered from a position of weakness it was more often humiliating and short-sighted.

Following the Boer War, in 1902, Churchill called for a just and magnanimous settlement in the Boer republics. He did so in the teeth of a defiant and jingoistic national mood; there were many who, flushed with victory, would have supported a more vindictive approach. Once the Boers had accepted defeat, he called for 'an honourable agreement' that foreswore revenge. In 1906, as Colonial Under-Secretary, he oversaw the granting of a constitution and responsible government for the Transvaal. One of his key arguments was that the abandonment of British control was bound to come soon, and it would be better to oversee it while Britain had diplomatic strength:

> What we might have given with courage and distinction, both at home and in South Africa, upon our own terms, in the hour of our strength, will be jerked and twisted from our hands – without grace of any kind – not perhaps without humiliation – at a time when the government may be greatly weakened, and upon terms in the settlement of which we shall have only a nominal influence.[239]

If independence was inevitable, it was better to grant it from strength rather than by appeasement from weakness.

Churchill was one of the first to argue for Franco-German conciliation after the First World War. In 1920 he said that the intransigent
French attitude towards Germany resulted from her people being
'terrified'. She could see German forces massing against her in the
East while she felt increasingly abandoned by both the United States
and Britain. He called for a binding alliance between Britain, France
and Germany, which would provide France with the security she so
desperately craved.

But he also believed that, to win German goodwill, there would
need to be 'a profound revision of the Treaty of Versailles', making
Germany 'an equal partner in the future guidance of Europe'. He
explained to the Imperial Conference in London in 1921 that his aim
was 'to get an appeasement of the fearful hatreds and antagonisms
which exist in Europe and to enable the world to settle down'.
Churchill clearly believed that, if the Allies failed to deal with post-
war grievances, these would fester and make a fresh round of fighting inevitable. Far from seeking to exacerbate the Franco-German
rivalry, Churchill sought to lessen it with British blessing. He told the
Imperial Prime Ministers: 'I am anxious to see friendship grow up
and the hatred of the war die between Britain and Germany. I am
anxious to see trade relations develop with Germany naturally and
harmoniously. I am anxious to see Britain getting all the help and
use she can out of Germany in the difficult years that lie before us.'
These positive developments, Churchill hoped, could 'mitigate the
frightful rancour and fear and hatred which exist between France and
Germany'.[240]

In 1925 Churchill reiterated these themes in a conversation with
French President Doumergue when he said that 'the one real security
against a renewal of war would be a complete agreement between
England, France and Germany'. But this would require an understanding and judicious settlement of German grievances with the
Treaty of Versailles. He argued that it would be entirely wrong to
have an Anglo-French alliance 'while the fundamental antagonism
between France and Germany continued unappeased'.[241]

But those grievances also had to be addressed while Britain and
France were strong enough to do so. A failure to address these concerns would lead to a tilt in the European balance of power towards
Germany. While Germany was 'prostrate' the Allies had 'breathing
space ... to end the quarrel'.[242] It was a classic statement of justifying
appeasement through strength.

As Colonial Secretary, Churchill played a key role in framing the Anglo-Irish agreement of 1921. Prior to the agreement, Ireland had descended into inter-communal violence and civil war. Sinn Fein, who demanded independence from Britain, started a guerilla campaign that targeted policemen and police barracks, mainly belonging to the Royal Irish Constabulary. Churchill welcomed the decision to fight Sinn Fein, claiming the government had no choice but to 'break the murder campaign and to enforce the authority of the law'.[243] He supported the Black and Tans in their policy of unofficial reprisals against members of Sinn Fein, though he was alarmed at suggestions of an all-out war with Sinn Fein.

But while he was prepared to use force against the IRA, he also hoped for an end to the killings so that peace talks could begin. As he wrote to the Archbishop of Tuam, 'No one desires more than I do a cessation of the conditions of strife which are ruining the happiness and the prosperity of the Irish people. It is my earnest hope that better days may come. It is in that sense that I have acted throughout; but the murders of the police and military must stop.'[244] And in another letter to Tuam he added, 'I need scarcely tell you how intensely I feel the desire and need for a truce and an appeasement in Ireland.'[245] What was unacceptable was a settlement based on surrendering to terrorism. In Parliament, in the same year, he called for Irish nationalists to 'press their constitutional claims ... in the great constitutional Parliamentary assemblies of the Nation'. This would lead to 'a release of all those harsh and lamentable conditions which are bringing misery upon Ireland'.[246]

When Britain subsequently offered concessions in the Anglo-Irish treaty, Churchill was at pains to defend a philosophy of appeasement from strength. He had used a severe level of force to subdue Irish militants and the treaty ended 'a period of brutal and melancholy violence'. Crucially Britain had not acted from weakness, so criticism from some MPs was misplaced: 'If we had shown ourselves a feeble nation, fat and supine, sunk in sloth, our mission impaired, our strength gone, our energies abated, our credentials impaired ... then indeed there would be some explanation and justification for such misgivings...' Instead Britain had taken a leading role in 'the great struggle which has overthrown the largest and most powerful military Empires of which there is a record', which meant that the charge of humiliating appeasement was an 'unjustifiable self-accusation.'[247]

Churchill also opposed a harsh peace treaty with Turkey after the First World War. Lloyd George seemed intent on awarding Turkish land to the Greeks but Churchill saw this would be disastrous. He feared the Allies would have to enforce a harsh peace on Turkey which would require military resources that they did not have. In addition, he was concerned that a resurgent Muslim nationalism in Turkey could spark unrest in Iraq and Palestine which would be costly for the British occupiers. In vain he counselled to Lloyd George 'prudence and appeasement' rather than a treaty which would mean 'indefinite anarchy'.[248]

Later Churchill made clear that reconciling Britain to Turkish nationalism would pay dividends in terms of imperial policy: 'We ought to come to terms with Mustapha Kemal and arrive at a good peace with Turkey which will secure our position and interests at Constantinople and ease the position in Egypt, Mesopotamia, Persia and India.'[249] Later he talked of the need for 'appeasement of the Middle East' and of 'appeasing Arab sentiment', vital if Britain was to avoid civilian unrest and insurgencies in Iraq and Palestine, which would prove to be expensive entanglements.[250]

It was not just in foreign affairs that Churchill advocated the need for reconciliation. During the parliamentary crisis of 1910-11 Churchill supported attempts to restrict the power of the Lords, but he also urged all parties to work together on social and imperial matters. He wrote to Herbert Asquith: 'I hope we may be able to pursue *une politique d'apaisement*'.[251] In 1925, as Chancellor, he told the British Bankers Association that his aim was 'the appeasement of class bitterness' and 'the promotion of a spirit of co-operation'.[252] On many occasions during his public career he had favoured the creation of a national party consisting of MPs from across the political divide who would work together free from the rancour of partisan politics.

Throughout his career Churchill had been a firm advocate of military action when necessary. He never shied away from conflict when a nation was belligerent, but nor did he reject pacific overtures if the enemy was defeated. As much as he was animated by conflict, he was also a passionate advocate of conciliation, settlement building and appeasement. As he put it in his autobiography, 'I have always urged fighting wars and other contentions with might and main till overwhelming victory, and then offering the hand of friendship to the vanquished. Thus I have always been against the pacifists during the quarrel, and against the Jingoes at its close.'[253] R.R. James put it even better in his masterful biography: 'Whenever confronted by an adversary in serious mood, he stood his ground. When the adversary was crushed, he would offer the hand of conciliation and friendship. It was an essential part of Churchill's philosophy that capitulation had to precede negotiation.'[254]

To be successful, peace-making, negotiation and appeasement had to be carried out from a position of unassailable strength. What Churchill would never advocate was a policy of appeasement and the granting of concessions from weakness or fear. When he felt that concessions were made under duress and intimidation, he was at pains to condemn them.

In 1921 a series of Arab riots in Jaffa left thirty Jews and ten Arabs dead. The High Commissioner's response was to halt Jewish immigration until subversive elements among Jewry had been expunged. While agreeing with Samuel's decision to call a temporary halt to immigration, Churchill was angered that the Arabs were using violence 'in the hope of frightening us out of our Zionist policy.' He also disagreed with Samuel's decision not to levy fines on the rioters, arguing that concessions had to be made 'on their merits and not under duress'.[255]

During one of the Indian debates in 1930, Churchill argued forcefully that it would be impractical to negotiate with Indian nationalists such as Gandhi. Concessions made in London, he declared, would only be 'the starting point for new demands'. He went on: 'It is no use trying to satisfy a tiger by feeding him with cat's meat.'[256]

As early as 1932, Churchill recognised that Germany had legitimate grievances with the Treaty of Versailles and urged the government to redress these. But he thought that these grievances had to be addressed by the victors while they were in a position of military strength. He condemned as 'folly' the attempts by the British government and the International Disarmament Conference to bring about 'equality of arms' between Britain, France and Germany. 'The removal of the just grievances of the vanquished ought to precede the disarmament of the victors', he said. To allow Germany equality of arms with the victors would be 'to appoint the day for another European war ... to fix it as if it were a prize fight'.[257]

To offer concessions when weak would lead to German demands becoming unreasonable and British acquiescence unavoidable. While desiring to 'live on terms of good feeling and fruitful relations' with German people, Churchill noted the fact that every concession which had been made was followed immediately by a 'fresh demand'.[258] 'It seems a mad business', he wrote later, 'to confront these dictators without weapons or military force'.[259] He likened Britain's negotiating with the dictators to 'a cow that has lost its calf, mooing dolefully now in Berlin, and now in Rome – when all the time the tiger and the alligator wait for its undoing'.[260]

He would become the Chamberlain government's chief critic during the Munich crisis of 1938. Churchill met Konrad Henlein, the leader of the Sudeten Nazi party, and sympathised with resolving German grievances. Churchill accepted Henlein's call for local autonomy for Sudeten Germans in German-speaking regions of Czechoslovakia, while preserving the territorial integrity of the Czech state. But throughout 1938 Churchill had called for a Grand Alliance of anti-fascist European states that could collectively negotiate with Hitler while defending the interests of lesser powers such as Czechoslovakia. Chamberlain rejected this proposal.

In the same year Churchill attacked Chamberlain's decision to give up British naval rights at Queenstown, Berehaven and Lough Swilly[261] as 'an improvident example of appeasement', and added: 'You are casting away real and important means of security and survival for vain shadows and for ease.'[262]

In 1939 he vigorously opposed the government's White Paper on Palestine. Under the terms of the White Paper, which was a response to growing pressure from Arab states as well as a rise in Arab violence in Palestine, there would be an absolute limit on Jewish immigration to Palestine for five years, after which there would be no further Jewish immigration unless the Arabs in Palestine agreed to it. For Churchill, this represented an egregious breach of British commitments 'for the sake of a quiet life' – by which he meant pacifying Arab nationalist feeling in the region. For Churchill this act of appeasement was particularly dangerous because of of how it would be interpreted by Britain's foes:

> What will our potential enemies think? What will those who have been stirring up these Arab agitators think? Will they not be encouraged by our confession of recoil? Will they not be tempted to say: 'They're on the run again. This is another Munich,' and be the more stimulated in their aggression by these very unpleasant reflections which they make?[263]

Churchill believed that appeasing Arab violence in this way would send a message to Britain's enemies that she would not defend her interests abroad. This point that appeasement from weakness would embolden Britain's enemies had been made before. In a speech in 1937 Churchill had lamented the government's complacency towards Nazi Germany and issued this stirring analysis: 'I feel our country's safety is fatally imperilled both by its lack of arms and by the Government's attitude towards the Nazi gangsters. It is fostering in them the dangerous belief that they need not fear interference by us whatever they do. That can only encourage those savages to acts of aggression and violence of every kind.'[264]

During the war itself he had to deal with the neutral countries that were refusing to commit themselves to either the Allies or the Axis powers. For the neutrals he had this message: 'They bow humbly and in fear to German threats of violence, comforting themselves meanwhile with the thought that the Allies will win ... Each one hopes that, if he feeds the crocodile enough, the crocodile will eat him last.'[265] It perfectly summed up his belief that appeasing dictators out of weakness was a short-sighted strategy. Far from ensuring survival, it would merely avert conflict to a time of the dictator's choosing. In 1950, in a Commons debate, Churchill summed up his lifelong political philosophy about diplomacy and power: 'Appeasement in itself may be good or bad according to the circumstances. Appeasement from weakness and fear is alike futile and fatal. Appeasement from strength is magnanimous and noble and might be the surest and perhaps the only path to world peace.'[266]

It was a philosophy that served him well in peace and war. 'Short of actually being conquered,' he once wrote, 'there is no evil worse than submitting to wrong and violence for fear of war. Once you take the position of not being able in any circumstances to defend your rights against the agression [*sic*] of some particular set of people, there is no end to the demands that will be made or to the humiliations that must be accepted.'[267]

Was Churchill a Zionist?

ON MAY 14th 1948 David Ben-Gurion announced the birth of the state of Israel, fulfilling the Zionist dream set out by Theodore Herzl half a century earlier. On the same day, the armies of five neighbouring Arab countries invaded the nascent state, declaring their intention to drive its Jewish inhabitants into the sea. By March 1949 Israel had achieved a significant victory, repulsing the Arab armies and expanding her borders in the process.[268]

Many British officials, particularly in the Foreign Office, had consistently favoured the Arabs over the Jews, and viewed Israel's survival with hostility or indifference. At the very least they believed that support for Arab nationalism best served Britain's long-term interests. Churchill's voice was noticeably absent from this clamour. For many years he had been critical of the anti-Zionist attitude of British politicians and urged the Labour government to recognise the Jewish state. Nor was this a sudden conversion to the Jewish national cause: he had expressed an interest in Zionism from his earliest days as a parliamentarian, and in the 1920s he played a crucial role in the pre-history of the Jewish state.

A number of factors had attracted him to the Zionist cause. His father Randolph was noted for his philo-Semitic sentiments. He befriended numerous wealthy Jews during his life, including the Rothschild family – something that gave rise to unfavourable comment in aristocratic circles. He often spoke up for Jewish causes, such as when he told the House of Commons in 1883 that it had been right to admit Jews to Parliament a quarter of a century earlier. He also strenuously attacked instances of anti-Semitic persecution, such as the Russian pogroms of 1881.

From an early age, Winston imbibed Randolph's philo-Semitic attitudes, including his positive view of Jewish values. He viewed the Jews as a 'remarkable' race who had enlightened the world with their devotion to monotheism and ethical purity. In an essay written in the 1930s, he wrote that the Jews 'grasped and proclaimed an idea of which all the genius of Greece and all the power of Rome were incapable. There was to be only one God.'[269] He viewed the Jewish people as a civilising influence on humanity, a force for progress, enlightenment and moral improvement in a world that was descending into barbarism. In similar vein, Churchill believed that the British Empire had a civilising influence on 'lesser' races by implanting the full benefits of Judaeo-Christian values.

In the 'religion' of Anglo-Saxonism, the imposition of Western values overrode any prior historical claim to territory. Churchill once declared: 'I do not admit, for instance, that a great wrong has been done to the Red Indians of America, or the black people of Australia.

I do not admit that a wrong has been done to these people by the fact that a stronger race, a higher grade race, or at any rate, a more worldly wise race ... has come in and taken their place.'[270]

In his racial world view, while the Jews and Zionists represented the forces of enlightenment, the Arabs (particularly the Palestinian Arabs) were backward, uncivilised and anti-British. He had a negative view of Islam from an early age and frequently described Arabs in pejorative terms, an attitude that was later to colour his views on the Palestinian conflict.

He also recognised that the Jews had a legitimate claim to Palestine based on their long-standing presence in the land, but rarely saw Palestine as a vital strategic asset to the British Empire. His belief in the restoration of the Jews to the Holy Land was primarily a romantic notion with historical and sentimental overtones. Makovsky is right when he says that Churchill's attachment to Zionism was a peripheral concern, subordinate to the more vital issue of promoting and protecting British (and imperial) power. When Zionism was perceived to conflict with these interests, he was indifferent to the movement and some of his decisions came to be resented by Zionist leaders. But when it synchronised with his wider concerns, particularly when there was a mood of grave international uncertainty in the 1930s and 1950s, he was an ardent champion of the cause.

Churchill's interest in Zionism can be traced back as far as 1904. In December of that year a commission set out for an area of the East Africa Protectorate,[271] in accordance with the wishes of the 6th Zionist Congress, to explore the possibility of setting up a Jewish state. When asked for his opinion on the matter, Churchill gave a favourable response: 'The proposal to form a colony of refugees in some part of the British Empire not less healthy but less crowded than these islands, deserves fair and patient consideration.'[272] Two years later, as a prospective Manchester MP, Churchill commended the vision of establishing a homeland for Jewish people. He told a constituent that he recognised 'the supreme attraction to a scattered and persecuted people of a safe and settled home under the flag of tolerance and freedom', and added that he did not feel the 'noble vision' should be allowed to fade.[273]

Here sincere conviction merged with political calculation, for in late 1905, with an election in Manchester looming, Dr. Joseph Dulberg, one of Manchester's leading Zionists, promised Churchill political help and votes in return for supporting Jewish aspirations. Churchill gratefully accepted the offer.

In 1908 Churchill wrote that he was 'in full sympathy with the historical aspirations of the Jews,' adding that, 'The restoration to them of a centre of racial and political integrity would be a tremendous event in the history of the world.'[274] Owing to demographic issues and splits within the Jewish community, a scheme for an East African homeland was quietly shelved. Despite his earlier backing for an East African settlement, Churchill now proposed that Palestine alone was viable. 'Jerusalem', he wrote, 'must be the only goal.' He ended by sounding a note of certainty that would have pleased Theodore Herzl himself: 'That it *will* some day be achieved is one of the few certainties of the future.'[275] Given that Zionism was then in embryonic form, this was a highly prescient sentiment.

During the First World War Ottoman Turkey, which controlled Palestine, was at war with Britain. In 1917 the British government produced the Balfour Declaration, a formal statement of sympathy with the aspiration of the Zionist movement to create a homeland for Jews in Palestine. The text of the Declaration read as follows:

> His Majesty's government views with favour the establishment in Palestine of a national home for the Jewish people and will use their best endeavours to facilitate the achievement of this object, it being clearly understood that nothing shall be done which may prejudice the civil and religious rights of the existing non-Jewish communities in Palestine or the rights and political status enjoyed by Jews in any other country.

Churchill played no role in drafting the Declaration as he was not a member of the War Cabinet at the time, but he also expressed little interest in Zionism throughout the First World War. Perhaps his only contribution in any War Cabinet meeting was a note he scribbled in 1915 to Foreign Secretary Sir Edward Grey that a postwar Palestine could be given to 'Christian, liberal and now noble Belgium'.[276] We cannot read too much into this hasty, passing thought, particularly from a minister who was consumed at that moment by events in the Dardanelles.

In 1920, at the San Remo conference in Italy, the victorious Allies sought to divvy up the defunct Ottoman Empire between them. France was given the mandate for Syria and Britain was awarded Mesopotamia (Iraq) and Palestine. The mandate for Palestine stated clearly: 'Recognition has thereby been given to the historical connection of the Jewish people with Palestine and to the grounds for reconstituting their national home in that country.' The area allotted for the development of the Jewish national home encompassed the present-day borders of Israel and Jordan.[277]

Churchill's Zionist sympathies were in evidence that year. In an article for the *Illustrated Sunday Herald*, he offered fulsome praise for 'Zionist Jews' who possessed 'a national idea of a commanding character'. 'If', he declared, 'there should be created in our lifetime by the banks of the Jordan a Jewish state under the protection of the British Crown, which might comprise three or four millions of Jews, an event would have occurred in the history of the world which would, from every point of view, be beneficial'.[278]

Despite these sentiments, Zionism was still a subordinate political concern. In the very same article in which he praised Zionists, Churchill condemned the 'international' Jews who were, in his view, the driving force behind Bolshevism. Using dark and conspiratorial language, he railed against 'a sinister confederacy' of Jews in Russia and Poland who were engaging in revolutionary violence and who had 'forsaken the faith of their forefathers'. He may have seen Zionism here as a powerful 'nationalistic' and spiritual antidote to the rootless atheism of the Bolshevik movement. In any case, the *Jewish Chronicle* rightly viewed this inflammatory article as part of his anti-Bolshevik crusade.

His fixation with countering Bolshevism also informed his view of Britain's Middle Eastern entanglements. Echoing his hero Disraeli, he urged Lloyd George to support Turkey as a counterweight to Russia. He feared that antagonising the Turks (which Lloyd George was doing by supporting Greece) would encourage them to form an alliance with Russia, allowing the Bolsheviks to further destabilise the British Empire. As he saw it, a moderately strong Turkey could be an invaluable buffer against Russian expansion, as Disraeli had argued half a century earlier. On more than one occasion Churchill urged Lloyd George to abandon the Palestine mandate altogether,[279] partly because of his overriding imperative to reduce Britain's military expenditure.

Churchill's main contribution to the Zionist project came in 1921-2 when he was Colonial Secretary. One of his first decisions was to visit Cairo in February 1921 to meet the government's leading advisors on Middle Eastern affairs. He appointed Colonel T. E. Lawrence

(Lawrence of Arabia) as his advisor on Arab affairs. Lawrence encouraged Churchill to adopt a regional pan-Arabist approach centred on the 'Sherifian' family. The head of this (Hashemite) family was a man Britain had supported during the First World War, Hussein Ibn Ali. Hussein, who had three sons, Abdullah, Feisal and Zaid, had been appointed sherif of Mecca in 1908 and became the self-declared King of the Arabs in 1916.[280]

The Sherifian policy Churchill implemented involved placing key members of Hussein's family on the thrones of Britain's mandate territories. In return for abandoning his father's claim to Palestine, Feisal obtained the throne of Iraq, while the throne of Transjordan was given to Abdullah. Both rulers agreed not to attack the French in Syria, and the advantage for Britain was that having pro-British Hashemites installed in these two countries would make them cheaper to administer. Churchill said that Abdullah, like his brothers, would be placed 'under an obligation to His Majesty's government in one sphere or another'.[281] Lawrence also argued that anti-Zionist agitation would be kept under control by appointing an Arab ruler loyal to Britain and serving British interests. He did not foresee that Abdullah and his sons would later covet all of Palestine.

In order to fulfil the promise to Abdullah, Churchill separated three quarters of eastern Palestine from the area allotted for a Jewish homeland, creating the new state of Transjordan. This was understandably viewed by Zionists as a betrayal of the Balfour Declaration. Chaim Weizmann, one of the most prominent Zionist leaders, asserted that western Palestine's economy was dependent on Transjordan for it formed 'the natural granary of all Palestine'.[282] In a stronger vein, another Middle East department advisor, Colonel Meinertzhagen, on hearing of the Transjordan decision, wrote in his diary: 'This reduces the Jewish National Home to one third of Biblical Palestine. The Colonial Office and the Palestine Administration have now declared that the articles of the mandate relating to the Jewish home are not applicable to Transjordan ... This discovery was not made until it became necessary to appease an Arab Emir...'[283] British economic interests, in particular the drastic need for economy in military spending, had dictated an agenda that hardly suited the Zionist movement.

Following the Cairo Conference, it fell to Churchill to defend the Balfour Declaration to Jews and Arabs, as well as British policymakers. In March 1921 Churchill was visited by a delegation representing

Haifa's Palestinian Arabs. They warned him against the 'unnatural partitioning' of their lands and sought to prove both that Palestine belonged to the Arabs and that the Balfour Declaration was 'a gross injustice'.[284] The memorandum contained passages of anti-Semitic prejudice, such as the following: "The Jew ... is clannish and unneighbourly, and cannot mix with those who live about him. He will enjoy the privileges and benefits of a country, but will give nothing in return. He encourages wars when self-interest dictates, and thus uses the armies of the nations to do his bidding.'[285]

Churchill rejected the memorandum for its 'partisan' statements. When asked to repudiate the Balfour Declaration, he declared: 'It is not in my power to do so, nor, if it were in my power, would it be my wish.' He went on: 'It is manifestly right that the Jews, who are scattered all over the world, should have a national centre and a National Home where some of them may be reunited. And where else could that be but in this land of Palestine, with which for more than 3,000 years they have been intimately and profoundly associated?'

In a rather cutting tone, he pointed out that British control of Palestine had come on the back of the Allied victory over the Ottoman Turks: 'I thought when listening to your statements, that ... the Arabs of Palestine had overthrown the Turkish Government. That is the reverse of the true facts ... You only have to look at the road here ... to see the graveyard of 2,000 British soldiers...' The mandate was 'one of the facts definitely established by the triumphant conclusion of the Great War'.[286] This was a profound indication of his belief that the Palestinian Arabs were hostile to British interests and that, by siding with Britain's enemies, they had effectively forfeited their right to self-determination.

Addressing a Jewish deputation later, Churchill said: 'A great event is taking place here, a great event in the world's destiny. It is taking place without injury or injustice to anyone; it is transforming waste places into fertile; it is planting trees and developing agriculture in desert lands; it is making for an increase in wealth and of cultivation...'[287]

He had a chance to see this transformation of waste land on a tour of Palestine in March 1921, where he visited a number of Jewish settlements. He paid tribute to the work of agricultural pioneers 'who changed desolate places to smiling orchards and initiated progress instead of stagnation'.[288] At a tree-planting ceremony at the still uncompleted Hebrew University in Jerusalem in 1921, Churchill addressed the assembled crowd in reverent tones: 'My heart is full of sympathy for Zionism ... I believe that the establishment of a Jewish National Home in Palestine will be a blessing to the whole world, a blessing to the Jewish race scattered all over the world, and a blessing to Great Britain.'[289]

However Churchill's Zionist sympathies sat uneasily with the prevailing climate of appeasement among British officials. After the war these officials urged their government to repudiate the Balfour Declaration, arguing that the country's Arab population would never consent to it. Having failed to secure this outcome, the same officials decided to appease Arab opinion, hoping to win over Palestine's Arabs by placing limits on Zionist policy and institutionalising Arab political power.

Thus in 1921 Herbert Samuel, the Palestine High Commissioner, appointed Haj Amin el-Husseini as the new Mufti of Jerusalem. The Mufti was an important religious figure who was treated as the head of the Muslim community in Palestine. However, the appointment made sense only in the light of an appeasement policy, for el-Husseini had instigated anti-Jewish riots in Jerusalem the previous year, receiving first a ten-year prison sentence and then a pardon from Samuel.[290]

In May 1921 attacks on Jews by Arabs in Jaffa left forty dead, while Arab mobs attacked other Jewish settlements including Petah Tikvah. Samuel's response was to suspend Jewish immigration into Palestine and propose the establishment of representative institutions which would block further Jewish immigration. Though Churchill did not demur on the immigration proposal, he accused Arab agitators of 'frightening us out of our Zionist policy'.[291] Far from wanting to appease this mob mentality, Churchill called on High Commissioner Herbert Samuel to maintain law and order, and to favour concessions only 'on their merits and not under duress'.

In June 1921 Samuel announced that the mass immigration of Jews into Palestine was unrealistic and that henceforth immigration levels would be limited to 'the economic capacity' of the country. In a speech to the House of Commons Churchill accepted the restriction on Jewish immigration but argued that Palestine was 'greatly under populated'. Though he stressed the need to reduce Britain's military expenditure, he also accepted the wartime pledge to the Jews. He repudiated the idea that Britain could 'leave the Jews in Palestine to be maltreated by the Arabs'. But, as *The Times* noted, one of the 'chief obstacles to peace' was 'a fixed scepticism amongst many of the agents of the government in Palestine about Zionism and the Jewish national home'.[292] While Churchill clearly did not share Samuel's scepticism, at least in private, he failed to influence the latter's appeasement mentality. Indeed, by not fully repudiating Samuel's attitude, and by supporting some of his measures, Churchill laid himself open to charges of appeasement.

In June 1922 the Palestine White Paper was published. This sent a mixed message to supporters of the Jewish National Home. There was a pledge to support the Balfour Declaration, a promise of 'further development of the existing Jewish community' and an acknowledgment that the community was in Palestine 'as of right and not by sufferance'. The community could increase its numbers through immigration but could not exceed the country's 'economic absorptive capacity' – which created a wholly unwarranted limitation on Zionist expansion. It also confirmed that the Palestine mandate would not apply east of the Jordan River where Abdullah Hussein ruled in Transjordan. There was little explicit mention of what a 'Jewish national home' would mean, though privately Churchill said that if the Jews became a majority they would naturally take over the government.[293]

The following month, in the House of Commons, it fell to Churchill to defend the Balfour Declaration. Countering charges that Britain was betraying the Arabs, he responded: 'Left to themselves, the Arabs of Palestine would not in a thousand years have taken effective steps towards the irrigation and electrification of Palestine. They would have been quiet content to dwell ... in the wasted, sun scorched plains ...'[294] Elsewhere he argued that the Zionists had 'created a standard of living far superior to that of the indigenous Arabs' and mentioned the agricultural settlements he had visited.[295] He would later tell friends that the Jewish colonists had 'made the desert blossom like the rose', while reminding Cabinet colleagues that under Ottoman rule Palestine was a wasteland.[296] As Makovsky points out, what mattered to Churchill above all was that the Zionists were 'agents of civilisation and progress'.[297]

Throughout the period Churchill consistently failed to appreciate the source of Arab anti-Zionism. When he met a group of local Arabs in March 1921, all of whom were professed opponents of the Balfour Declaration, he listened with incredulity to their stream of anti-Semitic invective. He tried to win them over with appeals to good economic sense: 'But we also think it will be good for the Arabs who dwell in Palestine ... You can see with your own eyes ... the work which has already been done by Jewish colonies; how sandy wastes have been reclaimed and thriving farms and orangeries planted in their stead.'[298]

In similar vein, Churchill argued that the decision to allow Jewish control of a hydro-electric power plant would win over Arab support. 'Was not this', he asked the House of Commons, 'a good gift which would impress more than anything else on the Arab population that the Zionists were their friends and helpers, not their expellers and expropriators ...?'[299]

But this strategy was based on the erroneous belief that Arab antipathy was economic in nature; in fact it was a cultural and religious antagonism to Jewish sovereignty. There was a failure to understand that deep-rooted Arab opposition to Jewish self-determination could not be minimised by an appeal to economic self-interest. The package of concessions offered by Samuel would only encourage more Arab violence, including violence against the British. As a report on pre-war British policy towards Palestine pointed out in 1945, 'by no concession, however liberal, were the Arabs prepared to be reconciled to a regime which recognised the implications of the Balfour Declaration.'[300]

Naturally, much of the blame has to rest on the British Palestine officials whose *raison d'être* was to placate the Arabs and reduce to a minimum Britain's Zionist obligations. Without root-and-branch changes in Palestinian bureaucracy, Churchill's course in Palestine would have been immensely difficult, whatever his strategy.

His next major involvement with the Zionist cause came in the following decade, the 'wilderness years'. Throughout this period he fulminated against what he saw as the unnatural appeasement of Britain's enemies, principally Germany, and the winding down of imperial commitments in India. Churchill was convinced that British power and prestige was unravelling at a time of grave international uncertainty, and that British policy in Palestine merely reflected this weakness.

He condemned the Arab riots in Palestine in 1929 that killed nearly two hundred Jews as a 'massacre and pillage of a horrible character'. He called on the authorities in Palestine not to appease the local Arab population and his argument reflected wider imperial concerns. He feared that perceived British weakness in Palestine would be exploited by subversive groups in Britain's colonies, sparking further uprisings and massacres. Unlike a decade earlier, Churchill insisted on maintaining British control in order to give the Jews 'a full and fair chance'. Again he argued that this was justified by the progress the Zionists had brought to Palestine: 'more wealth, more trade, more civilisation, new sources of revenue, more employment'.[301]

In 1936 Palestine witnessed a full-scale Arab revolt, involving attacks on Jews and Jewish farmlands, intended to prevent further Jewish immigration into the country. During the revolt, the British government appointed a Royal Commission to investigate the causes of unrest. Giving evidence to the Commission in March 1937, Churchill defended the Balfour Declaration and British control in forthright terms. Rebutting the notion that a continuing influx of Jews would harm the Palestinian Arabs, he said: 'Why is there harsh injustice done if people come in and make a livelihood for more, and make the desert into palm groves and orange groves? Why is it injustice because there is more work and wealth for everybody? There is no injustice. The injustice is when those who live in the country leave it to be desert for thousands of years.' Churchill believed that, by neglecting the country, the Arabs had forfeited their right to control Palestine. He made frequent derogatory comments about Arab rule, commenting that 'where the Arab goes, it is often desert'; 'the Arab' was a 'lower manifestation'.[302]

Responding to Sir Horace Rumbold's charge that the indigenous Arabs had been subjected to 'the invasion of a foreign race', Churchill argued that Arabs had entered Palestine after the Jews had arrived and that the 'great hordes of Islam' had 'smashed' Palestine. He opposed the partition plan recommended by the Peel Commission, feeling it was an egregious breach of the original mandate.[303] He wrote in an article for the *Jewish Chronicle* in September 1937 that the area allotted by the Peel Commission was 'wholly inadequate' and offered 'no real scope for future immigration and expansion'.[304]

Churchill believed that if Britain abandoned the Jews in Palestine it would represent a capitulation to violence which would embolden British enemies elsewhere. He was particularly alarmed at Mussolini's imperial ambitions which threatened British control of the Mediterranean, as well as Egypt and the Suez Canal. Indeed, he specifically warned that, if Britain abandoned her wartime pledge to the Jews, other less friendly powers would exploit her exit. He told the Commission: 'Someone else might come in [to Palestine]. You would have to face that. A power like Italy would have no trouble.'[305]

In Churchill's view, Zionism and British imperial interests now marched hand in hand.

The attitude of appeasement which characterised Britain's inter-war foreign policy was to be a decisive factor in the administration of Palestine. Violence continued unabated and in May 1939 a government led by the anti-Zionist Neville Chamberlain[306] submitted to pressure from some Arab states by setting an absolute limit on Jewish immigration for five years.[307] Over this period, 75,000 more Jews would be allowed into Palestine but after that the Arabs could veto further immigration. The plan was designed to ensure a permanent Arab majority in Palestine.

By any analysis, the 1939 White Paper was a total repudiation of the League of Nations mandate and Churchill offered a forthright denunciation: 'Now, there is the breach; there is the violation of the pledge; there is the abandonment of the Balfour Declaration; there is the end of the vision, of the hope, of the dream.'[308] Again he denied that the Zionist dream had greatly wronged the Arabs of Palestine, while the Jews had been struck 'a mortal blow'.[309]

Once again he linked Zionism to the wider arena of international affairs. 'What will our potential enemies think? ... Will they not be tempted to say: "They're on the run again. This is another Munich" and be the more stimulated in their aggression by these very unpleasant reflections which they make.' He was also thinking of Britain's potential friends, particularly the United States. Raising the notion of American Jewish influence, he declared: 'What will be the opinion of the United States of America? Shall we not lose more ... in the growing support and sympathy of the United States than we shall gain in local administrative convenience.'[310] Like many other politicians of his generation, Churchill took it as an established fact that American Jews exercised considerable influence on their government. Unlike some, he did not view this with alarm.

However, during the war, as Prime Minister, Churchill failed to alter the 1939 Palestine White Paper when it was within his power to do so. One of the principal Zionists opposing the White Paper was David Ben-Gurion. In his memoirs, he offered this interesting defence of Churchill: 'we were not so naïve as to think that he would conceive it as his primary task to set Britain's Palestine policy back on to a Zionist path. He was a Zionist sympathiser. But he was an Englishman first, and he was chiefly preoccupied with the conduct of the war, and the struggle for victory.[311]

Nonetheless, Churchill showed some sympathy for Jewish refugees who had travelled to Palestine to seek refuge from Axis-controlled Europe. A typical intervention came in 1942 when the Royal Navy intercepted a ship, *Darien II*, carrying 793 Jewish refugees. Churchill wanted them to settle in Palestine but Lord Moyne, the British High Commissioner in Cairo, insisted that they be sent to Mauritius. This was important, he argued, because it would confirm Britain's reputation in the Middle East for being a trustworthy power. Churchill's objection won the day and the refugees were allowed to enter Palestine.

However, he reluctantly accepted requests for further illegal immigrants to be sent to Mauritius until the end of the war, sensing that any further opposition would create unwanted tension with Whitehall. Nonetheless, he insisted that those interned on Mauritius be treated humanely and not 'caged up'.[312] And he remained convinced that British officers in Palestine were unwavering in their Arabism. 'Of every fifty officers who came back from the Middle East,' Churchill said, 'only one spoke favourably of the Jews.'[313]

Unlike those officers and Whitehall officials, Churchill perceived little cost to Britain from alienating Arabs. In 1941 Rashid Ali al-Gailani led a military coup in Iraq that overthrew the pro-British regent, Amir Abdul Illah. Following Churchill's orders, the rebellion was crushed, and it soon became clear that the rebels had received help from the Axis powers. Two years later Churchill reflected on the implications of the uprising: 'They [the Arabs] have taken no part in the fighting except in so far as they were involved in the Iraq rebellion against us.'[314]

Despite his concentration on defeating Hitler, Churchill did not forget the pledge to create a Jewish homeland in Palestine. Throughout the war he pursued a plan to create a pan-Arab federation headed by Ibn Saud, the ruler of Saudi Arabia. The plan involved paying Saud a £20 million annual subsidy in return for recognising a Jewish state. Churchill envisaged that, after the war, a state consisting of several million Jews would be established in Palestine which would 'be one of the leading features of the Peace Conference discussions'.[315] When Churchill initially proposed the scheme, he was rebuffed by the War Cabinet, including Foreign Secretary Anthony Eden. Nonetheless, he persisted with the idea on many occasions, arguing in July 1943 that he was 'committed to the creation of a Jewish National Home in Palestine' and that he supported arming the Jews of Palestine to aid their self-defence.[316] He was delighted when the plan was adopted (in private) by the War Cabinet early in 1944.

Churchill's zeal for Jewish statehood was to be severely affected by events in the Middle East. On November 6th 1944 Lord Moyne was assassinated by members of the militant Jewish group *Lehi*. The murder had a profound effect on Churchill, for Moyne had been a close personal friend from their years at the Treasury. Though comforted by Weizmann's assurances of support in rounding up the extremists, he took the killing as a personal setback.

In a speech to the Commons in which he paid tribute to Moyne, Churchill declared: 'If our dreams for Zionism are to end in the smoke of assassins' pistols, and our labours for its future only to produce a new set of gangsters worthy of Nazi Germany, many like myself will have to reconsider the position we have maintained so consistently and so long.'[317] This was somewhat insensitive given the vast scale of Jewish suffering at the hands of the Nazis, but it accurately reflected his personal anguish. After the Yalta conference in February 1945, Churchill met Ibn Saud in Egypt and urged him again to embrace a Jewish state. But he failed to win over the Saudi leader, who was an avowed anti-Zionist.

One year later Churchill lost the general election and a Labour government led by Clement Attlee took office. Attlee's government, in its determination to pursue an anti-Zionist agenda, refused to allow a hundred thousand survivors of the Holocaust to emigrate to Palestine, or to declare in favour of Jewish statehood. This led to a surge of violence in Palestine as militant groups such as Irgun and the Stern Gang battled against the British colonial authorities. In 1946 members of the Irgun bombed the King David Hotel in Jerusalem, killing 91 people in the process.[318]

Churchill's pre-war Zionist sympathies were strained by these terrorist activities and he fulminated against those he called 'the vilest gangsters'.[319] He told the House of Commons: 'It is perfectly clear that Jewish warfare directed against the British in Palestine will, if protracted, automatically release us from all obligations to persevere, as well as destroy the inclination to make further efforts in British hearts.'[320] He called for those involved in the King David Hotel bombing to be treated with the full force of the law. He then suggested that, if the government was unable to discharge its obligations in Palestine, it should hand over the mandate to either the

United States or the United Nations, a suggestion which echoed the comments he made in 1920.

Weizmann believed that the erratic trajectory of Churchill's Zionism had a easy explanation: he had simply become 'disgusted by the terrorists and terrorism'.[321] This is only partly true. In the immediate post-war years Churchill lamented the loss of British prestige and the 'clattering down' of the British Empire. Britain was in dire financial straits, dependent on American money and subject to a humiliating retreat (or 'scuttle' as he called it) from India. In this situation, he felt that the Attlee government was getting its priorities entirely wrong.

'To abandon India', he declared, 'but to have a war with the Jews in order to give Palestine to the Arabs amid the execration of the world, appears to carry incongruity of thought and policy to levels which have rarely been attained in human history.'[322] Palestine was not 'a twentieth part of the importance of India'.[323] In his view British power was being needlessly wasted in what was an imperial backwater.

But it would also be an overstatement to say that Churchill had lost his sympathy for the Zionists. While he thought that no justification could be given for the 'dark and deadly crimes' of 'fanatical extremists', he blamed the Labour government for reneging on its election pledges to the Zionists. This had created a 'deep and bitter resentment ... throughout the Palestine Jewish community'.[324] He continued to believe in a Jewish national home and told a friend in 1948 that he could 'put the case for the Jews in ten minutes', adding that Britain had 'treated them shamefully'.[325] Despite the upsurge in violent attacks on British soldiers and policemen, Churchill also decried the notion of reprisal attacks on Palestinian Jewry. Acts of terror were being carried out, he said, by a 'small, fanatical, desperate minority'.[326]

In the period after 1948 he revealed genuine generosity of spirit. From May 14th 1948 the nascent Jewish state was fighting for its survival after being invaded by five neighbouring Arab countries. After eight months of fighting, Britain still withheld recognition of the Jewish state and a perplexed Churchill called on the Labour government to modify its attitude: 'They have established a Government which functions effectively. They have a victorious army at their disposal and they have the support both of Soviet Russia and of the United States ... It seems to me that the government of Israel which has been set up at Tel Aviv cannot be ignored and treated as if it did not exist.'[327]

By January 1949 Britain's Foreign Secretary Ernest Bevin was still ignoring Churchill's pleas, arguing that it would be hasty to recognise a state whose territorial boundaries had yet to be established. Churchill pointed out that there were numerous European countries that Britain recognised whose exact boundaries were not yet established. He then cited the long view that he felt Bevin had entirely ignored: 'the coming into being of a Jewish state in Palestine is an event in world history to be viewed in the perspective, not of a generation or a century, but in the perspective of a thousand, two thousand or even three thousand years.' The government's refusal to accord recognition was due not only to 'mental inertia' but also 'to the very strong and direct streak of bias and prejudice on the part of the Foreign Secretary'.

The accusation of anti-Semitism against Bevin was a scathing (though fair) one to make in the House of Commons. Casting doubt on the claims made in 1948 that the Arabs would seal a momentous victory, Churchill paid tribute to the 'fighting qualities and tough fibre of the Zionist community'.[328]

Once Israel had been established, Churchill's attachment to Zionism was often conveyed in romantic terms. When he met Eliahu Elath[329] in 1950, he spoke in reverential tones of the fulfilment of the Zionist dream. According to Elath's account:

> The setting up of our state ... ranked as a great event in the history of mankind, and he was proud of his own contribution towards it ... Churchill was movingly eloquent on the sufferings of Jews throughout history, as a persecuted people and the faithful guardians of the Biblical heritage. The free Jewish nation, he declared, must preserve close association with the book; Israel must guard the people's spiritual and moral inheritance.[330]

In an address to the US Congress in January 1952 Churchill paid generous tribute to 'the achievements of those who have founded the Israelite state, who have defended themselves with tenacity, and who offer asylum to great numbers of Jewish refugees.'[331] Again in 1953, at a Commonwealth Conference, he stated that, while Britain had 'nothing but good feelings towards the Arab world', he would not 'allow Israel to be crushed by the Arab countries surrounding her', though he noted that until the question of Palestinian refugees was settled it would 'remain a festering sore'.[332]

Perhaps it was in this romantic vein that Churchill agreed with the suggestion made by James de Rothschild to include Israel in the British Commonwealth. In a conversation with Evelyn Shuckburgh in 1955 he discussed the implications of such a move. According to Shuckburgh, Churchill declared, 'It would be a wonderful thing. So many people want to leave us; it might be the turning of the tide.'333

But Churchill also saw Israel as a useful ally in the Cold War and many of his sentiments express a pragmatic viewpoint. Thus he took seriously a memorandum by the Chiefs of Staff that looked at the role that Israel could play in the defence of the Middle East. Churchill had in mind the strategic requirements in a possible war with Russia during which 'it was ... proposed that the Israelis should make their major fighting contribution in the air'.334

He was also aware of the hostility Israel had encountered from Egypt and of how the Egyptians had been receiving Soviet weapons. In 1951 the Egyptian Prime Minister Nahas Pasha denounced the Anglo-Egyptian treaty that had been signed in 1936 and which allowed Britain to station troops at Suez. In a fury Churchill told Eden: 'Tell them that if we have any more of their cheek we shall set the Jews on them and drive them into the gutter, from which they should never have emerged.'335 At best this was a backhanded compliment to Jewish military prowess, while it also revealed his animosity towards Arab nations. In less intemperate terms he told the Cabinet Defence Committee that Israel's army would 'constitute a useful deterrent against Egyptian aggressive aspirations'.336

In April 1956 Churchill wrote to Eisenhower about an impending confrontation between Israel and Egypt. Relishing the fact that 'this tiny colony of Jews should have been a refuge to their compatriots in all the lands where they were persecuted so cruelly', and praising them for having 'established themselves as the most effective fighting force in the area', Churchill went on to say that he was sure 'America would not stand by and see them overwhelmed by Russian weapons'.337 In November 1956 he made a public statement of support for the Anglo-French-Israeli trio fighting Egypt in the Suez crisis. Though he would later come to (privately) condemn the operation as 'bungled' and ill-executed, he could see a clear justification for the Israeli pre-emptive action. 'The frontiers of Israel', he wrote, 'have flickered with murder and armed raids' and Egypt, the 'principal instigator of these incidents', had 'rejected restraint'. Israel had invaded Sinai only 'under the gravest provocation'.338

Shortly before his death Churchill met David Ben-Gurion, whose admiration for the Englishman knew no bounds. According to the recollections of Yitzhak Navon, Churchill paid fulsome tribute to the Israeli leader and the achievements of the Jewish state. At the end of their short meeting Churchill turned to Ben-Gurion and said: 'You are a brave leader of a great nation.'339

There is no doubt that Churchill was sympathetic to the Zionist cause for much of his life. He championed a Jewish homeland after the First World War, argued its case eloquently during the 1920s and oversaw crucial developments as Colonial Secretary. He had only cordial relations with the Israelis once their state was established and consistently won the affection of Zionist leaders.

But, as a British politician with a sensitive eye to the national interest, Churchill regarded Zionism as a secondary and subordinate concern. He rarely viewed the movement in purely strategic terms and some of his decisions alienated Jewish leaders. Nonetheless, he perceived the historical and moral importance of the Zionist movement and for most of his public career his sentiments were sincere. On reflection, it seems Norman Rose's assessment is a fair one: 'Churchill has still earned the right to stand in the front rank of the Gentile Zionists of his day.'340

NOTES

1 M. Gilbert, *Churchill's Political Philosophy*, p.29.
2 Lord Wellington, one-time Conservative Prime Minister, summed this up nicely when he said in 1836: 'All that I hope for is that the change in the position of the country may be gradual, that it may be affected without civil war, and may occasion as little sudden destruction of individual interests and property as possible.'
3 Companion I (ii), p.1083.
4 V. Bonham-Carter, *Winston Churchill as I Knew Him*, p.120.
5 Speeches I, p.721.
6 Speeches III, p.2818.
7 WSC Bio 4, p.173.
8 P. Addison, *Churchill on the Home Front*, p.300.
9 M. Gilbert, *Churchill's Political Philosophy*, p.32.
10 V. Bonham-Carter, *Winston Churchill as I Knew Him*, p.99.
11 Companion II (i), p.103.
12 WSC Bio 2, p.278.
13 M. Gilbert, *Churchill's Political Philosophy*, p.47.

14 Speeches I, p.676.
15 WSC Bio 5, pp.114-15.
16 *Ibid.*, p.115.
17 P. Addison, *Churchill on the Home Front*, p.149.
18 *Ibid.*, p.149.
19 V. Bonham-Carter, *Winston Churchill as I Knew Him*, p.197.
20 I. Berlin, *Mr. Churchill in 1940*, pp.36-7.
21 J. Norwich, *The Duff Cooper Diaries*, p.234.
22 K. Theakston, *Churchill and the British Constitution*, pp.22-4.
23 'Whither Britain?', *Listener*, January 17th 1934.
24 R. Louis, *In the Name of God, Go*, p.105. In line with this conservatism went
    an acknowledgement that the constitution had to be adapted according to
    historical circumstances. Churchill had few qualms about taking on a joint
    role as Prime Minister and Minister of Defence in 1940.
25 Companion V (ii), p.1170.
26 Speeches VI, p.6276.
27 *Ibid.*, 6295.
28 R. Callahan, *Retreat from Empire*, p.26.
29 C. Ponting, *Churchill*, p.23.
30 A. Roberts, *Eminent Churchillians*, p.211.
31 Speeches V, p.4985.
32 F. Woods, *Artillery of Words*, pp.41-2.
33 WSC Bio 1, p.424.
34 M. Gilbert, *Churchill: A Life*, pp.99-100.
35 WSC Bio 1, p.276.
36 W. Churchill, *The River War*, p.23.
37 For a fascinating exploration of the philosophical underpinnings of this view
    read *Churchill as Peacemaker*, pp.64-72.
38 WSC Bio 2, p.32.
39 Companion II (i), p.328.
40 Speeches I, p.382.
41 *Ibid.*, p.435.
42 Companion II (i), p.582.
43 Speeches 1, p.575.
44 M. Gilbert, *Churchill: A Life*, p.183.
45 M. Gilbert, *Churchill's Political Philosophy*, p.40.
46 Companion II (ii), p.686.
47 M. Gilbert, *Churchill: A Life*, p.172.
48 W. Churchill, *The River War*, p.13.
49 W. Churchill, *My African Journey*, p.21.
50 *Ibid.*, p.25.
51 *Ibid.*, p.43.
52 *Ibid.*, p.59.
53 *Ibid.*, p.142.
54 *Ibid.*, p.84.
55 Companion II (i), pp.575-6.
56 All quotes from Speeches III, pp.3009-14.
57 Companion I (ii), p.751.

58 P. Addison, *Churchill*, p.135.
59 *Ibid.*, p.137.
60 Speeches VI, p.6695.
61 D. Stafford, *Churchill and Roosevelt*, p.202.
62 WSC Bio 8, p.301.
63 Blake/Louis, *Churchill*, p.468.
64 A. Seldon, *Churchill's Indian Summer*, p.354.
65 *Ibid.*, p.356.
66 A. Montague-Brown, *Long Sunset*, p.307.
67 WSC Bio 8, p.1330.
68 A. Montague-Brown, *Long Sunset*, p.302.
69 C. Ponting, *Churchill*, p.65.
70 A. Roberts, *Eminent Churchillians*, p.211.
71 Churchill and Black Africa, *History Review* 2005.
72 A. Roberts, *Eminent Churchillians*, p.213.
73 V. Bonham-Carter, *Champion Redoubtable*, p.252.
74 J. Colville, *Fringes of Power*, p.563.
75 D. Hart-Davis (ed), *King's Counsellor*, p.143.
76 W. Churchill, *The Story of the Malakand Field Force*, p.10.
77 Moran, *Diaries*, p.394.
78 V. Bonham-Carter, *Daring to Hope*, p.137.
79 C. Ponting, *Churchill*, p.546.
80 Companion V (iii), p.756.
81 Moran, *Diaries*, p.140.
82 Speeches II, p.1453.
83 V. Bonham-Carter, *Daring to Hope*, p.224.
84 Macmillan, *War Diaries*, p.382.
85 A. Seldon, *Churchill's Indian Summer*, p.126.
86 P. Addison, *Churchill*, p.137.
87 Companion V (iii), p.624.
88 A. Roberts, *Eminent Churchillians*, p.214.
89 R. Quinault, 'Churchill and Black Africa', *History Review*, 2005.
90 F. Woods, *Artillery of Words*, pp.41-2.
91 W. Churchill, *The River War I*, p.60.
92 *Ibid.*, pp.14-15.
93 Speeches I, pp.580-1.
94 *Ibid.*, p.577.
95 Speeches III, p.3173.
96 *Ibid.*, p.3117.
97 W. Churchill, *The History of the Second World War 1*, p.129.
98 WSC Bio 6, p.158.
99 W. Churchill, 'Zionism versus Bolshevism', *Illustrated Sunday Herald*, February 8th 1920.
100 W. Churchill, *Thoughts and Adventures*, p.224.
101 Speeches I, p.685.
102 Companion II (i), pp.354-5.
103 Companion IV (i), p.677.
104 M. Gilbert, *Wilderness Years*, p.111.

105 WSC Bio 5, p.681.
106 O. Rabinowicz, *Winston Churchill on Jewish Problems*, p.99.
107 WSC Bio 5, p.889.
108 C. Ponting, *Churchill*, p.230.
109 Companion IV (ii), p.918.
110 M. Cohen, *Churchill and the Jews*, p.56.
111 Companion IV (ii), pp.907-12.
112 J. Colville, *The Churchillians*, p.86.
113 J. Ramsden, *Man of the Century*, p.345.
114 War Speeches 1, p.37.
115 WSC Bio 5, p.1063.
116 WSC Bio 8, p.992.
117 Companion IV (i), p.433.
118 WSC Bio 7, p.722.
119 D. Stansky (ed), *Churchill: A Profile*, p.154.
120 D. Cannadine and R. Quinault, *Churchill in the Twenty First Century*, p.30.
121 Speeches II, p.1324.
122 Speeches III, pp.2546-7.
123 G. Best, *Churchill and War*, p.88.
124 Speeches III, p.2548.
125 S. Haffner, *Churchill*, p.69.
126 D. Cannadine and R. Quinault, *Churchill in the Twenty First Century*, pp.32-3.
127 Speeches IV, p.4213.
128 Speeches VI, pp.5788-9.
129 WSC Bio 5, pp.782.
130 Speeches VI, pp.5850.
131 Companion V (iii), pp.813.
132 May 22nd 1937 speech.
133 WSC Bio 5, pp.361.
134 Speeches VI, pp.6162.
135 *Ibid.*, pp.6331.
136 J. Wheeler-Bennett, *Action This Day*, pp.152.
137 Speeches VI, pp.6189.
138 See also Nicolson II, pp.236-324.
139 J. Wheeler-Bennett, *Action This Day*, p.229.
140 Speeches VII, p.7023.
141 *Ibid.*, p.7052.
142 War Speeches 3, pp.206-7.
143 M. Gilbert, *The Wilderness Years*, p.109.
144 K. Theakston, *Churchill and the British Constitution*, p.126.
145 S. Mansfield, *The Character and Greatness of Winston Churchill*, p.125.
146 K. Theakston, *Churchill and the British Constitution*, p.7.
147 Hayward, p.4.
148 Nowhere was he more oblivious to public (and parliamentary) opinion than in his support for Edward VIII during the Abdication Crisis.
149 W. Churchill, *Thoughts and Adventures*, pp.194-5.
150 K. Theakston, *Churchill and the British Constitution*, p.12.
151 J. Muller (ed), *Churchill the Peacemaker*, p.73.

152   V. Bonham-Carter, *Winston Churchill as I Knew Him*, p.102.
153   WSC Bio 5, p.549.
154   Speeches VI, p.5857.
155   *Ibid.*, p.6082.
156   Speeches III, p.2520.
157   K. Theakston, *Churchill and the British Constitution*, p.133.
158   *Ibid.*, p.152.
159   Speeches II, p.1688.
160   Speeches VII, p.7565.
161   N. McGowan, *My Years with Churchill*, pp.154-5.
162   K. Theakston, *Churchill and the British Constitution*, p.58.
163   WSC Bio 8, p.570.
164   I. Berlin, *Mr. Churchill in 1940*, pp.36-7.
165   Speeches VI, p.5849.
166   WSC Bio 7, p.251.
167   K. Theakston, *Churchill and the British Constitution*, p.217.
168   W. Churchill, *Great Contemporaries*, p.27.
169   WSC Bio 2, p.327.
170   K. Theakston, *Churchill and the British Constitution*, p.219.
171   D. Cannadine and R. Quinault, *Churchill in the Twenty First Century*, p.98.
172   Companion II (ii), p.908.
173   A. Allfrey, *Edward VII and his Jewish Court*, p.282.
174   Speeches II, p.1582.
175   Blake/Louis, *Churchill*, p.190.
176   D. Cannadine and R. Quinault, *Churchill in the Twenty First Century*, p.100.
177   J. Norwich, *The Duff Cooper Diaries*, p.118.
178   W. Churchill, *Great Contemporaries*, p.254-5.
179   *Ibid.*, p.257.
180   M. Soames (ed), *Speaking for Themselves*, p.76.
181   Churchill was run over in New York and hospitalised for several weeks.
182   J. Colville, *The Churchillians*, p.15.
183   WSC Bio 5, p.809.
184   Blake/Louis, *Churchill*, p.192.
185   WSC Bio 6, p.613.
186   Blake/Louis, *Churchill*, p.196.
187   *Ibid.*, p.197.
188   J. Colville, *The Churchillians*, p.120.
189   Speeches VIII p. 8336-7.
190   J. Colville, *The Churchillians*, p.120-1.
191   M. Soames, *Speaking for Themselves*, p.328.
192   Speeches VIII, p.8487.
193   *Ibid.*, p.8567.
194   J. Wheeler-Bennett (ed), *Action This Day* p.77.
195   J. Muller (ed), *Churchill the Peacemaker*, p.186.
196   WSC Bio 4, p.891.
197   J. Pearson, *The Private Lives of Winston Churchill*, p.146.
198   J. Norwich, *The Duff Cooper Diaries*, p.122.
199   WSC Bio 3, p.31.

200 M. Soames (ed), *Speaking for Themselves*, p.30.
201 M. Gilbert, *Churchill: A Life*, p.22.
202 G. Best, *Churchill and War*, p.14.
203 *Ibid.*, p.15.
204 Companion I (ii), p.788.
205 WSC Bio 1, p.424.
206 F. Woods, *Artillery of Words*, p.44.
207 M. Gilbert, *Churchill: A Life*, pp.99-100.
208 W. Churchill, *The River War II*, p.221.
209 *Ibid.*, p.226.
210 C. Sandys, *Churchill: Wanted Dead or Alive*, p.50.
211 F. Woods, *Artillery of Words*, p.51.
212 Companion II (i), p.23.
213 Speeches I, p.82.
214 *Ibid.*, p.728-9.
215 Speeches II, p.1252.
216 Companion IV (i), p.366.
217 WSC Bio 3, p.31.
218 Companion IV (i), p.241.
219 WSC Bio 3, p.120.
220 V. Bonham-Carter, *Champion Redoubtable*, p.25.
221 W. Churchill, *Thoughts and Adventures*, pp.198-9.
222 P. Addison, *Churchill on the Home Front*, p.212.
223 Companion IV (ii), p.1193.
224 M. Soames (ed), *Speaking for Themselves*, p.391.
225 W. Churchill, *Step by Step*, pp.164-5.
226 *Ibid.*, p.164.
227 F. Woods, *Artillery of Words*, pp.86-7.
228 Moran, *Churchill: Struggle for Survival*, p.273.
229 M. Gilbert, *Winston Churchill's War Leadership*, p.87.
230 WSC Bio 7, p.738.
231 *Ibid.*, p.437.
232 M. Soames (ed), *Speaking for Themselves*, p.512.
233 K. Larres, *Churchill's Cold War*, p.294.
234 J. Muller (ed), *Churchill as Peacemaker*, p.55.
235 G. Best, *Churchill and War*, p.ix.
236 J. Ramsden, *Man of the Century*, p.210.
237 M. Smith, *Britain and 1940*, p.126.
238 *International Herald Tribune*, 13th April 1999: 8.
239 M. Gilbert: *Churchill: A Life*, p.176.
240 Companion IV (iii), p.1546.
241 Companion V (i), p.340.
242 WSC Bio 5, p.124.
243 WSC Bio 4, p.454.
244 Companion IV (ii), pp.1265-6.
245 *Ibid.*, p.1274.
246 WSC Bio 4, p.469.
247 *Ibid.*, p.680.

248 Companion IV (ii), p.1055.
249 *Ibid.*, p.1249.
250 WSC Bio 4, p.513.
251 Companion II (ii), pp.1031-2.
252 WSC Bio 5, p.120.
253 W. Churchill, *My Early Life*, p.346 (original edition).
254 R.R. James, *Churchill: A Study in Failure*, pp.46-7.
255 Companion IV (iii), pp.1466-7.
256 Speeches V, p.4938.
257 *Ibid.*, p.5204.
258 *Ibid.*, p.5199.
259 Companion V (iii), p.94.
260 WSC Bio 5, p.907.
261 The three ports that were retained by the UK in the Anglo-Irish treaty of 1921. They were handed back to Irish control in 1938.
262 Speeches VI, p.5955.
263 WSC Bio 5, p.1070.
264 WSC Bio 5, p.862.
265 Speeches VI, p.6185.
266 Speeches VIII, p.8143.
267 Companion V (i), p.917.
268 See *Israel's Wars*, Chapter 1, for a more detailed account.
269 W. Churchill, *Thoughts and Adventures*, p.224.
270 P. Addison, *Churchill*, p.137.
271 Forerunner to the colony of Uganda.
272 O. Rabinowicz, *Winston Churchill on Jewish Problems*, p.187.
273 Companion II (i), p.496.
274 O. Rabinowicz, *Winston Churchill on Jewish Problems*, p.195.
275 M. Gilbert, *Exile and Return*, p.69.
276 M. Makovsky, *Churchill's Promised Land*, p.72.
277 Palestine was originally an administrative region of the Ottoman Empire, divided up into the sanjak of Jerusalem, the vilayet of Beirut and the vilayet of Syria. The current state of Israel, including the disputed territories of the West Bank and Golan Heights, constitutes approximately 22 per cent of the original mandated area for Palestine.
278 W. Churchill, *Illustrated Sunday Herald*, February 8th 1920.
279 M. Cohen, *Churchill and the Jews*, p.70.
280 In his quest to control Arabia, he was defeated in 1924 by Ibn Saud, who later founded the state of Saudi Arabia.
281 WSC Bio 4, p.553.
282 J. Muller (ed), *Churchill as Peacemaker*, p.239.
283 *Ibid.*, p.241.
284 WSC Bio 4, p.562.
285 Companion IV (ii), pp.1386-8.
286 J. Muller (ed), *Churchill as Peacemaker*, p.242.
287 WSC Bio 4, p.568.
288 M. Makovsky, *Churchill's Promised Land*, p.121.
289 *Ibid.*, p.117.

290 El-Husseini was to visit Berlin as a guest of Hitler during the Second World War. He was an ardent supporter of the final solution and urged the Fuhrer to extend it to Palestinian Jewry.

291 WSC Bio 4, p.586.

292 J. Muller (ed), *Churchill as Peacemaker*, p.248.

293 *Ibid.*, p.249.

294 WSC Bio 4, pp.655-6.

295 Companion IV (iii), p.1484.

296 M. Makovsky, *Churchill's Promised Land*, p.122.

297 *Ibid.*, p.119.

298 WSC Bio 4, p.565.

299 *Ibid.*, p.655.

300 J. Muller (ed), *Churchill as Peacemaker*, p.260.

301 M. Makovsky, *Churchill's Promised Land*, pp.145-6.

302 M. Gilbert, *Churchill and the Jews*, pp.113, 116.

303 *Ibid.*, pp.115-16.

304 *Ibid.*, p.132.

305 *Ibid.*, p.118.

306 At a Cabinet meeting in April 1939, Chamberlain told his colleagues of the overriding imperative 'to have the Moslem world with us'. He went on: 'If we must offend one side, let us offend the Jews rather than the Arabs.'

307 The policy was formulated in the White Paper of 1939, also known as the Macdonald White Paper.

308 Speeches VI, p.6133.

309 *Ibid.*, pp.6136-7.

310 M. Gilbert, *Churchill and the Jews*, p.159.

311 D. Ben-Gurion, *Ben-Gurion Looks Back*, p.102.

312 M. Makovsky, *Churchill's Promised Land*, p.187.

313 M. Gilbert, *Churchill and the Jews*, p.205.

314 M. Makovsky, *Churchill's Promised Land*, p.194.

315 *Ibid.*, p.200.

316 *Ibid.*, p.207.

317 Speeches VII, pp.7034-5.

318 Mainstream Zionist groups, both in Palestine and around the world, condemned this act and called for those responsible to be rounded up.

319 WSC Bio 8, p.430.

320 Speeches VII, p.7377.

321 Blake/Louis, Churchill, p.165.

322 Speeches VII, p.7404.

323 *Ibid.*, p.7476.

324 *Ibid.*, p.7375.

325 WSC Bio 8, p.430.

326 M. Gilbert, *Churchill and the Jews*, p.263.

327 WSC Bio 8, p.449.

328 *Ibid.*, pp.454-5.

329 A Russian-born journalist who emigrated to Palestine in 1925 and became Israel's first ambassador to the United States.

330 WSC Bio. 8, p.557.

331 *Ibid.*, p.689.
332 *Ibid.*, p.841.
333 *Ibid.*, p.1095.
334 *Ibid.*, p.825.
335 M. Makovsky, *Churchill's Promised Land*, p.251.
336 WSC Bio. 8, p.825.
337 *Ibid.*, p.1192.
338 *Ibid.*, p.1221, and see p.1191.
339 *Ibid.*, p.1324.
340 Blake/Louis, *Churchill*, p.166.

Acknowledgements

THE AUTHOR AND PUBLISHERS wish to thank Curtis Brown Ltd, London on behalf of the Estate of Winston Churchill for permission to reproduce copyright material from the following works: The 8-volume *Collected Speeches of Winston Churchill*, ed. R.R. James; Churchill's own works, *The History of the Second World War I* and *VI*, *The World Crisis I* and *II*, *My Early Life*, *Great Contemporaries*, *Step by Step*, *Thoughts and Adventures*, *The River War*, *My African Journey*; the Martin Gilbert biography, Volumes 2-8; and *The Collected Essays of Winston Churchill I* and *II*.

The author and publishers also wish to thank the following for their kind permission to reproduce copyright material from the following sources: *With Love and Kisses* by C. Sandys, Sinclair Stevenson Publishers; *Churchill: A Profile*, ed. D. Stansky, and *Action This Day*, ed. Sir J.W. Bennett, Pan Macmillan, London; *Masters and Commanders* by A. Roberts, Penguin, London; *Churchill as Peacemaker*, ed. J. Muller, and *Diplomacy and World Power*, ed. M. Dockrill and B. McKercher, Cambridge University Press; *The Myth of Rescue* by A. Rubinstein, Taylor and Francis Publishers; *Churchill and War* by G. Best, Continuum International Publishing Group; *Churchill: The Unexpected Hero* by P. Addison, and *Churchill*, ed. Blake and Louis, Oxford University Press. Every effort has been made to contact copyright holders. The publishers would be happy to include any omissions in future editions.

Select Bibliography

LIKE ALL CHURCHILL scholars, I am indebted to Sir Martin Gilbert's multi-volume 'official biography' which comprises 6 of the 8 volumes of narrative and 13 companion volumes of documents. I have also made extensive use of the 8-volume edition of Churchill's speeches edited by Robert Rhodes James. In the notes, these volumes are referred to as follows:

Official biography: 'WSC Bio', followed by the volume number.
Companion volumes: 'Companion', followed by the volume and page number. Where Companion volumes are themselves subdivided into volumes, I have inserted i, ii and iii before the page number.
Speeches volumes: 'Speeches', followed by the volume and page number.

Addison, Paul, *Churchill on the Home Front* (Pimlico, 1993)
Addison, Paul, *The Road to 1945* (Pimlico, 1994)
Addison, Paul, *Churchill* (OUP, 2005)
Aldritt, Keith, *Churchill the Writer* (Hutchinson, 1992)
Allfrey, Anthony, *Edward VII and his Jewish Court* (Weidenfeld & Nicolson, 1991)
Ashley, Maurice, *Churchill as Historian* (Secker & Warburg, 1968)
Balcon, Michael, *A Lifetime of Films* (Hutchinson, 1969)
Ben-Gurion, David, *Ben-Gurion Looks Back* (Weidenfeld & Nicolson, 1965)
Ben-Moshe, Tuvia, *Churchill: Strategy and History* (Lynne Rienner Publishers, 1992)
Berlin, Isaiah, *Mr. Churchill in 1940* (John Murray, 1949)
Berthon, Simon, *Allies at War* (HarperCollins, 2001)
Best, Geoffrey, *Churchill: A Study in Greatness* (Hambledon and London, 2001)
Best, Geoffrey, *Churchill and War* (Hambledon and London, 2005)
Birkenhead, F.E., *The Life of F.E. Smith* (Eyre & Spotiswoode, 1965)
Blake, Robert and Louis, W. Louis, *Churchill* (Oxford University Press, 1993)
Blake, Robert, *The Conservative Party from Peel to Thatcher* (Eyre & Spotiswoode, 1970)
Bonham-Carter, Violet, *Winston Churchill as I Knew Him* (Eyre & Spotiswoode, 1965)
Calder, Angus, *The Myth of the Blitz* (Pimlico, 1992)
Callahan, Raymond, *Retreat from Empire* (Scholarly Resources Inc., 1984)

Cannadine, David and Quinault, Ronald, *Winston Churchill in the Twenty First Century* (CUP, 2004)

Carey, John, *The Intellectuals and the Masses* (Faber & Faber, 1992)

Carlton, David, *Churchill and the Soviet Union* (Manchester Union Press, 2000)

Catherwood, Christopher, *Churchill's Folly* (Carroll & Graf, 2005)

Chaplin, E.D.W., *Winston Churchill and Harrow* (Harrow School Bookshop, 1941)

Churchill, Randolph, *Winston S. Churchill*, Volume I: *Youth* (Heinemann, 1966)

Churchill, Randolph, *Companion Volumes to Volume I*

Churchill, Randolph (1967), *Winston S. Churchill*, Volume II: *Young Statesman* (Heinemann, 1967)

Churchill, Randolph, *Companion Volumes to Volume II*

Churchill, Sarah, *A Thread in the Tapestry* (Andre Deutsch, 1967)

Churchill, Winston, *The Story of the Malakand Field Force* (Longmans Green & Co., 1898)

Churchill, Winston, *The River War* (Longmans, Green & Co., 1899)

Churchill, Winston, *My African Journey* (1908)

Churchill, Winston, *The People's Rights* (1909, reprinted 1970)

Churchill, Winston, *The World Crisis, 1911-18*, 2 volumes (Odhams Press, 1938)

Churchill, Winston, *My Early Life* (Odhams Press, 1930)

Churchill, Winston, *Thoughts and Adventures* (Odhams Press, 1932)

Churchill, Winston, *Great Contemporaries* (Odhams Press, 1937)

Churchill, Winston, *Step by Step* (Odhams Press, 1939)

Churchill, Winston, *The History of the Second World War*, 6 volumes (1948-54)

Churchill, Winston, *The Collected Essays of Sir Winston Churchill*, 4 volumes (Library of Imperial History, 1976)

Clarke, Peter, *Hope and Glory: Britain 1900-2000* (Penguin, 2004)

Clayton, Tim and Craig, Phil, *Finest Hour* (Hodder & Stoughton, 1999)

Cohen, Michael, *Churchill and the Jews* (Frank Cass, 2003)

Colville, John, *The Churchillians* (Weidenfeld & Nicolson, 1981)

Colville, John, *The Fringes of Power* (Hodder & Stoughton, 1985)

de Gaulle, Charles, *The Call to Honour 1940-2* (Collins, 1955)

Dear, I.C.B (ed), *The Oxford Companion to World War II* (OUP, 2005)

Desai, Meghnad, *Rethinking Islamism* (I.B Tauris, 2007)

Dockrill, Michael and McKercher, Brian (eds), *Diplomacy and World Power* (Cambridge University Press, 2002)

Donnelly, Mark, *Britain in the Second World War* (Routledge, 1999)

Eade, Charles (ed), *Churchill by His Contemporaries* (Hutchinson, 1953)

Gilbert, Martin, *Winston S. Churchill*, Volume III: *The Challenge of War* (Heinemann, 1971)

Gilbert, Martin, *Companion Volumes to Volume III*, 2 volumes

Gilbert, Martin *Winston S. Churchill*, Volume IV: *A Stricken World* (Heinemann, 1975)

Gilbert, Martin, *Companion Volumes to Volume IV*, 3 volumes

Gilbert, Martin, *Winston S. Churchill*, Volume V: *Prophet of Truth* (Heinemann, 1976)

Gilbert, Martin, *Companion Volumes to Volume V*, 3 volumes

Gilbert, Martin, *Winston S. Churchill*, Volume VI: *Finest Hour* (Book Club Associates, 1983)

Gilbert, Martin (ed), *War Papers I*

Gilbert, Martin (ed), *War Papers II*

Gilbert, Martin (ed), *War Papers III*

Gilbert, Martin, *Winston S. Churchill*, Volume VII: *The Road to Victory* (Stoddart Publishing, 1986)

Gilbert, Martin, *Winston S. Churchill*, Volume VIII: *Never Despair* (Heinemann, 1988)

Gilbert, Martin, *The Wilderness Years* (Macmillan, 1981)

Gilbert, Martin, *Auschwitz and the Allies* (Pimlico, 1981)

Gilbert, Martin, *Churchill's Political Philosophy* (OUP, 1981)

Gilbert, Martin, *Churchill: A Life* (Pimlico, 1991)

Gilbert, Martin, *In Search of Churchill* (HarperCollins, 1994)

Gilbert, Martin, *Winston Churchill's War Leadership* (Vintage Books, 2003)

Gilbert, Martin, *Churchill and America* (Free Press, 2005)

Gilbert, Martin, *Churchill and the Jews* (Simon & Schuster, 2007)

Graebner, William, *My Dear Mr. Churchill* (Michael Joseph, 1965)

Haffner, Sebastian, *Churchill* (Haus Publishing, 2003)

Harriman, W. Averell, *Special Envoy* (Hutchinson, 1976)

Hart-Davis, Duff, *King's Counsellor* (Weidenfeld & Nicolson, 2006)

Haste, Cate (ed), *Clarissa Eden: A Memoir* (Phoenix, 2008)

Hayward, James, *Myths and Legends of the Second World War* (Sutton Publishing, 2004)

Hayward, Steven, *Churchill on Leadership* (Gramercy Books, 2004)

Hickman, Tom, *Churchill's Bodyguard* (Headline, 2005)

Higham, Charles, *Dark Lady* (Virgin Books, 2006)

Hill, Malcolm, *Churchill: His Radical Decade* (Othila Press, 1999)

Holmes, Colin, *Anti-Semitism in British Society* (Holmes & Meier, 1979)

Howard, Michael, *The Continental Commitment* (Michael Howard, 1972)

Howells, Roy, *Simply Churchill* (Robert Hale, 1965)

Humes, James, *Churchill: Speaker of the Century* (Stein & Day, 1980)

Hylton, Stuart, *Their Darkest Hour* (Sutton Publishing, 2001)

Jablonsky, David, *Churchill: The Great Game and Total War* (Frank Cass & Co., 1991)

James, R.R. (ed), *Memoirs of a Conservative: J.C.C. Davidson's Memoirs and Papers 1910-37* (Weidenfeld & Nicolson, 1969)

James, R.R., *Churchill: A Study in Failure* (Weidenfeld & Nicolson, 1970)

James, R.R. (ed), *Churchill: The Complete Speeches* (Chelsea House Publishers, 1974)

James, R.R. (ed), *Chips* (Phoenix, 1996)

Jeffreys, Kevin, *Finest and Darkest Hours* (Atlantic Books, 2002)

Keegan, John, *Churchill* (Weidenfeld & Nicolson, 2002)

Knight, Nigel, *Churchill: The Greatest Briton Unmasked* (David & Charles, 2008)

Lamb, Richard, *Churchill as War Leader – Right or Wrong* (Bloomsbury, 1991)

Lamb, Richard, *Mussolini and the British* (John Murray, 1997)

Laqueur, Walter (ed), *The Holocaust Encyclopedia* (Yale University Press, 2001)

Larres, Klaus, *Churchill's Cold War* (Yale, 2002)

Lawlor, Sheila, *Churchill and the Politics of War* (CUP, 1994)

Lee, Geoffrey, *The People's Budget: An Edwardian Tragedy* (Shepheard-Walwyn, 2008)

Littman, Jonathan and Sandys, Celia, *We Shall Not Fail* (Portfolio, 2003)

Litvinoff, Barnet, *Weizmann* (Hodder & Stoughton, 1976)

Lloyd George, Frances, *The Years that are Past* (Hutchinson, 1967)

Lloyd George, Robert, *David and Winston* (John Murray, 2005)

Louis, W.M. Roger, *In the Name of God, Go!* (W.W. Norton, 1992)

Lukacs, John, *The Duel* (Ticknor & Fields, 1990)

Lukacs, John, *5 days in London* (Yale, 1999)

Lukacs, John, *Churchill: Strategy and History* (Yale University Press, 2002)

Lukacs, John, *Churchill: Visionary, Statesman, Historian* (Yale University Press, 2002)

-McDonough, Frank, *Neville Chamberlain: Appeasement and the British Road to War* (Manchester University Press, 1998)

McGowan, Norman, *My Years with Churchill* (Pan Books, 1958)

Macmillan, Harold, *War Diaries: The Mediterranean 1943-5* (Macmillan, 1984)

Makovsky, Michael, *Churchill's Promised Land* (Yale University Press, 2007)

Manchester, William, *The Last Lion: Visions of Glory* (Little Brown, 1983)

Mansfield, Steven, *The Character and Greatness of Winston Churchill* (Cumberland House, 1995)

Martin, Sir John, *Downing Street: The War Years* (Bloomsbury, 1991)

Menzies, Sir Robert, *Afternoon Light* (Cassell, 1967)

Moir, Phyllis, *I was Winston Churchill's Private Secretary* (Wilfred Funk, 1941)

Montague-Brown, Anthony, *Long Sunset* (Cassell, 1995)

Moran, Lord, *Winston Churchill: The Struggle for Survival, 1940-55* (Houghton Mifflin, 1966)

Morton, H.V., *Atlantic Meeting* (Methuen, 1943)

Muller, James (ed), *Churchill as Peacemaker* (CUP, 1997)

Nave, Eric and Russbridger, James, *Betrayal at Pearl Harbor* (Michael O' Mara Books Limited, 1991)

Nel, Elizabeth, *Mr. Churchill's Secretary* (Hodder & Stoughton, 1958)

Neville, Peter, *Churchill: Statesman or Opportunist?* (Hodder & Stoughton, 1996)

Nicolson, Nigel (ed), *Harold Nicolson: Diaries and Letters, 1939-45* (Fontana Books, 1970)

Norwich, John Julius (ed), *The Duff Cooper Diaries* (Phoenix, 2006)

Parker, R.A.C., *Churchill and Appeasement* (Papermac, 2001)

Paxman, Jeremy, *The English*

Pearson, John, *The Private Lives of Winston Churchill* (Simon & Schuster, 1991)

Pelling, Henry, *Britain and the Second World War* (Collins, 1970)

Ponting, Clive, *1940: Myth and Reality* (Hamish Hamilton, 1990)

Pottle, Mark (ed), *Lantern Slides: The Diaries and Letters of Violet Bonham-Carter 1904-14* (Weidenfeld & Nicolson, 1996)

Pottle, Mark (ed), *Champion Redoubtable: The Diaries and Letters of Violet Bonham-Carter 1914-45* (Weidenfeld & Nicolson, 1998)

Pottle, Mark (ed), *Daring to Hope: The Diaries and Letters of Violet Bonham-Carter 1946-69* (Weidenfeld & Nicolson, 2000)

Rabinowicz, Oscar, *Churchill on Jewish Problems* (Lincolns-Prager Publishers Ltd, 1956)

Ramsden, John, *Churchill: Man of the Century* (Columbia University Press, 2003)

Ranson, Edward, *British Defence Policy and Appeasement Between the Wars, 1919-39* (The Historical Association, 1993)

Rattigan, Neil, *This is England* (Associated University Presses, 2001)

Reynolds, David, *In Command of History* (Penguin, 2004)

Robbins, Keith, *Appeasement* (Blackwell Publishers, 2004)

Roberts, Andrew, *Eminent Churchillians* (Weidenfeld & Nicolson, 1994)

Roberts, Andrew, *Secrets of Leadership* (Weidenfeld & Nicolson, 2003)

Roberts, Andrew, *Masters and Commanders* (Allen Lane, 2008)

Robertson, Derek, *Invasion, 1940* (Constable, 2005)

Rose, Norman, *Churchill: An Unruly Life* (Simon & Schuster, 1994)

Rowse, A.L., *Memories of Men and Women* (Eyre Methuen, 1980)

Rubin, Gretchen, *Forty Ways to Look at Winston Churchill* (Ballantine Books, 2003)

Rubinstein, David, *The Myth of Rescue* (Routledge, 1997)

Sandys, Celia, *From Winston with Love and Kisses* (Sinclair Stevenson, 1994)

Sandys, Celia, *Churchill: Wanted Dead or Alive* (Carroll & Graf, 1999)

Sandys, Celia, *Chasing Churchill* (HarperCollins, 2003)

Seldon, Anthony, *Churchill's Indian Summer*

Smith, Malcolm, *Britain and 1940* (Routledge, 2000)

Soames, Mary (ed), *Speaking for Themselves: The Personal Letters of Winston and Clementine Churchill* (Doubleday, 1998)

Stafford, David, *Churchill and Secret Service* (Abacus, 2000)

Stafford, David, *Roosevelt and Churchill* (Little Brown & Company, 1999)

Stansky (ed), *Churchill: A Profile*, Macmillan (1973)

Stewart, Graham, *Burying Caesar* (Weidhorn & Nicholson, 1999)

Storr, Anthony, *Churchill's Black Dog* (HarperCollins, 1989)

Taylor, A.J.P., *The War Lords* (Book Club Associates, 1978)

Taylor, A.J.P. (ed), *Lloyd George: A Diary by Frances Stevenson* (Hutchinson, 1971)

Theakston, Kevin, *Winston Churchill and the British Constitution* (Politico's Publishing, 2004)

Thompson, Walter, *60 minutes with Winston Churchill* (Christopher Johnson, 1961)

Weidhorn, Manfred, *Sword and Pen* (University of New Mexico Press, 1974)

Weisberg, Jacob, *The Bush Tragedy*

Weizmann, Chaim, *Trial and Error* (Hamish Hamilton 1949)

West, Nigel, *Unreliable Witness* (Grafton Books, 1986)

Wheeler-Bennett, Sir John (ed), *Action this Day: Working with Churchill* (Macmillan, 1968)

Williams, Susan, *The People's King* (Penguin, 2003)

Woods, Frederick, *Artillery of Words* (Leo Cooper, 1992)

Index